D1577030

John Heartfield

John Heartfield

Edited by Peter Pachnicke and Klaus Honnef

With contributions by Petra Albrecht , Hubertus Gassner, Klaus Honnef, Michael Krejsa, Heiner Müller, Peter Pachnicke, and Nancy Roth

Harry N. Abrams, Inc., Publishers, New York

Published on the occasion of the exhibition *John Heartfield*

Akademie der Künste zu Berlin
Altes Museum
May 16–July 11, 1991

Rheinisches Landesmuseum Bonn
September 5–November 3, 1991

Kunsthalle Tübingen
January 11–March 1, 1992

Sprengel Museum Hannover
March 15–May 14, 1992

Barbican Art Gallery, London
Carol Brown, Senior Exhibition Organiser,
Brigitte Lardinois, Exhibition Organiser
August 13–October 18, 1992

The Irish Museum of Modern Art, Dublin
Ruth Ferguson, Curator
November 20, 1992–January 10, 1993

Scottish National Gallery of Modern Art, Edinburgh
Keith Hartley, Assistant Keeper of Art
January 30–March 25, 1993

The Museum of Modern Art, New York
Magdalena Dabrowski, Curator, Department of Drawings
April 15–July 6, 1993

San Francisco Museum of Modern Art
Sandra Phillips, Curator of Photography
July 23–September 19, 1993

Los Angeles County Museum of Art
Stephanie Barron, Curator of 20th-Century Art
October 7, 1993–January 2, 1994

This catalogue has been adapted from the original German-language book published on the occasion of the exhibition *John Heartfield*, organized by the Akademie der Künste zu Berlin, the Landesregierung Nordrhein-Westfalen and the Landschaftsverband Rheinland.

Concept and curators:
Peter Pachnicke on behalf of the Akademie der Künste zu Berlin; Klaus Honnef, Rheinisches Landesmuseum Bonn, on behalf of the Landschaftsverband Rheinland

Project directors:
Beate Reisch, Akademie der Künste zu Berlin; Hans-Jürgen von Osterhausen, Landschaftsverband Rheinland

Reconstruction of the 1920 Dada Room:
Helen Adkins

Reconstruction of the 1929 Heartfield Room at the FILM UND FOTO Exhibition:
Elisabeth Patzwall

Editors:
Karin Thomas, Sebastian Zeidler, and Nora Beeson

Designers:
Peter Pachnicke and Winfried Konnertz

Translators:
Patricia Crampton (from the French); Keith Hammond (from the Russian); Alice Isenberg, William A. Mickens and Sue Picket (from the German)

Library of Congress Cataloging-in-Publication Data

Heartfield, John, 1891–1968.
    John Heartfield / edited by Peter Pachnicke and Klaus Honnef : with contributions by Hubertus Gassner . . . [et al.].
        p.   cm.
    Catalogue of an exhibition.
    Includes bibliographical references and index.
    ISBN 0–8109–3413–2
    1. Composite photography—Exhibitions. 2. National socialism—Caricatures and cartoons—Exhibitions. 3. Heartfield, John, 1891–1968—Exhibitions.   I. Pachnicke, Peter. II. Honnef, Klaus. III. Gassner, Hubertus, 1950–   . IV. Title.
TR685.H39213   1992
779′.092—dc20   92–19588
ISBN 0-8109-2534-6 (pbk.)   CIP

Published in 1992 by Harry N. Abrams, Incorporated, New York
A Times Mirror Company
No part of the contents of this book may by reproduced without the written permission of the publishers

Printed and bound in Germany

Frontispiece: Aleksandr Rodchenko. Portrait of John Heartfield. *Photograph, Moscow 1931*

The exhibition was made possible by the kind support of the Department of the Interior of the Federal Republic of Germany, the Foundation for Art and Culture of the State of North Rhine-Westphalia, the Foundation for Cultural Endowment, Berlin, and the Department of Foreign Affairs of the Federal Republic of Germany, Bonn.

The showing of the exhibition at The Museum of Modern Art, New York, has been made possible by a generous grant from the Robert Lehman Foundation, Inc.

Table of Contents

We are now so used to the ubiquitous use of photomontage in advertising and other forms of propagandistic artwork that we find it hard to conceive of them without its witty, disruptive, or startling contribution. We are no longer surprised to see two or more different realities juxtaposed in the same image. The satirical and the surreal have become part of our way of thinking about and seeing the world. We are suspicious of an homogeneous image and almost automatically try to deconstruct it, to try and show the true realities that lie behind its seamless surface. If the Surrealists have taught us to seek out the hidden sexual motives of human behaviour, John Heartfield has shown the base materialism of so much political power, the links between war and money. No one has been more effective than Heartfield in exposing the lies of fascist politicians. His work speaks powerfully to us today despite the intervening half century and more. The basic subjects which he treats – war, poverty, political misuse of power, injustice – have not disappeared from the world. They are still unfortunately universals that can arouse feelings of pity, fear, and anger.

We are extremely pleased to be able to present this major exhibition of Heartfield's work that shows not only the range of his achievements, from political satire to book covers, from posters to theatre sets, but how he achieved the eye-deceiving brilliance of his montaged images. For the first time in a touring exhibition Heartfield's original montages will be shown, thus allowing an unique opportunity to observe his working methods at close quarters. In addition the recreations of the First International Dada Fair held in Berlin in 1920 and of the FILM UND FOTO exhibition held in Stuttgart in 1929 will show the importance that Heartfield (and his colleagues) gave to the installation of his works, so as to achieve their maximum impact.

We would like to take this opportunity of thanking the Director of the Akademie der Künste zu Berlin for lending works so generously from their Heartfield Archive and the Director of the Berlinische Galerie for lending works connected with the 1920 Berlin Dada Fair. The exhibition has been conceived and planned by Dr. Peter Pachnicke and Dr. Klaus Honnef. We wish to thank them in particular for helping to edit the English-language version of the catalogue. Through all the stages in the planning and realisation of this exhibition Dr. Beate Reisch of the Akademie der Künste zu Berlin has been an invaluable colleague. We are very grateful to her.

Heartfield (who anglicised his name from the German Herzfeld as a protest against nationalism during the First World War) spent the years from 1938 to 1950 as a refugee in London. The impact and appreciation of his art were limited at that time. We hope that this exhibition will do much to broaden an awareness in Britain and Ireland of the contribution he made to an uniquely twentieth-century art form.

John Hoole, Curator
Barbican Art Gallery, London

Declan McGenagle, Director
The Irish Museum of Modern Art, Dublin

Richard Calvocoressi, Keeper
Scottish National Gallery of Modern Art, Edinburgh

Foreword

For scholars of avant-garde and early twentieth-century art John Heartfield represents the quintessential *operierende Künstler* (activist-artist). To many he embodies the very notion of the engaged critical artist. He is, in essence, an early model of the artist whose singular oppositional voice carries for us all the banner of social and political conscience. As a Dada provocateur, Heartfield worked to undermine the very notion of art as a purely aesthetic entity separated from the fabric of the society in which it is produced. In his efforts to disseminate information to the public, Heartfield made extensive use of photomontage and was, indeed, one of the first artists to use the techniques of the mass media to question, probe, and satirize the growing tyranny of a political regime. Through his innovation of combining contradictory images into spatially unified compositions, Heartfield created a means of communication that was uncompromising in its harsh directness.

In the politically fragile and tumultuous world of today, the role and significance of art and the artist is again being questioned, and it is perhaps in looking at Heartfield's work that lessons of the past can be applied to the present. His politicizing of art and use of the mass media as a critical tool have a special relevance to the contemporary practice of many European and American artists. Nevertheless, for all the art-historical importance scholars have assigned to Heartfield, few exhibitions have been devoted to his work, and it is with special pride that we are pleased to present the first extensive showing of John Heartfield's photomontages to the American public.

We are grateful to Dr. Beate Reisch of the Akademie der Künste zu Berlin for her unsparing efforts in bringing this exhibition to the United States and to Dr. Peter Pachnicke, Dr. Klaus Honnef, and Mr. Hans-Jürgen von Osterhausen for their help in organizing this project. The members of the editorial and production staffs of DuMont Buchverlag, particularly Karin Thomas and Peter Dreesen, and the editorial staff at Harry N. Abrams, Inc. made essential contributions to this publication. Without the enthusiasm and professional commitment of the responsible curators at our respective institutions – Magdalena Dabrowski of The Museum of Modern Art, Sandra Phillips of the San Francisco Museum of Modern Art, and Stephanie Barron of the Los Angeles County Museum of Art – this exhibition might not have been seen in this country, and they all deserve our warm thanks. Finally, The Museum of Modern Art is deeply appreciative to The Robert Lehman Foundation, Inc., for generously supporting the presentation in New York.

Richard E. Oldenburg, Director
The Museum of Modern Art, New York

John R. Lane, Director
San Francisco Museum of Modern Art

Earl A. Powell, III, Director
Los Angeles County Museum of Art

June 1992

Heiner Müller

On Heartfield

John Heartfield is a classic artist in the sense that his work had impact, more in the arts than in politics: German workers, to whom it was primarily addressed, preferred dancing fairies or bellowing stags at the edge of the woods to Heartfield's photomontages. The dictators of the century had the same conception of art, with the exception, perhaps, of Mao Tse-tung: after all, he loved *Immensee* just as Napoleon loved *Werther*. Even the majority of visual artists at the Academy of Arts in the German Democratic Republic needed seven years to accept Heartfield's work as art, to accept the assemblyman [*Monteur*] as artist. His photomontages are part of the class warfare of his day, but they are not only documents that keep alive the recollection of the past. They gain in substance from hatred of injustice, just as Tintoretto's frescoes gained in substance from belief in salvation, a new beauty that can be used for other things. The first lines of Brecht's unsuccessful attempt to cast the Communist Manifesto in poetry: *Kriege zertrümmern die Welt und im Trümmerfeld geht ein Gespenst um* [*Wars are wrecking the world, and a spectre is haunting the ruins*], in perfect verse remain in one's memory, even if the spectre of communism will probably never materialize. The empires, as well as the cults that are committed to it, come and go; the statues remain. That sentence loses some of its solace with each new war. Recollection of the past presupposes the survival of the species, which is now endangered; the liquidation of the planet is in progress. Surgical war should not be the last resort in order to save the memory of mankind—works of art.

Peter Pachnicke
Klaus Honnef

On the Subject

In 1939, John Heartfield was honored in England with the exhibition *One Man's War Against Hitler.* In fact, this vivacious, little, five-foot-two David had openly challenged the fascist Goliath with his satirical picture montages and was the only one, with the exception of Charlie Chaplin, who was able to make a laughing stock out of him.

When he returned from emigration in England in 1950, we Germans, though, put our hero in cold storage for the time being. During the Cold War, the petty-minded opportunists, who solicitously sought to placate the victors' standards and enemy's profiles, were incapable of realizing and comprehending Heartfield's genius. In the West, he was ignored because he was a communist and did not express himself in the international idiom of abstract art; in the East, he was accused of cosmopolitan formalism because, in giving socialism a sensual countenance by means of avant-garde art, he contravened the know-it-all state-ordered doctrine of art, according to which the artist could make himself comprehensible to the man on the street only in the form of nineteenth-century genre painting.

Heartfield was still able to experience the renaissance of his work during the thaw of the sixties. Due to the unwavering commitment of, above all, his brother Wieland Herzfelde and his friends Brecht, Heym, Uhde, and others, a comprehensive Heartfield exhibition was finally held at the Academy of Arts in the German Democratic Republic in 1957, and in 1962 a monograph, still valid today, was published by the Verlag der Kunst, Dresden. He also received all kinds of government distinctions and tributes. In exhibitions that he arranged himself, his works were sent out around the world as ambassadorial messages from an anti-fascist state – thus reaching the other Germany. If Heartfield's fate in the German Democratic Republic at that time was more that of the ineffectual classic artist, he certainly struck the nerve of a generation in the German Federal Republic during those years. He became a father-figure for the generation of 1968. His operative conception of art, whereby art should not be shut up in the seclusion of the museum but should instead strive to be active in the political day-to-day life of the street and in the mass media, was for them a basic model for the emancipation of a truly democratic, socialist society.

These dreams did not blossom in the West, and real socialism, in whose all-liberating power Heartfield staunchly believed until his death, is now in a phase of tragic, tragicomic self-destruction. In the year of John Heartfield's centennial birthday, his works will therefore have to speak for themselves. The philosophy of this exhibition is to put these works under scrutiny – not just examine how they function within the operative conception of art. The starting place was the Heartfield Archive of the Akademie der Künste zu Berlin, where virtually all the designs for his photomontages as well as their printed reproductions in newspapers, magazines, on dust jackets and posters are preserved. Intensive study of the original montages has made it clear that Heartfield's works were not only of agitatorial use for the cause of the revolution, but, when released from the concrete historical situation, also prove to be varied and ambivalent artistic creations reflecting and penetrating the totality of a world full of contradictions. In this exhibition and catalogue we endeavored to present in a tangible way the original montages in their refined graphic structure and the reproductions from the *AIZ (Arbeiter-Illustrierte-Zeitung)* [*Workers' Illustrated Newspaper*] in their abundant tonal values. We did so to make it clear that Heartfield's montages did not – like a well-told joke – simply combine picture and text in a provoking manner. For him, montage was more a symbolic form in which, apart from photos and texts, tonal values, the colors and structure of the material, the precisely calculated organization of the visual plane, and the imaginary visual space devised by means of retouching produced many levels of meaning. Heartfield is not being aestheticized. Instead, the diversity and ambivalence of his montages become obvious. Thus his works extend beyond political current events, allowing the viewer to develop his thoughts, imagination, and sensual perceptiveness. The fact that the current political trend has not faded is assured by reality itself, which tries even nowadays to live up to the satirical montages in a violent and impertinent manner.

The debate in the press during this exhibition in Berlin and Bonn demonstrates just how solidified prejudices are when the subject concerns Heartfield in Germany. The Left complained that the exhibition aestheticized Heartfield's work. The Right contended that the exhibition only confirmed its firmly held opinion that Heartfield was nothing more than a clever propagandist of communist ideology. There is no doubt that Heartfield was a dyed-in-the-wool communist. There is even much less doubt that he handled art as a weapon: against bigoted conservatives, against Nazis and fascists, and even against Social Democrats. Heartfield was a typical representative of the German intelligentsia in the Weimar Republic.

Heartfield was a rigorous moralist and an aesthetic fireball. This at least is emphatically seen in this exhibition. He consistently used a wide range of artistic media of the day for his political and aesthetic ideas – the new media of film and photography, illustrated magazines published for the masses, the theatre. He was an artist to whom impact mattered. He was not one of those whose only ambition is to go down in the annals of art history. Nevertheless, Heartfield is one of the great figures in the history of German art in the twentieth century. He was certainly the first German artist who was capable of looking beyond conventional practices and, as a matter of fact, anticipated most of what is now celebrated as innovation: interrelated media and disciplines. Heartfield did not think, feel, or work in such divergent terms as fine or commerical, legitimate or illegitimate, high or low art. He took every job with equal seriousness, regardless of whether it was an advertisement, a dust jacket, a newspaper, a stage set, or a display. Every aspect of everyday living was also to be aesthetically revolutionized, and was to acquire a face and body in which people could also see the NEW with their own eyes, hear it with their own ears, taste it with their own mouths, smell it with their own noses, and touch it with their own hands. He was not only the most significant satirist of the German plight; he would have been the most significant designer of a socialist world had he been, to use his own words, "left alone to do it."

The idea for this exhibition originated in 1988. It did not need to be altered in the period of political change because it came from the Akademie der Künste specifically from Heiner Müller. This exhibition would not have been possible without the special political and financial involvement of the Landesregierung Nordrhein-Westfalen, the Landschaftsverband Rheinland, the Foundation for Art and Culture of the State of North Rhine-Westphalia, as well as the Ministry of the Interior of the Federal Republic of Germany.

The overall organization of the project was in the hands of Beate Reisch on behalf of the Akademie der Künste zu Berlin, and Hans-Jürgen von Osterhausen at the Landschaftsverband Rheinland. The staff of the Heartfield Archive, above all Elisabeth Patzwall, Michael Krejsa, Petra Albrecht, and Lia Manouri, have made a variety of scholarly and archival contributions. The first reconstruction of the Heartfield Room from the Stuttgart FILM UND FOTO exhibition is the scholarly merit of Elisabeth Patzwall. The interpretation of the *Dada Fair* on the basis of the *Stationen der Moderne* exhibition was rendered by

Helen Adkins and supported by generous loans from the Berlinische Galerie, Berlin.

The editors thank the staff of DuMont Buchverlag, Karin Thomas, Winfried Konnertz, and Peter Dreesen, who supervised the editorial work, the layout, and the technical production of this catalogue with tremendous personal commitment. Thanks go also to Nora Beeson and the staff of Harry N. Abrams, Inc. for the English edition.

Additional thanks go to Dieter Ronte of the Sprengel Museum in Hannover, Götz Adriani, of the Kunsthalle Tübingen, and especially to Magdalena Dabrowski of The Museum of Modern Art in New York, and to all the museum directors and curators who are showing this exhibition in London, Edinburgh, Dublin, New York, Los Angeles, and San Francisco.

The editors are especially pleased with the extraordinary interest shown by prominent art institutions abroad, not only because Heartfield is finally receiving the international recognition that his work deserves, but also because it can prove abroad what a diverse intellectual heritage the reunified Germany possesses.

Self-portrait, 1920

John Heartfield, 1967

[…] how I got the idea of making photomontages. I'd say […] I started making photomontages during the First World War. There are a lot of things that got me into working with photos. The main thing is that I saw both what was being said and not being said with photos in the newspapers. The most important thing for me was that I intrinsically became involved in the opposition and worked with a medium I didn't consider to be an artistic medium, photography. […] I found out how you can fool people with photos, really fool them. […] You can lie and tell the truth by putting the wrong title or wrong captions under them, and that's roughly what was being done. Photos of the war were being used to support the policy to hold out when the war had long since been settled on the Marne and the German army had already been beaten. […]

I was a soldier from very early on. Then we pasted, I pasted and quickly cut out a photo and then put one under another. Of course, that produced another counterpoint, a contradiction that expressed something different. That was the idea. It still wasn't all that clear to me where it would lead to, or that it would lead me to photomontage.

From a conversation with Bengt Dahlbäck
(Moderna Museet, Stockholm)

ca. 1917/18
(Cat. no. 173)

The painter paints his pictures with paint, and I do it with photographs.

Wieland Herzfelde, 1913

My brother is small [. . .] the opposite of robust, the upper part of his body is bent forward [. . .] he walks with broad strides [. . .] his whole figure clearly shows that it doesn't know what repose is. [. . .] He can be and look grotesque, sad, arrogant, haggard, friendly, irascible, but never profane or vacuous. [. . .]

His critical judgment may be just average, but he has a critical sense of such power and certainty, clarity and sensitivity that it is reflected in every movement, every expression in his eyes and every pose. If it were possible to record those movements, for instance, as fluctuations in temperature and air pressure, I believe the movements of my brother's hands when he's deep in thought, when he's formulating an idea or even when he's trying to explain something to someone, would make wonderful Futurist pictures. Those hands are [. . .] careworn [. . .] sensitive [. . .] the hands of one who draws, of one who draws pictures in black and white. [. . .]

The same can be said about my brother's face. It doesn't have wrinkles, but it is full of lines that are hardly there but can be felt. An infinite amount of pain, sadness, longing, combativeness, and love lies in those features. [. . .] There's nothing sweet, dreamy, nobly romantic, or elegiac in Helmut's eyes, and the expression in them is neither remote from reality nor dark, melancholic, or bright. They are blue, chaste, and honest. They are very large and always observant. [. . .] The expression in his eyes reveals the soul of a person of such naiveté, such love and openness in a fashion you perhaps never would have imagined. His head is proudly, seriously, and tempestuously set. He has high-combed, bushy hair that shines reddish gold depending on the weather, and it blazes, sometimes dangles wearily on his brow. [. . .] That brow is marble that has become alive [. . .] white, defiant, glowing high above the smiling eyes. [. . .] His mouth is virtually the opposite. [. . .] A short, trimmed beard [. . .] vouches ostensibly for the wearer's energetic appearance. [. . .] Persistence, ardor, care, and embitterment mark that mouth, which is always closed. [. . .] Perhaps it is worth mentioning that he doesn't wear any of the clothes that have become typical of artists.

Letter to Else Lasker-Schüler, December 6, 1913, in Wieland Herzfelde, "George Grosz, John Heartfield, Erwin Piscator, Dada und die Folgen oder Die Macht der Freundschaft," *Sinn und Form*, 23, 6, 1971, pp. 1221–51.

Berlin 1929

Moscow 1931

Prague 1935 (?)

London 1949

Leipzig 1950

London 1950

Berlin 1962

Moscow 1957

Peking 1957

17

Nancy Roth

Heartfield and Modern Art

In the debates of the European avant-garde of the 1920's and 1930's, John Heartfield repeatedly figured as a reference point, an instance of a particular kind of success. Often he appeared as the very type of the successful "operierende Künstler" (activist-artist), one whose work actually reached mass audiences with a steadfastly anti-fascist, anti-capitalist message. Always he was the *Photomonteur:* using photographs, texts, and color – the very tools with which the mass media of his time constructed "reality" – he represented instead the incompetence, greed, and hypocrisy behind appearances.

It is perhaps ironic, but hardly coincidental, that Heartfield should now need an introduction to English-speaking audiences. The continental debates of the interwar years figured little in the postwar construction of modernism in Great Britain and the United States. In the conception of modernism that *did* come to prevail – art defined as a self-contained activity pursuing goals unique to itself – there was little place for an artist whose medium of choice was the mass-circulation press and who openly announced that his work served the cause of world socialism. (Heartfield was a loyal member of the Communist Party to the end of his life.) Heartfield became a "neglected" artist. As Douglas Kahn has put it, "the neglect is almost as famous as he is."[1]

In the absence of comprehensive exhibitions or books about the artist,[2] Americans broadly familiar with twentieth-century art are likely to have heard of Heartfield in connection with Berlin Dada,[3] 1918–1920, or as one of the contenders for the title "inventor of photomontage," before 1918.[4] And yet it is certainly the work from 1929 to 1939, namely the body of 237 full-page photomontages that Heartfield furnished – sometimes weekly – for the communist newspaper *Arbeiter-Illustrierte-Zeitung (AIZ)* [*Workers' Illustrated Newspaper*] that characterizes Heartfield best. Most of the Heartfield literature, almost all in German, and the exhibitions have focused on this work, sometimes to the exclusion of everything else, such as book jackets, posters, stage sets, etc. Further, the literature has, until recently, tended to distance Heartfield from an avant-garde that had been discredited within the context of Socialist Realism. Substantial exhibitions of his photomontages have appeared in England,[5] where they have generally shared the orientation of the German literature. By focusing on the photomontages and stressing the artist's political orientation, they have sustained Heartfield's isolation in terms of modernist art.

Now, at a moment when the model of an autonomous, socially isolated art seems increasingly inadequate, renewed interest in Heartfield is associated with a broad reconsideration of modernism itself. He offers, among other things, an entrypoint into a "lost," or profoundly obscured, body of thought about what art might be and what it might accomplish in a democratic society. For Heartfield was always categorically opposed to and impatient with any art that sought autonomy or detachment from the political and social conditions of the moment. He embodies, on the contrary, the very idea of an artist who works in critical opposition to existing social conditions. And because so much of his work still so effectively marks the presence of one passionate, angry, resistant consciousness, it holds out the possibility of reenacting such an art in the present. Certain contemporary artists – Klaus Staeck in Germany and Peter Kennard in England perhaps most prominent among them – have consciously turned back to Heartfield as a model; many others, the Americans Barbara Kruger and Jenny Holzer, for example, make critical use of Heartfield's same tools: – mass media technology or photomontage itself – without any particular reference to historical precedents. The issue, in any case, concerns Heartfield's specific techniques only to the extent that they contributed to the critical success of his project as a whole. And it is the whole project – a conjunction of aesthetic judgment and political commitment, personal experience and technique, all against the background of specific historical conditions – that the present exhibition promises to clarify. Heartfield's entry into the avant-garde was abrupt and decisive. After an extraordinarily traumatic childhood,[6] a three-year training program in advertising and graphic design in Munich, and about a year of work experience, Helmut Herzfeld came to Berlin in 1913 – just before the outbreak of the First World War – expecting to become a plein-air painter. *Jugendstil* was the fashion during his years as a design student. He particularly admired the work of Ludwig Hohlwein, an admiration reflected in his first book jacket, made for an anthology of his father's writing (Fig. p. 19). What little remains of his painting of that time suggests a connection with the Romantic landscape tradition (Fig. p. 19). Much later, however, in recounting his experience around the First World War, he mentioned having seen an exhibition of Futurist painting in Berlin in 1912, which had made the most lasting impression. "Obviously one opposed Romanticism, and that and lots of other things had to do with Italian Futurism, and of course I saw the exhibition here in the Sturm [Gallery] of Herbert [sic] Walden, a large Futurist exhibition. [...] I was especially [impressed] with the political situation, the taking sides. [...]"[7] When the Herzfeld brothers first arrived in Berlin, in any case, they became attached to the Expressionist circle centered in the Cafe des Westens, and particularly to the writer Else Lasker-Schüler.

A decisive moment was Heartfield's first encounter with Georg Grosz's drawings in 1915. As his brother Wieland Herzfelde later put it, the experience was "a revelation. At the same time, a cold shower; shocking, sobering, tingling and invigorating. My brother and I had been accustomed to thinking of art as that which makes beauty visible and audible. [...] Grosz suddenly made us stop seeing the everyday world as dry, dull, and boring, and start seeing it as a drama in which stupidity, crudity, and sloth played the starring roles. He awakened in both of us a new highly critical attitude toward our previous efforts of the artistic sort: Helmut burned everything he had made in charcoal, pencil, chalk, ink, tempera, and oil up to that time."[8]

The same year Herzfeld, along with Grosz, began using anglicized versions of their own names: Georg Grosz became George Grosz; Helmut Herzfeld became John Heartfield.[9] Ostensibly done as an act of anti-war, pro-English sympathy, the change, more dramatic in Heartfield's case, served to publicly disconnect the artist from family and country, and to clear the way for a new "engineered" identity. Disdaining his own previous artwork, Heartfield initially turned his energy to publishing Grosz's work, and then recognized publishing itself as a medium suited to his new ambitions. From 1915 on, John and his brother Wieland, whose literary ambitions complemented Heartfield's artistic ones, produced print portfolios as well as various small fliers and newspapers, in which highly unorthodox typography was combined with sharp political satire. More than once these publications succumbed to the censors. On March 1, 1917, in a ploy to continue publishing despite a ban on the existing periodical *Neue Jugend* [*New Youth*], Heartfield founded the Malik-Verlag (publishing company).[10] This press, despite chronic financial problems, published the work of socialist authors throughout the Weimar period (1918–1933), with Herzfelde running the business and Heartfield steadily designing book jackets, posters, and so on.

It was primarily in the course of his work for the Malik-Verlag and other publishing enterprises during the 1920's, work that demanded eye-catching, clear, easily readable messages, that Heartfield honed his particular approach to photomontage. The beginnings, however, are usually traced to his association with Berlin Dada, 1918–1920.[11] Like the earlier Zurich Dada movement, the Berliners printed fliers and staged events designed to mock the conventional

John Heartfield, title page for Franz Held, *Selected Works*, Berlin, 1912

The Cottage in the Woods, oil painting by Helmut Herzfeld, 1907

"sense" and "logic" that had culminated in the bitter, brutal absurdities of war. In Berlin, however, the events had a keen political edge. The city was reeling from food shortages, economic instability, utter disillusionment with the recently lost war, and more recently the brutal quashing of the workers' revolution of 1918 by troops ostensibly under the control of the centrist Social Democrats, subsequently the founders of the new Weimar Republic.

Within the loose configuration of personalities that Berlin Dada embraced – Richard Huelsenbeck, Franz Jung, Raoul Hausmann, Hannah Höch, Johannes Baader, and Grosz – Heartfield was known for his fierce, uncontrolled outbursts of anger. Huelsenbeck later recalled an all-night drinking and drug-taking episode, in which Heartfield had to be forcibly restrained and dragged back to Wieland Herzfelde's top-floor garret. "Here, amid boxes, rolls of paper, books, manuscripts as well as wine bottles in heaps around the room, we continued. [...] John Heartfield was bound to a chair, and we said and did things to annoy him, as one might provoke an animal at the zoo."[12]

Although the Berlin Dadaists were apparently united in their exasperation with Expressionism,[13] Heartfield vented his anger, perhaps more specifically than did others in the circle, on "bourgeois" art. He was particularly careful to separate his own effort as *Photomonteur* – the term *Monteur* approximates "machinist" – from that of an artist. The tone of sweeping, angry rejection permeates Grosz's and Heartfield's infamous article, "Der Kunstlump," which appeared in the political monthly *Der Gegner* in 1920.[14]

After a blanket condemnation of museums, past art, and famous artists – including Rubens and Rembrandt – as merely bourgeois tools for blinding and controlling the proletariat, Heartfield and Grosz narrowed in on a personal attack against Kokoschka. "He is a scab," they wrote, "who wants his brushing business honored as if it were a mission from God. Today, when the cleaning of a Red soldier's gun is more significant than the whole metaphysical œuvre of all painters. The concept of art and artist is a bourgeois invention, and within the state it can only take the side of the ruling, that is, the bourgeois caste."

At the time "Der Kunstlump" appeared, Grosz and Heartfield were officially communist artists, having joined the KPD (German Communist Party) at its founding, the last day of 1918. In part for this reason, their pamphlet provoked a lively response, notably in the KPD's newspaper, *Die Rote Fahne* [*The Red Flag*]. More specifically, it stimulated the first serious debate about what a bourgeois cultural heritage might mean in a socialist society. Gertrude Alexander, for example, argued that while works of art have functioned as luxury wares in the past, they would not necessarily continue to do so, and that established masterpieces (she excluded contemporary movements, such as Expressionism, Cubism, and Futurism) embodied historical conditions that the working class wanted and needed to understand.[15] The last word in the discussion came from August Thalheimer, the editor-in-chief of *Die Rote Fahne*, who flatly stated that the proletariat, rather than rejecting, must *reform* an inherited bourgeois culture according to its own needs.[16] This marked the end of Heartfield's radical denunciations of past art. Although he continued to be highly critical of contemporary movements – Expressionism, Neue Sachlichkeit, New Vision photography, and later Surrealism – his own work began to reflect the party-sanctioned "umfunktionieren" (reusing for a different purpose) of familiar past art.

Many years later, in an interview with the English art historian Francis Klingender,[17] Heartfield described Dada as an effort to disturb the higher impulses of the intellect – the spiritual, mystical, and subjective – but only in order to get at the truth behind them. Dada was the first "ism," he said, to insist on a new *content* rather than simply a new form. "The chaotic eruption of resistance, the protest against everything, gave way to a systematic and conscious pursuit of art propaganda in the service of the Workers' Movement."

Heartfield's reputation grew quickly during the 1920's, though less as a political activist or as a fine artist than as a graphic designer.[18] His notable design innovations move in a discernable direction toward a combination of photographs, text, and color that abruptly switches the expected meanings of each separate element and yields a new meaning. He is credited, for example, with the introduction of a book jacket conceived as a three-dimensional object, its two surfaces bearing related images that together convey an abstract idea central to the book in question. One effective example was the jacket for Ilya Ehrenburg's *Most Sacred Possessions* – in German, *Die heiligsten Güter* (Pl. 30). The front cover shows a montage of bullets, stacks of silver and gold coins, boxes of matches, and a small crucifix arranged as if on an altar. The back cover has another montage, this time of diverse single figures set up like chessmen on a checkerboard – a cardinal, a female nude (white), a naked black woman carrying a large basket, a "proper" bourgeois businessman, a soldier with a gas mask, etc. Together, the two images imply that religious institutions function within a larger, highly structured "power game" that controls everyone.

Later, in discussing his own development, Heartfield pointed out a pair of photographs that appeared on one page of the Malik-Verlag yearbook for 1924 as illustrative of his photomontage principles (Pls. 23a and 23b). "It isn't photomontage yet [...] above there's a picture of a general [who died] at headquarters, how he is buried [...] with all ceremony. Then [...] how a poor soldier is buried at the front line, where grenades have been thrown, with plaster sprinkled over everything [...] so, the juxtaposition above and below. [...]"[19] In the same year, Heartfield designed a poster for the Malik-Verlag called "After Ten Years: Fathers and Sons 1924," generally acknowledged to be the first of the characteristic photomontages in which two or more contrasting elements are integrated into a single image (Pl. pp. 22–23).

By the late 1920's, Heartfield had emerged as something of a model for other revolutionary artists, someone whose work was acclaimed even in mainstream exhibitions. In FILM UND FOTO, the vast and highly influential exhibition sponsored by the Deutsche Werkbund in 1929, for example, one room was devoted almost exclusively to his work. According to its organizer, Gustav Stolz, the exhibition sought to show what was intrinsic, characteristic about the photographic medium, and to do so by presenting, as comprehensively as possible, the work of those individuals who "were the first to recognize the camera as the means of image-making most appropriate to our time."[20] Heartfield's prominence and his works' position in the exhibition testify to his status as an innovator, specifically in the use of photographs with typography as well as in social criticism and political agitiation.

A number of historians have recently suggested that FILM UND FOTO marked not so much a beginning as the celebratory end of a decade of enthusiasm about rapid technical and formal innovation in photography. After this point, which corresponds to the end of a period of relative economic stability and prosperity in the Weimar Republic, divisions among those supporting different forms and uses of photography widen, and a sharply polemical tone enters the discussions. Within Communist Party circles, the broader question of the best way to visually "mobilize the masses" centered on photomontage, and it was against the background of that debate that Heartfield was invited to in Moscow.

Between April 1931 and January 1932, with Sergei Tretyakov acting as his main guide and translator, Heartfield worked, exhibited and taught about his ideas

John Heartfield, "After Ten Years: Fathers and Sons
1924." Photomontage, 1924. Cat. no. 178

and methods in Russia.[21] The invitation itself represented a shift in attitude. A certain suspicion lingered about Heartfield as a result of his past association with Dada, the art movement that party adherents regularly cited as the example *par excellence* of bourgeois decadence. Heartfield's use of allegories, his reliance on word plays, above all his "organic" integration of montage parts emerged in sharp contrast to the Constructivists' – particularly Gustav Klutsis's – reliance on startling contrasts, dynamic compositions, and repetitions. Initially, Heartfield was officially singled out for special praise for the unity and clarity of his messages, as well as for the supremacy of idea over form in his work; over the period of his visit in Moscow, the terms of the debate as well as his place in it shifted. Good points and bad points were enumerated: some of the montages were overly complex and contradictory, others were exemplary. It was at this time, too, that the very negative charge of "formalism" was first leveled against Heartfield.[22]

Although Heartfield apparently did not participate in it, a parallel debate about the merits and appropriate forms of photomontage was underway during the same years in a small publication, *Der Arbeiterfotograf* [*The Worker-Photographer*], published by the Neuer Deutscher Verlag [New German publishing company]. This press, under the direction of Willi Münzenberg, was communist in its convictions, although not directly affiliated with the German Communist Party. Its main publication was the mass-circulation newspaper *AIZ,* which by the end of the decade had become the third-largest circulation newspaper in Germany. In 1926, partly in order to serve the photographic needs of the *AIZ,* Münzenberg founded a nationwide network of "worker-photographers," primarily readers of the newspaper with an interest in photography.[23] The organization, the Union of Worker-Photographers of Germany (VdAFD), set out to provide interested individuals with enough technical, political, and aesthetic education to take usable photographs. Between 1928 and 1932, about a dozen short articles appeared in *The Worker-Photographer* that sketch the relationship of photography to art, and more specifically of worker photography to art photography. Although a sharp distinction is always maintained between Heartfield's work and bourgeois art, the position of photomontage and that of Heartfield shifts within these discussions as well. Writing in 1928, for example, Franz Höllering, the editor-in-chief of the *AIZ,* set out to dispel the idea that art is somehow different and detached from everyday life; it is, he wrote, simply an extraordinary solution to an ordinary problem. He roundly condemns Neue Sachlichkeit photography and the cameraless photography of an artist like Moholy-Nagy; Heartfield, now the exponent *par excellence* of photomontage, becomes his example of an effective artist. Three years later, Alfred Durus, the art critic of the German Communist Party, found it appropriate to take up the issue of photomontage itself, differentiating among its various forms and goals, as party representatives were doing at that moment. His judgment on form was different from Höllering's: he praised, for example, a piece of cameraless photography by Alice Lex-Nerlinger for its critical stance toward the Weimar constitution. Heartfield again emerged as exemplary, now not simply as photomontagist but a particular kind of photomontagist who used the technique in a critical rather than promotional way. Although Heartfield's own theoretical interests were very limited, he clearly shared *The Worker-Photographer*'s broadly dismissive view of contemporary art photography movements. In these circles, the startling new shooting angles, extreme close-ups, polarization, and abstract photograms, etc., embraced by what Moholy-Nagy enthusiastically called "New Vision" photography, appeared simply as new forms of old, bourgeois self-indulgence, as so many fresh diversions from the primary task of social change.

In 1929, the Neuer Deutscher Verlag published Heartfield's hugely successful satirical collaboration with Kurt Tucholsky, *Deutschland, Deutschland über alles,*[24] an irreverent picture-survey of the Weimar Republic. In this book, the photographs – selected from images taken by anonymous worker-photographers[25] – function as snippets of the Republic itself, which Tucholsky's text variously questions, mocks, compares, and contrasts, with devastating effect (Pls. 60a–60g, 61).

Later the same year, Heartfield began his long collaboration with the *AIZ*, furnishing full-page photomontages, on an average monthly. In the resulting body of work, he directed his montage techniques, developed over the preceding decade, to the political events of the moment. He used images not only from current newspapers and magazines, but also from photography archives, agencies, and books; he also had photographs taken for specific purposes. He usually began with a detailed drawing of what was needed, then supervised every stage, from shooting, to developing, to sizing, to printing, regularly exhausting and frustrating the photographers who worked for him.[26] He did not take pictures himself.[27]

Through the early 1930's, as the Nazis rose to power, Heartfield's situation became increasingly dangerous. He left Berlin literally steps ahead of the Gestapo in April 1933. Traveling on foot, with nothing but what he could snatch up in the last harrowing moments, he joined the exiled *AIZ* staff in Prague, where he continued to work for almost six years. Conditions were difficult: he had been forced to abandon his own huge collection of materials, especially photographs, in Berlin. Since the *AIZ* staff was greatly reduced, he helped with editorial work and production, in addition to steadily supplying photomontages. Nevertheless, the years in Prague were remarkably prolific and yielded some of the most succinct, memorable work of his career. They also brought him international political notoriety.

In April 1934, Heartfield participated in an exhibition of caricature held at the prestigious Mánes Verein in Prague. Of the thirty-six montages on view, the German government was officially offended by seven, above all by Heartfield's montage of Hitler, "Adolf the Superman: Swallows Gold and Spouts Junk" (Pl. 94). Formal notes of protest from the German and Italian embassies were sent to the Czech government, asking that those works be removed from the exhibition. The Czech government resisted. Publicity and visitorship to the exhibition rose sharply. The tension mounted, and finally the Czech government was forced to give in. When the montages were removed, Heartfield responded with another montage, a grid of his own photomontages against a prison wall with several missing: "The More Pictures They Remove, the More Visible Reality Becomes!" appeared in the May 3 issue of the *AIZ* (Pl. 86).[28]

Among the letters and articles of support for Heartfield, one came from the French artist Paul Signac, offering his help in organizing a French exhibition of Heartfield's work. This in fact took place at the end of April the following year. Sponsored by the Association of Revolutionary Writers and Artists (AEAR), the exhibition of 150 photomontages included all of Heartfield's work since April 1933. It immediately preceded the International Congress of Writers in Defense of Culture, an event organized by the French Communist Party in an effort to present itself as the supporter not solely of revolutionary culture but of culture altogether and of national cultural traditions, especially French ones.[29] To clarify and publicize the AEAR's position in advance of the international gathering, the Heartfield exhibition was accompanied by a public symposium. Louis Aragon, since 1933 formally excluded from the Surrealist group and actively supporting Socialist Realism, read his essay, "John Heartfield and Revolutionary Beauty."[30] In it, he constructs a legacy of great realist artists, to which Heartfield becomes the contemporary, and specifically German, heir.

The parallel between Heartfield's and the Surrealists' approach to photomontage has been noted by several critics. The "organic" blending or integrating of parts into a coherent picture in terms of space and composition – the same qualities that set him apart so decisively from the Constructivists – had much in common with the Surrealist approach. However, Heartfield could not accept the Surrealist address to unconscious processes as "revolutionary" art. In his 1944 interview with Klingender, Heartfield described Surrealism as a reactionary movement because it reinterpreted Dada's revolt of the "lower" against the "higher" impulses solely in terms of individual psychology, rather than in terms of social struggle.

During his visit to Paris in 1935, Heartfield met various illustrious German emigrés who were living there, among them probably the critic Walter Benjamin. It would have been close to the time Benjamin began writing the now-famous essay, "The Work of Art in the Age of its Mechanical Reproducibility," which was published the following year. He never addressed himself to Heartfield in any extended way. But the same artist whose technique, as he had written earlier, "made the book cover into a political instrument,"[31] was also one whose early work as a Dadaist "hit the spectator like a bullet, it happened to him, thus acquiring a tactile quality. It promoted a demand for film, the distracting element of which is also primarily tactile, being based on changes of place and focus which periodically assail the spectator."[32] That is, Benjamin saw Heartfield's work as delivering the constant shocks and interruptions in the viewer's associative processes that mark the coming of a new form of art.

By December 1938, the Nazis were demanding Heartfield's extradition to Germany. Again steps ahead of the Gestapo, and again taking only the barest necessities with him, Heartfield flew from Prague to London. His first English hostess, Yvonne Kapp, had been awaiting the arrival of this "very special refugee" for weeks, through several postponements of the flight. She described him as a small, nervous gentleman, who turned down an offer of food, and asked to be allowed to lie down immediately. The next morning, she tried repeatedly to wake him for breakfast, to no avail. Worried, she called friends to assist in taking the door off the hinges. Despite all the noise, Heartfield was still, she reported, "sleeping like a baby [...] it must have been the first time he had slept in safety in many years."

Heartfield's initial success in England was promising: soon after his arrival, some of his photomontages appeared in *Lilliput* under the title "A Master of Political Art: John Heartfield."[33] After staying at Mrs. Kapp's home a short time, he moved into the home of the painter Fred Uhlmann in Hampstead, where the art historian Klingender also lived. In July 1939 Heartfield helped initiate and produce a satirical review at the Arts Theatre about the Third Reich entitled "4 and 20 Black Sheep." In December, an exhibition of his photomontages, "One Man's War Against Hitler," was held at the Arcade Gallery in London.

Later the same month, England declared war against Germany. Almost all enemy nationals were interned, and although Heartfield received the most benign classification – "C" meant political refugee – he spent six weeks in camps under conditions that aggravated a long-standing problem with headaches.[34] After war was declared, refugees were subject to severe work restrictions. The review "4 and 20 Black Sheep" had been among the more ambitious projects of the Free German League of Culture (Freier deutscher Kulturbund), an organization aimed at demonstrating a united front of German opposition to the fascist regime in power and at maintaining some sense of a continuous German culture apart from the immediate conditions in Germany itself. It kept a small library, sponsored lectures, concerts, and discussions, published a newsletter, and ostensibly provided Heartfield and other political exiles with a core of social and cultural life.

On January 1, 1943, Heartfield and Gertrud Fietz, whom he had met in England, moved into their own apartment in Highgate, 1 Jackson's Lane. The landlord, Dr. Otto Manasse, entrusted part of the house garden to Heartfield, where he promptly not only planted fruit trees but kept a pair of rabbits he had received as a gift, along with their offspring. Later, there were cats and chickens as well; Manasse apparently accepted it all in good humor. Heartfield was eventually able to work as book designer with the firm of Lindsay Drummond, and, near the end of his stay, with Penguin as well; however, whether for reasons of health, language, or political climate, his work in England never achieved the same topicality as it had enjoyed before 1939.

After the war, health problems prevented Heartfield from traveling back to Germany immediately. When he did return to the newly formed German Democratic Republic (East Germany) in 1950, he was not immediately readmitted into the good graces of the party. The ideals of Socialist Realism demanded that art represent social reality richly and completely enough to support the audience's reflection on its own situation. By this standard, largely shaped through the efforts of Georg Lukács, Heartfield's cut-and-pasted snippets of "reality" were insubstantial, no more than "a good joke."[35] Without official party support, Heartfield could find little work and so was largely dependent on his brother and friends. In addition, he suffered two heart attacks during the first years after his return.

Through the efforts of friends and supporters, among them Bertolt Brecht, the party reversed its position toward Heartfield in 1956. With a professorship at the Akademie der Künste der DDR (National Academy of Arts), he received a lifelong pension and the first large, state-sponsored exhibition of his work the following year. Until his death in 1968 he lived quietly, working occasionally as a set designer for productions in East Berlin theatres. He was showered with honors. For the first time in his life he supported and was supported by the political regime in power.

The present exhibition provides the groundwork for a more complete view of Heartfield than has ever been possible before. It includes some hand-finished, camera-ready boards for his photomontages[36] – evidence of the artist's own facture. And above all, it embraces work and documents from the artist's entire career, broadening the historical framework within which his work can be examined. It becomes possible, for example, to see the fury of the photomontages made in exile in Czechoslovakia (1933–1938) against the generally cautious work made in exile in England (1938–1950), or the continuity between the early Dada graphics and the biting insight of the montages from Prague.

It becomes possible, too, to see Heartfield's critical strengths more clearly in light of some limitations. As the artist's brother once wrote, Heartfield was possessed of "perhaps only average critical intellect, but a critical feeling of such strength and certainty, clarity and sensitivity, that it was reflected in every movement, every glance, every posture."[37] A different kind of critical intellect might have balked at the sort of conflicts John Berger has outlined: "Politically revolutionary artists hope to integrate their work into a mass struggle. But the influence of their work cannot be determined, either by the artist or by a political commissar, in advance. And it is here that we can see that to compare a work of imagination with a weapon is to resort to a dangerous and farfetched metaphor."[38] The rhetoric of art with a purpose *does* permeate Heartfield's own statements, as well as much of the discourse surrounding him; he did not publicly acknowledge conflicts. Near the end of his life he was asked whether his photomontages were made in the framework of party function or on personal artistic initiative. His answer was quick and pointed: "I was never a functionary."[39]

Many of Heartfield's images are still instantly comprehensible, even though they rely on a general familiarity with figures and events of fifty and more years ago. Yet certainly this recognition does not depend so much on our sensing parallels to the present, as to the sheer infamy of those particular figures and events, their ongoing identity in contemporary consciousness with the complete and disastrous failure of democratic institutions. Nor can Heartfield's solution – the triumph of world socialism – have much resonance with contemporary viewers. What remains current is surely less his specific accomplishments than the nature and scope of his criticism. He did not stop the rise of fascism. But in some of his work, for part of his life, Heartfield *was* able to turn the very technology of "making real" – the mass media – to the purpose of social and political criticism. As a historical figure, he marks a place, a set of conditions under which such criticism once was possible, a fixed point from which to measure how much those conditions, those possibilities have changed.

1. Douglas Kahn, *John Heartfield: Art and Mass Media* (New York: Tanam, 1985), p. 2.
2. In addition to Kahn's (see footnote 1), English-language books that include substantial information about Heartfield include *Grosz/Heartfield: The Artist as Social Critic* (Minneapolis: University of Minnesota Press, 1980); *Photomontages of the Nazi Period/John Heartfield* (New York: Universe Books, 1977); David Evans and Sylvia Gohl, *Photomontage: a Political Weapon* (London: Gordon Fraser, 1986). Evans's comprehensive study of the *AIZ* and *VI* photomontages, *John Heartfield: AIZ/VI* was published by Kent Fine Arts, New York, 1992.
    Heartfield's work was first exhibited in the United States under the auspices of the Photo-League in 1938. There were two more small exhibitions during the 1940's under the same sponsorship, but no other exhibitions until the early 1980's.
3. Although Heartfield was mentioned several times in the catalogue for New York's influential historical exhibition, *Dada, Surrealism, and Their Heritage* (New York: The Museum of Modern Art, 1968), his work was not reproduced there, nor was it included in the exhibition.
    In fall 1981, the New York art journal *Artforum* published a short exchange of letters between William Rubin, then Director of Painting and Sculpture at The Museum of Modern Art in New York and the organizer of the *Dada/Surrealism* exhibition, and the prominent conceptual artist Hans Haacke. Haacke felt that Heartfield had gotten "rather short shrift," and implied that the reason was the overtly political messages in Heartfield's work and their potential to offend the exhibition's funders. Rubin denied any such connection, saying that there had been difficulty in borrowing the Heartfield works he had wanted, but that in any case Heartfield, "hardly a major figure," had been treated in as much depth as any of the other Dadaists in what was by design a brief catalogue text, *Artforum*, No. 20 (September, 1981), p. 2.
4. The issue of who "invented" photomontage has been debated often, the prime contenders being Raoul Hausmann, Heartfield, and Gustav Klutsis. In fact, photomontage was a common feature of both advertising and commercial photography well before the First World War. Sergei Tretyakov took this for granted in his monograph on Heartfield, published in 1936; Sally Stein has recently investigated early commercial photomontage more thoroughly ("The Composite Photographic Image and the Composition of Consumer Ideology"), *Art Journal* (spring, 1981), pp. 39–45.
5. The first English exhibition of the photomontages was held at the Arcade Gallery in London, in December 1939, shortly after Heartfield had arrived in England as a political refugee. Further exhibitions of his work were held in 1969 (Institute of Contemporary Arts, London); 1980 (Camden Arts Centre); and 1989 (Goethe Institute, London, Glasgow Arts Centre, Bluecoat Gallery, Liverpool).
6. See "Biographical Chronology," p. 300 ff.
7. "From an Interview with John Heartfield" (1967), in Roland März, ed., *John Heartfield: Der Schnitt entlang der Zeit. Selbstzeugnisse – Erinnerungen – Interpretationen*, (Dresden, 1981), pp. 464–69.
8. Wieland Herzfelde, "George Grosz, John Heartfield, Erwin Piscator, Dada und die Folgen oder die Macht der Freundschaft," *Sinn und Form* (June 23, 1971), pp. 1224–51, in März, *Der Schnitt*, p. 78. Translation mine.
9. See "Biographical Chronology," pp. 302, 317.
10. A very good history of the Malik Press appears in an exhibition catalogue by James and Sibylle Fraser, *The Malik-Verlag, 1916–1947: Berlin, Prague, New York* (New York: The Goethe House in association with the Madison Campus Library, Fairleigh Dickinson University, 1984).
11. George Grosz, in a rather Dada-spirited statement, pinned the moment of invention to "5:00 some May morning in 1916, in my studio at the south end of town," in Hans Richter, *Dada: Art and Anti-Art* (London, 1965), p. 117.

12. Richard Huelsenbeck, *Mit Witz, Licht und Grütze. Auf den Spuren des Dadaismus* (Wiesbaden, 1957), pp. 98–99, in März, *Der Schnitt*, p. 64.

13. The Berlin Dada Manifesto of 1918 explicitly rejected Expressionism; Heartfield did not sign it. In notes from an interview made in 1944 by the English art historian Francis Klingender, however, Heartfield refers to Expressionism as "the biggest lie of the twentieth century." Francis Klingender, "Diskussion mit John Heartfield über Dadaismus und Surrealismus, 1944," in März, *Der Schnitt*, pp. 48, 57–64.

14. *Der Gegner*, Vol. 1, No. 10–11 (1919/20), pp. 48–56, in März, *Der Schnitt*, p. 112. The "Kunstlump" – loosely "art scab" – refers to the painter Oskar Kokoschka, at the time a professor at the Dresden Academy of Art. The incident in question concerned a stray bullet that had damaged Rubens's painting *Bathsheba* during the Kapp putsch on March 15, 1920. Kokoschka had, at his own expense, printed and distributed posters around the city asking, in an imperious tone, that further hostilities be conducted at a safe remove from the cultural treasures, or better, that two champions – the political leaders of the opposing factions – be designated to fight on behalf of the larger group, as in ancient times.

15. *Die Rote Fahne*, Vol. 3, No. 99 (June 9, 1920), in März, *Der Schnitt*, pp. 112–14.

16. "Das Proletariat und die Kunst. Politische Bemerkungen," *Die Rote Fahne*, Vol. 3, No. 112 (June 24, 1920), in März, *Der Schnitt*, p. 123.

17. Klingender's unpublished notes from a discussion of April 2, 1944, in März, *Der Schnitt*, pp. 48, 57–64.

18. Background of Heartfield's graphic design in particular is given in Maud Lavin, "Heartfield in Context," *Art in America*, Vol. 73 (February, 1985), pp. 84–93.

19. From an interview with John Heartfield, 1967, in März, *Der Schnitt*, pp. 464–65.

20. Gustav Stolz, "Die Ausstellung," *Film und Foto* (Stuttgart, 1929), p. 12. Reprint edited by Karl Steinorth, with a preface by Manfred Rommel (Stuttgart: Deutsche Verlags-Anstalt, 1979).

21. From notes made during Heartfield's visit, Tretyakov later wrote the first monograph on the artist, published in 1936.

22. Aleksei Fedorov-Davydov, "Kämpferische Kunst. John Heartfield, ein proletarischer Künstler," *Brigada khudozhnikov* (Moscow, 1932), in März, *Der Schnitt*, pp. 279–84.

23. Worker-Photography is the subject of an exhibition currently traveling in the United States, *Camera as Weapon: Worker Photography between the Wars.* The catalogue, published by the Museum of Photographic Arts, San Diego, contains a comprehensive essay by guest curator Leah Ollman.

24. A spirited English translation by Anne Halley, with an afterword and notes by Harry Zohn, was published by the University of Massachusetts Press, Amherst, in 1972.

25. Angelica Wilhelm, in "Nicht gefallen, sondern wirken…," *Bildende Kunst*, No. 32, pt. 4 (1984), p. 150.

26. One of the photographers who worked closely with Heartfield, Janós Reismann (professional name Wolf Reiss), later described the exacting demands the artist sometimes made, observing that Heartfield "hated all photographers" – he included himself – because of "the nuance […] they could no longer perceive." Wolf Reiss, "Als ich mit John Heartfield zusammenarbeitete," *Internationale Literatur* (Moscow, May 1934), pp. 186–88, in März, *Der Schnitt*, p. 190.

27. According to his son Tom, Heartfield did enjoy taking amateur snapshots later in his life (personal conversation).

28. Documents pertaining to the 1934 events, "Mánes I," along with others from further attempts to censor Heartfield's work that occurred in 1936 and 1937, respectively, are assembled in März, *Der Schnitt*, pp. 331–50 and 362–76.

29. Julian Jackson, *The Popular Front in France: Defending Democracy, 1934–38* (Cambridge: Cambridge University Press, 1988), pp. 119–20.

30. Louis Aragon, "John Heartfield et la beauté revolutionnaire," *Commune*, No. 20 (April, 1935), pp. 985–91. The essay appears in English translation in *Photography in the Modern Era: European Documents and Critical Writings, 1913–1940*, Christopher Phillips, ed. (New York: The Metropolitan Museum of Art/ Aperture, 1989), pp. 60–67.

31. Walter Benjamin, "The Author as Producer," in *Reflections: Essays, Aphorisms, Autobiographical Writings*, translated by Edmund Jephcott (New York: Schocken, 1986), p. 229. First published as "Der Autor als Produzent," *Versuche über Brecht* (Frankfurt, Suhrkamp Verlag, 1966).

32. Walter Benjamin, "The Work of Art in the Age of Mechanical Reproduction," [sic] in *Illuminations*, Hannah Arendt, ed. (New York: Schocken, 1969), p. 238. Translated by Harry Zohn.

33. *Lilliput*, Vol. IV, No. 5 (London, 1939).

34. Details of Heartfield's life in England are drawn from an account given by Gertrud Heartfield, the woman he met in England and whom he married in 1952. "Im englischen Exil," 1977/78, in März, *Der Schnitt*, pp. 419–32. A brief and anecdotal account by Richard Carline also appeared in the catalogue for the Heartfield exhibition organized by the Arts Council of Great Britain in 1969.

35. The remark is from Lukács's "Realism in the Balance," originally published in the journal *Das Wort*, 1938. It is part of the famous "Realism-Expressionism" debate carried by that journal in the mid-1930's, in which Lukács, Brecht, Ernst Bloch, and Walter Benjamin confronted one another on broad questions of what art should be and do in a socialist society. In these debates, Heartfield's work is mentioned specifically on occasion; more often it is treated within the broader issue of montage. The debates are outlined in English in *Aesthetics and Politics: the Key Texts of the Classic Debate within German Marxism*, Ronald Taylor, translation ed. (London: Verso, 1977). Lukács's reference to Heartfield's work being "like a good joke" is on page 43.

36. Heartfield himself insisted that his cut-and-pasted, drawn-on, airbrushed "originals" actually represented a preliminary stage. The finished work was the one that appeared in the newspaper, in editions of thousands.

37. Letter of December 12, 1913, to Else Lasker-Schüler, in Wieland Herzfelde, "George Grosz, John Heartfield, Erwin Piscator, Dada und die Folgen oder die Macht der Freundschaft," *Sinn und Form*, Vol. 23, No. 6 (1971), pp. 1221–51.

38. John Berger, "The Political Uses of Photo-Montage," *Selected Essays and Articles: The Look of Things* (Hammondsworth: Penguin, 1972), pp. 183–88.

39. In Eckhard Neumann "Das Comeback des visuellen Agitators John Heartfield," *Format*, Vol. 13 (summer, 1968), p. 25, in Roland März, *Der Schnitt*, note 9, p. 171.

P. 30–31
"War and Dead Bodies – The Last Hope of the Rich."
Arbeiter-Illustrierte-Zeitung (*AIZ*, Berlin) No. 18, 1932, pp. 420–421. Cat. no. 210

KRIEG UND LEICHEN — DIE L

TE HOFFNUNG DER REICHEN

Peter Pachnicke

Morally Rigorous
and Visually Voracious

Whenever I have the task of designing a title page or cover for a book or brochure of our political front, I try to do it in such a way that it appeals irresistibly to the public at large, that is to say, guarantees the widest possible promulgation of revolutionary literature, is a faithful reflection of the contents, and, furthermore, is an autonomous paper that promotes our aims. [...] Every scrap of printed paper, every line of print, every book cover must be a help in the great struggle, for the only way that can save us is the way shown us by the Communist Party.

John Heartfield, 1932[1]

I actually believe that the more exceptional the individual, the more startling the sensual delight he experiences in being abruptly absorbed into the mass and detached from himself.

André Gide, 1935[2]

Why important intellectuals in the thirties ostentatiously devoted their talents to the service of the proletariat has never been satisfactorily explained. For Brecht, Eisler, Grosz, Heartfield, Herzfelde, and Piscator were just the very ones who in their youth were so loud in their protests against all forms of restriction of their individuality through ideology, order, and bureaucracy, and whose favorite occupation was to provoke the good, industrious, obsequious petit bourgeois. They, of all people, now wanted to join the proletarian mass movement, to serve the Communist Party, to be a spearhead in the class warfare. Later, Walter Mehring wrote the following about this transformation in the life of the Herzfelde/Heartfield brothers: "[...] disgusted at its [sic. Dadaism's] asocial shallowness, its privileges of profuse talents, horrified at its own frivolity – rather as St. Augustine was by the Manichean heresy of Carthage – they sought consolation in the bosom of universal Mother Russia, under the rod of a severe father, the international working class, and in the fold of bolshevism."[3]

This comment is malicious, but it betokens a deep-seated longing of not a few intellectuals for a common human society – and that yearning did in fact link Heartfield more closely to the proletariat than a theoretical realization of the "historical mission of the working classes." He was not following any intellectual insight: "No, our dear Jonny was prompted by only one thing – a bruised heart that reacted very strongly to any kind of adverse, unjust, ominous, or undeserved utterance affecting our common society. That tortured, crushed heart of his, and that alone, showed him the way."[4]

Hate and Longing

Heartfield, who in his earliest childhood had experienced emotional hardship and physical punishment, had not broken down under everyday cruelty but had developed a resilient, aggressive, and even choleric sense of justice, "which reacted to every suffering he witnessed as violently as to any attack against himself."[5] This rigorous moralism was expressed not only in an implacable hatred of the bourgeois class and all who sought to preserve it, but also in an almost ingenuous faith in the communist society as the fulfillment of an unsatisfied social longing. Heartfield was, according to Oskar Maria Graf, "a fanatical moralist and Don Quixote rolled into one."[6] He was a romantic artist who, on the one hand, was disgusted with capitalist reality, flogged it with merciless satire, and, on the other hand, drew a sentimental picture of the movement of the masses as an embodiment of unadulterated hope. Sharp criticism of the times and ecstatic pathos, satire, sentimentality, hate, and a striving for harmony are indissolubly mingled in Heartfield's works – as in those of Tucholsky and Chaplin.

Scholarship so far may often have belittled Heartfield's works depicting the ideals of the workers' movement, because these works do not apply the same critical criteria in showing up the inconsistencies of that movement as do his works about the capitalist class; but the fact remains that the function of those works – as dreams of a harmonious world order free from such discord – has not been duly appreciated. A comparison of the dust jackets for *Der Abgrund* [*The Abyss*] and *Staat ohne Arbeitslose* [*State without Unemployed*] shows an emphatic, socially critical point of view with a strong utopian perspective: *Staat ohne Arbeitslose* as a utopian place where the individual is no longer engulfed by the masses but is able to rise up from a mighty movement in which the common man is no longer humiliated but resurrected. We are faced with a pathos, the touching naiveté which we can only understand if we read these works in the meantime as historical products of what at the time was still an unspoiled Romanticism; the movement of social realism has since become estranged from its ideals to the point of self-destruction, and – that is the historical tragedy of those works of Heartfield's – many of the images and symbols of the working classes created by him have been ridiculed and misused as clichés, to idealize oppressive inconsistencies (Figs. pp. 36, 37).

What may be the most satirical book in German literature, the picture-and-text-montage *Deutschland, Deutschland über alles* by Tucholsky and Heartfield, is also a very sentimental one. The ruling class and those subservient to it are mercilessly caricatured in it, the oppressed, however, are subtly exalted (Fig. p. 35; Pls. 60–69). While members of men's choral societies, officer cadet corps, dueling fraternities, and men's clubs stand or sit stupidly and stiffly in rows, the faces and attitudes of the common people in all their misery give the impression of being sensitive and capable of suffering; they are dignified and proud – as if the formerly bourgeois ideals had come home to roost in the countenances of the almost iconlike portrayals of the exploited and dispossessed. By contrast, the aristocracy, landowners, petite bourgeoisie – although these are authentic photographs – look as though they have been taken from the pages of the magazines *Simplicissimus* or *Der Wahre Jakob* [*The Real McCoy*]. When the book appeared, the readers must have been particularly astonished to learn that such types really existed. Or had the Weimar Republic gone through such an anachronistic development that reality had become a farce: reality as satire in real life? If so, that meant that photography was indeed the modern medium for documentation *and* caricature.

Thus, *Deutschland, Deutschland über alles* became both a social satire and a sociological study of "specimens of the German mentality" between the two wars. For the sociologist Theodor Geiger, the "mentality specimens" were characteristic types of people of different classes and social strata, who in their specific lifestyle, way of moving, speaking, and posing, as a whole convey a holistic impression of a given society.[7] In an endless flood of photographs from the illustrated mass tabloids and from photo agencies, Heartfield discovered with his visual and social flair the "mentality specimens" that are to the present day our idea of a German civil servant, teacher, banker, officer of the guard, captain, judge, pastor, emperor, bar regular, member of the Reichstag, general, military chaplain, soldier, and laborer. "Once you've studied the pictures a while," writes Tucholsky in the preface, "they begin to speak. The people in the pictures hold still – so patiently, that you can study them at your leisure. [...] They open their hearts to you. This is how we love, they say, and this is how we hate, and this is

Left:
John Heartfield, dust jacket for Oskar Maria Graf, *Der Abgrund* [*The Abyss*], London 1936

Right:
John Heartfield, dust jacket for Ernst Glaeser/Franz Carl Weiskopf, *Staat ohne Arbeitslose* [*State Without Unemployed*], Prague 1934

why we didn't get anywhere, and this is our youth, and these are our dreams of glory, and this is what our parents looked like, and here is my weak point, and here my strength, and, they say, I'm a good guy, but I don't want to admit it, and I'm a bastard at the office – more and more crowd around, and the pictures have no ending: faces and backsides and the well-to-do and the rich and the millions who work, the places where they work, and the houses they live in, the fields around the house, the meadows, the little lakes, the oceans, the towers of the city, the forest, the workshops, foundries, plowland, the factories, the offices, movie-houses – an unending picture book: Germany."[8]

Visual Voracity

Photographs not only depict reality, but they can – if properly selected and intriguingly mounted with other photos and captions – express something of social significance both sensuously and compellingly just like traditional art works. That was why Heartfield wrote in capitals above the door in his show-room at the *Werkbund* exhibition FILM UND FOTO held in Stuttgart in 1929: "MALE MIT FOTO/DICHTE MIT FOTO" ["PAINT WITH PHOTOGRA-PHY/MAKE POETRY WITH PHOTOGRAPHY"]. To credit the hitherto illegitimate medium of photography with the same power of artistic expression as painting and sculpture was part of the "material revolution" that dominated the aims and discussions of avant-garde artists of the time. Neither the authenticity nor the informative value of photography was disputed (although even then it was a more effective vehicle for distorting the truth than the typewriter), but Heartfield's claim that photomontage was the most satisfactory instrument for expressing normal human perceptions certainly was questioned. And, as if that was not enough, he challengingly wrote on one of the walls of his showroom in Stuttgart the words of an art stylite: "VAN GOGH: EIN GEFUEHL FÜR DIE DINGE ALS SOLCHE IST VIEL WICHTIGER ALS EIN SINN FUER DAS MALERISCHE" ["VAN GOGH: A FEELING FOR OBJECTS AS SUCH IS MORE IMPORTANT THAN A FEELING FOR PAINTING"].

A medium commercially manipulated by bourgeois society for press and advertising, and politically and economically corrupt, was given precedence over traditional independent art. A sacrilege, especially as Heartfield not only declared photomontage to be the most modern and creative of artistic media, but also because, instead of claiming the venerable aura of the museum for his works, he preferred the triviality of the mass media newspapers, magazines, books, and posters, since there he could reproduce his ideas technically and publicize them. Art was to penetrate into the daily life of the masses, was to make use of the media and techniques familiar to them. This drastic art program was at that time defined as "operative art."[9] This was not simply another term for art with a proletarian bias, which made use of traditional forms of the visual arts in order to make itself understood by ordinary people. On the contrary, the intention behind "operative art" was to operate in everyday life with the most modern means available to avant-garde artists, who up to then had been confined within the isolation of the bourgeois art world. Above all, they aimed to activate the passive observer with the avant-garde strategy of provocation, to startle him out of his lethargy by involving him in the process of art and inducing him to be productive himself. In this process, montage was the most enlightening and rewarding method of depiction. After all, the perceptive faculty of the masses was being daily manipulated by an industrial production run on the assembly-line principle as well as by a technically reproduced culture industry. Furthermore, montage works – by the irritating heterogeneous nature of their component parts – can stimulate independent thought much more effectively than traditional works of art that call for meditative appreciation.

Kurt Tucholsky, *Deutschland, Deutschland über alles*, Berlin 1929, p. 149

The theorists of the operative art concept were particularly fascinated by Heartfield. Newspaper, book, poster, etc., were for him not only sources that opened new methods of depiction, but at the same time were the essential operative scope for promulgating them as effectively as possible. After all, the new media were not only intended to be the scene of a search for the "aesthetic building blocks" of a material revolution but also the everyday field for their mass development. "We don't need to wait for Tolstoy, we have our epic. Our epic is the newspaper. [...]"[10] While Heartfield "operated" quite unabashedly in this vein, Tretyakov and Brecht were trying in an exemplary manner to integrate into the theatre the "aesthetic building blocks" they had obtained by studying newspapers, radio broadcasts, films, etc. This approach mostly lent these didactic dramas an artificial, pedantic quality, the atmosphere of a laboratory experiment to activate the public. Faced with so much artistic pedagogical zeal, it was virtually impossible for the spectator to enjoy the vital energy emanating from the innovations hidden in the trivial media. Brecht also seems to have been shocked by the truly elementary forces of the more lowly media, for on May 12, 1942, in American exile, he noted down in his working diary: "A hundred times a day one can hear rousing music on the radio, choirs encouraging one to buy Coca Cola, and one cries desperately for l'art pour l'art."[11]

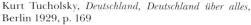

Kurt Tucholsky, *Deutschland, Deutschland über alles*, Berlin 1929, p. 169

Heartfield, on that point, was quite different: He was obsessed by visual curiosity. Reared in the advertising world, he never worried about whether certain "low" means of expression were worthy of his works, but was constantly in search of visual discoveries with which to convey his intentions even more graphically and precisely on posters, dust jackets, and news sheets. According to Hans Reimann, he was one of the few in Germany who knew the meaning of advertising: "that Odol [brand name of a mouthwash] has no meaning as long as nobody understands what Odol is."[12]

During his student days in Munich and Berlin, and his employment as commercial artist in Mannheim for Edelweiss, the producers of cheese and sparkling

Red Front, 1927

wine, Heartfield's visual voracity covered all forms of art, legitimate and illegitimate. For example, he "lapped up Beardsley and Thomas Theodor Heine, who blossomed forth magnificently at the end of the nineties, a veritable *praeceptor Germaniae* for the great among Germany's illustrators. John Heartfield toyed with ornamental art as practiced by the Japanese, which the stout-hearted Brecht presented at the Pinakothek. He rooted about among typecases and devised up typographical experiments. He flung himself, so to speak, on oriental carpets, devoured faience ware (again, in a metaphorical sense), and, for some considerable time, was fanatically devoted to Turkish folk art, which he cast aside after Wertheim and the KaDeWe [department stores] came into being."[13] While studying under Ernst Neumann in Berlin, he learned that an object from the street or a department store is as interesting as a plaster head from an art school, and that it need not be depicted only with a pencil but can be reproduced from colored paper: "Neumann did not present his pupils with dead imitations but with real objects such as zeppelins, dynamos, turbines, dogs, fleas. Before beginning his lessons, he would ask, 'Now, my boy, what did you see on your way here?' And that would be drawn, or cut out and assembled from colored paper."[14]

The art historians, with their unwavering devotion to the time-honored arts, made great efforts to discover forerunners of the collage and montage principle in painting and graphic art; but the enormously innovative impetus that the avant-garde creative methods received from the "low" arts was for the most part overlooked (with the exception of film). However, what Heartfield demonstrated impressively at the 1929 *Werkbund* exhibition was taken particularly from formal innovations from the trivial arts. Since his Dada period, for instance, especially American illustrated periodicals had great influence on his artistic work; not just because their antithetical contents were often flung together in a way that (for the German mentality at the time) was almost profane, but also because photography and typography seemed to be staging a sensational fight for recognition on every page. Graphic photos with texts in large and small print – sometimes emphasized in color – provided exciting contrasts. Heartfield's montage art was permanently molded by these newspaper and magazine pages. It was here that he got the idea of how to create a three-dimensional effect on a flat surface by means of the very dissimilar elements of photography, typography, and color. In his Dada period, that had been an exuberant game with as many components as possible; later, when he felt committed to the concept of "operative art," this developed into meticulous montage composed of just a few elements. Regarding the most striking photomontages shown at the Stuttgart exhibition, Tretyakov wrote that Heartfield often used "no more than two elements [. . .] a photo and a photo, a photo and text, a photo and paint, a photo and a drawing."[15]

Incidentally, as a commercial artist he had learned to organize a flat surface simply and impressively with a minimum of elements through his study of the posters of Hohlwein and others. What kept him on the alert for innovations from the world of posters, packaging, and window displays was, as mentioned before, his artistic flair: not to depict himself in his works but to subordinate himself for the sake of the subject, and invest it with a face, body, and clothing in which the spiritual content makes the greatest possible optical impact. By designing the jackets of books for the Malik-Verlag [Malik Publishing Company] and the Neuer Deutscher Verlag [New German Publishing Company] as advertising vehicles combining photography, typography, and color, he made them "come to life," made them "'fight' for the author."[16] To design a book not merely as a two-dimensional entity but in a three-dimensional way was a sensation at that time, but for a commercial artist interested in packaging techniques, this was quite natural: the book in its entirety was attractively wrapped all around (front, back, spine). The usual tricks of the window dresser to intensify the interest of the observer in a given product also included the serial presentation as practiced by Heartfield with certain posters and books on the walls and in showcases at the Stuttgart and Moscow exhibitions. In this way, he introduced everyday designing devices of commercial art into his practice of operative art.

Productivity of Satire

Heartfield admittedly enticed the observer into the scene with the suggestive methods of the trivial media; he did not, however, permit himself to settle down comfortably with these methods. His book jackets, posters, and layouts of newspaper pages do not allow the observer to wallow in a "world of illusion," but confront him in his photomontages with the contradictions and conflicts of reality.

For example, the attractive red spot on the jacket of Maxim Gorki's *Der 9. Januar* [*The Ninth of January*] turns out on closer inspection to be the blood of Russian revolutionaries. And the book *Drei Soldaten* [*Three Soldiers*] by John Dos Passos (Pl. 20), with the romantic scene under a starry sky in the front, shows on the back a road with fallen soldiers. That was the aim of "operative art": *to turn the*

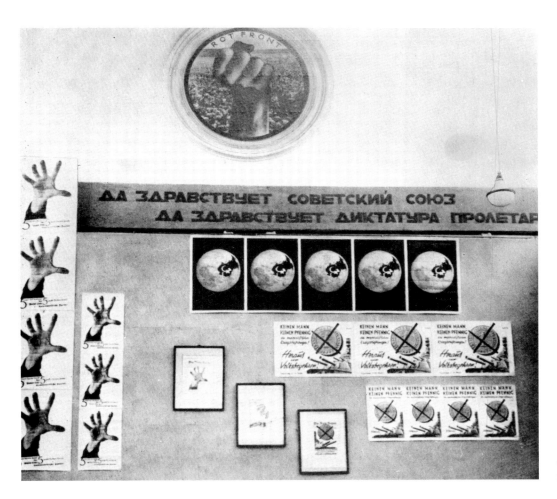

Wall display at the Heartfield Exhibition in Moscow, November 20–December 10, 1931

Portrayal of the Times – No Comment

John Heartfield, "Pillars of Society: 'Everything's in Perfect Order!'" *Arbeiter-Illustrierte-Zeitung* (AIZ, Prague), June 29, 1933, p. 436

stimulating and suggestive methods of the bourgeois mass media in a way calculated to irritate and enlighten. The idea was to provoke, to unmask, to get to the bottom of the beautiful masquerade of the "drama in which stupidity, brutality, and rottenness play the main roles."[17] This "disturbing, sobering, and animating view of reality"[18] took hold of John Heartfield as a result of his contact with George Grosz. In the latter's works he sensed that satire held many artistic possibilities for him with which he could find a powerful outlet for his characteristic trait to feel morally assaulted by each and every humiliation. This led, as Elias Canetti has put it, to that highly individual way Heartfield had of learning and expressing himself: "[...] he could only learn aggressively; and I believe one could show that this is the secret of his montages. He brought things together, he confronted things after first leaping to them, and the tension of these leaps is preserved in his montages. [...] He learned only from things that he regarded as attacks; and in order to experience something new, he had to see it as an attack."[19] Thus, paradoxically, his artistic talent developed to classic greatness, in the photomontages of the *Arbeiter-Illustrierte-Zeitung (AIZ)* in the intellectual militancy of the Weimar Republic and under the physical and psychological threat of the Nazis.

"In Heartfield's art there is an element that serious artists have always avoided like the plague. It is the comic element in all its forms – jokes, fun, satire, irony, sarcasm. In Western art, the comic artist was never highly respected, because art was used to idealize."[20] And in fact, the essence of caricature, to expose false idealization to ridicule, was particularly in keeping with Heartfield's artistic bent. For the whole point of caricature is to underline a different, "opposite view of the world, to protest against a world of beauty, meaningfulness, propriety, to lay bare weaknesses and defects, to emphasize tendentiously the caustic, the callous, the wicked [...], its basic form of criticism being directed against the world of illusion."[21]

This strategy to create, from protest, images in opposition to the prevailing world of pictures led, as Werner Hofmann discovered, to caricature's bridging role in the nineteenth century for the development of avant-garde art in the twentieth century. This applies to caricature as avowed antiart, as persiflage and travesty of artistic beauty, as a potential resistance against anachronistic conditions, as the artist's right to an abnormal way of thinking and to a playful representation governed solely by his subjective slant, as well as a strategy to stimulate the observer to independent thought and feeling. "Caricature means scepticism. [...] The caricaturist sees below the surface of the world and behind the scenes of its drama the confusing scenery of a 'topsy-turvy world.' He puts on the motley of the scoffer, whose jests turn nonsense into profundity. [...]"[22] In the process, caricature emerges as a "critical manifestation of an artistic personality,"[23] which "contrives distortion as a deliberate protest, the playful transformation of forms as an intentional, subjective creative whim."[24] In Dadaism, these productive forces of caricature caused a tremendous upheaval in modern art. In the classic montages of the *AIZ,* Heartfield pursued his confusing, obsessive sport in the form of precise constructions with few elements. An analysis of the creative materials and motifs of Heartfield's photomontages in the *AIZ* shows how closely they were related to caricature, not to Daumier's, but in particular to that in *Simplicissimus* and *Der Wahre Jakob,* then obtainable at any kiosk. Thus, in his classic photomontages, Heartfield expressed himself mainly by means of portrait caricatures and created pictorial satires using text and image quotations and comparing people with animals, employing their symbolic forms (large and small, light and dark, etc.). Furthermore, his best montages, like all clever satires, depend entirely on the wealth of pictorial and text comparisons, the maze of concepts and illustrations, the aptness of parallels, ambiguity, and surefire wit.

His favorite way of ridiculing a political opponent was with the latter's own weapons. For example, Heartfield would take him at his word ("Hurray, the butter is all gone! Goering in his Hamburg speech: 'Iron has always made a country strong; butter and lard, at most, have made the people fat'" [Pl. 77]); or he would show what really was *behind* their words ("Millions are behind me") [Fig. p. 290]; or, again, the adversary really keeps his promise ("Through light to night. Thus spoke Dr. Goebbels: 'Let us again fan the flames to make sure the blinded won't awaken'"); and a slip of the tongue is taken to be meant seriously ("I Will Lead You to Splendid Bankruptcy") [Fig. p. 42]. His versatility is an object lesson ("German Natural History; in the history of the Weimar Republic: the logical consequence: Ebert-Hindenburg-Hitler") [Pl. 72], and he can be dead serious when he wants to be ("The Peaceful Fish of Prey") [Pl. 81]. The impact of his symbols is clear ("The Old Slogan in the 'New' Reich: Blood and Iron") [Pl. 98], as is the fact that his allusions go far back ("As in the Middle Ages . . . So in the Third Reich") [Pl. 101].

The adversary is not only beaten with the *intellectual substance* of his hypocritical words and metaphors but also with the *form* in which he lies like the devil and which conjures up grand illusions. In Daumier's time this was done with lithographs in illustrated newspapers and with the commentaries of their captions; in the twenties and thirties, there were the large-format magazines with their documentary photos and their authentic atmosphere, the headlines and headings screaming out the essential message in large letters, and the news, reports, and commentaries in small print redolent of objectivity. Heartfield did his unmasking by adhering to these same forms, down to the type and size of typography. He not only parodied, ridiculed, vexed, and put the subject at a distance, but also made a travesty of the subject as well as the forms of illusion, thereby evoking in the reader that sense of irritation and surprise that is for him not only a mental challenge but produces that perceptive enjoyment with its reward of laughter and a vicarious feeling of superiority. That is what gives "caricature its knowing quality, the deliberately contrived punch line, the hid-

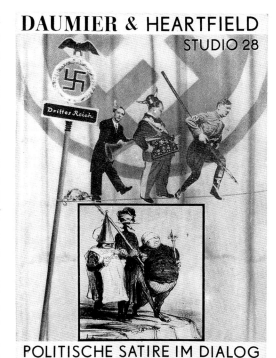

Exhibition catalogue *Daumier & Heartfield – Politische Satire im Dialog*, Altes Museum, Berlin 1981, front page

Left:
Geiss, *The Worker in the Reich of the Swastika*. Election poster of the SPD [German Social Democratic Party], 1932

Right:
A. Segue, *The Red Week: The Advertising Appeal of the Party*. Poster

Honoré Daumier, *Will There Be a Total Eclipse of the Sun?* Lithograph, 1871

John Heartfield, "Eclipse of the Sun Over the 'Liberated' Rhine." (*AIZ*, Berlin), no. 31, 1930, p. 603

Locarno? Vote German Nationalist! Poster, 1928

den allusion that depends on the spectator to grasp fleeting implications and random notations. Caricature depends on having a knowing public that enjoys the interchange of ambivalent forms and subject matter."[25] Thus, caricature caused the activation of the public's "visual intuition," which the avant-garde artists in the twentieth century regarded as the essential objective of their artistic work in a world of passive consumers.

Heartfield's "Imaginary Museum"

"Picasso was the first to paint 'glued-together junk,' to the horror even of the cultured among the population; Heartfield is so close to the people that many a cultivated person will have nothing to do with montage."[26] What Ernst Bloch wrote in 1938 denotes a paradox that reflects the contradictory reception of the montage principle by the masses. The intention of the avant-garde, of activating people's minds by means of montage, was *repudiated* by the masses in those instances where artists were trying to revolutionize traditional arts, whereas an appreciation of montage was quite a matter of course in the familiar world of the trivial arts. That explains the extraordinary influence of Eisenstein, Chaplin, and Heartfield: by remodeling the forms of depiction familiar to the general public from the trivial (commercial) media, they achieved a "material revolution," which managed truly to galvanize the recipients.

Heartfield's decision in this context, as a *Monteur* to make use primarily of photographic material, was particularly important for his impact, for that medium had, by and large, introduced a new element of sensuality into the world of illusion. In the days before the circulation of large-format illustrated newspapers, people's dreams and longings could only be roused through words and drawings, but now, by means of photographic reproduction techniques, every conceivable idea and desire was rendered almost palpable as a pseudo-reality within easy reach before their eyes. The pictorial world became a second,

vicarious reality: "Today art does not consist of experience [...] but art consists of artifacts."[27]

Now that all sorts of things and people, irrespective of time and place, size and state, could be brought into the livingroom in the form of illustrated newspapers, not only was a suggestive and seductive collection of images created, but also a completely new opportunity for the satirist to debunk illusion; for he now had a pile of images lying before him that put the whole world in equally large photos at his scissors' disposal. He now only needed to cut out from his material the things that, when combined, revealed the reality behind them: he had before him the material for their reconstruction. "Schwitters took the material debris of society – bus tickets, nails, every conceivable rubbish – to create his reality. Heartfield took the ideological debris of society to make his picture of society. [...] Heartfield put reality in its true perspective, and that is an unforgivable sin because the true image of the ruling class must remain invisible to the common people."[28]

Heartfield's "imaginary museum," the images stored in his voracious visual memory and incorporated in his montages, must have contained visual motifs taken from the "high" and "low" arts. At all events, it is evident that he took motifs from sculpture, painting, graphic arts, films, newspapers, advertisements, caricatures, and postage stamps. His creative adaptation of traditional imagery has been repeatedly stressed: the dove as a symbol of peace ("The Meaning of Geneva") [Pl. 88], the crucifixion motif as the expression of the depths of human suffering ("As in the Middle Ages ... So in the Third Reich"), the Samson legend as a depiction of the old order ("Pillars of Society"). A study of the history of caricature and poster art,[29] however, suggests that even such "classical" motifs often found their way into his work indirectly via caricature and posters. The idea for the illustration to "As in the Middle Ages ... So in the Third Reich" probably came from the Social Democrat poster "The Worker in the Reich of the Swastika";[30] "Pillars of Society" from a caricature such as "Portrayal of the times – without words";[31] "Gale Force 1917" [Pl. 70] from the poster advertising *The Red Week*;[32] and "The Meaning of Geneva" from a postage stamp [Fig. p. 43].[33]

The fact that no systematic search for such trivial pictorial stimuli had been undertaken can only be explained by the underestimation of the innovative power of the popular arts by art historians, who were fixed on tradition. It was Roland März alone who revealed a variety of motif correlations in Daumier's work.[34] But if one leafs through *Simplicissimus, Der Wahre Jakob*, the *Süddeutscher Postillon*, or contemporary poster collections, one realizes that they contain works that did not originate directly from Daumier's caricatures but from later adaptations of those motifs. For example, the photomontage "The Watch on the Rhine" cannot be entirely attributed to a knowledge of Daumier's lithograph "Prussia and Freedom," but also to the poster "Locarno? Vote German Nationalist!" Heartfield, too, when he produced "H. M. Adolf: I Will Lead You to Splendid Bankruptcy!," was at least familiar with Durrer's drawing "S. M." from *Simplicissimus* as well as Daumier's lithograph of the "Citizen King" Louis Philippe.[35]

Basically, the question that really arises – and not only as regards Heartfield – is whether the productivity of avant-garde artists in this century was not stimulated in a much stronger degree by innovations and impulses of the trivial media than has been supposed until now. This is an issue that, considering the phenomenon of pop art, was quite naturally to force itself onto art scholarship, especially in view of art trends that, like "operative art," had the avowed intention of deliberately opening the door to the mass-produced, day-to-day imagery. This kind of motif investigation must, above all, take into account the heterogeneous structure of Heartfield's visual memory, that is to say, ideas for one and the same image may stem from works of different genres. For instance, the Swiss stamp is not likely to be the sole source of inspiration for "The Meaning of Geneva." The idea of pitting the sharp point of a sword against soft, hovering downy feathers can probably be traced to Lang's Nibelungen film, in which the sharpness of Siegfried's sword was graphically shown with the same downy feathers. Another important thing would be to find out if other artists worked on certain motifs at the same time as Heartfield, and whether he took these versions into consideration in later variations. In 1928, when he created the poster "The Hand Has 5 Fingers" (Pl. 53; Fig. p. 294), Buñuel and Dalí's film *Un Chien Andalou* had its premiere, with the take of a symbolic hand crawling with ants; in 1942, the *Freie Deutsche Kultur* published Heartfield's crucified hand. The program aspired to by Tretyakov, Brecht, Piscator, Heartfield, and others, to effect a mental transformation in capitalist society by permeating everyday life with "operative art," was dependent on having access to the production and distribution machinery of mass-appeal movie theatres, films, radio, and the press. A good deal of this had to remain experimental and did not get beyond the laboratory stage, because this "huge machinery" could not be made available to the artists by the workers' movement at the time of the Weimar Republic. The one exception was the Münzenberg concern. "MÜNZENBERG's Neuer Deutscher Verlag, with its extensive book and newspaper production, did not have as wide a range of the market as such concerns as ULLSTEIN, MOSSE, and SCHERL, but their illustrated workers' press, which was edited with deliberate party-line bias as a reflection of social conditions, was considered to be an instrument of enlightenment. [...] In 1925, the *AIZ*, a biweekly publication, had a circulation of 200,000."[36] Heartfield without the *AIZ* and Münzenberg would be just as inconceivable as Daumier without the newspapers *Charivari* and *Caricature,* and the publisher Philipon. The constant challenge to "deliver" works to a politically hypersensitized circle of readers, in which he could develop his political views and all

Left:
Honoré Daumier, *The Past – The Present – The Future.* Lithograph, 1834

Center:
Durrer, *H [is] M [ajesty]. Simplicissimus,* March 5, 1906, title page

Right:
John Heartfield, "H [is] M [ajesty] Adolf: I Will Lead You to Splendid Bankruptcy!" *(AIZ,* Berlin), August 21, 1932, p. 795

of his artistic capabilities, gave Heartfield the feeling that he was needed to play a part, in a personal and concrete manner, in the proletarian, anti-fascist movement. In so zealously devoting their services to the proletariat, the "operative artists" did so not as submissive "soldiers" prepared to take orders on the subject of art, but as "officers," who at the "cultural front" believed in bringing their artistic instruments – initially developed in the isolation of the bourgeois avant-garde – into the proletarian movement. They were convinced that their mission consisted in making their mark on the social revolution by revolutionizing artistic ways of depiction and their "material." The *AIZ* offered one of the rare examples of how to learn first-hand what proletarian culture is capable of when it has the *material and intellectual* conditions at its disposal for its development. One of the basic reasons for the fact that Heartfield, after his return to the German Democratic Republic after his emigration, did not continue the production of photomontages was that, although the proletariat was now in power and had monopolized the major cultural machinery, it did not enable those employed in it to develop their spiritual and mental powers.

Die von der Schweiz anläßlich der Abrüstungskonferenz herausgegebene Briefmarke — rechts die von der Moskauer „Prawda" veröffentlichte Karikatur auf die wahren Absichten der Konferenz.

Clipping from the (*AIZ*, Berlin), no. 26, 1932

The Operative Process and Autonomy

Shortly before the beginning of the Second World War, a discussion was conducted in the exile magazine *Das Wort* – as previously in the *Kunstlump* debate and in the Heartfield-Behne confrontation – a discussion on the socially most effective artistic strategies and devices; it was a "conflict of opinions between kindred spirits," in which, as before, each of the dissenting parties was adamant about its own artistic program.

Heartfield did not participate in the debate, but montage was a central subject of the dispute. Bloch and Eisler argued that montage was a new, important way of expression, developing along with radio, film, and the press to activate the masses. For Lukács, on the other hand, montage was the "height" of late bourgeois decadence: instead of the powerful effect of an autonomous work of art which, in its complexity, is able to give creative shape to the world as a whole, the montage of isolated fragments, torn from reality, produces pictures that, no matter how striking and in some cases impressively agitatorial, are intellectually – like a well-told joke – unable to penetrate the surface of life's reality.[37] Lukács, therefore, did not dispute the potential impact of Heartfield's photomontages, but he did contest the intellectual depth of this mode of depiction.

Furthermore, the futility of this discussion lay in the fact that it was carried on without regard to the works themselves. For Heartfield's photomontages did show that their effect was lasting. They abandoned their role as political instruments in a process of emancipation that was almost bizarre in its inconsistency, and thus proved to be precisely what Lukács had defined, namely, a complex intellectual creation reflecting the world in its entirety.[38] To understand this, it is enough to investigate Heartfield's works with the traditional instruments of art history; they prove to be considerably more subtle than Tretyakov's assertion, that "his most perfect works [. . .] involve no more than two elements," would lead us to expect. Photomontage is not, however, merely a matter of scissors and paste by means of which the *Monteur* takes the ready-made pictorial material and remodels it into rhetorical symbols of human gestures and speech; on the contrary, as regards the artistic resources, at least the spatial treatment, tonal value of photography, technique of retouching, and photogravure retain their importance.[39]

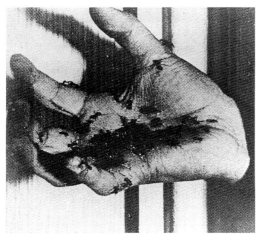

Luis Buñuel/Salvador Dalí, *Un Chien Andalou*, 1928. Film clip

In this book, we have tried for the first time to reproduce adequately Heartfield's designs for photomontages in their subtly graphic arrangement, as well as the *AIZ* pages with the aesthetic impact peculiar to photogravure in order to facilitate a *perceptive appreciation of the complexity of Heartfield's works*. In comparing the "original" *AIZ* pages with the usual black-and-white reproductions common until recently, the viewer is directly confronted with the oddly contradictory conclusion that the montage that surprised him with its intellectual, witty incisiveness is not printed in the *AIZ* with multiple contrasts and sharp contours, but with warmth and abundant tones. This lends the work not only spatial unity but also conveys a picturesque, "romantic" atmosphere – a word we would not hesitate to use if we were not referring to Heartfield. That was exactly what Heartfield wanted, for he deliberately decided in favor of photogravure as the only adequate means of reproducing his montages. Furthermore, according to the sensitive description of his montage designs by his photographer, Kuhnert, Heartfield, in order to avoid a high-contrast reproduction, used "mat, brownish photographic paper in varied tonal values."[40] In addition, there is "in the original montages [...] never a dead black, it is always a deep, luminous shade. When he used white script on dark tones [...] he never chose a hard white but used Chinese white that has a touch of gray in it, and thus produced a transition to the sepia tones."[41] This spatial atmosphere, this picturesque effect is important in itself: the longing for inner harmony stands in striking contrast to problematic, caustic satire. If we compare Heartfield's montage designs with the photographic works of the turn of the century, we can scarcely fail to notice that the special picturesque atmosphere in his works was enhanced by the tonal value of photography.

Harmony was also achieved by the almost "classic" pictorial layout to which Aragon drew attention when he stated that "the dove impaled on a bayonet in front of the League of Nations palace [Pl. 88] or the Nazi Christmas tree with its branches twisted into swastikas [Pl. p. 295] – there the viewer would detect not only Dada's heritage but also that of centuries of painting as a whole. There are still lifes by Heartfield, such as [...] the Hitler house of cards [Pl. 105] that unfailingly remind me of Chardin."[42] Above all, the later montages, with their often symmetrically balanced, systematic layout, have a simplicity and dignity that, in contrast to illustrated satire, lend them ambivalence and ambiguity. On closer inspection, the perceptive space of the picture is no less important than the assembled photographic pieces. With its differentiated structure, photomontage takes over its own operative function. Already in 1969, Marina Schneede-Sczesny and Uwe Schneede had remarked, with reference to Heartfield's legendary photomontage "Fathers and Sons" [Pl. pp. 22–23], that the "intentionally 'painterly' composition with the dark background [...] lends it at once spatial unity, perspective, self-containedness, and 'atmosphere'."[43] In contrast to the earlier collages, the photomontages were now permeated with an atmosphere that lent the space an *imaginary* quality. When Heartfield harassed his photographers, retouchers, and photogravure printers to pay more attention to what they considered to be unimportant details (the size of the photographic parts and the tonal value of the retouched spot), he did so endeavoring to construct from the photographic parts and gray tones *a pictorial space that is in itself coherent and intact*.

John Heartfield, photomontage for *Freie Deutsche Kultur* [*Free German Culture*] (London), no. 3, March 1942

This imaginary pictorial space often recalls the relatively flat expanse of studio photography. In the tradition of pictorial photography, people and objects in the foreground stand out in relief, with a sharp focus on details, against the softly lighted studio backdrop. This produces the effect (as Eckhard Siepmann comments on the montage "The Meaning of the Hitler Salute" [Pl. p. 292]) whereby "the surface around the body [...] remains 'soft' [...] because of the gentle gradations of light [...]; the surface because of its abstractness remains undefined, the interior structure of the body is highly defined."[44] Conforming to pictorial tradition, Heartfield in his montages (particularly in his satirical portraits) accentuated heads or significant gestures with a halolike pool of light, produced by means of studio lighting or retouching. A close scrutiny of the montage designs reveals how Heartfield created his imaginary space with much retouching. "Dissimilar tonal values of assembled photo parts had to be merged, and pasted edges made invisible for the printing process by means of an airbrush. [...] In addition to this, there is a deep mat airbrush effect in the greatest variety of tones ranging from light gray merging into ochre, pale blue to sepia and Chinese white, so as to divide or intensify lines. [...] A pale blue paint was sprayed over dark areas of the montages to prevent them from turning black during printing. When dark brown photo pieces are assembled, this effect is achieved by spraying them with sepia brown in order to make them appear as a uniform whole after printing."[45]

Thus his photomontages are not just products made up of single photographs and texts with a single – merely agitatorial level of meaning. They are complex, polysemantic pictorial structures, which give the impression of a *surreal* event with the intriguing interplay of parody and baffling pictures and texts. They also convey the impression of a harmonious composition by means of a wealth of tonal values of the surface, symbolic distribution of light and shadow, and imaginary space. "What is one to do," wrote Hans Hess, "when everyday reality is absurd...? That was precisely the problem of Heartfield, who was engulfed in an absurd situation. He had to discover ways of describing the nonabsurd. And he found them in typical examples taken from normal life, which in itself was so preposterous that he created a realistic art form with his surrealist approach. What he had to do, and did, was to turn the surrealist process inside out. He transformed fake poetry into genuine prose."[46] An art historiography free from ideology will be able to assess in the analysis of Heartfield's classic photomontages just how close he was to Surrealism. Heartfield himself rejected the ideological principles of Surrealism, but not its artistic innovations. "All this," he

NUR KEINE ANGST – ER IST VEGETARIER

Left:
Etienne Carjat, portrait of Giacchino Rossini. Photograph, 1860

Right:
John Heartfield, "Have No Fear – He's a Vegetarian." *Regards* (Paris), May 7, 1932

45

said to Francis D. Klingender, "does not mean that in the [...] atmosphere of the twenties and thirties, Surrealism might not have provided a stepping stone for some artists toward a more positive attitude regarding reality. In a number of cases, this undoubtedly happened, for instance from 1937 to 1939."[47]

In the most striking of the montages created in Prague before his escape to London, space as such had, in increasing measure, become the really significant factor. "Illustration for Grimms' Fairy Tale of the Cat and the Mouse," "The Fox and the Hedgehog," "This is the Salvation They Bring," "War" [Pls. 85, 113, 82, 97] – these are no longer satires, and nothing is exposed to ridicule any more. There are few snappy witticisms. Here the message is conveyed by depressing backgrounds, oppressed figures and objects, horror and panic, the time "shortly before darkness falls."[48] These are "grotesque scenes concerned not so much with concentrated forms as with a broad panorama of the world, or visions of the sheerly incredible."[49] In the early 1980's, Laszlo Glozer presented his retrospective *Westkunst* with works created shortly before the outbreak of the Second World War. Mondrian, Klee, Picasso, Moore, Beckmann, Schlemmer, Kokoschka, and Heartfield, who had been separated years before by their programmatic, quietly reflective or vociferous intentions, moved closer together – alarmed by their own ineffectuality in the face of the burning of pictures and the portents of a world conflagration. "The separation from the initial point of departure, the clipping of the wings of the avant-garde in the thirties, have become clearly discernible in art. [...] Their common interests are to be found here, an ambivalent revival of the atmosphere and expression of the not so much new as typical art of the late thirties. Dramatic subjects increase, pictorial backgrounds expand [...] with watered-down but no less striking pathos. [...] What is actually happening is an intensified reflection on a surrealist outside world in pictures with no limits on the possibilities of expression. In this context, pictures of different schools and outlooks are moving closer together. [...]"[50]

Pablo Picasso, *Chat à l'oiseau* [*Cat and Bird*]. Oil on canvas, 1939. New York, Mr. and Mrs. Victor W. Ganz Collection

Cat and Bird by Picasso dates from 1939. "Here the projection into the gigantic fills the whole picture. Simultaneously, the powers of the monstrous creature are shown, the ability to arch itself toward the hard ground, and the strength to hold down, to seize, and kill. Those could be hilltops, a fleeting glimpse of a broad landscape, where the towering beast has stopped short in its prowling, digging its claws in complete control. Three or four concentric rings for eyes suggest a staring, hypnotic look: a flash photo of an attack at close range."[51] A year earlier, Heartfield had created his montage for Grimms' fairy tale of the cat and the mouse [Pl. 85]. Here, too, the cat becomes a monumental figure of menace, the forest, a place filling people with dread. It recalls the German forest where Hansel and Gretel were abandoned by their parents – and Wieland Herzfelde's description of the place where Heartfield must have learned once and for all the meaning of anxiety, fear, forlornness. "For four days he searched for his mother, knowing that we, his younger brothers and sisters, were alone in the cottage. [...] Time and again he ran into the woods, full of fear and helplessness and with despair that increased from hour to hour, from day to day, kept calling and screaming only one word: 'Mother!' Those four days and nights of forsakenness have been indelibly etched in my brother's character."[52]

1. John Heartfield, "Heimkehr," in *Rote Post* (Berlin, January 1932), in Roland März, ed., *John Heartfield: Der Schnitt entlang der Zeit. Selbstzeugnisse – Erinnerungen – Interpretationen* (Dresden, 1981), p. 284.
2. Claude Martin, *André Gide par lui-même* (Paris, 1963), p. 172. Trans. Patricia Crampton.
3. Walter Mehring, *Verrufene Malerei. Berlin DADA: Erinnerungen eines Zeitgenossen* (Düsseldorf, 1983), p. 161.
4. Oskar Maria Graf, "John Heartfield. Der Photomonteur und seine Kunst," in *Deutsche Volkszeitung* (Paris, November 11, 1938).
5. Wieland Herzfelde, *Immergrün* (Berlin and Weimar, 1976), p. 13.
6. Graf, *John Heartfield* (see footnote 4).
7. Cf. Gert Selle, *Kultur der Sinne und ästhetische Erziehung* (Cologne, 1981), p. 132 ff.
8. Kurt Tucholsky, *Deutschland, Deutschland über alles,* trans. Anne Halley (Amherst, Mass., 1972), p. 2.
9. Cf. Fritz Mierau, *Erfindung und Korrektur. Tretjakows Ästhetik der Operativität* (Berlin, 1976), p. 19 ff.; Werner Mittenzwei, "Brecht und die Schicksale der Materialästhetik," in *Kampf der Richtungen* (Leipzig, 1978), p. 7 ff.; Eckhard Siepmann, *Montage: John Heartfield* (Berlin, 1977), p. 180 ff.
10. Sergei Tretyakov, in Mierau, *Erfindung und Korrektur* (see footnote 9), p. 62.
11. Bertolt Brecht, *Arbeitsjournal,* Vol. I (Frankfurt am Main, 1973), p. 439.
12. Hans Reimann, "John Heartfield," in *Das Stachelschwein* (Berlin, June 1927), p. 36.
13. Ibid., p. 37.
14. Ibid.
15. Sergei Tretyakov and Solomon Telingater, *John Heartfield. A Monograph,* trans. from the Russian by Keith Hammond (Moscow, 1936), p. 65.
16. Lilly Becher, "Beseelt von unserer Sache. Zur Heartfield-Ausstellung, Akademie der Künste" (East Berlin, 1957), in Wieland Herzfelde, *John Heartfield,* 2nd ed. (Dresden, 1971 [1962]), p. 345.
17. Wieland Herzfelde, "George Grosz, John Heartfield, Erwin Piscator, Dada und die Folgen – oder Die Macht der Freundschaft," in *Sinn und Form* (Berlin, June 23, 1971), pp. 1224–51; here p. 1226.
18. Ibid.
19. Elias Canetti, *The Torch in My Ear,* trans. Joachim Neugroschel (New York, 1982), p. 271.
20. Hans Hess, "John Heartfield und das Wesen der künstlerischen Realität," in *John Heartfield* (see footnote 1), pp. 477–501; here p. 490.
21. Werner Hofmann, "Die Karikatur als Gegenkunst," in Gerhard Langemeyer et al., eds., *Karikatur als Waffe* (Munich, 1984), p. 355.
22. Ibid., p. 365.
23. Ibid., p. 367.
24. Ibid.
25. Ibid., p. 368.
26. Ernst Bloch, "Diskussionen über Expressionismus," in *Das Wort* (Moscow, June 1938), p. 111.
27. Hess, "John Heartfield" (see footnote 20), p. 489.
28. Ibid.
29. Cf. Friedrich Arnold, ed., *Anschläge. Politische Plakate in Deutschland 1900–1980* (Frankfurt am Main, Olten, and Vienna, 1985); H. Olbrich et al., eds., *Sozialistische deutsche Karikatur 1948–1978* (Berlin, 1979).
30. Illustrated in Arnold, *Anschläge* (see footnote 29), p. 100.
31. Illustrated in *Sozialistische deutsche Karikatur* (see footnote 29), p. 32.
32. Illustrated ibid., p. 132.
33. Illustrated in Siepmann, *Montage* (see footnote 9), p. 273.
34. Roland März, *Daumier und Heartfield, Deutsche Satire im Dialog* (Berlin, 1981).
35. Illustrated in Arnold, *Anschläge* (see footnote 29), p. 84; cf. März, *Daumier und Heartfield* (see footnote 34), pp. 34, 10; *Karikatur als Waffe* (see footnote 21), p. 135.

36. Selle (see footnote 7), p. 140.
37. George Lukács, "Es geht um den Realismus," in *Das Wort* (Moscow, June 1938), p. 125.
38. Just how productive are the analyses of Heartfield's collages and montages is demonstrated in the contributions by Hanne Bergius ("Life and Times in Universal City at 12:05") and Eckhard Siepmann ("The Meaning of the Hitler Salute"), in Siepmann, *Montage* (see footnote 9), p. 43 ff. and 240 ff.
39. Bernd Kuhnert, "Die Tonwerte bei Heartfield-Montagen," in Siepmann, *Montage* (see footnote 9), p. 283.
40. Ibid.
41. Ibid.
42. Louis Aragon, "John Heartfield und die revolutionäre Schönheit," in Siepmann, *Montage* (see footnote 9), p. 256.
43. Marina Schneede-Sczesny and Uwe M. Schneede, "Zur Technik und Kunstform der Fotomontage bei Heartfield," in März, *John Heartfield* (see footnote 1), p. 197.
44. Eckhard Siepmann, "Die Millionen-Montage," in *Montage* (see footnote 9), p. 246.
45. Kuhnert, "Tonwerte" (see footnote 39), p. 283.
46. Hess, "John Heartfield" (see footnote 20), p. 492.
47. Francis D. Klingender, transcription of an interview with Heartfield (March 2, 1944) on Dadaism and Surrealism, in März, *John Heartfield* (see footnote 1), p. 63.
48. Oskar Schlemmer, in Laszlo Glozer, ed., *Westkunst*, Catalogue (Cologne, 1981), p. 74.
49. Hofmann, "Die Karikatur als Gegenkunst" (see footnote 21), p. 371.
50. Glozer (see footnote 48), pp. 35–36.
51. Ibid., p. 25.
52. Herzfelde, *Immergrün* (see footnote 5), p. 13.

Klaus Honnef

Symbolic Form as a Vivid Cognitive Principle

An Essay on Montage

I

"Editing [cutting] is the arrangement of disassembled details into an ordered sequence in which not only entire scenes (however brief they may be) but also takes of the smallest units within a scene follow each other (a similar process also occurs on the Shakespearean stage). Like the stones from a time mosaic that are laid one after the other, the scene develops as a whole. This is montage, editing."[1]

This brief and concise definition by the early film theorist Béla Balázs is more than a mere description of an important aesthetic principle in twentieth-century art; it reaches far beyond and simultaneously highlights the effect of this methodological element on most, if not all, of aesthetic production both past and present. It does not confine itself to film, for which it was initially coined; by using the specific words "scene" and "mosaic," it also incorporates the theatre arts and the visual arts into a concept of something that is sometimes referred to as "scene," sometimes as "montage." In the language of film theory, both expressions stand for one and the same thing: the common practice of initially dismantling the individual elements of a film comprising various frames and scenes[2] (generally shot at different locations and not in the order of the film plot but in terms of length existing on a standardized film roll) and consequently, reassembling these elements according to an overall film concept. The term "cut" reflects the instrumental process whose tool is a pair of scissors, while the term "montage" already implies an aesthetic dimension, which bears diverse socio-cultural characteristics. In German and English, the process is referred to as *Schnitt* or *cutting*, while the French speak of *montage*. Correspondingly, the term "montage" may also be used to describe the result of separating and then reassembling fragments from an aesthetic creation that sees itself as a whole in terms of its pictorial structure. It is thus an "assembled" creation, an aesthetic product consisting of heterogeneous elements.

Both expressions "montage" and "product" imply an industrial aspect in creating works of art. As soon as they replace traditional expressions such as "work," or its exalted version "creation," in aesthetic terminology, they signalize a change in the self-perception of both the artistic work and its theoretical reflection. Simultaneously, these definitions – which have long since been aesthetically coined – show the change in social and cultural premises and conditions that underlie art. Particularly the term "montage" has been adopted in aesthetic discussion, and it is not only film that regards montage as one of its most crucial principles. It happens in literature, in the theatre, especially the "documentary theatre," and not least in the visual arts; however, only in film has it acquired a significance as a principle, whereas in the other artistic fields it is restricted to characterizing special poetic, dramatic, or visual disciplines.

In the fine arts, a distinction is made between collages, montages, and assemblages. Compositions made out of cut-and-pasted paper come under the term "collage"; the combination of objects and materials of different origin and composition, which is the result of an artistic will, is described as "assemblage." In the field of photography, which has always been under a certain "pressure to legitimize itself" (Wolfgang Kemp) with regard to aesthetic recognition, the term "montage" has emerged as an expression for the results of a balancing act between photography and art. Nevertheless, montage breaks the boundaries of all these restrictive terms, and on closer examination rises to become, in every respect, a symptomatic formal and structural principle of artistic development since the end of the undisputed supremacy of perspective as "symbolic form."[3]

Although it is generally film that offers the most convincing examples of the outstanding significance of montage within the spectrum of art, this indicates,

49

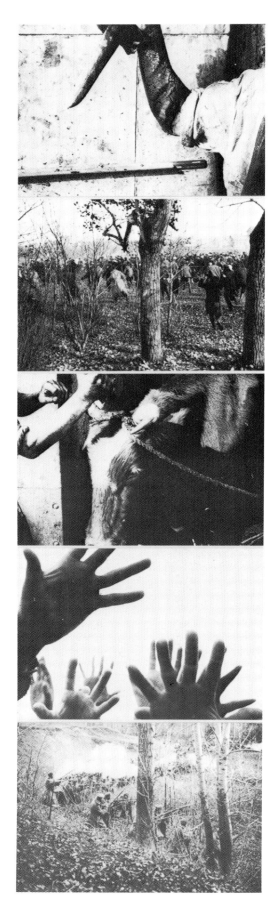

on the one hand, the creative power that it possessed during the artistic revival in the first quarter of the twentieth century – affecting the arts in general – and, on the other hand, the fascination that it held for the authoritative aesthetic theorists at that time. Consequently, Arnold Hauser's observations, inspired by the pioneering films of Russian directors such as Sergei M. Eisenstein and Vsevolod Pudovkin (both prolific theorists of the principle of montage), by no means apply only to this medium. The author formulates them against the background of the dramatic changes in the theatre, film, and fine arts: "The revolutionary aspect of this montage technique, however, was not actually the shortness of the cut, the tempo or rhythm of the alternating images, nor was it the extension of the limits of what can be portrayed in film, but the fact that heterogeneous, ontological elements rather than homogeneous material were confronted with each other."[4] And taking the most famous of all Russian montage films as an example, Hauser clearly demonstrates what the montage technique was capable of achieving: "In *Battleship Potemkin*, Eisenstein showed the following sequence of shots: men working excitedly; the engine room inside the battleship; frantic hands; rotating wheels; faces contorted by exertion; the maximal distance of the pressure gauge; a perspiring chest, a red-hot kettle; an arm, a wheel; a wheel, an arm; machine, man; machine, man; machine, man. Two totally different realities, one conceptual and one material, were joined together here and not only joined but identified as having developed from each other. Such a conscious and intentional frontier crossing, however, presupposes a world view that denies the autonomy of individual spheres of life. [...]"[5]

In film, montage interrupts the continual flow of the film narrative, shortens or extends it as required, and also destroys the impression of homogeneous space as the narrative's scene of action, which the images of paintings – and subsequently the images of photography – suggest as a result of the plane-perspective arrangement of the pictorial contents. In this visual art, space loses its rational logic, its calculated clarity, its apparent objectivity. First and foremost, however, it loses its irrefutable validity, supposedly reinforced by the discovery of a mechanical method of producing images, namely photography, which, according to its first empirically obsessed advocates, was the "means of recording concrete details, a fixed reflection of nature or more essentially an imprint of nature."[6] The "perceptual space of the Renaissance"[7] was replaced in the medium of film by the fragmented, faceted, changeable space of montage. Only the enormous implications of the moving images of film hide the fabricated, artificial character of the assembled, spatial structure. However, when Balázs compares this nonuniform, discontinuous space of montage, for the sake of greater clarity, with the pictorial nature of a mosaic, he neglects what is probably the most important difference. The many mosaic stones (tesserae) hardly differ in terms of size, all of them possess the same formal and thematic significance, and their order obeys an overall pictorial plan. By comparison, the formal and thematic significance of the individual segments in an assembled sequence of images is totally different, and the discontinuous arrangement is its most important structural principle. The pictorial organization of montage assigns to individual elements a certain degree of autonomy,[8] replaces the uniformity of "seeing through"[9] into the material world in one-point perspectival painting with a multi-perspectival framework of diverse views, and releases the viewer from his fixed position as prescribed by "plastic space."[10]

Although the aesthetic principle of montage has so far developed most effectively in film (it was not completely coincidental that Hauser gave to the last chapter of his impressive *Social History of Art and Literature* the succinct title of "Under the Sign of the Film"[11]), montage only gradually became an influential means of formal and thematic structure in this "seventh" art – as film was once called – and it has no claim to its invention. Nevertheless, montage had already matured greatly as a crucial aesthetic element before the outbreak of the First World War. The American film director David Wark Griffith is credited with having used it consistently for the first time and for having recognized and tested its artistic effectiveness: a credit that is not reduced by the fact that he was capable of benefiting from the experiments of the Brighton School and of motion picture pioneer Edwin S. Porter.[12] Even Eisenstein acknowledged his status as a remarkable pioneer.[13]

Montage's sphere of influence, however, is by no means restricted merely to film. Although we can agree with Sergei Tretyakov's evaluation that film, or in his words "the cinema," was a kind of "cradle of photomontage,"[14] montage is not alien to the traditional visual arts. On the contrary – even before film began to utilize its aesthetic possibilities, similar early forms of montage had begun to take shape in the fine arts. In the "long ancestral line"[15] of collages and "material pictures," Herta Wescher cites examples from Japanese background painting for twelfth-century calligraphies, engraved ornaments in icon painting, Baroque quodlibets, Dutch seventeenth-century silhouettes, as well as folkloric collages with "fascinating" orientation, and popular nineteenth-century photocollages sent as picture postcards. Even genuine photomontage is not a child of the "film era," since its real fathers were the British art photographers Oscar Rejlander and H. Robinson.[16] As an artistic tool, albeit more for "craft products, folk art, and popular art" and thus "on the fringes of artistic development,"[17] montage is familiar in art history. And in the history of photography, it already fulfilled decidedly agitatorial purposes before the photomonteurs of the avant-garde[18] made use of it: "In a primitive example of montage, representing the shooting of hostages that took place in the courtyard of the La Roquette prison under the regime of the Paris Commune on 24th May 1871, the portrait heads of the hostages, most of them clerical dignitaries, and of the Communards supervising the execution are stuck onto figures positioned in front of the prison wall on a kind of stage. In order to make the executioners appear closely lined up, the same detailed shot has been copied side by side several times."[19] It is also interesting that numerous writers such as Victor Hugo, Joachim Ringelnatz, and Hans Christian Andersen were involved with creating collages. The fairy-tale writer, for example, made a collage "folding screen" (1873/74),[20] whose formal conception anticipates much of Dada photomontage or the montage film *Berlin – Die Symphonie einer Großstadt (Berlin: the Symphony of a City)* (1927) by Walter Ruttmann. And it was not by chance that Eisenstein frequently quoted the works of authors such as Maupassant and Pushkin[21] to historically substantiate his theoretical reflections on montage; indeed, he even established a link between the literary works of Charles Dickens and Griffith's films, claiming that the American film director gave the English author's montage technique a vivid form.[22] "It is therefore quite natural that Griffith's conception of montage is like a reflection of his dualistic view of the world, that is to say, a world which, in the two parallel lines of the rich and the poor, reaches a nebulous, hypothetical 'reconciliation' as soon as these two parallel lines converge, i.e., in an infinity as unattainable as the promised 'reconciliation' itself."[23]

The instruments were ready and the technology available. The technology, however, was lacking the material through which montage was finally to evolve as a contemporary symbolic form. The aesthetic dimension was still missing, and we may justifiably question whether the literary figures thrown into the discussion by Eisenstein utilized the montage technique as the film author had envisaged. On the other hand, a new medium among the visual arts soon took advan-

David Wark Griffith, *The Birth of a Nation*, 1915. Sequence

tage of montage, a medium that has accompanied modern industrial society as constantly as the light of cathedrals shining over the feudal society of the late Middle Ages, and that – although occasionally stimulated by artists – was to become the most serious threat to art, like the sirens to the crew of the delayed returning soldier Odysseus, with its increasing demands for an autonomous status: the advertisement. At the beginning of the nineteenth century, the methods of montage and collage were very common forms of expression in advertising.[24]

II

Since the pioneering achievements of the Renaissance, the world view of the fine arts has rested in the established structure of the one-point perspective. In a central-perspective picture, the visible and, of course, the metaphysical, world appeared as though we were examining it through a window.[25] Albrecht Dürer spoke of a "seeing through" to characterize what was taking place on the canvas. As artists and scientists conquered the visible world against the background of an emerging bourgeois society with its gradually refining rational strategies of coping with immediate life, the question of a representation appropriate to the increasing insights and knowledge had arisen. The result is – measured against the notion of the Middle Ages with its purely metaphysical orientation – a reorganization of the pictorial composition. It manifests itself in the planimetric organization of depicted objects within the network of lines of the central-perspective construction that lead toward a single vanishing point. In literature, it is defined as a cut through the cone of vision, although it is supposed that a visual center emits rays onto the object to be illustrated (or vice versa), which, in the construction of the planar perspective picture, are treated as connecting lines between this and the objects.[26] "By inventing the one-point perspective, the convergence of the sciences and the arts is achieved. It is the expression of an endeavor to 'generate a synthesis of fantasy and ratio as basic impulses of every artistic creation' (Heydenreich 1972), i.e., no longer being content with subjective observation and experience but – to quote Max Dvorák – 'raising general,

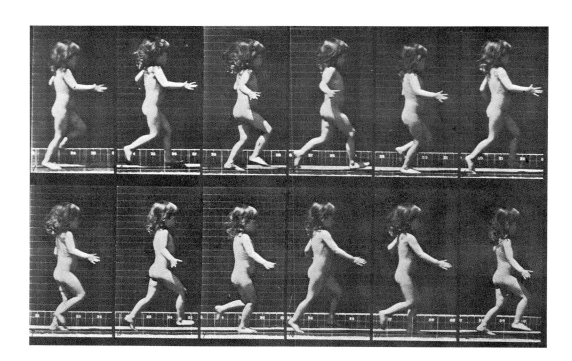

Eadweard Muybridge, photo sequence, ca. 1873

natural causality, which underlies perception and experience, to an indicator of that which is truly of artistic significance' (1927)."[27]

To transform what artists had acquired empirically into a picture that reflected this vivid experience, a parameter was required to simultaneously recast coincidental experiences in a kind of regularity. Geometry offered the necessary assistance. Artistic endeavors were generally directed toward both the depiction and the recognition of what was represented. The procedure was carried out in three stages, as Arnold Gehlen ascertained with the assistance of the works of Leonardo: the study of natural phenomena was followed by the epistemological investigation into complicated processes, enabling the experiences gained to penetrate human consciousness, and subsequently the conversion of the results of visual and mental effort by means of "technique" into artistic representation. "Only the combination of these three steps results in what would today still be called science in the broadest sense of the word; as an idea, it is still valid in unchanged form today, but it has *never*, not even in the present day, been so extensively realized as in Renaissance painting!"[28]

Its affinity to the beginnings of scientific research is undoubtedly one of the causes for the almost "natural" plausibility of the planar perspective. Nevertheless, this pictorial structure is nothing more than a construction with a comparatively high degree of abstraction. It abstracts totally from the physiological conditions of the act of seeing by presupposing that one is only capable of seeing with an unmoving eye. Because only under this condition would the cut through the cone of vision be the appropriate representation of the visual picture. Moreover, "the structure of an infinite, unchanging and homogeneous space – in short, a purely mathematical space – is quite unlike the structure of psychophysiological space."[29] Erwin Panofsky quotes Ernst Cassirer: "Perception does not know the concept of infinity; from the very outset it is confined within certain spatial limits imposed by our faculty of perception. And in connection with perceptual space we can no more speak of homogeneity than of infinity. The ultimate basis of the homogeneity of geometric space is that all its elements, the 'points' which are joined in it, are mere determinations of position, possessing no independent content of their own outside this relation, this position which they occupy in relation to each other. Their reality is exhausted in their reciprocal relation: it is purely functional and not a substantial reality."[30]

H. P. Robinson, *Nor' Easter*, Combination print, 1890. Combination of two photographs (landscape with figure, sky) into a third

Despite its surprising proximity to the subjective visual impression, perspective was not automatically accepted by contemporaries. When this convincing pictorial view of the world lost the irrefutability that it had preserved over the centuries, Pierre Francastel was able to diagnose: "The inventors of the perspectival representation of space are creators of illusion, and not more or less discriminating imitators of reality. Moreover, they cannot agree among one another, at least not at the beginning, with which modus operandi they can best encourage their contemporaries to accept this illusionism, in which both technical and scientific insights as well as visual and mental habits of their time were assimilated. The new space is a mixture of geometry and symbolic representation, where technical knowledge is the tool of individual and collective beliefs."[31] The fact that contemporaries also regarded perspective as an artificial construction verifies the statement of one of its most virtuoso practitioners: "There are three branches of perspective: the first deals with the reasons for the (apparent) diminution of objects as they recede from the eye, and is known as (Diminishing) Perspective. The second refers to the way in which colors vary as they recede from the eye. The third and last is concerned with the explanation of how the objects (in a picture) ought to be less finished in proportion as they are remote, and the names are as follows: Linear Perspective; Perspective of Color; Perspec-

Walter Ruttmann, collage for his film *Berlin: Die Symphonie einer Großstadt* [*Berlin: the Symphony of a City*], 1927

tive of Disappearance."[32] In spite of this, Leonardo confirmed the proximity of the linear perspective to the subjective visual experience: "[...] perspective is a rational demonstration by which experience confirms that every object sends its image to the eye by a pyramid of lines; and bodies of equal size will result in a pyramid of larger or smaller size according to the difference in their distance, one from the other. By a pyramid of lines, I mean those that start from the surface and edges of bodies, and, converging from a distance, meet in a single point. A point is said to be that which [having no dimensions] cannot be divided, and this point placed in the eye receives all the points of the pyramid."[33]

Neither montage nor perspective were unanticipated developments in the history of art. Perspective amalgamates artistic developments in the field of Gothic sculpture as well as notions passed on in written form of ancient *Scenographia* and its "angle-perspectival" pictorial arrangement[34]; it is also closely associated with the simultaneous emergence of a rational attitude among the increasingly influential urban, bourgeois merchant class, encouraging research into the laws of nature and social behavior. In the planar-perspective picture, every detail has its calculable place, and the mathematically substantiated vision of the infinity of these pictures tacitly suggests that this is also acceptable and sanctioned for eternity. We may justifiably doubt whether the perspectival definition of infinity has gained significance only on the formal level. When Eisenstein shrewdly transposed this pictorial convention, which was undisputed for centuries, to the social level as a result of his observations about the use of montage by Dickens and Griffith, he resolutely challenged the widespread notion that art had nothing to do with social reality.

Even if the numerous attempts to interpret works of art as dull reflections of social conditions and conflicts have failed, the contrary conclusion that works of art only obey their own norms and are not "bearers of prescribed programs [...] an expression of concealed intentions or ideas [...] and thus a mirror reflecting the unfamiliar and not itself"[37] is also refuted by empirical examinations. Even avant-garde art, whose self-perception is based on the postulation of autonomy, can be easily interpreted in a social context as a significant "text," or even *ex negativo*.

The problem therefore reaches the point where we have to clarify whether perspective is nothing other than a mere means of reproducing the subjective visual impression in a plausible illustrative model, or whether perspective does not reveal a collective, vividly formulated world view of things and notions, which, in accordance with the prevailing intellectual and spiritual trends of the time, knew how to objectify these adequately. The optical signature of a changeable epoch, as it were? Already in the title of his essay "Perspective as Symbolic Form,"[38] Panofsky leaves no room for doubt that perspective is strongly linked to the philosophical and anthropological influences in human society. According to his thesis, it is "no accident if this perspectival view of space ["Raumanschauung," which he carefully distinguishes from mere perspective construction – K. H.] has already succeeded twice in the course of the evolution of art: the first time as a sign of an ending, when antique theocracy crumbled; the second time as the sign of a beginning, when modern 'anthropocracy' first reared itself."[39]

Raoul Hausmann, *Dada siegt!* [*Dada Triumphs!*]. Collage, 1920. Whereabouts unknown

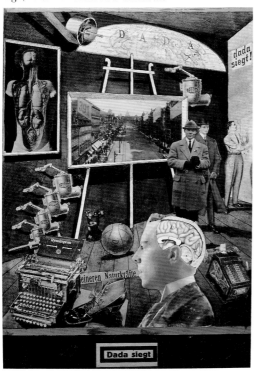

III

In light of Panofsky's essay, perspective manifests itself as a "symbolic form" as defined by Ernst Cassirer. The philosopher regards myth, language, technology, law, art, religion, science as well as history, and only once the field of economics, as symbolic forms: "By a 'symbolic form' is to be understood any mental energy through which a spiritual meaning is attached to a concrete, material sign and is intrinsically given to this sign."[40] There is no doubt that perspective, if seen as a "concrete, sensual symbol" according to Cassirer, has a "spiritual meaning." Yet what is right and proper for perspective is not necessarily proper for montage. Although photographic and cinematographic visual arts and also television – whose electronic conditions ought to produce a completely new view of the world – still adhere to the planar-perspective representation in individual pictures (and due to their technical conditions cannot do otherwise), they exist in the former terrain of the fine arts as a mere quotation whose task is to reveal or to expose the illusory character of the perspectival space. And if one imagines the chronological sequence of the images on a film roll projected next to one another on a surface, the homogeneous space of the planar perspective painting of the Renaissance breaks up in favor of a kaleidoscopic "mosaic,"[41] reminiscent more of an evenly arranged rag carpet than of a standardized "looking through" the material world. From this point of view, photography had a dual significance with respect to perspective: on the one hand, an optical fixation, or so to speak an "absolutizing" by virtue of its technical precision and verifiability; on the other hand, a complete elimination of its conventional claim to competence due to the arbitrary change in perspective of the immense flow of images.

The collapse of perspective's unlimited control over the world of pictures in the fine arts was heralded during the last half of the nineteenth century. Although actually still in existence, its stable framework began to crumble in the atmospheric shimmer of Impressionist paintings. As the objects lost their bold contours, "perspectival space" lost its external structure. The homogeneous space of painting was transformed step by step into an aggregate space. "Here the system of the colored representation of the universe is superimposed on the canvas supplied by a few linear elements borrowed from the Renaissance representation of space."[42] Parallel to this, new subjects that had previously attracted no attention entered painting. It inconspicuously shed its idealized apparel. The everyday bourgeois world and occasionally the industrial working world received increasing attention. "It has often been said [...] that Impressionism was the art of the era which confronted philosophically the problem of analyzing the modalities of sensory perception. Rather, it is the art of an era which relinquishes the mechanical idea of a universe whose external appearance had been accepted as unalterable, in order to work out an analytical concept of nature."[43]

However, it was not Impressionism but an almost opposing artistic trend that paved the way for montage and finally canceled out perspective. The "peinture conceptuelle"[44] of Cubism, which splintered into an analytical phase represented in particular by Braque and Picasso, and into a synthetic phase on which Gris had a lasting influence, laid the foundations parallel to the cinematographic experiments of the Brighton School and the American work of Griffith. It delayed the tendency toward ornamentation in painting, which a reduced representationalism had initiated through Impressionist artistic practices. Daniel-Henry Kahnweiler, the authoritative theorist on Cubist art, regarded "peinture conceptuelle" as conceptual art whose aim was to give a new foundation to the relationship between subject and outside world, which was disrupted by a number of unrelated factors. The dynamic, rapidly progressing radical changes in economics, politics, and science had also reached the cultural world and sharpened the awareness of receptive minds to the fact that the one-point perspective arrangement of painting was merely feigning an illusory fictitious world of reality and, in view of the demand to illustrate adequately the

Otto Dix, *Prager Straße* [*Prague Street*]. Oil on canvas and collage, 1920. Düsseldorf, private collection

experience of what appears to be an increasingly complex world, was bound to fail. Even the increase in individualism, which found extensive expression for the first time in Romanticism, ran counter to the tacitly accepted assumption that a slightly subjective visual experience is reflected in the planar perspective image. According to Kahnweiler, the "peinture conceptuelle" of Cubism forged links between the subjective "experience" of the painter and the no less subjective visual experience of the observer by creating symbols that evolved from the creative imagination of the artist and the nature of the work of art, at the same time characterizing "the outer world."[45] In order to carry out this task, the "conceptual painting" of the Cubists made use of a specially developed "pictorial language," by virtue of which not the mere appearance of the material world but the essential and material characteristics of the "portrayed" objects were embodied.[46] Because Kahnweiler (obviously prompted by Guillaume Apollinaire) drew analogies between what is articulated in painting, and in language and writing,[47] he also relieved painting of the obligation to imitate visible reality and transferred responsibility for the acception of painted pictures as well as their creative act to the imagination of all those participating in the artistic process of communication.

The homogeneous, continual perspectival space of the Renaissance finally disappeared into the chasms of the interrupted perspectival space of Cubist painting. Even if the Cubist painters initially left the pictorial surface untouched, they replaced the "plastic" and comprehensible space of the now traditional painting with the heterogeneous and discontinuous space of montage. This tendency was reinforced when they began adding objects from everyday life, such as scraps of wallpaper, newspaper clippings, and letters onto the picture, thus eliminating the homogeneity of this very same surface. The hand-crafted creation blended with the fabrications in the collages and montages of the Cubists. If indeed an element of collective world view manifests itself in images of art – where the sum of individual world views would allow a conclusion to be drawn about the general attitude of a society toward the world – then the Cubist pictures reveal the collapse of traditional notions, a condition that was to be confirmed in the dreadful industrial combat of the First World War with its far-reaching consequences.

Related artistic aspirations (albeit of a considerably lesser intellectual significance), such as Futurism, picked up the pictorial experiments of chronophotography, as carried out by Eadweard Muybridge and Etienne-Jules Marey, as well as the dynamic spatial conception of film, attacking the homogeneous spatial picture of "Euclidean linearity" (Virilio) with cataractlike forms of presentation. And as the avant-garde visual arts destroyed the "perspectival space" and instead gave preference to a multi-perspectival or dynamic space conception in painting or stressed the intrinsic value of space, the overwhelming mammoth film *Cabiria* (1914) by Giovanni Pastrone destroyed the continuity of the chronological narrative in film. *Cabiria* originated in the land of the Futurists, whose manifesto had appeared three years earlier. For both Pastrone and the Futurists, the linear Euclidian organization of thought had come to an end, human sight was on the same footing as energetic propulsion. Quite intentionally, Pastrone downplayed the element of plot in favor of technical effects and the dynamic improvement of cinematic photography. Brownlow: "Obsessed by the third dimension, director Pastrone (under the pseudonym Piero Fosco) created shots of remarkable depth, separating the planes with a constantly moving camera."[48] Perspective was suddenly in a state of agitation. The safe ground that had always been guaranteed by the contemplation of the planar-perspective image accelerated because the suggestive effect of the moving camera positively absorbed the viewer of the film into the flexible cinematographic spaces. "After Pastrone, however, what was 'false' in cinema was no longer the effect of accelerated perspective but the very depth itself, the temporal distance of the projected space. Many years later, the electronic light of laser technology and integrated-circuit computer graphics would confirm this relativity, in which speed appears as the primal magnitude of the image and thus the source of its depth."[49]

The architecture of the conventional conception of images in the visual arts already revealed obvious rifts and deep ruptures by the time the "antiartistic" impetus of the Dada movement caused its complete collapse. The Dada artists, who did not see themselves as such because they wanted to have nothing to do with all the traditions of an art that was totally discredited by its appearance, identified the "high" art of the past with a social system that had declared itself bankrupt in the First World War. Dadaism, which was a European phenomenon, found its political orientation primarily in Berlin, where the social conflicts following the devastating failure of the German Empire and its allies vented themselves most strongly. Young intellectuals, literary figures, painters and draftsmen, doctors, pacifists, and people catapulted out of their walks of life by the experiences of war came together spontaneously and informally in the frontierless movement of Dadaism to remove the cultural burdens from what they considered to be a dilapidated social system. Half in unconcealed anger, half from an impetuous desire, they violated the prevailing cultural conventions, defied traditional values, destroyed familiar symbols, swam against the tide of established notions, and created a cultural *tabula rasa* situation. Like George Grosz and John Heartfield, they dissected coherent pictorial units and combined them with slogans, occasionally incomprehensible messages; or like Hannah Höch, Raoul Hausmann, and Heartfield, they concocted bewildering visual impromptus from a host of selected photographic images. These "photomontages" had to be read like a text, although the discovery of a plausible meaning was unlikely. Everything that the social establishment of the imperial era had considered exemplary[50] was regarded as false by the Dadaists. "The revolutionary strength of Dadaism consisted of examining art for its authenticity."[51]

IV

The test of authenticity threw the world of art into a profound crisis, affecting everything that had previously been permanent. Although it reached a special climax in Dadaism, the symptoms of a fundamental change in the self-perception of art had already been accumulating since Goya, in Romanticism, and notably since Impressionism. And perhaps it is not unreasonable to believe that the fine arts have existed in a state of permanent crisis since the loss of perspective as symbolic form – that this moment of constant crisis is actually the sign of its advancement. In any case, not only have several different attitudes to the problem of representing subjective experiences been in conflict in the visual arts ever since then, but the means and media have also multiplied and given themselves over to curious conglomerations in artistic practice, especially at the end of the twentieth century. In painting, developments have branched off, on the one hand, into a direction that has abandoned contact with empirical reality and insists either on autonomous artistic means or seeks the transcendental experience of mysticism; on the other hand, it follows a direction that continues to cling to the vivid visualization of the subjective perception of the pictorial plane – however, in a contemporary symbolic form. Montage has established itself as that very symbolic form, wherever the visual arts are not content with exhibiting their aesthetic material but are striving for a reflection of the emotional, intellectual,

PP. 58–59
John Heartfield, "Resurrection." Photomontage, 1932. Cat. no. 209

Kurt Schwitters, M[er]z[bild] 379: Potsdamer. Collage, 1922, New York, Collection The Museum of Modern Art

59

and social existence. Even in photography, which is still subject to the planar-perspective principle, montage has achieved an important position thanks to advertising, illustrated newspapers, and the artistic use of photomontage. Montage has also become a common organizational principle in literature and in the theatre. The influential power of montage is strikingly shown in one of the most popular figures in cinema. As montage personified, Jan Mukařowsky analyzed the figure of Charlie Chaplin as a symbol of the contradictoriness of modern man. Mukařowsky noted "[…] that the unity of image presupposes its duality, rather than obliterates it. Charlie's costume has two parts: the top part includes an elegant bowler hat, shirt-front and bow-tie, while the bottom part includes baggy trousers and enormous shoes. […] The combination in his dress of extreme elegance […] and extreme shabbiness and degradation was continued in the gestures and mimicry of Charlie. Elegant, faultlessly aristocratic motions with which Charlie raised his hat or straightened his tie, are combined with gestures and mimicry of a tramp. Charlie was, in effect, two people."[52]

Montage asserted itself only very hesitantly in art – at best, Constructivism favored a spatial design that revealed a montagelike character, whereas in the Neo-Classicism of a Picasso, and in the artistic orientations of the *Neue Sachlichkeit* and the Novecento, pronounced retardative moments emerged – but it took complete hold of film as its very own domain. And after Dadaism, Höch, Hausmann, and others – with Heartfield leading the way – developed photomontage into an autonomous, artistic discipline, a territory that mediated, so to speak, between art and reality (the photos). The numerous constellations of current experiences of reality, the conflict-laden and contradictory aspects of modern industrial civilization, the sudden decline of social emotional states, the complex messages of the natural sciences, the constant acceleration of city life, and the more or less unambiguous feeling that the world is immense, difficult to comprehend, and full of insoluble contradictions, gradually made montage a vivid synonym of *Zeitgeist*. However, these were all artistic ideas, reflecting the energetic efforts to achieve an interpretation and reflection of the concrete world of experience, which found expression in montage. They unambiguously rejected the tendencies developing in traditional visual arts that aimed at complete autonomy. It is not surprising that photography, a medium closely related to reality, played a key role. Nevertheless, its limited possibilities of adequately representing complex reality were evident. "In short, the beginnings of photomontage lay in the conscious reinterpretation of photographs."[53] The famous objection by Bert Brecht, who incorporated the montage concept in his theatre practice and later theory of the "epic theater," that the photographic shot of an industrial plant revealed nothing about the inner conditions and fate of the workers, best illustrates the scrupulous relationship of artists to photography.

The theoretical basis of montage was first put into practice – hardly surprisingly – in the art of film, a medium rooted in photography. Admittedly, the most distinguished representatives of the "film" theory of montage were familiar with experiments in advanced art. While still in the theatre, Eisenstein referred to these works in an essay written in 1923 about the production of the play *Even a Wise Man Stumbles* by A. N. Ostrovsky and developed his theory on the "Montage of Attractions" completely "analogous to the montage sections of the pictures of George Grosz or elements of the photo-illustrations by Rodchenko."[54] What is even more interesting, however, is that he demonstrates this influential montage theory, which is later dealt with in literature as the "montage of conflicts," with "that understanding of immediate reality" practiced in vaudeville and circus. This was in spite of the fact that he never intended montage to be used as a means for psychologically massaging the viewer – as in circus and vaudeville.

Aleksandr Rodchenko, *Another Cup of Tea*. Photomontage, 1923, for Vladimir Mayakovsky's book *About This*. Prague, Lubomír Linhart Collection

What the opposing montage concepts of the Soviet film directors and theorists, and also of the photomonteur Heartfield were aiming at was a "penetration" of the confusing and seemingly muddled weave of reality in order to discover the laws governing the visible and accessible reality – laws that were objective according to their ideological convictions. In Russian films, two different viewpoints represented by the great directors Pudovkin and Eisenstein competed against each other. One confined itself to ordering and coordinating the film material; it interpreted the illustrated story. "'Interpretation' here implies decoding, analyzing, elucidating, explaining. This kind of interpretation can produce a particularly interesting and subtle style of narration but is unable to invent or create a new story. The story already existed before the camera arrived and the camera does little more than interpret what already exists, although this can be a great deal."[56] The other viewpoint is capable of "creating a new story, producing a plot or situation that does not yet exist outside the film. [. . .]"[57] "It is associated with the order of film images in their totality."[58] This montage of associations, or "montage of ideas," as Eisenstein referred to it, is consequently a process that accords the individual film images a significance which they do not possess in a state of isolation. This occurs through a conflict-laden combination of heterogeneous individual images, which brings about a new, comprehensive meaning. "What advantages do we really have from the view of montage? It implies that each individual montage section no longer exists as something unrelated but is a 'special portrayal' of the unified general theme which penetrates all these parts equally. The confrontation of special details in a certain montage structure produces that 'generality' in our perception which has in turn created all individual parts and combines them to form a 'whole,' namely a generalized 'image' in which the artist and subsequently the viewer are exposed to the given theme."[59] Despite some differences of opinion, Eisenstein, who moderated his conflict theory in the course of time, agreed with his rival Pudovkin, with whom he was in constant contact, on the fundamental evaluation of montage: "For my purposes, I define montage as a universal exposure and explanation of correlations using all possible artistic means among the phenomena of real life in film art. Film montage in this sense presupposes a level of general culture on the part of the film director, allowing him not only to be familiar with life but also to understand it correctly. Likewise, it presupposes his capability to observe life, to cope with observations, and to think about them independently. Finally, it presupposes a certain degree of artistic ability, which enables him to transform the inner, hidden context of real phenomena into a bare, clearly visible and immediately comprehensible context. If the emaciated children of ruined farmers appear on the screen next to mountains of wheat filmed for commercial reasons, this is montage. The association achieved through reasoning astounds as a result of the immediate spectacle of a scandalous contradiction (Paul Rotha)."[60]

If perspective was a symbolic form, which, according to Dürer, assisted the "seeing through" of empirical reality, montage was regarded by Pudovkin and Eisenstein as the "penetration of reality through the use of technical equipment."[61]

These points of view were shared by Heartfield, and even Kahnweiler acknowledged the aesthetic principle in the use of montage that could provide access to an art characterizing the material world and yet remaining autonomous. Although the two viewpoints diverged greatly in terms of ideology, in the final analysis the different notions of montage reveal themselves as two sides of a coin. Montage "is therefore not confined exclusively to film. It is merely a technical term for a compositional problem that arises in the same way in film as it does in literature and the fine arts. Thus, Eisenstein comes to the correct conclusion in

UMBO (Otto Umbehr), *Bildnis Egon Erwin Kisch* [*Portrait of Egon Erwin Kisch*]. Photomontage, 1926. Wassenaar, Paul Citroen Collection

Richard Hamilton, *Just What Is It That Makes Today's Homes So Different, So Appealing?* Collage, 1956. Tübingen, Kunsthalle, Prof. Dr. Georg Zundel Collection

one of his later essays, by means of comparisons with painting (Leonardo da Vinci) and with epic (Maupassant) and lyrical poetry (Pushkin), that the 'montage principle in film is merely a sectorial application of the general montage principle.' The view that editing is something special, something peculiar to the art of film, or that it is cutting that confirms the uniqueness of the film is thereby omitted. In this respect – and this is the most elementary aspect of the composition issue – there is no difference between the cinematographic art and the narrative and visual arts."[62] While the technical aspect played only a subordinate role in the aesthetic debate, and the technical aspect attracted comparatively little attention, the opportunity, offered by montage, to introduce the time element provoked greater interest. The Dadaists were already fascinated by the optical experience of the simultaneity of what montage assembled in the individual pictorial fragments on the picture plane. The photographic fragments, each of which represented a fleeting moment while the photographic depiction inevitably documents the actual absence of what is present,[63] extended the access of the fine arts to the domain of time. The collage of the Cubists had neglected this, and some time elapsed before painting made use of this possibility.[64] In the heterogeneous and discontinuous spaces of montage, it was the factor of time that caused the disappearance of the concrete location of pictorial representation after the actual destruction of spatial homogeneity and continuity. However, the harder it was to identify a certain picture in its local environment, the more incomprehensible the category of the transitory had to become, so that the montage image could become a symbolic form, even transcending time and space, regardless of the temporal relationship of some of its fragmentary elements.

By removing the journalistic traits from his montages, Heartfield released them from any temporal contingency and heigthened them – according to his political point of view – to generally valid pictorial metaphors, in which the supposed law of history was vividly enforced. "A photomontage by the Dadaist Heartfield

Edward Kienholz, *A Portable War Memorial*. Installation, 1968. Cologne, Museum Ludwig

consisted of a large number of small details. But over time Heartfield's language became increasingly laconic, his photomontages were constructed more and more sparingly, greater expressiveness being achieved with fewer elements. His most perfect works are those which involve no more than two elements. We should not forget that a photomontage is not necessarily a montage of photographs. No – it may be a photo and a photo, a photo and text, a photo and paint, a photo and a drawing."[65] As a result of technical progress, the American film of the forties finally succeeded in interweaving the different time planes with each other in a single pictorial frame without interfering with spatial coherence. In one of the most famous takes in the film *Citizen Kane* (1940/41) by Orson Welles, we see demonstratively positioned in the foreground of the picture an empty bottle, which, according to the label, contains sleeping pills; in the center, the head of a sleeping woman; and in the background, through the open door, the woman's husband – everything captured within the space of a room. Without cutting, Welles combined the moment of discovery of an obvious suicide with the recognition of the cause. In the conventional use of the montage principle, the scene would have unfolded over several phases: the taking of the tablets, the gentle passing away of the woman, and the discovery of the victim.

The simultaneity of the unsimultaneous in film and modern theatre, in literature, and not least in the fine arts, corresponds not only to the heterogeneous and discontinous structure of spatial and local conditions but also to the eclectic attitude in the advanced arts of the so-called Post-Modernists shortly before the turn of the millennium, which expresses itself in the relationships of artists to historical art epochs and to the disparate use of material. The principle of montage has ultimately reached the arts in general and has since become so established in human consciousness that we can confidently speak of an internalization. In this respect, montage appears not only as a symbolic form of our time but also as a model of a view of the world and its experience, as self-evident as perspective was to our ancestors.

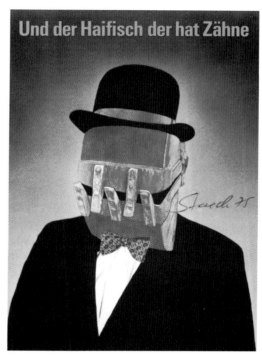

Klaus Staeck, *Baulöwe* [*Building Tycoon*], Postcard, 1975

1. Cited in Walter Dadek, *Das Filmmedium* (Munich, 1968), p. 219. The quotation cannot be found on the page indicated in Balázs' *Der Film. Werden und Wesen einer neuen Kunst* (Vienna, 1961). A more thorough examination revealed that the literary references in this useful and almost inexhaustible book are not especially exact.
2. This rather unnecessary differentiation is intended to distinguish between the takes that are customary especially in contemporary films and that can extend over one or several scenes and close-ups, or "Stehkader."
3. The reference is to Erwin Panofsky's influential essay "Die Perspektive als symbolische Form" (1924/25), in his *Aufsätze zu Grundfragen der Kunstwissenschaft* (Berlin, 1974), pp. 99ff. (Engl. *Perspective as Symbolic Form*, trans. Christopher S. Wood [New York, 1991]), which will be referred to frequently in this essay.
4. Arnold Hauser, *Sozialgeschichte der Kunst und Literatur*, Vol. II (Munich, 1953), p. 511.
5. Ibid.
6. Wolfgang Kemp, *Theorie der Fotografie 1839–1912*, Vol. I (Munich, 1980), p. 25.
7. Pierre Francastel, "Destruction d'un espace plastique," *Peinture et société*, Oeuvres, Vol. I (Paris, 1977), pp. 139–222; p. 141. Translated by Patricia Crampton.
8. Cf. in film, especially close-up. Highly remunerated film stars have the number of close-ups desired included in their contracts. For further reference, see François Truffaut, *Mr. Hitchcock, wie haben Sie das gemacht?* (Munich, 1973).
9. "Item Perspectiva ist ein lateinisch Wort, bedeutt ein Durchsehung," Dürer's definition of perspective as cited and translated in Panofsky, *Perspective*, p. 27.
10. This is true only in a visual sense.
11. Hauser (see footnote 4), loc. cit.
12. See Walter Dadek (see footnote 1), for references to further literature; or Ulrich Gregor and Enno Patalas, *Geschichte des Films* (Gütersloh, 1962), pp. 13–43.
13. Sergei Eisenstein, "Dickens, Griffith und wir," in *Gesammelte Aufsätze*, Vol. I (Zürich, n. d.), p. 60f.
14. Sergei Tretyakov, "John Heartfield montiert," in Eckhard Siepmann, *Montage: John Heartfield. Vom Club Dada zur Arbeiter-Illustrierten-Zeitung* (Berlin, 1977), p. 169.

15. Herta Wescher, *Die Collage* (Cologne, 1968), p. 7.
16. See Margaret F. Harker for further reference, *Henry Peach Robinson* (Oxford, 1988).
17. Wescher (see footnote 15), p. 19.
18. The term here is used exclusively in a descritpive way.
19. Wescher (see footnote 15), loc. cit.
20. Cf. Wescher (see footnote 15), illustration 9.
21. Sergei Eisenstein, "Montage 1938," in *Gesammelte Aufsätze,* Vol. I (see footnote 13), p. 229 ff.
22. Ibid., *Dickens, Griffith und wir* (see footnote 13), loc. cit.
23. Ibid., p. 113.
24. Cf. the exhibition catalogues *Art et Publicité* (Paris: Centre Pompidou, 1990) and *High and Low* (New York: The Museum of Modern Art, 1990).
25. L. B. Alberti, *Della pittura,* in *Kleinere Kunsttheoretische Schriften,* ed. Hubert Janitschek (Vienna, 1877), p. 79: "scrivo uno quadroangulo (…) el quale reputo essere una fenestra per donde io miri quello que quivi sara dipinto" (*On Painting,* trans. John R. Spencer [New Haven, 1966], p. 56: "I inscribe a quadrangle […] which is considered to be an open window through which I see what I want to paint"), cited in Panofsky, *Perspective,* p. 76, n. 4.
26. Panofsky (see footnote 3), p. 99.
27. Joscijka Gabriele Abels, *Erkenntnis der Bilder – Die Perspektive in der Kunst der Renaissance* (Frankfurt am Main, 1985), p. 77.
28. Arnold Gehlen, *Zeit-Bilder* (Frankfurt am Main and Bonn, 1960), p. 31.
29. Panofsky, *Perspective,* pp. 29–30.
30. Ernst Cassirer, *Die Philosophie der symbolischen Formen,* 2: *Das mythische Denken* (Berlin, 1925), pp. 107 ff.; Engl. *Philosophy of Symbolic Forms* (New Haven, 1955), pp. 83–84, cited in Panofsky, *Perspective,* p. 30.
31. Francastel (see footnote 7), loc. cit.
32. Jean-Paul Richter, ed., *The Literary Works of Leonardo da Vinci,* Vol. 1 (London, 1970), p. 130.
33. Ibid.
34. For further reference see Panofsky, *Perspective,* pp. 38 ff.
35. Eisenstein, *Dickens, Griffith und wir* (see footnote 13), loc. cit.
36. Cf. Klaus Honnef, "Bilder und Abbilder," in *Romantik und Gegenwart. Festschrift für J. Chr. Jensen* (Cologne, 1988), p. 99 ff.
37. Andreas Beyer, "Privileg des Rätselhaften," in *Frankfurter Allgemeine Zeitung,* 266 (November 14, 1990), N3.
38. Panofsky, *Perspective,* loc. cit.
39. Ibid., p. 72.
40. Ernst Cassirer, "Sprache und Mythos," in *Wesen und Wirken des Symbolbegriffes* (Darmstadt, 1956), p. 175. This translation adapted from Panofsky, *Perspective,* p. 41 (no reference).
41. "Mosaic" to be understood here only in a descriptive and not in a psychological sense, which affects the formal structure of the individual film image.
42. Francastel (see footnote 7), p. 159.
43. Ibid.
44. A term that Arnold Gehlen (cf. footnote 28) uses in reference to Daniel-Henry Kahnweiler's reflections on Cubism and whose argumentation is applied in parts of this text.
45. Daniel-Henry Kahnweiler quoted by Gehlen (see footnote 28), p. 75.
46. See Daniel-Henry Kahnweiler for further details, *Juan Gris – Leben und Werk* (Stuttgart, 1968), p. 63 ff.
47. Ibid.
48. Paul Virilio, *War and Cinema. The Logistics of Perception* (London and New York, 1989), p. 16; translated by Patrick Camiller Virilio cited in Kevin Brownlow, *Hollywood. The Pioneers* (London, 1979), p. 71.
49. Ibid., p. 61
50. Opposition to the bourgeois avant-garde is in my opinion the result of the express political commitment of the Left.
51. Walter Benjamin in a lecture in Paris on the opposing artists, cited in Siepmann (see footnote 14), p. 166.
52. Cf. Jury Lotman, *Semiotics of Cinema,* trans. Mark E. Suino, *Michigan Slavic Contributions* 5 (Ann Arbor, 1981), p. 51.
53. Tretyakov (see footnote 14), p. 169.
54. Sergei Eisenstein, *Schriften,* Vol. I, ed. Hans-Joachim Schlegel (Munich, 1974), p. 218.
55. Ibid.
56. I. M. Peters, "Bild und Bedeutung. Zur Semiologie des Films," in *Semiotik des Films,* ed. Friedrich Knilli (Munich, 1971), p. 67.
57. Ibid.
58. Ibid.
59. Eisenstein, "Montage 1938" (see footnote 21), p. 234.
60. V. I. Pudovkin, "Über die Montage," in *Theorie des Kinos, Ideologiekritik der Traumfabrik,* ed. Karsten Witte (Frankfurt am Main, 1972), p. 116.
61. Walter Benjamin, *Das Kunstwerk im Zeitalter seiner technischen Reproduzierbarkeit* (Frankfurt am Main, 1963), p. 62.
62. Dadek (see footnote 1), p. 244 f.
63. Cf. Robert Castel, "Images et phantasmes," in Pierre Bourdieu et al. *Un art moyen. Essai sur les usages sociaux de la photographie* (Paris, 1965), pp. 289–331; p. 293.
64. E.g., Bernhard Heisig in his "Fritz-Bildern;" cf. catalogue by Klaus Honnef, *Bernhard Heisig* (Munich, 1988), p. 62 ff.
65. Tretyakov (see footnote 14), p. 169.

Catalogue

John Heartfield, 1931

[...] under the impact of the imperialist war of 1914–1918 the foundations of bourgeois culture and morality began to crumble one by one. Artists no longer kept abreast of events. The pencil was too slow and was overtaken by the lies spread by the bourgeois press. Revolutionary artists did not keep pace, but fell behind and failed to record each stage of the proletariat's struggle.

Sergei Tretyakov/Solomon Telingater, *John Heartfield. A Monograph*, p. 63. Moscow, 1936. Translated by Keith Hammond.

Hanne Bergius, 1989

The Dadaists tossed their laughter as a joint anarchic impulse of their revolt into a society shaken by the First World War. Laughter was the "favorite tool" of the Dadaist art and culture guerillas, which they subversively implemented as an instrument of scepticism, disruption of meaning, and re-evaluation, with the full impact of modernism. Dadaist laughter assumed many forms: irony, humor in varying shades, cynicism, and sarcasm. [...] The "mad simultaneous concert of murder, fake culture, the erotic, and veal roast" escalated to a Dionysiac state of euphoria – "to the sanctity of the meaningless" and to the "jubilation of Orphic nonsense." In this way the Dadaist celebrated a newly won creativity and put Dada at the "beginning." He dared to go way out onto the open "sea" of irony. [...]
The Dadaist, continually on the road and always role-playing, outwitted his rootlessness with a laugh, and turned the burden of disorientation into an exoneration. He sought refuge in attack. He transformed the loss of meaning into a renunciation of meaning.

Hanne Bergius, *Das Lachen Dadas: Die Berliner Dadaisten und ihre Aktionen*, Werkbund-Archiv 19, pp. 9, 15. Anabas-Verlag, Gießen, 1989.

1 *Grosz-Heartfield mont.*, "Sonniges Land" [*The Sunny Land*]. Collage, 1919. Cat. no. 302

2   *Grosz-Heartfield mont.*, "Dada-merika." Collage, 1919. Cat. no. 65

Udo Rukser, 1919

Dadaism as struggle, as polemic is the artist's protest against the educational ideals of the Philistine who considers compulsory education to be the epitome of all cultural achievement; it is the artist's retaliation against the bourgeoisie for keeping him hungry, making him suffer, for wanting to make him bend under the yoke of narrow-mindedness and a wretched life-style and outlook on life; it is the whip with which he can shock the bourgeois out of his snug, epicurean composure. For the bourgeois, life is one of habit and materialism; the artist's life is a permanent revolution of the mind. [. . .]

Thus Dadaism is not a trend; it is the affirmation of a feeling of independence, a distrust of society, of everything that smacks of the herd; it is the protest against the *sinologizing of Man*, against his transformation from a beast into a tame domestic animal of blue-eyed docility and with horns, as large as possible. Dada is not a formulated program in the conventional sense; it is the unrestricted natural instinct for life as preached by Nietzsche, which spits everything that is polemical into the grotesque mugs of the bourgeois and turns somersaults in the bourgeois world. Put aside what is oppositional in it, and it is essentially *the allegiance of Man to Himself, to Nature*; it is a life-style that has the courage

and the honesty to be as Nature has made one, without the whitewash of all the fake conventions of bourgeois life. In this sense, Dada is the logical cult, the enthronement of one's own person, of individuality, the appeal to true humanity and honesty; it is, in fact, nothing other than – the Humboldtian notion of humanity understood properly.

Udo Rukser, "Dada. Aufführung und Ausstellung im Salon Neumann, Kurfürstendamm," in *Freie Zeitung*, (Berlin, May 5, 1919).

3   "Leben und Treiben in Universal-City, 12 Uhr 5 mittags" [*Life and Times in Universal City at 12:05 Noon*]. Collage, 1919. Cat. no. 72

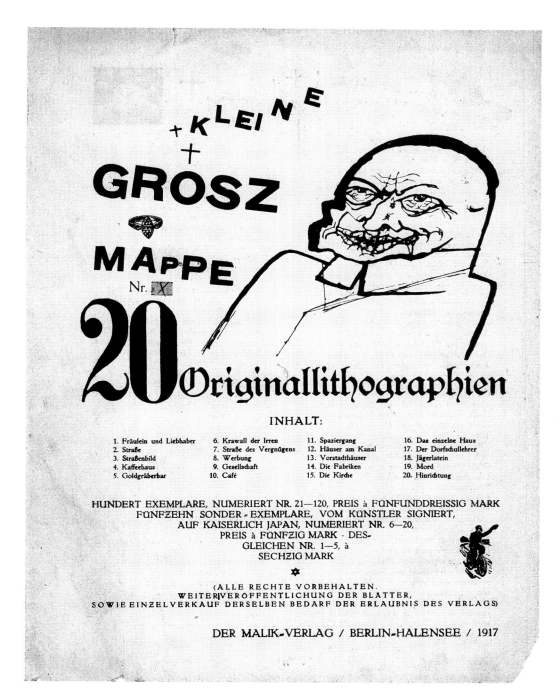

Jan Tschichold, 1928

Die Neue Jugend [*New Youth*], the brochure for the *Kleine Grosz-Mappe* [*Small Grosz Portfolio*], was published in Germany in 1917; it represents one of the earliest and most significant documents of New Typography. There, we already find its typical characteristics: Liberation from "traditional" typographical design, tremendous contrast in type size, form, and color, use of all kinds of fonts and line arrangement, and of photography. The feverish impotence against the capitalist war finds its literary expression in political articles: "One Has to Be a Rubber Man," "Pray with the Skull Against the Wall," "Work, Work, Work, Work: Triumph of Christian Science," etc. All the chaos of these times is reflected in the outer form of the brochure.

Jan Tschichold, *Die neue Typographie: Ein Handbuch für zeitgemäß Schaffende*, p. 58. Berlin, 1928.

Eckhard Siepmann, 1977

The decomposition of the traditional "illusionistic space" was carried over into typography. The simple function of typography, to arrange words and sequences of words, was suspended in favor of creating a synthesis of word and image; typography took care of iconic functions such as rhythm and color; the composition of the word intervened in the image. In this way the ground was prepared, not only for the typography of the dust jacket, but also for a specific structural element of Heartfield's photomontage, which consists in the meaning of the image being inflected by the word. The typography of *Neue Jugend* [*New Youth*] can therefore be considered as the negation of the word's function of commentary; but instead, as a dialectic prerequisite for integrating the word into the photomontage, no longer as supplement or commentary, but as a semantic intervention in the image; as an alteration, even reversal, of the meaning of the image through the word.

Eckhard Siepmann, *Montage: John Heartfield. Vom Club Dada zur Arbeiter-Illustrierten-Zeitung*, p. 38. Elefanten Press, Berlin, and Eckhard Siepmann, 1977.

Wieland Herzfelde, 1971

John and I were of a different nature than he [George Grosz], not exactly humorless, but essentially emotional and sentimental. Still, cruelty repelled us as it did him. We shared his hatred of war and of all who were to blame for it, excused it, or glorified it, and our spontaneous friendship developed into a working alliance that lasted almost without friction over the next fifteen years. We loved Grosz's appearance and character, his original way of telling a story and of listening – his art, moreover, was a revelation to us. Altogether like a cold shower: shocking, sobering, thrilling, and invigorating. My brother and I were used to understanding art as making Beauty visible and audible, which is as inherent to life as metal is to stone. However, from then on Grosz made us see the ordinary world as far from dull, banal, and boring, but rather as a drama in which stupidity, brutality, and corruption play a major role. He aroused in both of us a new, highly critical appreciation of our previous dabblings in art: Helmut burned everything he had created in charcoal, pencil, chalk, ink, tempera, and oils.

Wieland Herzfelde, "George Grosz, John Heartfield, Erwin Piscator, Dada und die Folgen – oder Die Macht der Freundschaft," in *Sinn und Form*, (June 23, 1971), pp. 1224–51. Aufbau Verlag, Berlin and Weimar, 1976, for id.; *Zur Sache*, Berlin/Weimar, 1976.

AUS DEN GESÄNGEN

Ha! in Kopenhagen fallen die Börsen!!
Ha! in New York fallen die Börsen!!
Betlehems Steel Aktien — wer kanns wissen?!
Die Menschen drängen, krank,
verlogen brüllt alter Faulgreis Friedensgerücht,
Druckerschwärze, noch frisch geleitartikelt — —
weiter: Die Straßen klitschig,
Der Regen strähnt,
die Omnibusse torkeln,
beinschwarz stoßen Regenschirme ineinander,
nur die Lichtreklamen blühn:
Rheingold, Manoli, Steiners Paradiesbett.
Der Antichrist kam wieder, er trägt Konfektion.

Krahne und Lohrenbahn,
unterfressener Asphalt — wie seltsam!!
Abenteurer ziehn vorüber, steifen Hut,
schwarz auf Glatthaar, nach hinten.
Des Syphilitikers buntes Profil schimmert
durchs Dunkel — auch ohne Nase läßt sichs leben —!!!

Die Schnapskneipe wartet schon — die Feengrotte,
schon der Coctail, der Gin, der Grog, der steife.
Heidi, Musik — eine richtige Negermusik!
Kann jemand Ragtimes??!!
Tanz — bitte!
: Rio taucht auf — Hafengassen
und Matchiche, hallo! nackt, geil — — —
Oh, Südamerika!! Deine warmen Küstenbuchten!
Oh, Argentinien, Sehnsuchtland!
Schokolade trink ich,
früh auf Veranda aus Bambus,
und schwarze Zigarre,
großer Baststrohhut übern Kopf —
und Nilpferdpeitsche —
Mestizen stolz und Rinderheerden in Fray=Bentos —
Den Revolver knall ich ab
früh, wenn ich aus dem Blockhaus trete
breit, mit roter Bluse und braun —
wild bellt der Hund —
und der Papagei singt englisch.
Ha!! ich lebe auf! Früh! Tau auf allem Gras,
meine beiden Revolver, das große Schottenmesser,
mein schwarzer Zottelhund — — oh!! Colorado!
Freiheit!!!

Kobaltenblau singt der große Fluß
um uralte Bäume,
unberührt von Kreiselsäge und Aktienunternehmer.
Das Canoe liegt bereit,
bemalt mit Rot — —
Bisamburgen treiben vorbei,
Pisang und Banane und bunte Vögel —
Der Himmel cölinblau,
weiß segelt eine Wolke nach Europa.
Wir fahren an Stromschnellen vorbei,
wirbelnd zu den tausend Inseln —

Perlbesäter Sammetmantel — Du, oh Rio!!
— Cuba hör ich, seh grün und roten Schwanzaffen
oben am Brotfruchtbaum —
und die tausend Masten und den
gemütlichdummen wollbraunen Neger
und amerikanischen Matrosen mit der Shagpfeife,
bogenspuckend — an blauer Küste.

Immer noch die tolle Sehnsucht nach Hitze —
ih, — im Coctail ist Leben!
im Coctail so farbig
fließt der Rio grande del Norte,
mit tausend kleinen Booten,
und der großen Korvette,
und dem blauen Kapitain,
unbeugsam am Steuerruder und gelber Messingstange,
ih — im Coctail ist Leben —
die Hafengassen sind belebt —
es gibt schon Tote,
zwei Matrosen — — — —
im Bordell von rosa Licht schwül umhaucht —
und wankende Schenkel, riesig und wüst —
Der Schnaps fließt die Bordellgassen entlang —
ist das ein Leben!!!!
Die Speicher mit Tabak und Baumwolle — —
und alte Dame, würdig,
mit Gouvernanten aus Osteuropa —
im Coctail ist Leben — — —
Auch Porter ist da,
alter noch, von
Perkins & Co., London. — —

4b   *Kleine Grosz-Mappe*, 1917. Pamphlet, p. 2. Cat. no. 301

Hans Richter, 1961

Wieland Herzfelde, together with his brother John, published *Die Neue Jugend* [*New Youth*] just as the First World War was winding to an end and the empire was visibly crumbling. They put forward the demands of the new generation in a literary, aggressive, and political way. But it wasn't until Dada that this Stress found the Storm that made it public. John, Wieland's brother, called himself Heartfield and differed in many ways from Wieland, who kept the name Herzfelde. Wieland was as methodical, businesslike, more brains than heart, as John was erratic, unpredictable, and emotional.

Wieland, the publisher, became an "important man," the editor of leftist German magazines and books, of modern rebellious literature including Lasker-Schüler and, above all, books and drawings by George Grosz. [...]

With the vigorous assistance of the two brothers, Berlin's Dada program became a politically radical trumpet of doom of the Last Judgment, which no longer acknowledged the silvery notes of art, but preferred to stake everything on a radical change of society. Jonny and Wieland never left any doubt as to where they stood politically: somewhat left of left. [...]

John seemed to be infinitely weaker than Wieland, but a lot wilder by contrast. Nothing of the iron will, but all the more explosive. A cat on a hot tin roof, an electric eel, a glass of water slipping and sliding on a wet table, an artist. I cannot decide whether he or Hausmann invented photomontage. Hausmann, the self-styled Edison of Berlin, claims he did. But in fairness I would divide it up between the two of them [...] if I did not have serious doubts in the first place as to whether before them Rodchenko in Moscow had invented and used photomontage when the Russian Revolution was in full swing. Be that as it may, Hausmann's gaping, bellowing mouths spewing slogans, Heartfield's almost classically composed political graphics, and later Hannah Hoech's lyrics, demonstrated the artistic potential which by now has been explored by other generations in every more or less civilized country. It is Heartfield's achievement to have torn apart static photography by cutting it into pieces and then reassembling it. That is the reason why he was called the *Dada-Monteur* [*Dada assembler*]. In this way his art helped him to kick to hell a world dissolving into ruins. What was then meant as a political pamphlet and a statement about "what's bothering me," can be included today in the history of art; no advertising agency anywhere in the world can do without photomontage.

Hans Richter, "John Heartfield–Wieland Herzfelde: Die H-Brüder," in *Dada Profile*, pp. 62–63. Verlags AG Die Arche, Zurich, 1961.

4c   *Kleine Grosz-Mappe*, 1917. Pamphlet, p. 3. Cat. no. 301

George Grosz, 1955

When Wieland was called to the front once again, a new man joined the editorial board: the boisterous poet Franz Jung. The *Neue Jugend* [*New Youth*] at once assumed a new face: it became aggressive. Its new format was based on that of American journals, and Heartfield used collages and bolder type to develop a new style. Black index-fingers stood between arbitrarily-placed capital and small letters; beside them could be found two gigantic crossbones, a small coffin, a lady with a roguish grin behind a mask, part of a concertina, a lead soldier. It all added up to a message that frightened the uninitiated and went far beyond anything most people expected. It reflected the spirit of the age, of a world in the process of being dismembered.

A Small Yes and a Big No. The Autobiography of George Grosz, translated by Arnold J. Pomerans, p. 149. Allison and Busby, London and New York, 1982.

4d   *Kleine Grosz-Mappe*, 1917. Pamphlet, p. 4. Cat. no. 301

IM JUNI 1917 — NEUE JUGEND — PREIS 20 PF.

PROSPEKT
zur Kleinen Grosz Mappe.
Der Malik-Verlag, Berlin-Südende

Prospekt zur Kleinen Grosz Mappe.

34, Steglitzer Strasse, Südende.

CHRONIK Friedrich Adler ist zum Tode verurteilt, Stockholm-Getöne gegen internationale Teuerung - das Leben weiterhin billiger, Lebensmittel bleiben in Cornerstimmung. Nach Reuter verhungern in Ovamboland die Ovambos, keine Kaffern - in den European Dominions niemand! Verhungert doch - Steigerung!! Spinoza ist eingestampft für Bedarf diplomatischer Sendschreiben - Liberia, Pseudoliberia - Molière verrieselt in Sternheim (Zukunft vom 26. 5. 1917), Umfassungsmanöver gegen Wallner in Wien, Durst! - das Aktionsbuch ist erschienen. Frühlingswende fiebert Sexualität, Heufieber. Liebeich-la-l'au! Sich hinzu-schmeissen! Lichtmord!! — unsere Seelen sind so wund. **Amokläufer** . . . . Die Messer raus !!!

Man muß Kautschukmann sein!

Ja, Kautschukmann sein — eventuell den Kopf zwischen die Beine stecken oder durchs Faß springen — und spiralig in die Luft schnellen! sieh, ein Paragraph rempelt Dich an, eine Affiche, ein Flohzirkus . . .

EIN „MARSIAS" INTERESSENT

(sämtliche Flöhe liegen an Schlingen — desertieren ausgeschlossen — Springen von Flöhen auf Kommando, Paradenmarsch der Flöhe . . . .)

Immerhin wichtig ist, das Gleichgewichtzu behalten! Wo vordem die gotische Kirche, messelt sich heute das Warenhaus hoch — !

— Die Fahrstühle sausen . . . Eisenbahnunglücks, Explosionskatastrophen . . . — quer durchrast den Balkanzug Mitteleuropa, doch gibts auch Baumblüte und Edelmarmeladenrationierung . . .

Wie gesagt, Kautschukmann sein beweglich in allen Knochen nicht blos im Dichter-Sessel dösen oder vor der Staffelei schön getönte Bildchen pinseln.

Den Bequemen gilts zu stören beim Verdauungsschläfchen ihm den pazifistischen Popo zu kitzeln, rumort! explodiert! zerplatzt! — oder hängt euch ans Fensterkreuz . . . . . .

Laßt euren Kadaver in die Branntweingasse baumeln! Ja! Wieder elastisch werden, nach allen Seiten höchst federnd — sich verbiegen — anboxen! Kinn- oder Herzgrubenhieb!

Ladies and gentlemen!!
jeder hat Zutritt!

Nur nähertreten !! . . . nur nähertreten !! . . . Schon beulen sich die Weihrauchkessel ein. Nervös rutscht das weiche Gesäß hin und her!

— — — Ja! Wenn nicht sämtliche Flöhe an Schlingen lägen ! . . . . . .

Dieses Blatt ist der

PROSPEKT
ZUR KLEINEN
GROSZ-MAPPE

Die Sekte 1917

Die Sekte Neunzehn Siebzehn wächst aus dem Intellekt der umstehenden Zuhörer empor und zwingt ihre Mitglieder gegen den Block der Überzeugten. Die ohnmächtige Wut unserer Leser verpflichtet, einen bereits in Schwingung umgesetzten Glauben wieder zu fixieren, um mit den Gläubigen von neuem dagegen loszugehen. Die Leute wollen halt nichts alleine tun.

Sekten. Mehr Sekten. Noch mehr Sekten.

Das Wunder der Christian Science ist über unseren kürzlich veranstalteten Werbe-Abend gerauscht und schüttet Glück aus über diejenigen, die uns lieben, um uns hinterrücks zu erdolchen.

Darum muss Einer seine Stimme erheben: Nicht mehr glauben, überhaupt nicht glauben. Sich selbst. (Sich und selbst) Beten.

Wenngleich jeder schuldig ist an der Unfähigkeit der andern, Feind zu sein, sondern schlotternder Neidhammel, soll keiner an dieser Schuld sich selbst beruhigt genug sein lassen. Nicht das Peinliche dieser Schuld schmatzend zu fressen, soll es ankommen, sondern Genuss auch noch auszukotzen — und wiederum zu fressen und wiederum!

Es ist in jeder Sekunde, die ein hundertmalverfluchtesLebenschenkt (unsägliche Wonne durstend das galizische Petroleumgebiet zu durchfahren, die Gestänge der Bohrtürme verrusst!) so unendlich vieles zu tun.

Betet mit dem Schädel gegen die Wand!!

Wir — aha! — wir treten gegen die Menschen nicht auf. Wir treten geduldig noch mit den Menschen auf. Die Sekte Neunzehn Siebzehn schlägt gegeneinander, Sturmflut aus unseren Gebeten, die aus der Ohnmacht der Gläubigen emporgewachsen sind. Unsere Mitglieder verrecken, weil die Sekte sie nicht mehr locker lässt. Betet aus

98.8 Tempelh. TELEPHON

REKLAMEBERATUNG

unseren Gebeten zu diesem Ende. Damit ihr endlich in die Schlinge kommt. Es ist ein so ungleiches Spiel mit diesen Sanften, Zappelnden. Der Magen der Neunzehn Siebzehn will das alles nicht mehr verdauen, immer wieder dasselbe, die Ohnmacht der Gläubigen, der Block der Ueberzeugten, das Einfangen, Verarbeiten, Auskotzen, Fressen,

---

das Ich triumphierend über Puntas Arenas, Michigan See, Sachalin bis Sorau. Dort wurde der Dichter Heinrich Steinhausen geboren, steht in der Zeitung.

Halt dich, Junge.

Die Frist ist um. Her die neue Ladung. Sektierer, los! Wieviel zappeln schon wieder?

Die Arbeit Arbeit Arbeit Arbeit: Triumph der Christian Science. **Das Wunder der Sekte Neunzehn Siebzehn.** 1917. SCHREIT!!

Kannst du radfahren ?

Zu den reinsten unverbildeten Erklärungen und Dokumenten unseres Lebens gehören jene Bilder aus den Rückfronten der Häuser, diese Erlasse des Kaufmanns (des wahren Herrn dieser Zeit) — von unerhörter Sachlichkeit vorgetragen, gigantisch eingeätzt wie auf alten Pyramiden, pressen sie das psychologische und formale Erleben des in knallenden Stadtbahnzug Dahinrollenden. Fabelhaft bunt und klar, wie mie ein Tafelbildchen, — von kosmischer Komik, brutal, materiell, bleichsüchtig, verwaschen — drohend und mahnend gleich Ragtimestepptanzmelodie immer wieder sich ins Gehirn bohrend —

Das grölüt in einem fort!

Zwingt uns zum prallenden Marineblau, zu Grellrots (ganze Straßen Buchstaben), Varietégrün, Spezialitätengelb, Wollwarengraus, und fistelndes Rosa —

Mozialtionen tauchen auf . . . . . .

Champagner-Flasche — der Korken knallt davon, ho! ho!

Sekt Schloss Vaux.

Ich, Dannemann-Zigarre schief im Maul, Zeitung — vor mir knerzen die Knattermotore — hart überholt mich Backbord der rote Autobus!

Ho! ho! schon wieder brüllen die Häuserwände:

Regie-Zigaretten, Satrap, Palast-Hotel, Teppich-Thomas, bade zu Hause, Steiners Paradiesbett . . . . . ho! . . . . Sarg's Kalodont . . . . . Passage-Café . . . . . AEG . . . . . Ceresit.

z. B., vom Training kommend, am Punching Ball . . . . Den Joe hiebst Du nieder.

z. B., Du segeltest fabelhaft in die Chaussee, eben noch flog Dir der Fußball an die klemmerlose Nase, Du hingst oben im Aeroplan unter der Bergsonne — zwischen den Stämmen knallte Deine Winchesterbüchse (Gott ließ ja Eisen wachsen, bravo)

Abends in den Asphaltbrüchen, in Geldsack-Hills, zwischen Porter-Bierplakaten, oder an der Bar bei Kantorowicz, in Zooquellen oder piklein mit steifem Hemd aalglatt bei Adlon, strömendes Pils Coctails Ersatz und Agoston, Apollotheater und Kinohäuser . . . . und dem Treiben der beiden Herzfelder!

Sag mal? — . . . . . . graults Dir da nicht in den Kunstsalons? . . . in den Ölgemäldegalerien . . . . . . ? in den literarische Soirèen . . . . ?

Lieber Leser! Ein guter Fußballspieler enthält immerhin eine ganze Menge Wert — obwohl er nicht dichtet, malt und Töne setzt!

Bleibt die Frage? Kennst Du Schiller und Goethe — ? — ja! **Aber kannst Du radfahren?**

Weitere Marsyas-Interessenten wollen sich noch melden!

Dara geht ins Hotel.

Ein Stück aus dem Roman „Ehrlich zu sich selbst" von W. Winnischenko. Hier veröffentlicht, weil der Roman dieses Kleinrussen, der aus dem Arbeiterstande hervorgegangen ist, bei aller grob aufgetragenen Sentimentalität, trotz aller Verzerrungen in der gemeinschaftspsychologischen Einstellung und der übertriebenen Werbelmessung soziale Probleme (wie eben nur der Sozialist denken kann) eine über literarischer Tasten hinausgehende Kraft zum Erleben des Einzelnen kundtun möchte. Mag die vielfach irrig, weil unerläßlich sein, in folgendem nur auszugsweise wiedergegebenen Kapitel, so ist dieser Glaube im Menschen restlos und über die Auflösung aller Konflikte hinausgehend. Und mehr wie das gerade noch Für-uns-Richtiges vielleicht wesentlicher wiedergibt.

Der Gatte hielt im Sprechen inne und warf Dara flüchtige Blicke zu. Dann bat er sie plötzlich leise, diese Nacht bei ihr bleiben zu dürfen, wobei er gleichsam schuldbewußt errötete und verwirrt vor ihr stehen blieb. Dara sah erstaunt zu ihm auf. In seinem betretenen Blick war etwas Furchtsam-erwartendes, als ängstige er sich vor ihrer Absage und wünsche sie zugleich.

Dara errötete, erhob sich spöttisch lächelnd und führte Ssergei, ihn umarmend, aus dem Zimmer.

'Geh, geh . . . Du mußt jetzt schlafen. Mach, daß du fortkommst. Das wäre unhygienisch . .

Und sie lachte sogar, — mit einem trockenen, scharfen Lachen. Ssergei protestierte nicht weiter, murmelte etwas vor sich hin und lachte ebenfalls gezwungen. Aus seinem Benehmen fühlte man etwas wie Dankbarkeit, wie Schuldbewußtsein und etwas Unruhiges-verzehrendes, Ungelöstes. An der Schwelle blieb er nochmals stehen und wollte ihr in die Augen sehen, aber sie stieß ihn mit weicher Entschlossenheit hinaus und schloß die Tür.

Gegen zwei Uhr nachts war sie noch immer auf. Ungestüm, mit düster zusammengezogenen Augenbrauen ging sie auf und ab, setzte sich zuweilen auf den Diwan, schloß die Augen und warf den Kopf auf die Lehne zurück. Dann zeigte sich auf ihrem, vom Lampenlicht voll erhellten Gesicht brennende Röte auf den unteren Teilen der Wangen und das bebende Eigenleben der erregten Nasenflügel. Und wieder sprang sie auf und ging rubelos im Zimmer auf und ab.

Auch im Bett konnte sie sich nicht beruhigen, wälzte sich seufzend, hüllte sich bis oben zu und schlug die Decke wieder zurück.

Am Morgen waren ihre Augen mit einem dunklen Müdigkeitsstreifen umrändert, aber im Gesicht lag der Ausdruck einer sonderbar spöttischen, erregten Entschlossenheit.

Oft blickte sie beim Mittagessen über die Gesichter der anderen und lächelte heimlich in sich hinein, um dieses Lächeln sofort wieder zu verstecken. Und etwas Feindseliges folgte diesem Lächeln aufblitzend in ihren Augen, etwas Feindseliges und Unerschütterliches.

Abends zog sie sich ohne jemand ein Wort zu sagen um, zählte das Geld in ihrer Börse und verließ das Haus. Sie lächelte ebenso wie beim Mittagessen, während sie auf der Straße ging.

Sie schlug eine vorher offenbar überlegte Richtung ein, obzwar sie sich öfters umsah und die Häuser aufmerksam betrachtete. In einer kleineren Straße angelangt, wurde ihr Schritt sicherer. An der nächsten Kreuzung blieb sie stehen. Zwei Schritte weiter war der Eingang zu einem Hotel. Ueber der Tür brannte eine große Laterne, auf deren Scheiben die Aufschrift zu lesen war „Imperial" vor der offenen Tür schlummerte friedlich ein livrierter Portier mit einer betreßten Mütze.

Dara trat entschlossen zu ihm und fragte laut:

„Haben Sie freie Zimmer?"

Der Portier warf den Kopf hoch, besann sich einen Augenblick schlaftrunken, riß dann die Mütze vom Kopf und antwortete eifrig und mit vielen Verbeugungen:

Das Aktionsbuch ist erschienen!!

„Bitte, bitte treten Sie ein! . . Hierher, wenn ich bitten darf, wünschen Sie ein großes Zimmer?"

„Das ist gleich. Nur sauber muß es sein."

„Sofort . . ."

Der Portier drückte auf einen Knopf, oben schellte laut eine Glocke, und gleich darauf hörte man weiche, über den Läufer laufende Schritte. Auf dem Treppenabsatz zeigte sich ein Kellner.

„Darf ich Sie bitten, — man wird Ihnen oben zeigen . . ." verbeugte sich der Portier.

Dara stieg langsam und gelassen die wenigen Stufen und folgte dem Kellner an einer langen Reihe von Türen vorbei. Der Mann hatte eine Glatze, die bis zum Halse hinabreichte, ein kleines, spitziges Gesicht, mit versteckten, klugen und durchdringenden Aeuglein darin.

Er stieß eine der Türen auf, zündete die Kerze an und hielt sie in der erhobenen Hand. Das Zimmer war groß, sauber und sogar behaglich.

„Gut. Ich nehme es", sagte Dara.

„Soll das Gepäck vom Bahnhof abgeholt werden?"

„Nein. Ich bin ohne Gepäck."

„Ist eine Teemaschine gefällig?"

„Nein. Ich brauche nichts. Stellen Sie die Kerze auf den Tisch und warten Sie."

Dara nahm vor dem Spiegel stehend den Hut ab, steckte die Nadeln langsam in einen Filz, legte ihn auf den Tisch, drehte sich zu dem ehrerbietig wartenden Kellner um, und sagte ruhig und befehlend:

„Besorgen Sie mir einen Herrn und führen Sie ihn zu mir ins Zimmer."

Des Kellners Augen wurden größer.

„Sie wünschen? . ." fragte er behutsam, als fürchte er sie nicht recht verstanden zu haben.

„Ich wünsche von Ihnen, daß Sie mir einen Herrn heraufbringen. Sie führen doch den Männern, die bei Ihnen wohnen, Mädchen zu. Nun, und ich verlange von Ihnen, daß Sie mir einen Herrn zuführen. Ich werde Sie und ihn bezahlen."

Die Tür öffnete sich langsam und ein kleiner Herr schob sich mit kurzen weichen Schrittchen durch den Spalt ins Zimmer. Als sich die Tür, durch die der Glatzkopf und das weiße Vorhemd des Kellners - sichtbar wurden, schloß, begann sich der Herr seitwärts und die Hände reibend, als wüsche er sie der Herr Waschschlüssel, zu Dara hinzuschleichen. Die Haare auf der Stirn waren sorgfältig gescheitelt, an seinem Kinn hing ein dichtes, wie aus schwarzer Watte gemachtes Bärtchen, die Augen waren groß und vorstehend und mit lauernder, lüsterner Neugierde auf sie gerichtet.

Daras Blicke überflogen rasch seine Gestalt, ihre Augen verengten sich kühl: sie wartete.

„Guten Tag . . ." sagte er überraschend weich, mit süßlich zärtlicher Stimme.

„Guten Tag", antwortete Dara.

Der Herr schlich sich noch näher an sie heran und musterte sie mit einer immer größer werdenden Gier. In den vorstehenden Augen zeigte sich jetzt eine durchaus nicht heuchlerische Bewunderung.

„Sie sind erst kurze Zeit hier?"

„Ja."

Daras Blick überflog noch einmal seine ganze Gestalt, dann wandte sie sich plötzlich zur Tür. Der Herr wollte ihr galant zuvorkommen.

„Darf ich für Sie etwas bestellen? . . Wünschen Sie den Tee?"

„Nein. Ich will ihm sagen, daß er Sie hinausbegleiten soll. Sie gefallen mir nicht."

Die Blutwelle schoß dem Herrn ins Gesicht, er warf den Kopf in den Nacken.

„Wie Sie wünschen . . ." sagte er würdevoll und fügte spöttisch lächelnd hinzu: „Nur sind Sie auch nicht ganz so sehr . . . Weil wir doch auch . . . uns mit Dämchen auskennen, so zu sagen . . . He! . . ."

„Gehen Sie von selbst fort, oder soll ich den Kellner rufen?"

Dara blieb an der Glocke stehen.

Mit komisch verletzter Würde seinen Kopf schüttelnd, wandte sich der Herr zur Tür.

„Ganz wie Sie belieben . . ." warf er verächtlich, aber mit leichter Drohung hin. Die Klinke in der Hand, fügte er hinzu: „Ja-a . . . sehr jugendhaft . . . Mein Kompliment."

Und die Tür schloß sich hinter ihm.

Dara mußte unwillkürlich lachen und läutete nach dem Kellner.

In der nächsten Minute stand er vor ihr.

„Hören Sie, mein Lieber," wandte sie sich streng an ihn. „Sie hätten es doch selbst begreifen können, daß ich Greise und Alten nicht brauchen kann. Der Mann muß jung und hübsch sein. Verstehen Sie?"

Der Kellner verbeugte sich ehrfurchtsvoll.

„Vielleicht befehlen Sie einen Studenten?" Er neigte den Kopf treuherzig-schmeichlerisch zur Seite. „Ein Student wohnt hier bei uns, ein ganz junger und sehr . . . passender. Ich hatte gleich an ihn gedacht, er war aber nicht zu Hause. Eben ist er vom Spaziergang zurückgekommen. Er geht jeden Tag spazieren."

„Gut. Führen Sie ihn her."

Der Kellner drehte sich um und glitt geräuschlos aus dem Zimmer.

Dara preßte ihre Hände auf das brennende Gesicht und wurde nachdenklich. Seufzend warf sie einen kurzen Blick auf ihren Hut, heftete ihn eine Weile unentschlossen auf die blitzende Hutnadel und begann hartnäckig den Kopf schüttelnd und wieder mit verschränkten Armen auf und ab zu gehen; sie warf ungeduldige Blicke zur Tür.

Man klopfte jetzt ebenso leise und vorsichtig wie vorhin.

„Herein!"

Der Kellner musterte sie mit kurzen Blicken und schien noch immer nichts zu verstehen.

Dara stand stolz und unnahbar vor ihm und runzelte ungeduldig die Brauen.

„Nun, was stehen Sie? Können Sie das?"

„Ganz wie Sie befehlen . . . Nur . . . Wünschen Sie das sofort . . ."

„Ja, sofort."

Dem Kellner schien ein Licht aufzugehen.

„Zu Befehl . . . Wie darf ich Sie anmelden?"

„Anna Iwanowna Iwanenko."

„Und der Paß? . . "

Dara sah ihn auffahrend an.

„Verfügen Sie sich gefälligst hinaus: Sie sind mir zu gesprächig. Gehen Sie und schicken Sie mir einen anderen."

„Ich bitt' um Verzeihung . . . Ich meinte nur . . . Da wir jeden anmelden müssen . . ."

„Es ist gut. Gehen Sie, und tun Sie, wie ich Ihnen gesagt habe . . ."

„Zu Befehl . . ."

Der Kellner wich rückwärts zur Tür und verschwand. Er mochte das Gefühl gehabt haben, daß die Welt nahe dem Untergang sei.

Dara nahm den Mantel ab, hing ihn auf den Kleiderständer, trat zum Spiegel und ordnete ihr Haar. Die Augen waren glänzend, und um die Wangen spielte leichte Röte. Schwere goldene Flechten krönten die reine, hohe Stirn. Sie lächelte ihrem Spiegelbild zu und begann auf und ab zu gehen.

Es verging ziemlich viel Zeit. Dara ging immer noch mit leicht vorgeneigtem Kopf, mit auf der Brust verschränkten Armen und biß sich auf die Unterlippe.

Als sie das leisen Klopfen an der Tür gewahr wurde, erhob sie den Kopf, sah sich erstaunt um und sagte laut und ruhig:

„Herein!"

Die Tür öffnete sich unsicher, und auf der Schwelle erschien eine schmächtige, leicht gebeugte Gestalt in einem Studentenkittel. Ein junges, verwirrtes Gesicht und schüchterne Augen sahen zu Dara auf.

„Verzeihung . . . Ich glaubte . . . Darf man eintreten?"

Er war sehr verlegen, aber sein Blick wich keinen Augenblick von Dara. Die Tür hinter ihm schloß jemand, der im Korridor gewartet haben mußte.

„Sie dürfen. Kommen Sie nur herein," sagte Dara in einem befehlenden Ton.

Der Student trat einige Schritte näher, blieb stehen und lächelte, wie es Kinder zu tun pflegen, gleichsam schuldbewußt.

MANNHEIM

5b *Neue Jugend*, June 1917, p. 2. Cat. no. 62

Seine Lippen waren frisch und zeigten, sich öffnend, eine gleichmäßige Reihe weißer Zähne.

Auch Dara lächelte.

„Nun, setzen Sie sich . . .“ sagte sie freundlich, ihn aufmerksam betrachtend.

Der Student war wirklich jung und hübsch wie ein Mädchen. Rosafarben, mit tiefroten, weichen Lippen und blauen Augen. Auf der Oberlippe — ein zarter, goldner Flaum.

Er setzte sich etwas linkisch und lächelte von neuem.

„Man sagte mir, daß . . . Sie es allein . . . langweilig haben,“ begann er, immer tiefer errötend, „aber ich dachte, daß . . . Ich dachte, das würde irgend so eine . . . sein . . .“

„Und bin ich denn nicht ‚irgend so eine‘?“ fragte ihn immer noch lächelnd musternd Dara.

„Ja . . . Das heisst . . .“

„Wissen Sie, weshalb ich Sie herkommen ließ?“

Der Student sah sie furchtsam an.

„Verzeihung . . . Ich weiß nicht . . . Vielleicht habe ich mich geirrt . . . Mir sagte der Kellner . . .“

Dara lächelte spöttisch.

„Sie haben ihn ganz richtig verstanden. Wie alt sind Sie?“

„Dreiundzwanzig.“

„Stimmt das? Haben Sie nicht ein paar Jahre draufgeschlagen?“

„Oh nein. Ich sehe nur so aus . . .“

„Das erste Jahr auf der Universität?“

„Nein, ich bin schon im dritten Semester . . .“

„Hm! Sie sehen aus, als wären Sie im ersten. Nun, und jetzt, — sind Sie sehr erstaunt . . . über all das?“

Der Student sah sie mit etwas mehr Mut an und heftete seinen Blick sogar eine Weile lang auf ihre Augen.

„Nein . . . Das heißt, natürlich . . .“

Er schwieg betretenen . . .

Der Fall Grosz

Der Preis des Buches beträgt ordinär . . . . **25** Mark.

Die vom Verfasser und Zeichner signierten Exemplare kosten **50** Mark.

Bei Subskription ermäßigt sich der Preis jedes Buches um **15** Mark

Der Malik-Verlag, Berlin-Südende, Steglitzer Str. 34

„Nun, und wenn Ihre Schwester dasselbe täte, was würden Sie dazu sagen? . . . Haben Sie eine Schwester?“

„Ja.“

„Nun?“

Der Student schien sich jetzt sehr schlecht zu fühlen.

„Ich weiß natürlich nicht . . . Vielleicht sind Sie unzufrieden . . . Ich werde fortgehen, ich wollte Sie nicht verletzen . . . Der Kellner sagte mir . . .“

„Was hat Ihnen der Kellner gesagt?“

Der Student erschrak wieder und wollte sogar aufstehen.

„Bleiben Sie doch sitzen!“ fuhr ihn Dara an. „Was sagte Ihnen der Kellner? Wie hat er sich ausgedrückt? Uebrigens — Unsinn . . . Das ist einerlei . . . Ich habe Sie zu mir rufen lassen, wie Sie es mit Prostituierten zu tun pflegen. Hören Sie? Sie werden wahrscheinlich kein Geld annehmen . . . Aber wenn Sie wollen, werde ich Sie bezahlen. Ich brauche Sie, wie einen Mann. Verstehen Sie? Das ist alles. Sind Sie einverstanden?“

Er warf ihr hilflos-erstaunte, ungläubige Blicke zu.

„Nun? Warum schweigen Sie?“

„Ich bin einverstanden . . .“

„Und das Geld werden Sie auch annehmen?“

Dara sah ihn mit Neugierde an.

Ihm schoß das Blut zu Kopfe.

„Nein . . . Wie können Sie?!“

„Warum denn? Ihre Lage ist doch die einer Prostituierten?“

Er erhob sich und warf ihr unruhige Blicke zu.

„Dann . . . Dann muß ich . . . Ich werde fortgehen . . .“

„Sind Sie beleidigt? Und wenn ich Sie mit einem Arzt vergleiche? Ich brauche Sie, wie man einen Arzt brauchen könnte, und bezahle Sie dafür. Das macht doch nichts?“

Sie lächelte seltsam und abwartend.

Der kleine Student sah sie von der Seite an, — scherzt sie, oder ist das ihr Ernst?

„Das ist etwas anderes . . .“ sagte er vorsichtig.

Dara stand lächelnd auf.

Als der Student wieder fortging, sah er Dara mit einer flehenden, schüchternen Demut an, daß man auf den Gedanken kommen konnte, ihm einen Fußtritt zu versetzen.

„Nehmen Sie das Geld?“ fragte Dara, ohne sich umzudrehen, während sie vor dem Spiegel stand und ihren Hut aufsetzte.

„Warum sind Sie so?“ flüsterte er mit bittendem Vorwurf. „Ich werde Sie . . . wie eine Göttin verehren, und Sie . . .“

„Ich will, daß Sie es annehmen. Reichen Sie mir bitte die Tasche.“

Er reichte sie ihr demütig. Sie öffnete sie, entnahm dem Portemonnaie zehn Rubel und reichte ihm den Schein hin. Sein Gesicht bedeckte sich mit tiefer Röte.

„Nehmen Sie!“ sagte Dara stirnrunzelnd. „Hören Sie? Ich will, daß Sie es annehmen. Ich sehe nichts Häßliches darin. Sie haben mir einen Dienst erwiesen. Nehmen Sie. Sonst gebe ich es Ihnen in Gegenwart des Kellners . . .“

Sein Gesicht überzog eine qualvolle Röte, nahe am Weinen, streckte er die Hand aus. Dara sah ihn an und steckte das Geld wieder in das Pörtemonaie zurück.

„Ach, Sie! . . . Na, meinetwegen. Gehen Sie jetzt und schicken Sie mir den Kellner. Hören Sie, noch eins: der Kellner hat mir zuerst einen Herrn geschickt, mit dem ich aber nichts zu tun haben wollte. Es ist anzunehmen, daß er mich aus Rache wird ausspionieren wollen. Wollen Sie ihn daran hindern?“

„Oh, natürlich!“ fuhr der Student erleichtert auf.

„Ich danke Ihnen. Aber auch Sie selbst werden mir nicht folgen?“

„Wenn Sie das . . . nicht wünschen . . .“

„Natürlich wünsche ich das nicht. Also leben Sie wohl. Schicken Sie mir den Kellner.“

Dara bezahlte die Rechnung, schickte nach einer Droschke und ging ebenso langsam und streng hinaus, wie sie gekommen war. Aus einer Tür sahen ihr neugierige Gesichter nach. Man lachte laut. Dara lächelte, ohne sich umzusehen.

Vor der Einfahrt standen der Portier und der Student. Die Droschke fuhr vor.

„Adieu!“ Dara nickte dem Studenten und dem Portier zu. Beide verbeugten sich tief.

Dara sagte dem Kutscher „geradeaus!“ und fuhr ab.

Gleich darauf, als sei er die ganze Zeit auf der Lauer gewesen, stürzte der Herr mit dem dichten Bärtchen mit einem steifen Hut auf dem Kopfe aus der Tür und begann hinter der Droschke herzulaufen. Im nächsten Moment aber schon holte ihn der Student ein und packte ihn am Oberarm. Dann wälzten sie sich am Boden.

DINGE UND MENSCHEN

I.

Du hast die Messe in dem großen Dom gehört, taumelst beseligt zwischen den Pfeilern aus aegyptischem Marmor, hältst mit deinen Blicken das unsagbar elfenbeinerne Gerüst der Kuppel über Deinem Kopf. Da sind die Sarkophage der verstorbenen Helden, die mit den Tartaren um die Ehre Gottes kämpften, da sind die Fahnen der besiegten Barbaren, die rotbärtig und wüst, plump wie Kühe, verfressen und fett, das Feuer an geheiligte Grundmauern legen wollten, ehe sie der Blitzstrahl des Erzengels traf. Da ist der leuchtende Stein, von den geschicktesten Händen als Emblem der großen Inspiration zwischen die Quader gefügt, da ist — mir zittert die Stimme, indem ich es ausspreche — das Bild der Mutter Christi, der großen Gebeugten, der ewig Duldsamen, der unfaßbare Ausdruck der Milde, vor dem die Jahrhunderte sich nicht schämten, ihre heißesten Tränen zu vergießen, vor dem die Grafen und Könige ihre ziselierten Schwerter zerbrachen und die Damen des Hofes, die Lukrezien und Leonoren, ihre Kniee beugten ohne Aufenthalt. Die weißen Mützen der Dreifaltigkeit gehen durch den Raum, auf deinen Fingerspitzen balanzieren die Flämmchen des ausgegossenen Geistes, und sieh, du Mensch, du Zwillingsbruder, ehe du dich von dem Halbdunkel wendest, das Größere erschüttert hat, bevor deine Ohren wieder auf die hellen Töne der Sonne gerichtet sind, die deinem Herzen wohler tun werden als je — sieh sieh — da wirfst du dich auf die ausgehöhlten Steine und schreist: Herr, Herr mein Gott! Herr, Herr mein Gott! Ich sehe von den bunten Bastionen in ein fremdes Land, das angefüllt ist mit seltsamen feindlichen Bäumen, Basaltfelsen und heißen Quellen. Ich sehe Aethiopier, Leoparden und Ratten im Kampf. Glut sehe ich, Glut der von der Flamme zerfressenen Häuser, Glut der Flüße, in denen sich der erbarmungslose Brand spiegelt, Glut der Mordgier, Glut der Rache. Ich sehe das Weltall in der Stunde seiner Niederkunft, die Leiber der großen Sterne entwanden sich ihren Ketten, die Lippen des Makrokosmos haben sich gelöst Da ziehen die Scharen der Halbentseelten, der Scheintoten und Dämmerkranken, aufgeschwollen an Bäuchen und Füßen, Affen und Pauke an dem Genick. Rette du mich mein Gott vor dem Hauch der Verwesten, der Pestilenzler und Seelenkranken — alle Freudenhäuser sind geöffnet und schon dringt der Strom des Giftes über uns hin. Die Luft ist schwarz — Vögel seh ich — Elefanten groß, groß wie Häuser, groß wie Berge — hahahaha — sie schlagen mit ihren Schnäbeln in das weiße Fleisch, sie schlagen mit ihren Krallen in das weiße Fleisch. Aus' den Glaskuppeln stiegen die Drachen, Lanzettfische und Molche. Papp-Drachen, Papp-Fische, Papp-Molche. Hahahaha — was hilft mir mein Herz, was hilft meine Frömmigkeit, die Reinheit meiner Augen. Die Erde brach auf und spie die Kohorten der Teufel aus — Dickteufel, Krummteufel, Gallertteufel, Klabautermann um Klabautermann. Wie die Harpyen hocken sie auf den Agaven, den Rotdornsträuchern, den Hollunderbäumen mit verzerrtem Gesicht. Rette mich Gott, rette meine Seele vor den Teufeln. Jetzt kommt das Bombardon, jetzt kommt das Bombardon — wieder die Stunde des Todes Jesu Christi — Fluchen der Kriegsknechte — Heulen des Donners über dem Tempel. Allzulange wartest Du — rette mich Gott.

II.

Man ist wie das Meer, das sich zurückzieht auf die hohen Sandufer, die Felsvorsprünge und Steine der Riesenmolen. Man ist wie das Meer, das die Süße des Mondes anzieht, zurückgerufen von der Geliebten, den Flöten- und Zimbelklängen. Einen hellen klirrenden Tag lang donnerte es seine Wut aus, zerwühlte seine Brust, schlang Schiffe auf den Grund. Einen heißen unerhörten Tag lang schrie's seinen Kampf in die Himmel, Fetzen von Schaum um seine Stirn gelegt. Einen Tag lang umsprang es das Kap und die Küsten der Negerländer als wütender Tänzer, zersplitterte Holz, sprengte Steine, spie, lachte, grollte, überschlug sich und wand sich auf seinem Weg. Einen Tag lang — nur einen Tag lang. Die Augen der Nacht riefen uns zurück, der Duft der Weingärten und die Glocke der kleinen Städte. Die Stille tastet nach unseren Augenliedern, schon sind wir erschüttert, ohne es zu wissen, schon öffnen sich die Kelche der großen Blumen für uns. Die Bäume schreiten von der Anhöhe nach dem Gesang der Priester mit hochgerichteten Zweigen — ja, das ist die heiligste der Nächte, die uns umgeben hat, das ist die Fülle der Liebe, die uns durchdringt. Das ist das unerhörte Ereignis, auf das wir warteten, ehe wir zur Welt gekommen waren, das ist das Wunder, an dem sich unser Leben erfüllt. Aus ihren harten Rahmen haben sich die Farben gelöst, als freie beseelte Geister dienen sie der Nacht und dem Mond, der uns erhebt. Rot ist Grün und Gelb ist Blau. Vor Symbolen kann man nicht sehen, muß sich die Hand vor die Augen legen, muß Lippen und Herz in Schlaf singen wie ein Kind. Alle Standarten sind versteckt, niemand will Führer sein. Derwische haben sich zur Ruhe gelegt — es herrscht nur der Glanz, stiller Glanz der Seligkeit, mattleuchtendes Fanal des Glücks. Ach — was ich erlebe kann ich euch nicht sagen. Wo ist die Hand, nach der ich tasten kann, wo das Gewand, das ich küssen darf? Wo ist die Geliebte, die mir die Verse des Tasso rezitiert, für die die Besten ihr Leben gelassen haben? Boote will ich und sanften Gesang — Boote unter Fackeln und die Phosphoreszenz der Paläste an der Riva Schiavoni — Lieder will ich aus einfachem Mund, die mich das Leben der schönen Frauen lehren — Worte will ich von Freunden, die den Lauf der Gestirne kennen und weise sind. Eine unendlicne Nacht will ich, in der der Himmel schwingt — unendliche Horizonte und den Atem der Nacht — vor allem den Atem der Nacht, der in die Adern dringt und mich berauscht. Korso seh ich — Korso und Fächerschlag — ach wie du lachst Seraphina — wie du lachst Seraphina — verdammt — verdammt — lautlos — lautlos — wahnsinniger als je.

Das griechische Feuer sitzt also doch in meiner Brust — o — o — schon fühle ich den neuen Sturmwind, der mich hinaustragen wird, aber ich bin so fromm wie ihr. Ich bin so fromm wie ihr — das ist das einzige, worauf ich Wert lege. Ich habe Kassenbücher gefälscht, meinen Vater geschlagen, ein kleines Kind in die Jauche geworfen — ich habe die Hosen des Ministers lackiert — o — o — aber ich bin so fromm wie ihr. Zwillingsbruder hör mich an, sieh die Gerechtigkeit auf meinen Lippen — verdammen kannst du mich nicht. Denn ich habe mich in allen Erdteilen um die Phantasmen Gottes bemüht — frage den Inder in Ceylon, frage den Neger, laß das Tamtam umgehen in Samothrake — ganz kann man mich nicht verwerfen. Wenn es Gerechtigkeit gibt, darf man es nicht tun.

III.

Diese Beschreibungen genügen bei weitem nicht. Man muß hier mit ganz einfachen und harten Worten sprechen (Haben wir nicht zu viel erlebt, gesehen, gehört, um uns noch auf Umwege einzulaßen?) man muß diesen Menschen beschreiben, als er mit düsteren Augenbögen, verkniffenem Mund, napoleonisch gefalteter Toga die Caféhaustische umkreiste, als er es verstand, die Harmlosen, Neugierigen und Ehrlichen mit einem leichten Hochziehen seiner schmalzigen Oberlippe fernzuhalten. „Wer ist das? — was tut er? — er sieht bedeutend aus — welch ein Mensch — welch ausgezeichneter Schwachkopf“. Voilà quel homme! Das Augenzwinkern der verschüchterten Backfische, das dienstfertige Gesäßheben der Kellner, die Begeisterung literaturidealistischer Studioten — welch ein Fest das alles für ihn, den Dichter, den Genius, den Raubmenschen, den Land- und Weiberusurpator. O — wie sein Herzlein zitterte und wie ihm das Fett eigener Begeisterung an den dünnen Waden herablief, wenn er die glücksverdrehten Augen eines Hundes sah, der mit Schwanz und allen Beinen zu ihm hinaufwedelte. O — wie er diese Augenblicke eingebildeter Größe in seinem Platthirn genoß — wie er zitterte und schwitzte. Doch nur nichts sehen laßen, Standbild sein, Größe sein, Genius, Genius, — **„Der Dichter ruft euch Zwanzigjährige —“** Du sprichst mit ihm — er kennt die Welt, Japan, Indien, China — alle Frauen — alle Toxine — aber er hat noch eine Pose, dies alles nicht zu kennen, über und neben allem zu sein, er ist noch der Farceur seiner selbst, es bleibt noch das Monokel, durch das er seine Seele beschaut. Wir sehen dies und staunen. Wir haben das Gymnasium besucht, kennen Göthe und Heine, fraßen eins zwei drei deutsche Literaturgeschichten. Wir sind Konpatrioten der Patrioten, die für jedes Volk eine Literaturgeschichte verfertigt haben. O — wir sind imstande, das dichterische Ingenium zu verstehen, wir dichten selbst, wir sind zukünftige Journaille, bald kräftige Totschweiger, auch Tottreter — Journaille, Journaille. So sind wir, so ist er. Er ist größer. Er ist Kind und Orkan zugleich. Er ruft die Schlampen und Lumpen des Jahrtausends zur Revolution und läßt sich die Haare über der Stirn schneiden wie eine Priesterin der Vesta. Er hat ganz die Seele eines Kindes, die himmelblaue Seele eines Kindes, verstehst Du — sodaß die älteren Weiblein eine neue Mutterschaft an ihm einüben, ihn aus ihrem gelblichen Leib austragen (mit Geld und guten Worten) ihn aufpäppeln und aufschreien, ihn auf seinen Thonfüßchen festhalten, daß er ja nicht umfalle. Denn er ist so schwach, so anämisch und mattherzig — es fällt ihm so schwer, immer genial sein zu müssen, sich immer zu „üben“, daß er das beste Mitleid verdient (wir wollen ihm die Backenknochen streicheln, wir Jonrnaille, Journaille). Ach — er ist nur die Sentenz seiner Persönlichkeit, nur der Begriff seines eigenen Wollens. Er ist so unklar, so verlogen, so bereit zu jeder Imitation, daß er wie keiner den schöngeschorenen Pudeln gleicht, die nach der Flöte tanzen. Wenn Frieden ist, brüllt er Krieg — beginnt der Krieg die Leiber der Völker zu zerfetzen, winselt er Frieden und zeigt sich dem erstaunten Publikum als Demokrat und Pazifist, ist es still, ersehnt er den Sturm, fegt aber der Sturm über die Dächer und hebt die tiefen Brunnen aus, quäkt er nach Ruhe — sentimental erregt, Korallenkettlein auf dem Grund. Ach du ausgezeichneter Hokuspokusmacher, Vivatschreier und Schlangenmensch — ach Du wundervoller Kulissenschieber, Du Chamaeleon, Proteus und Serpentintänzer der Seele. Du chaotische Schweinsblase, Du lärmender Säuselwind — wie lange werden wir uns deine Seilkunststücke noch gefallen lassen? Wir kennen die geheimsten Falten deiner Seele, wir kennen die Kochkiste deines Herzens — Ruhm möchtest Du, Ruhm und Geschrei um den großen Dichter. Du Tapezier-Genie aller Dichtkünste — du ungleich tiefere Salami. Du bist der Typus der Gestenschwinger und lallenden Seladone, Du bist die oberste Froschmolluskenbreinatur von Berlin und darum — wie stolz kannst Du sein — einer unerhörten Attake wert. Es gibt keinen Menschen, den man besser prügeln könnte als dich, darum weise deine Hinterbacken her und beginne dein masochistisches Freiheitslied. Du bist mein Antipode und Antischreier ersten Ranges — darum laß mich dich lieben, verflixter Prügelknabe — ich will meine Peitsche an dir erproben und dein Leib ist gerade weiß genug für mein Schwert.

IV.

Kaum hat sich der Mensch in den Abendwinkel seines geohrten Sessels gesetzt, kaum beginnt er sich nach den Formen seines Weibes umzusehen und an die Phantastik kommender Träume zu denken, die die Geburt härtester Wirklichkeiten sind, da läuten sie wieder dies verfluchte Sinngedicht, dieses Epos aller Impotenzen aus und der Rhythmus stört seine Nachtruhe: **das ist der Hans im Schnakenloch, ta, ta — — Schnakenloch, der weiß nicht was er will.** Er bekommt eine maßlose, geschmacklose, berserkerische, fast teutonische Wut. Er läßt sich sein Gong und seine Topfdeckel kommen und spricht dies **poème bruitiste** zu einem schnell versammelten Publikum: Ich denunziere diesen Hans im Schnakenloch als ein fatal chauvinistisches Stück, als eine Dependence der deutschen Tageszeitung, als den Gegensatz alles dessen, was wir in unseren besten Stunden groß haben wollen. Der Autor dieses Stückes muß einer jener typischen Halb- und Lemurenmenschsn sein, einer jener Taster nach allen Seiten, einer jener Praefektoren und Protagonisten lauwarmer Literatenbanden, die wir endlich, endlich — nun aber ganz — abtun müssen. Das ist ein Bruder, der es äußerst geschickt versteht, schöre Liberalismen hinter shakespearschem Donner und Halbdonner hören zu lassen — — das ist ein Kerl, der für die Jungen zu sein scheint und sich sehr fest an den Rockschößen der Alten hält. Das ist einer von den Unerhörten, die es sich nicht nehmen lassen „reif zu werden“. Dies Stück ist die steif gekochte Sentimentalität — der Krieg, der hier beschrieben ist, ein Froschmäusekrieg, ein Kolophoniumkrieg, ein Krieg der Kriegfremden. Man muß begreifen wie das Publikum auf dies Spektakel reagiert, um die ganze geistige Inferiorität des Gewinsels verstehen zu können, man muß das freudig erregte Gesicht der Herren von der Preße und der Herren von der Schwerindustrie gesehen haben, um die wirklichen Instinkte dieses Schnakenlochs, dieses Unkenlochs, dieses dumpfsten aller Löcher fühlen zu können. Nieder mit ihm, für immer nieder mit ihm. Seien wir schnell und entschlußfest, gründen wir einen **Anti-Schickelébund** und gebrauchen wir die **Weißen Blätter** als Papier timbré. Was sagen Sie „Kameradin“ Kolb? Haben Sie einen Einwand, eine Rechtfertigung für Ihren Spielgefährten — wie? Ich finde keine — für mich besagt es garnichts, nach teutobaldischen Excessen von der Bühne zn hören, daß die Franzosen ein stolzes und tapferes Volk sind. Nein — sie sind genau so gemein, so brutal, so hinterhältig wie wir — sie sind ein Volk von unglaublichster Infamie, wie ich teuflischer noch keins gesehen habe und dieu merci — das ist ihr Glück, sonst hätten sie weder die Revolution von 1789

Der Malik-Verlag verlegte seine Geschäftsräume nach Berlin-Südende, Steglitzer Straße 34

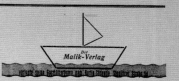

Subskription!!

FRANZ JUNG: DER FALL GROSZ

15 Mark Ermäßigung
bei Subskription / Der Malik-Verlag, Bln.-Südende

Der Fall Grosz

ANTON GROSZ AUF DER FLUCHT

ZEICHNUNGEN VON GEORGE GROSZ

DER NOTZUCHTSVERSUCH DES WENZEL GROSZ

DIE DENUNZIATIONEN DES JO[illegible]

BILDBEILAGEN VON GEORGE GROSZ

TITELWAP[illegible] VON GEORGE GROSZ

ERLEBNIS DES ANTON W. GROSZ

FAKSIMILE PAUL GROSZ

SEIDEL STELLT SEINE LETZTEN FALLEN

VIGNETTEN VON GEORGE GROSZ

FRANZ JUNG

Der Fall Grosz ?

5c *Neue Jugend*, June 1917, p. 3. Cat. no. 62

gemacht noch jene Dichter hervorgebracht, denen wir nicht die Schuhbänder lösen können. Mich ekeln diese Halbweisheiten an, Kameradin Kolb, Halbweisheiten nnd Literatursprüchlein, deren Konjunktur — jetzt nach dreijährigem Gemetzel — ach so gut ist. Warum lassen sich in diesem Pseudodrama, in diesem Gallert und Syrupdrama alle Menschen von dem Krieg bestimmen, warum lösen sich Familienverhältnisse, wenn die erste Granate einschlägt — wie? — hé? — sind wir nicht genau das, was wir vor dem Kriege waren — wir die wir den Mut haben, für den Geist zu sterben?

Der Autor dieses Schnakenlochs, dieses Unkenlochs, dieses dumpfsten aller Löcher gehört zu denjenigen, die nach der Schweiz gelaufen sind, als es hier wichtig zu werden begann, Dinge zu tun, Geistiges durchzusetzen, vielleicht das zu tun, was — Sie müssen noch verstehen Madame — eine unerhörte und überraschende Neuigkeit bedeuten kann.

Das sind die Herren, die nach den vollbesetzten Tischen streichen — para sition — para sition — wenn es hier nichts mehr gibt, gehen sie nach der Schweiz, wenn dort die Lebensmittel knapp werden, müssen sie weiterwandern. Auch Sie — göttlicher Meister und Herausgeber dieses Zeit-Echos, das aus allzu versteckten Winkeln wiederhallt — auch Sie Ranunculus acer, Mensch in der Mitte, Rubiner, Dichter kriminalistischer Sonette — Sie sind auch gemeint. Stecken Sie sich beizeiten eine Kladde vor das Gesäß und lassen Sie mich in Ruhe einen neuen Stock schnitzen — dann kann der Tanz losgehen und ich verspreche Ihnen, weißhaariger Meistersänger, Führer der Menschheit — es soll ein Duo geben, wie Sie trotz Ihrer Literaturerfahrung noch keins erlebt haben.

R. Huelsenbeck

Verantwortung zum Glück

fg Wer sich selbst leben sieht, fühlt — daß niemand zum Kompromiß gebunden ist. Die Schwache, die sich erkennt, trägt das Glück schon in sich. Die Forcierung jenes Glückskeimes — gegen den Kompromiß, als Erleben — ist das Glück. Die Entfaltung dieses Glücks bedingt, solange im Rahmen der Umwelt Kompromisse noch erkennbar sind, den Zwang, zur Auflösung, Revolution und Erlebensbestätigung. Eine Form des Glücks, zu der ich keine Stellung nehmen kann, die durch die Auflösung dieses Ichs zertrümmernd, eine neue weite Welt aufreißend, zitternd und einem unsagbar tiefen Erlebenspunkt konzentrisch aus den Erlebnisspannungen der Einzelnen zueinander zuströmend, hinausgegliedert ist.

Noch ist es besser, gegen dieses Glück zu sündigen. Die Verkrampfung im Rahmen unser Umweltserscheinungen trägt mehr Glauben in sich als der Versuch, im reinen Glauben sich an der Ichzertrümmerung dieser Kompromisse zu schonen.

Aber die Wir — wir wollen nur glauben.

Denn die Wir pfeifen auf das Leid. Hohnlachend der Zerstörung Die Wir glauben an das Glück. So zu glauben, daß aus der Explosion dieses Wir — fixiert als Zwang, der die Spannungen als Motor bewegt — das leid-überladen und verwittert sich herausschält.

Für das Ich ist es verhängnisvoll, an das Glück zu glauben. Muß es sich nicht sichern — durch immer wieder den neuerkannten Zwang, hier zum Widerspruch —?

Glauben und Zweifel zu einem gemeinsamen Dritten gebären lassen, das Alle samt dem Ich tragen kann und das Ich auch als Teilchen der motorischen Kraft nicht ausschalte.

Dafür lohnt es sich, gehangen zu werden.

Das Glück trägt restlos alles, auch das Ich vollinhaltlich. (Die Zersplitterung in Erlebenskompromisse, die die Schlampigkeit unseres Widerspruchs gegen Naturgesetze bedingt hat, bleibt so wie so jedem Einzelnen, der auf einmal den Vorzug bekommt, „allein" zu sein, überlassen.) Der **Tod** ist Privatsache. Wobei unklar bleibt, ob damit nicht mehr geschieht, **wenn man dem einzelnen dazu verhilft**, als diese Schweinearbeit jedem sich selbst zu überlassen.

Laßt uns lieber das Glück binden, damit wir es zerpflücken können, ehe es verdorrt. Leierkasten.

Es wird vergessen: Das Ich hat mit dem Glück als Begriff nichts zu tun, wohl aber als Inhalt — im differenziertesten Unterbewußtsein. (Um ernst zu bleiben.) Die lebenfressende Spannung von Begriff und Inhalt (Erleben — gesehen als Verantwortung zum Glück, schaltet gottlob Gott aus.

Es ist eine Sensation, daß die Wir eins noch nicht fertiggebracht haben, den Zwang zum Schweigen. Dieser Zwang kann damit beginnen, vom Glück zu reden. Ließe sich ein einzen Zwang zum Glück fixieren, auch nur in drei Lebewesen, so würden sich die restlichen Milliarden anderer **nicht** auf die drei stürzen, sondern augenblicks krepieren, wie man sich häufig den Weltuntergang vorstellt.

Ich vertrete den Zwang zum Glück.

Ich — Selbst bin der Zwang.

Weil ich mir unter Glück nichts vorstellen kann.

VARIETÈ

Palast-Theater am Zoo

Zuviel Humor, Paul **Göbel**, sächsischer Humorist, **Georg Neumüller**, süddeutscher Komiker, die Gesangssoubrette Lilly mit Hund Foxel, einen Steierischen tanzend — sehr schwach. **Margit und Lener** arbeiten gut im akrobatischen Akt: „Frisch gestrichen". **Bellonis** Wunder-Kakadus und die jetzt reichlich veraltete Lustspiel-Pantomime „der zerschossene Spiegel" — als Diener **Camillo Schwarz** annehmbarer Durchschnitt. Die Hauptnummer: **Josef Milos**, Darstellung berühmter Meisterwerke der Plastik, wirkt in dem perspektivisch beengten Raum nicht so gut wie vor wenigen Monaten

im Wintergarten. Die Tänzerin **Else Russel** scheint einer Ballettschule entlaufen zu sein. Die Direktion sollte darauf achten, daß sich der Kostümwechsel etwas schneller vollzieht, die Leute schlafen sonst ein. Gut sind die Equilibristen **Maximilian und Sohn**. Der jüngere arbeitet an der Stange mit verblüffender Sicherheit. Die Begleitungsmusik wird immer ärmlicher. Es scheint fast, daß man nächstens ausgraben wird: Puppchen . . ., dagegen sind die Dekorationen im Palast-Theater geradezu hervorragend.

Apollo-Theater.

Der Hauptpunkt des Apollotheaterprogramms ist diesesmal der ausgezeichnete Illusionist **Ernest Thorn**, dessen Tricks durchaus erstklassig sind (verblüffender Zauberer, der aus Wasser Wein macht, und noch nach neun Uhr Liqueur ausschenkt) . . . . unter anderem: es gelingt ihm überraschend, bei hellstem Licht einen Baum samt Vogel, mitten im Publikum, spurlos verschwinden zu lassen Obwohl man Ernest Thorn schon oft auf Berliner Varietébühnen begegnet ist, sieht man seine Darbietungen stets mit neuem lebhaften Interesse. Von den rein akrobatischen Leistungen sind die drei Schwestern **Ploetz-Larellas** zu nennen, graziös molchhaft als Handtänzerinnen und als biegsame Kautschukdamen. **Käthi Sandwina** (eben von der Ostfront zurückgekehrt!) . . . . auch keine Unbekannte . . . . zeigt uns wieder einmal ihren rosanen athletischen Körper . . . bizarr und unbewußt masochistisch wirkt das Männchenkarussel, wobei ihr Körper die Axe ist . . . . **Arlo und Dolo** . . . Humor-Radfahrer, haben ihre Nummer noch nicht im ganzen so konzentriert und schlagend durchgearbeitet um als erstklassige Radnummer zu gelten — **Fritz Steidl**, durchaus populärer deutscher Humorist, Tierstimmenimitator und Komiker, erntet natürlich stets größten Beifall (besonders bei dem Friedens-Couplet!)

Zirkus Albert Schumann.

Aus dem sehr abwechslungsreichen Programm sind besonders **Fato und May**, komische Fangkünstler hervorzuheben, eine Nummer allererſten Ranges. Fabelhafte Durcharbeitung von Grotesk-Wirkungen. Ferner die Spaßmacher **Adolf und Coco**. Die Zuhörer werden in die überaus einfache Handlung der Komik unweigerlich eingefangen, die Ruhe Adolfs ist der größten Wirkung sicher. Die vornehme Selbſtbeherrschung des Direktors Albert Schumann in seinem hervorragend gearbeiteten Dreßsurakt ist zu bekannt, als daß noch besondere Worte darüber zu verlieren wären. Gut sind auch die **4 Veras**, Drahtseilkünstlerinnen. Sie wirken in der Manege fast noch besser, als unlängst im Apollo-Theater. Das übrige ist Kriegsdurchschnitt. Dem großen Publikums gefallen **Turl Damhofers** Bayrische Alpen-Spiele. (Die Claque auf der Szene schlagen gottfeidank das Theater aus dem Feld.) Die Pantomine **Halali**, Parforce-Schnitzeljagd, gehört nicht gerade zur besten Tradition des Unternehmens.

KINO

Die rote Nacht

Der Film, der in den U. T's, später in den Kammerlichtspielen am Potsdamer Platz gezeigt wurde, führt eine allerdings etwas knappe Handlung sehr straff durch. Unter dem gegenwärtigen Tiefstand der Lichtbildkunst ist es besonders sympathisch, den Versuch zu sehen, in die Bildwirkung Rythmus zu bringen. Das Einfangen des Interesses beim Zuschauer in der Darstellung des Brandes der Petroleumquellen von Palis ist vorbildlich. Nirgends häufen sich merkwürdigerweise auch Geschehnisse. Man kann sagen, die Führung der Handlung glättet sich später etwas ab, beruhigt sich — und wirkt gerade darum fein. Die Aufnahmen sind überaus geschickt. Evelyn, in der Brandung laufend, immer wieder gleich aufgenommen, fällt, steht auf, fällt, darüber Gischt — ohne daß man die Verfolger sieht, prägt sich außerordentlich ein. Bleibt noch zu sagen, daß die Darstellerin, Frau Clara Sandberg, darstellerisch ohne Starmanieren sehr Wertvolles leistet.

Neue Zeitschriften

Titel vermögen nicht immer den Inhalt zu vertuschen. Nach dem „Falken", der in der Tat eine Ente ist, braust jetzt der „**Orkan**" in die Literatur — als Brause. In der Ankündigung wird festgestellt, daß er mit dem „Sturm" im Austauschverhältnis steht, — ob das der „Sturm" weiß? Außer einer Reihe Gutachten über den Zweck der Kultur und des Orkans inbesondere, unter denen sich neben Leo Heller und sonstiger ähnlich veranlagter Herren auch merkwürdigerweise auch Paul Adler befindet — man lacht mehr, wenn als Mitarbeiter der künftigen Hefte Erich Mühsam angekündigt wird — werden aus dem Inventar der Verlage S. Fischer und Kurt Wolf Proben veröffentlicht und besprochen. Die Autoren erhalten je nach der Eigenart der vorerwähnten Verleger besonders abgestimmtes Lob. Zum Schluß heißt es wo: Besprochen werden die Publikationen der **gerade führenden** Verleger. An der Spitze marschiert die deutsche Handelsgesellschaft sogundso, Abteilung Verlag, die neben dem Orkan gleich eine ganze Romanserie verlegen will. Die Aufmachung spottet jeder Beschreibung, jeder Marienkalender ist besser. Paul Adler, im Zeichen höchster „Deutschheit" — sagt er, hat das Wort!

Heinrich Michalski, Gründer von Beruf, hat mit der Europäischen Staats- und Wirtschaftszeitung Pech gehabt — er ist trotz Gründung ausgebootet worden. Dort übrige jetzt andere Herren am Tisch. Es ist zu begrüßen, daß Heinrich bald was Neues gemanagt hat: **Die Drei!** Sehr bescheiden. Michalski sollte ruhig sagen: Die Tausend! Man lese aber dies Blatt, das in München mit irgendwelcher Politik und sonstwie erscheint. Man lese es um Heinrichs willen.

DER MALIK-VERLAG, BERLIN-SÜDENDE

6a *Der dada 3* [*The dada 3*], 1920, brochure cover. Cat. no. 64

DADA in Europa.

Marschall ·G. GROSZ

Begreifen Sie, bester Leser — was DADA ist, weiß am genauesten der Dadasoph. Dada, sehen Sie, Dada wurde erfunden von drei Männern: Huelsenbeck, Ball und Tzara. Zunächst bedeutete Dada nichts, als vier Buchstaben, und damit war sein internationaler Charakter gegeben. Nachdem man also den eigentlichen Gehalt und die Reklamemöglich-keiten dieses Wortes DADA erfaßt hatte, gründete man das „Cabaret Voltaire" (Zürich 1916), in dem zwischen Musik, Tanz, Montmartre-Chansons, Kubismus und Futurismus ironisiert und neue Arten der Dichtung propagiert wurden. DADA war zunächst ein Bekenntnis zur unbedingten Primitivität, von dem Züricher Publikum teils verständnis-los, teils erheitert begrüßt. DADA wurde aber die große Elasti-zität der Zeit, die ihren Maßstab an dem Bürger fand:

Die Int. Dada-Company, Berlin sendet **Charlie Chaplin,** dem größten Künstler der Welt und guten Dadailten, Sympathie-grüße. Wir protestieren gegen die Ausschließung der Chaplin-Films in Deutschland.

GROSZ HEARTFIELD HUELSENBECK HAUSMANN BLOOMFELD PICABIA GUTTMANN ARP TZARA SERNER SWITTERS ERNST KOBBE HERZFELDE ARCHIPENKO CHIRICO HUSTAEDT NOLDAN PISCATOR

je seniler und steifer dieser wurde, um so beweglicher wurde DADA, das heute über den ganzen Erdball ver-breitet ist. Denn, dies müssen Sie wissen, DADA ist die Wahrheit, die allein zutreffende Praxis des realen Menschen, wie er heute ist, stets in Bewegung durch die Simultanität der Ereignisse, Reklame, des Marktes, der Sexualität, der Gemeinschafts-dinge, der Politik, der Oekonomie; ohne überflüssige Gedanken, die zu nichts führen. Ja, erlauben Sie, DADA ist (und dies ärgert die meisten Menschen gr nzenlos) **sogar ganz gegen jeden Geist; DADA ist die völlige Abwesenheit**

Der Monteurdada JOHN HEARTFIELD lehrt die intellektuellen Esel Dada.

20. Juni: Beginn der großen DADA- AUSSTELLUNG BERLIN Kunstsalon Dr. Otto Burchard Lützowufer

437 l

dessen, was man Geist nennt. Wozu Geist haben in einer Welt, die mechanisch weiterläuft? Was ist der Mensch? Eine bald lustige, bald traurige Angelegenheit, die von ihrer Produktion, von ihrem Milieu gespielt und gesungen wird. Sehen Sie, Sie glauben zu denken und Beschlüsse zu fassen, Sie glauben original zu sein — und was geschieht? Das Milieu, Ihre etwas staubige Atmosphäre hat den Seelenmotor angeworfen und die Sache läuft von allein: Mord, Ehebruch, Krieg, Frieden, Tod, Schiebung, Valuta — alles entglitt Ihren Händen, es ist Ihnen unmöglich, etwas aufzuhalten: Sie werden einfach gespielt. Sie sind das Opfer Ihrer Anschauungsweise, Ihrer sogenannten Bildung, die Sie aus den Ge-

schichtsbüchern, dem Bürgerlichen Gesetzbuch und einigen Klassikern gleich en gros generationsweise beziehen. Sie scheitern an Ihren Voraussetzungen . . . Der dadaistische Mensch kennt keine Vergangenheit, die ihn bindet, er ist gestrafft von der lebendigen Gegenwart, durch seine Existenz . . . . DaDa gestaltet die Welt praktisch nach ihren Gegebenheiten, es benützt alle Formen und Gebräuche, um die moralisch - pharisäische Bürgerwelt mit ihren eigenen Mitteln zu zerschlagen. Sie werden einwenden: DADA, das ist der Bluff. Nun, die Menschen sind Sensationstiere, die das Gruseln nicht erst zu lernen brauchen; der dadaistische Mensch überspringt im Bluff seine eigene Sensationsgier und Schwere. Der Bluff ist kein ethisches Prinzip, sondern praktische Selbstentgiftung; da DADA und Bluff miteinander gleichzusetzen sind, so ist der Bluff Wahrheit — denn DADA ist die exakte Wahrheit. Demnach ist DADA eher ein Lebenszustand, mehr eine Form der inneren Beweglichkeit, als eine Kunstrichtung. DADA, das ist die Einsicht in die verlogene Art der dichterischen Tragik und der Feierlichkeit, die Einsicht in die Unverschämtheit der Wissenschaft. Dem Dadaisten dreht sich heute noch die Sonne um die Erde . . . sollte sie es aber nicht tun, so wird ihn auch dies nicht erschüttern. Wenn Sie bedenken,

15 Minuten tägliche Übungen für DaDa.

RAOUL HAUSMANN:
Abendliche Toilette.

642 kg

daß nach sechstausend Jahren vergeblicher geistiger Anstrengung die Philosophie kläglich versagte und daß Ihnen die Naturwissenschaften ebensowenig ein festes Programm bieten können, so müssen Sie einsehen, daß DADA, geboren aus der Unerklärbarkeit eines glücklichen Augenblicks, die einzig praktische Religion unserer Zeit darstellt. **Sagen Sie sich von allen Hemmungen los, vergessen Sie Ihr Kartenspiel und die Wärme Ihrer Familientraulichkeit** — und Sie werden des Schwindels, den die Künstler, die Dichter mit Ihnen treiben, inne werden; Sie werden begreifen lernen, daß diese Dinge nur einer besonderen Technik bedürfen, Eigenverkehrsprobleme sind, die durch DADA aller Prahlerei und Ambition entkleidet werden: werden Sie Dadaist und Sie erwerben sich Angriffslust und die unbesiegbare Macht der Ironie!

RAOUL HAUSMANN.

RAOUL HAUSMANN: **Heimatklänge!**
Aus: „Hurra, Hurra!" Grotesken. Der Malik-Verlag, Berlin-Halensee.

DADA in Amerika.
(Colliers, The National Weekly, February 14, 1920.)

A 50

Durch Post u. Buchhandel à Nummer 40 Pf.
Abonnement: Quartal (6 Nummern incl.
Zustellung) 2 Mark. Vorzugs-Ausgabe:
100 numm. Exemplare 1-20 sign. auf echt
Zanders Bütten à 10 M., 21-100 à 3 M.

Preis 40 Pf.

Anzeigenpreise: 1 Quadratzentimeter 0,50 Mark, einmal wiederholt 10%
Rabatt, zweimal wiederholt 20% Rabatt.
Exzentrischer Satz: 1 Quadratzentimeter
1,00 Mark, bei gleichen Rabattsätzen.

"Jedermann sein eigner Fussball"

Illustrierte Halbmonatsschrift

1. Jahrgang   Der Malik-Verlag, Berlin-Leipzig   Nr. 1, 15. Februar 1919

Sämtliche Zuschriften, betr. Red. u. Verl. an: Wieland Herzfelde, Berlin-Halensee, Kurfürstendamm 76. Sprechst.: Sonntags 12—2 Uhr

Preisausschreiben!
Wer ist der Schönste??

Deutsche Mannesschönheit 1   (Vergl. Seite 4)

Die Sozialisierung der Parteifonds

Eine Forderung zum Schutze vor allgemein üblichem Wahlbetrug

(Diese Ausführungen sollen den Unfug unserer Nationalversammlung selbst vom Gesichtspunkt der Demokraten aus illustrieren, jener Leute, die meinen, ein Volk dürfe keine Regierung besitzen, deren Niveau dem seines eigenen Durchschnitts überlegen ist.)

Man mag Demokrat sein, deutsch-sozialistischer Untertan oder Kommunist, man mag mit Schiller sagen: Verstand ist stets bei wenigen nur gewesen oder behaupten auf jede Stimme komme es (sogar mit Recht) an, die Tatsache wird man nicht bestreiten: Wahlen gehören zu den ge-

---

7a   *Jedermann sein eigner Fussball* [*Everybody His Own Football*], February 1919, front page.
Cat. no. 174

81

wichtigsten politischen Faktoren der Gegenwart und nächsten Zukunft — ob nun Wilson, Lenin oder der Imperialismus die Welt erobert.

Wahlen sollen der Ausdruck des freien politischen Willens innerhalb einer Gemeinschaft sein. Sind sie es? Nein! Können sie es sein? Nein — denn nur verhältnismäßig wenige Menschen besitzen einen bewußten, in eigener Erfahrung, Denkkraft und Kenntnis wurzelnden politischen Willen; und unter diesen Wenigen wiederum schenkt nur eine geringe Anzahl einem der zu wählenden Kandidaten tatsächlich Vertrauen; und schließlich dürfte sich bis zur Wiederkehr der Wahlen auch in diesen seltenen Fällen das gewährte Vertrauen nur ganz ausnahmsweise als wirklich berechtigt erweisen. Dies „Nicht-wissen-können wen man wählt" bleibt jedoch relativ unwichtig, weil die Massen meist nicht wissen, wie der Träger ihres Vertrauens überhaupt beschaffen sein soll. Die Wahl ist in der Regel lediglich Instinkt-Angelegenheit. Das wäre wohl zu bejahen, wenn jene Urinstinkte, jener Witterungssinn der unausrottbar und unwandelbar im Menschen verankert ist dabei den Ausschlag gäben. Mitnichten: die zahllosen passiven Instinkte widersprechendster Art, die durch äußere (d. h. vom Individuum nicht zu verhindernde und doch nicht kontrollierte) Einwirkung umso stärker und bequemer ausgelöst werden, je (politisch) unentwickelter ein Mensch ist — diese Instinkte sind die treibende Kraft aller Wahlen. Um aber auf die Millionen Willensarmer einwirken zu können — dazu gehört Macht. Macht = Geld. Geld findet sich und bleibt am wenigsten im Besitz altruistisch handelnder Menschen und Gruppen: daher sind die Wahlen in Wahrheit Seismographen und Regulatoren der Machtschwankungen zwischen den undemokratischsten und unsozialsten, den egoistischsten Cliquen innerhalb einer Gemeinschaft.

Da sich vorläufig unser Staatsgebilde ohne Wahlen nicht lenken lassen wird, lohnte es sich, den (übrigens internationalen) Wahlbetrug dadurch einzudämmen, daß allen Parteien ihr ausschlaggebendstes und gleichzeitig imperialistischstes Machtmittel, der Parteifonds genommen würde. Die Parteifonds sollten in Händen einer exparlamentarischen Institution liegen, die völlig mechanisch jedem Staatsbürger (solange dies nationale Vorurteil noch herrscht) der seine Mitbürger parlamentarisch zu führen, d. h. eine Partei zu gründen oder zu vertreten wünscht, kostenlos die Veröffentlichung seines Programms sichert. Aus der Vertriebsziffer jedes (selbstverständlich zu gleich billigem Preis und durch gleiches System verbreiteten) Programms ließe sich leicht eine Skala der öffentlichen Anteilnahme aufstellen, der entsprechend die Geldmittel der vereinigten Parteifonds zu Propaganda-, Reklame- und Parteizwecken den einzelnen Parteien zugewiesen würden.

Parteien, die durch irgendwelche Manöver die Vertriebsziffer ihres Parteiprogramms zu erhöhen suchten, oder irgendwelche Organisation oder Propaganda mittels anderer als solcher zugewiesenen Geldmittel betrieben, würden rücksichtslos von der Wahl ausgeschlossen.

Damit wäre noch lange kein idealer Zustand erreicht. Wir wissen indessen genug von den Zielen, zu wenig von den Wegen. Zweifellos wäre die „Sozialisierung" der Parteifonds bejahenswert aus moralischen Gründen seitens ehrlicher Demokraten, aus realpolitischen seitens der Sozialisten und Kommunisten. Falls aber (was ich nicht bezweifle) die meisten Parteien der „Deutschen Republik" sich krampfhaft gegen die Sozialisierung der Parteifonds wenden würden, erwiese sich aufs neue, daß n i c h t die berühmte „Achtung vor j e d e s Staatsbürgers politischem Willen" (für die außer den Kommunisten doch alle Parteien einzutreten behaupten) sondern Wille zur vielgeschmähten „Diktatur" ihre Begierde ist. Wieland Herzfelde.

UNSERE GEGNER

I.

B r u c h m ü l l e r sen., Dezernent im Auswärtigen Amt, (persönlicher Feind Radeks) versucht auf siderischer Basis mittels einer im Regenschirm verborgenen Wünschelrute geheime Spartaccidische Waffen- und Munitionslager zu entdecken.

II.

B r u c h m ü l l e r jun., Oberprimaner, nahm erfolgreich an der Aktion gegen Liebknechts Sohn teil, gründete einen Schülerrat zur Bekämpfung kommunistischer Umtriebe in den deutschen höheren Lehranstalten.

III.

Gutsbesitzer Josef Bürr, aus Stolp i. P., Mitglied der Nationalversammlung, (vielfach prämierter Mastviehzüchter), hielt in Weimar eine aufsehenerregende Rede für die Wiedereinführung der Wehrpflicht und Gründung einer wendisch-kaschubischen Republik auf monarchischer Grundlage.

Der nachträgliche Heldentod

Eines Abends erinnerte sich ein armer, alter Mann seines verstorbenen Jugendfreundes. Da klopfte es bescheiden an die Tür, und herein trat ganz offenbar dieser Freund.

„Aber Julian, lebst Du denn?" fragte erschrocken der alte Mann. Julian verneinte das kopfschüttelnd. Er sagte mit einer Stimme, die schon lange nicht gebraucht worden zu sein schien:

„Ich lebe nicht mehr, Marcus, ich kann das kein Leben nennen. Als ich vor nunmehr etwa 25 Jahren starb oder jedenfalls als tot begraben worden war, überkamen mich Ruhe und Vergessen. Zirka sechs Jahre lang dachte ich nur an das hellgrüne Tischtuch meiner Mutter. Es ist unglaublich, eine Art Traum. Eigentlich hat es gar keine Dauer. Erst beim Erwachen scheinen es lange Jahre gewesen zu sein. — Warum, frage ich Dich, macht man die Gräber nicht schalldicht? Warum verstopft man die Ohren der Leichen nicht mit Watte? Nämlich seit etwa zwei Jahren begann mich in meinen monotonen Träumen irgend etwas zu stören. Auf ein Mal merke ich, das ist Artillerie. Erinnerst Du Dich: ich habe doch als Kanonier gedient. Es bummt. Es poltert. Ich unterscheide mehr und mehr. Hölle und Teufel, d a s Geräusch erkenne ich noch im Tode wieder. Ich befand mich bestimmt unter einer Kanone. Plötzlich saust und zischt es um mich herum. Ich fühle mein Bett, meinen Sarg, hoch gehoben, fliegen, wieder auffallen. Der sorgfältig angelötete Deckel klappt auf, mein Leichnam, holterdipolter — rollt in eine Art Jauche — brrrr in Blut, in lauter Blut. Aber im nächsten Augenblick packten mich einige Leute. Ich verlor mein (ohnehin schwaches) Bewußtsein. Erwachen tat ich in einem Krankensaal. Ich hörte, wie der Arzt sagte: „stark unterernährt, deliriert, beste Pflege; Ablenkung von diesen Leichenphantasien. Kerl bildet sich ein, aus dem Grabe zu kommen." Ich wandte mit schwacher Stimme ein: „Herr Stabsarzt, beim wunderbaren Gott, ich bin schon Anfang der 90 er Jahre begraben worden." — „Schnauze gehalten, Mann!" war Alles, was ich zur Antwort bekam. Sie pflegten mich nun soweit ganz ehrlich. Sie gaben mir dann Proviant, Kleider, etwas Geld und entließen mich. Da, lieber Marcus, entsann ich mich Deiner. Hier bin ich. Du weißt, ich stand schon dazumalen allein da. Du warst mein einziger Verkehr, mein Halt. Verlasse mich nicht! Und erkläre mir: was ist das für ein Krieg oder Manöver?"

Marcus war während der Rede seines verstorben gewesenen Freundes bemüht, es diesem behaglich zu machen. Er hatte ihn in einen weichen Sessel niedergezogen, ihm ein warmes Getränk und einige Speisen vorgesetzt. Er legte ihm jetzt die Hand auf die Schulter und beugte sich vertraulich zu ihm herab. „Julian" sagte er, „so lebst Du also wirklich! Ich muß es ja glauben, obgleich mir der Verstand still steht. Es ist aber auch eine Zeit! Sie haben uns von allen Seiten überfallen: Russen, Franzosen, Japaner, Belgier, Rumänen, Montenegriner, Italiener, Portugiesen, Kanadier, aber allen voran die Engländer und Amerikaner." Julian sprang auf wie e i n Dämon. „Siehst Du", schrie er, „sogar Tote in ihren Gräbern spüren es doch, daß unser Deutschland in Gefahr ist. Glaube mir, die echte Vaterlandsliebe ist mit den Toten im Bunde wie mit Unsterblichen, wie mit der Auferstehung. Mir kroch es prickelnd bis ins Gebein. Aber mein Fall mag nicht vereinzelt sein; d e n n k e i n F a l l ist jemals vereinzelt. Ich prophezeie Dir, daß Deutschland nicht untergehen kann, weil eher noch die Toten sich wieder beleben und die Waffen ergreifen werden. Ich melde mich gleich morgen bei meiner alten Kompagnie." Und so geschah es. Julian machte sein Wort am andern Tage wahr. Übrigens, so sehr sich beide Freunde auch Mühe gaben, die Welt von dem wunderbaren Ereignis zu überzeugen, so wenig glaubte man ihnen, so daß sie es schließlich aufgaben, es zu erweisen. Der wackere Julian focht an der Somme mit. Lange Wochen hörte sein Freund Marcus nicht das Geringste mehr von ihm. Endlich, eines Abends . . . . er war im Begriff, schlafen zu gehen, stand ein Schatten vor ihm, lichte Augen sahen sekundenlang strahlend in die seinigen . . . . die Gestalt zerging in Nebel. Mitten in der Nacht traf ein Telegramm ein, das d e n Heldentod Julians meldete. Mögen die prophetischen Worte des doppelt Gestorbenen erfüllt werden! Möge der Ameronger . . . . ! Mynona.

DER KIRCHENSTAAT   DEUTSCHLAND

Grosz

✴ ✴ **POLITISCHE STERNWARTE** ✴ ✴

Das dreieckige Verhältnis

Von Tag zu Tag wird es klarer: Deutschland ist antibolschewistisch. Eine alte Wahrheit: „Wer nicht für mich, der ist wider mich" möchte den Schluß rechtfertigen: Deutschland schließt sich der Entente an. Die Entente dankt: Kapitalistische Staaten können einen Staat, der vorm Bankrott in jeder Hinsicht steht, nicht coordinieren, höchstens subordinieren. Dabei hilft Erzberger ja redlich. Man wird aber doch nicht meinen, Erzberger sei so devot aus Verlegenheit. Hat er Victor Naumann vielleicht auch aus Verlegenheit zum Deutschen Pressechef ernannt? Naumann, den Hauslehrer der ehemals königlichen Wittelsbacher (u. a. der heutigen Königin von Belgien) den Intimus Czernins, Exkaiser Karls? Wenn Erzberger nach der Entente tanzte, was kann der an jenem — sagen wir — indirekt „kompromittiertem" Herrn Naumann liegen? Wem kann überhaupt mit dieser Ernennung gedient sein? (Man lanciert doch keinen Pressechef ohne gleichzeitig einer Großmacht Reverenz zu leisten.) Wilson? — verzichtet. Lenin? — niemals! Bleibt (ja ja, er hat sich tot gestellt) — der Papst! Die Öffentlichkeit verkennt die Gefahr des Klerus! Was liegt Erzberger an Deutschland, das verschachert er ruhig der Entente, (je ärmer, umso frommer) wenn er nur seine Macht genügend ausbaut, das Deutsche Reich zu klerikalisieren. Er schiebt nicht schlecht: Ebert, ehrfürchtiger Katholik: Präsident! Nun Victor Naumann: der hat die Presse in der Hand. Das deutsche Volk, nachdem aus seinem irdischen Preußenhimmel nichts geworden — müde der politischen Freiheit infolge der Kämpfe, die sie brachte, ist für das päpstliche Sklaven-Jenseits geradezu disponiert. — Wetten — binnen kurzem, zu spät natürlich — wird jedes Kind in Deutschland das Trio: Lenin-Wilson-Benedikt erkennen. Was Wunder auch — die Weltrevolution schafft Leichen, da lassen die Geier nicht lange auf sich warten: — Herr Erzberger verkuppelt Germania den westlichen Imperialisten (Gott, machte es ihm Wilson nur nicht so schwer). Sein Gehilfe Naumann bläst ihr indessen den „Bolschewismus" in die Augen (à propos: lasen Sie die Hirtenbriefe?) damit sie nicht inne wird, was ihr blüht: Der Klerus frißt das „70 Millionen-Volk" auf, um sich über Wasser zu halten, wenn eines Tages die Entente den Bolschewismus bejaht und sich dann, über Deutschland hinweg, mit Rußland vereint zu einer Macht — die keinen Papst braucht. Getrost, heiliger Vater in Rom — man nennt uns nicht umsonst das dümmste Volk der Welt.   *He*

+KLEINE
+
GROSZ
MAPPE

20

Berlin mit
den Augen
eines
Bolsche-
wisten
gesehen

Orig.-Lith.

Nr. 1—20 auf echt
Japan, nur noch
2 Expl. à 90 M.
(erhöhter Preis)
Nr. 21—120 (inkl.
Teuerungsauf-
schlag) à 38,50M.
Zu beziehen durch
den Malik-Verlag

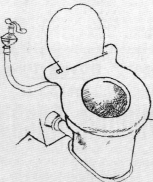

Kurt Tucholsky, 1920

A Dada exhibition is on now at Lützow-ufer 13. Because we don't have any cares otherwise. When you strip away what's bluff, there's not a whole lot left. I know exactly what these people want: the world is topsy-turvy, meaningless, pretentious, and intellectually inflated. This they want to ridicule, needle, disavow, destroy. There's a lot to be said about that. (Like art, bolshevism, questioning the legitimacy of the value of art, is a matter that cannot be dismissed simply. Doubt is contagious.) But I don't like those formats.

He who hates ardently must have loved very much at one time. He who wants to negate the world must have affirmed it very strongly at one time. He must have embraced once what he now burns. But what is the effect? Petty writers somewhat desperately try to shock ordinary citizens and spit on what is sacred to other people. That's the word: desperation. From nine to seven one is continuously, subversively funny and in a satirically good mood. One Dadaism at three Marks and thirty Pfennigs admission charge. "The real thing here. Beware of imitations."

The exhibition itself looks like a cute junk shop. (Although I think hundreds of generations of artists have done the same thing at their studio parties in a more witty, more striking, more daring way.) A large stuffed sailor hangs from the ceiling and blissfully stares down upon the disarray of old hatboxes, cardboard containers, rusty nails, very inappropriately placed dentures, and paintings. It's rather quiet at that small exhibition, and nobody really gets upset anymore. Dada — oh well.

Berliner Tageblatt, July 20, 1920; Kurt Tucholsky, *Gesammelte Werke*, I, p. 702. Rowohlt Verlag, Reinbek, 1960.

Wieland Herzfelde, 1920

In the past, the express purpose of painting was to offer people depictions of things, landscapes, animals, buildings, etc., which they could not watch with their own eyes. Today, this task has been assumed by photography and film, and they solve it with an incomparably greater perfection than painters throughout the ages ever have achieved.

Painting, however, did not die with the loss of this objective but sought new objectives. All subsequent artistic endeavors, no matter how diverse, can be classified as having the common tendency to seek emancipation from reality.

Dadaism is the reaction to all attempts to deny the factual, which was the driving force of the Impressionists, Expressionists, Cubists, and of the Futurists as well (unwilling as they were to capitulate to the film); but this does not at all mean that once again the Dadaist undertakes to compete with the camera or even breathe a soul into it by leaving everything (as the Impressionists do) to that worst lense of all, the human eye, or (like the Expressionists) by turning the camera round and forever depicting merely his interior life. The Dadaists are saying: While once vast amounts of time, love, and effort went into the painting of a body, a flower, a hat, a hard shadow, etc., we now only need to take scissors and cut out what we need from among the paintings and photographic depictions of all these things. If the things in question are on a small scale, we do not even need illustrations; we take the objects themselves instead, e.g., pocketknives, ash trays, books, etc., things which, to be sure, can be found, beautifully painted, in the museums of traditional art. But that's just it, merely painted.

And now for the famous question: Yes, but what about the content, the spiritual? In the course of the centuries, the unequal

8b *Erste Internationale Dada-Messe*. Catalogue, 1920, p. 2. Cat. no. 63

Für diesen Nachdruck wurde das Exemplar der Berlinischen Galerie benutzt · © 1988 Verlag der Buchhandlung Walther König, Köln · Litho: Miess & Voswinkel · Druck: Farbo · ISBN: 3-88357-082-4 · Printed in Germany

Bild Nr. 126 Hans Citroen: „Das Netz".

Eine Zusammenstellung verschiedenartigster Kleinigkeiten, wie sie das Hirn eines jungen Menschen ausfüllen, der von Problemen unbelastet der Welt gegenüber eine aufnehmende, sammelnde, kaum registrierende Einstellung hat. Dazwischen Begriffe, die im Bewußtsein eine große Rolle spielen, hingegen im wesentlichen noch keine Vorstellung ausmachen und daher so dargestellt sind, wie sie kennen gelernt wurden z. B. als Zeitungsüberschriften. Ueber das ganze ist ein Netz gespannt, das die Leidenschaftlichkeit, mit der all diese Eindrücke gesammelt werden, symbolisiert, und in dessen Mitte eine Koralle hängt, die wohl zu betrachten ist als Hirn, das einer Spinne gleich die Welt mit seinen Fäden umklammern möchte.

Bild Nr. 153 Baader: „Gutenberggedenkblatt".

Hier unterläßt es Baader, Kritik oder Symbolik zu schaffen, vielmehr macht er mit derselben Freude, wie ein Häusler sein Gärtchen abbildet, ein Blatt, das die Mannigfaltigkeit des Gedruckten und seine Inhaltsmöglichkeiten betont. Auffällig ist die Vereinigung der rein ästhetischen Freude an den Formen der Schrift mit der Ueberraschung, daß das Nebeneinander solcher Figuren und Buchstaben plötzlich den Ausdruck für die umfangreichsten und verschiedenartigsten Vorstellungen ergeben kann.

Bild Nr. 62 George Grosz: „Der Sträfling" Monteur John Heartfield nach Franz Jungs Versuch ihn auf die Beine zu stellen. 1920.

Das Bild zeigt den Verbrecher weder in menschlich-sentimentaler noch in bürgerlich moralischer Auffassung, lediglich als vitales Geschöpf. Wir sehen einen deformierten Körper, dessen Formen ungewöhnliche Energienvorräte verraten, welche nach allen Richtungen gegen die gleichgültigen Wände hin anschwellen. Außerdem die einzigen und wesentlichen Reflexionen: das sind die Vertrautheit mit der Maschine (die ja auch die Kunst des Verbrechers ausmacht) und der Drang nach guter Nahrung und Freiheit, der symbolisiert ist durch das über ihm schwebende neue Heim, in dem gleich ein Wein- und Delikatessenladen eingebaut ist. Menschliche Fähigkeiten, Verbitterung, Illusionslosigkeit, Neid, Pessimismus und Unnachgibigkeit sind im Gesicht in der für Grosz typischen Eindeutigkeit ausgeprägt.

Bild Nr. 118 Rudolf Schlichter: „Verbesserte Bildwerke der Antike — Venus von Milo".

Hier zeigt sich am faßlichsten das Verhältnis der Dadaisten zur Antike. Die Bourgeois, welche dauernd lamentieren, man wolle das Vergangene sinnlos ruinieren oder zertrümmern, mögen hier stehen bleiben und Abbitte tun. Hat je ein Meier-Gräfe oder Lessing es verstanden, der Antike derart alle Scheuklappen zu nehmen, d. h. sie gegenwärtig zu machen wie hier Schlichter, indem er ein Götzenbild, das nur für Altertumsforscher verständlich und beachtenswert war, mit einem für unser Empfinden menschlichen Kopf versieht und dadurch den ganzen Körper in den Fassungsbereich unserer Sinne rückt. So mag der Marktwert vernichtet werden, die Plastik hat dadurch wieder Leben und ihren ursprünglichen sinnlichen Reiz bekommen.

Bild Nr. 40 George Grosz: „Ein Opfer der Gesellschaft."

Ein großes Fragezeichen liegt vor der Stirn des Mannes. Der Inhalt der Frage ist abgestorben. Sie ist verblaßt, hat sich niedergelegt und ist so zu einem gewohnheitsmäßigen Nichtbegreifen geworden, hinter dem das dumpfe Bewußtsein des Mißgeborenseins den Schädel wie ein Stein belastet. Die Arme des Mannes hängen schlapp hernieder. Halb aufgerollt liegt ein Schlauch auf der Schulter: Es ist dem Manne nicht gelungen, sich gänzlich aufzurollen und zu -pumpen. Diese Enttäuschung erweckt Selbstmordabsichten: Das offene Rasiermesser sitzt dicht am Halse, aber es bleibt bei den Absichten, denn wenn auch das eine Auge die Trostlosigkeit des Daseins durchdringt, das andere schielt ängstlich umher. Der Mann lebt, weil er nun einmal damit angefangen hat, er fragt sich aber umsonst wozu, und schlaff hängt das Rad, mit dem er dies Leben zu durcheilen gedachte, ins Nichts. Schlaff hängt der Bart über einen Mund, der in seiner Jugend (man sieht es deutlich) unternehmungsfroh und entschlossen war. Jetzt aber ist das einst kräftige Kinn schwammig und aufgedunsen. All die Entwicklungsansätze sind stecken geblieben, nur die pedantische Gewohnheit blieb übrig, sich sorgsam zuzuknöpfen — „zwar einfach, aber ordentlich".

Dada-Oz Otto Schmalhausen: „Antwerpen".

Bevor wir auf die Erläuterungen seiner Bilder eingehen, einige Daten:

Der in Deutschland bei weitem nicht genügend gewürdigte Dada-Oz einer der frühesten Dadaisten, der in Antwerpen schon vor dem Kriege, als niemand an Dada dachte, in Zusammenhang mit seiner reklameorganisatorischen Tätigkeit „dada-works" konstruierte und in den Ländern der Entente bald Schule machte, war so freundlich, die Internationale Dadamesse zu beschicken. Wir lassen einige Zeilen folgen, die das charakteristische Schaffen des Dada-Oz würdigen.

Bild Nr. 98 Dada-Oz: „Beethoven".

Dada-Oz hat sich die Aufgabe gestellt, uns die „Heroen der Vergangenheit" zu vergegenwärtigen, unter anderen auch Beethoven. Tatsächlich vermittelt die bekannte Totenmaske aus weißem Gips ein verfälschtes und schwaches Bild. Nachdem sie aber durch die Hände des belgischen Dadaisten gegangen ist, blickt uns schier glasiger Schmerz aus treuen Blauaugen an, störrisch zwirbelt sich der Schnurrbart, ungeordnet hängt dem Sonderling das Haar in die Stirn. Jetzt begreift man, wie es möglich war, daß dieselbe Gesellschaft, die heute Beethoven zu ihrem musikalischen Idol erhoben hat, ihn bei Lebzeiten für einen unangenehmen Menschen hielt.

Bild Nr. 152 John Heartfield: „Leben und Treiben in Universal-City 12 Uhr 5 mittags" (Besitzer Lämmle, Kalifornien).

Dieses Bild, von dem der Dichter Wieland Herzfelde aussagt, daß es ihm ausgezeichnet gefällt, schildert mit den Mitteln des Filmes das Leben und Treiben in Universal-City. Es handelt sich um kein futuristisches Bild, es ist nämlich ein dadaistisches Bild, und zwar ein ausgezeichnetes. Um zu einem richtigen Gesamteindruck zu kommen, trete man am besten 40 Schritte durch die Wand (Achtung, Stufe!) zurück. Dann ergibt sich von selbst, daß der Dadaist John Heartfield der Feind des Bildes ist. Er hat es auch für sich zerstört. Eine sehr einfache nutzbringende Probe darauf kann man in jeder beliebigen Straße anstellen, in welcher gewöhnliche Straßenlaternen sind.

Bild Nr. 75 Dada-Oz: „Traum der Mütter am Zuidersee".

Hier ist offen und einfach angezeigt, was in so vielen Romanen lang und breit geschildert wird, ohne je solche Anschaulichkeit zu erreichen: Was wahre Mütter ihren Töchtern wünschen —: einen Mann, der herrschend in seiner Vaterstadt dasteht, stets im Frack mit weißer Weste, verfügend über alle Mittel, die ein sorgloses Leben garantieren. Dieser Mann muß sein junges Weib auf Händen tragen, muß Lakai sein, dabei aber doch stark und treu. Und er muß küssen können — wie, das sieht man nicht recht, da Liebesleute den Müttern dabei den Rücken zukehren.

Bild Nr. 46 George Grosz: ‚Der Städter auf dem Lande".

Ein Oeldruck — See, Bauernhaus, Wiese mit Baum, Insel — reizt Grosz, aufs Land zu gehen. Wie Künstler sind — er stellt dar (und zwar auf dem Oeldruck), was für Erwartungen er mit aufs Land bringt: da wird Nachen gefahren (gut für die Blutzirkulation) nach der Insel rüber (wie das die Lungen weitet). Und wer weiß, ein schlankes Geschöpf mit durchsichtigen Sommerkleidern ist sicher da zu finden. Darum — auch auf dem Lande, Haltung, gute Kleidung. Aber auch nackt! Luft, Körperübung! Milchtrinken! Cigarren nicht vergessen (wegen der Mücken). Und den Elektrisierapparat, der tut Wunder, wenn man den ganzen Tag der Gesundheit lebt. Gleich einer üppigen Rose blüht da der Körper auf. Und auch die Seele: Man träumt wieder beim Spiel der Wolken, der Wellen von lieblichen Mädchenköpfen — und von zuhause: den Autos, den Wolkenkratzern, den Lackschuhen, den angenehmeren hygienischen Einrichtungen. Wieland Herzfelde.

Bild Nr. 73. Groß-Heartfield mont.. Korrigiertes Meisterbild

1—3 Porträts der Veranstalter der Ersten Internationalen Dada-Messe Berlin 1920

1 Porträt des Dadasophen Raoul Hausmann
2 Porträt des Monteurdada John Heartfield (*)
3 Porträt des Propagandada Marschall G. Grosz
} Dadaphotos von John Heartfield

4 George Grosz: Vierundzwanzig Dada-Spiesser besteigen einen Pudding
4a George Grosz: Der Schuldige bleibt unerkannt
5—9 John Heartfield, Raoul Hausmann: Druckbogen aus dem Dadaco (bei Kurt Wolff Verlag, München) (*)
10—12 John Heartfield: Druckbogen für die „Kleine Grosz-Mappe" (bei Der Malik-Verlag, Berlin- Halensee, Kurfürstendamm 76) Die ersten dadaistischen Druckversuche in Deutschland.
13 John Heartfield: Druckblatt Vorderseite „Neue Jugend, Wochenausgabe". Druckblatt der ersten dadaistischen Revue in Deutschland 1917 (bei Der Malik-Verlag, Berlins siehe auch Saal II No. 99, 150, 151 (*)
14 dadamax Ernst (Köln a. Rhein): dadafex maximus (*)
15 Hanna Höch-Hausmann: 2 Dadapuppen
16 John Heartfield: dadaistisches Umschlagbild für Programmheft „Schall und Rauch No. 6 Mai 1920" und Dada 3 (siehe Originalbild No. 138)
17 Raoul Hausmann: Plakat ‚Der Malik-Verlag Berlin-Halensee Kurfürstendamm 76"
18 John Heartfield: (siehe No. 13) (*)
19 Hannchen Höch: Plakat Ali Baba-Diele, Berlin
20 Hannchen Höch: Schnitt mit dem Kuchenmesser Dada durch die letzte weimarer Bierbauchkulturepoche Deutschlands
21 Hanna Höch: Diktatur der Dadaisten (relief)
22 Hanna Höch: Mechanisches Brautpaar (relief)
23 Johannes Alberts, Berlin-Steglitz: A. Preiss †, der erste wahre unvergeßliche Obermusikdada in seiner Szene „dadaistischer Holzpuppentanz". Aus dem Dadaco (bei Kurt Wolff-Verlag, München)
24 Raoul Hausmann: Dada im gewöhnlichen Leben
25 George Grosz: Germania ohne Hemd
26 Raoul Hausmann: Plakat Dada
27 Raoul Hausmann: Selbstporträt des Dadasophen
28 Raoul Hausmann: Tatlin lebt zu Hause (*)
29 Raoul Hausmann: Ein bürgerliches Präcisionsgehirn ruft eine Weltbewegung hervor. (*)
30 Raoul Hausmann: Industrieller Umsturz im Jahre 1919
31 Raoul Hausmann: Der eiserne Hindenburg 1920 (*)
32 Raoul Hausmann: Schriftkonstruktion aus dem Dadaco (bei Kurt Wolff Verlag, München)
33 Raoul Hausmann: Ein altes Meisterwerk
34 Raoul Hausmann: Deutsche Freiheit 1920 a
35 Raoul Hausmann: Deutsche Freiheit 1920 b (*)
36 Raoul Hausmann: Die Schieberger (*)
} Aus: „Hurra, Hurra, Hurra!" Grotesken von R. Hausmann. Der Malik-Verlag, Berlin 1920
37 Raoul Hausmann: Der Kunstreporter
38 Raoul Hausmann: Portrait einer alten Frau (Dr. S. Friedlaender-Mynoud)

distribution of opportunities for life and personal development has produced, as in all other spheres, outrageous conditions also in the art world: On the one hand, a clique of so-called artists and talent who, partly through decades of training, partly through protectionism and tenacity, partly also through inherited special gifts, have monopolized all matters of art evaluation; on the other hand, the many people whose naive, unpretentious urge to express their own ideas and the events in their lives, to give them constuctive shape, are being suppressed by this clique of trendsetters. Today, every young person, unless he is willing to forego all training or broadening of his innate aptitude, has to submit to the authoritarian-structured system of art education and the public judgment of art. Whereas the Dadaists are saying that to produce pictures is no big deal; if it does happen, at least there should be no despotic standpoint laid down, and the broad masses should not have their pleasure in creative activity spoiled by the arrogance of experts from some supercilious guild. That is why the content of the Dadaist pictures and creations can be extremely varied and so can their means of expression. Any creation is Dadaist that is produced uninfluenced by, and heedless of, public authorities and values, provided the depiction is anti-illusionist and motivated entirely by the urge to keep on eroding the present world which is obviously in a state of disintegration, of metamorphosis. The past is only important and relevant in so far as its cult must be fought. The Dadaists agree in this respect; they say that what antiquity, the classical age, and all the "great minds" have created must not be judged in respect of the period in which it was created (except through a scientific, historical approach), but rather as if it were produced today;

8c *Erste Internationale Dada-Messe*. Catalogue, 1920, p. 3. Ex. cat.

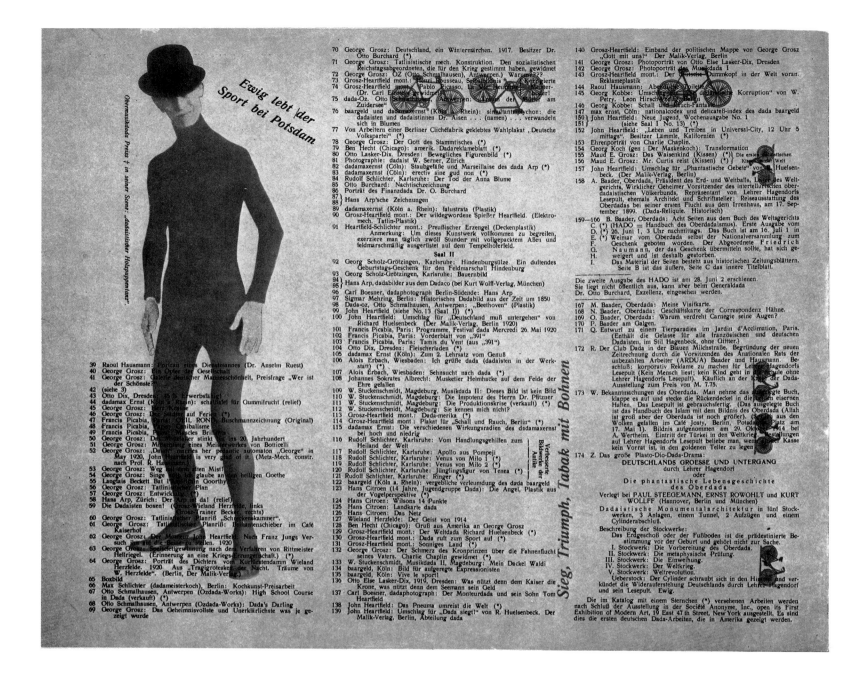

John Heartfield, 1967

and nobody will doubt that today not a single person, even if he were, to use an art term, a genius, could produce works the conditions of which were prevalent hundreds and thousands of years ago. The Dadaists take credit for being the vanguard of dilettantism, for the art dilettant is nothing but the victim of a prejudiced, arrogant, and aristocratic conception of life. The Dadaists acknowledge as their sole program the obligation to make what is happening now in time and in place the content of their pictures, which is the reason why they consider as their sources the illustrated journals and the editorials in the press, rather than *The Arabian Nights* or *Bilder aus Hinterindien* [*Views of Southeast Asia*].

Wieland Herzfelde, "Zur Einführung," in exhibition catalogue *Erste Internationale Dada-Messe*, Kunsthandlung Dr. Otto Burchard. Malik-Verlag, Dada Department, Berlin, June 1920.

And it even went so far that we disrupted our friend Theodor Däubler when he was giving readings, a great poet with his *Nordlichtgedichte* [*Northern Lights Poems*], yes, a very pleasant, likeable person, a great man whom we loved very much. [...] He would give readings, we would disrupt them, and he would always say, "Oh, tonight. The Dadaists are coming." That became our cue. [...] We would put on our performance. [...]

An old codger with a goatee would come along [...] so inhibited and decrepit. Then we would say, "You're the very one; didn't

8d *Erste Internationale Dada-Messe*. Catalogue, 1920, p. 4. Cat. no. 63

te. And, would you believe it, it happened. The door opened and he came in, old and frail – wonderful – went forward with the thing, and we stood up and sang, "We'll make you a bridal wreath of azure silk." Everyone froze. He too, the messenger-boy. He stumbled. The box fell open, the wreath fell out. Our friend Däubler fled to the rear. The reading broke up.

From an interview with John Heartfield (1967), in Roland März, ed., *John Heartfield: Der Schnitt entlang der Zeit. Selbstzeugnisse – Erinnerungen – Interpretationen*, p. 465. Verlag der Kunst, Dresden, 1981.

Walter Mehring, 1959

But the sole authoritative standard book of Berlin Dada was the DADA-AL-MANACH (Berlin, Erich Reiss-Verlag, 1920, 160 pp. Or. Br – With cover illustration: Beethoven's death mask, painted and with a mustache pasted on it – See also: Bern catalogue, 1958, No. 45: Truly unique!)

This work was commissioned by the central office of the GERMAN DADA MOVEMENT and edited by Richard Huelsenbeck. Or, more precisely, it should have been the originally planned DADAKO-ATLANTE MONDIALE DADAISTICO *Dedicated to Gabriele d'Annunzio with (Dadaist) Respect*. However, the design, realization, and typography, entrusted to our capable *Monteurdada* [Dada assemblyman], grew and swelled to such an enormous folio of universal kitsch that the publisher, shying away from the increasing cost estimate running into the thousands (at the dollar exchange rate), published only fragments. And thus world literature missed a unicum, at least as regards its extent...

Walter Mehring, "Berlin DADA" (1959), in *Verrufene Malerei – Berlin DADA: Erinnerungen eines Zeitgenossen*, pp. 139–212; here: pp. 177–78. claassen Verlag, Düsseldorf, 1983.

Chaplin send you? Did Chaplin send you? We'll have to telegraph our thanks right away." [...] And so, we engaged him on the spot. Then we had a cardboard box. We had a big wreath of violets and those dear Dadaists of yours. Those dear Dadaists of yours. Those dear Dadaist friends of yours put it in the cardboard box with silk and ribbons. We then ordered the man to carry it up front. And that was an order, when we gave him the signal, when we stood up and sang. We drummed that into him. Then he had to go in, go through the doors, carry the box up front to the rostrum where Däubler was reading the wonderful *Nordlichtgedich-*

9   Richard Huelsenbeck, *DADA siegt!* [*Dada Triumphs!*]. Brochure cover, 1920.
Cat. no. 303

Chirico

10   Giorgio de Chirico, trial sheet for *Dadaco: Dadaistischer Handatlas* [*Dada Handatlas*] (unpublished, planned for 1920). Cat. no. 171

Paysage

Le soir on se promènera sur des routes parallèles

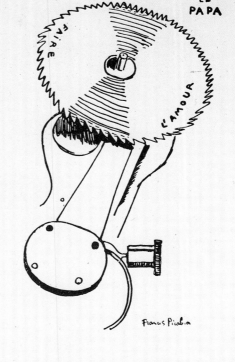

L'ARBRE
ETAIT
PLUS
HAUT
QUE LA
MONTAGNE

MAIS LA
MONTAGNE   LE
              FLEUVE
ETAIT SI LARGE   QUI
QU'ELLE DEPASSAIT   COULE
                    NE
LES EXTREMITES   PORTE
                PAS
DE LA TERRE   DE
                POISSONS

ATTENTION A NE PAS
JOUER SUR L'HERBE
FRACHEMENT PEINTE

Une chanson conduit les brebis vers l'étable

Vincente HUIDOBRO

11   Francis Picabia, "Paysage" [*Landscape*]. Trial sheet for *Dadaco: Dadaistischer Handatlas* (unpublished, planned for 1920). Cat. no. 171

91

Unser John

John Heartfield, der große Häuptling, wurde im Jahre 1888 in New Orleans geboren, wo sein Vater, der „weiße Bär" seit Jahrzehnten sein Wigwam aufgeschlagen hatte. Die Mutter des besagten Heartfield ist die bekannte Lady Noccer Boccer, deren Großvater der berühmteste Zirkusinhaber Kanadiens war. Dieser Zirkus zeigte zum erstenmal in der Welt dressierte Löwen, es ist mir sehr gut in Erinnerung; denn die Jugend meiner Heimatstadt stand vier Wochen Kopf, ehe er kam (mit Schreien und Trompeten machten sie laute Reklame) und vier Wochen, nachdem er verschwunden war, und an der Stelle, wo die Manege gestanden hatte, nur noch ein ausgebranntes Loch mit faulenden Gemüse-resten lag, sprachen die Mägde und Koppelknechte von ihm wie von einem großen Wunder und einem leuchtenden Ballon, der durch die Köpfe der Menschen gegangen war. Lady Noccer-Boccer, eine temperamentvolle Dame mit schwankendem Busen, leicht angedeutetem Doppelkinn und etwas angegrautem Haar, hatte schon in frühester Jugend die hohe Schule geritten, fühlte sich nur glücklich, wenn die Zeltbahn mit den Riesen-Initialen

über ihrem Kopfe schwebte, trug Hosen aus Seegras und rauchte einen Tabak, der so stark war, daß der Wind vor ihm seine Richtung wechselte. Lady Noccer-Boccer kam eines Tages mit ihren Eltern, dem Zirkus, 120 Pferden, 5 Elefanten, 2 Löwen und einem Nashorn nach New-Orleans. Sie fand dort den weißen Bären in einer schlimmen Lage. Er hatte als rassereiner Indianer sein letztes Geld in Whisky angelegt und lebte nun schlecht und recht von den Abfällen und Fußtritten, die ihm Wohlmeinende zukommen ließen. Das war eine fatale Existenz. Aber Lady Noccer-Boccer erkannte in ihm, obwohl er im Rinnstein lag, den Mann von Ehre, sie verliebte sich in seine Waden und sein Brust-korb begeisterte sie. Sie betrank sich mit ihm, ließ sich ent-führen, verführen und schenkte nach neun Monaten auf natürliche Weise oben besagtem Heartfield das Leben. Die erste Aeußerung, die genannter John dem Leben gegenüber für am Platze hielt, war DADA, wodurch ersichtlich ist, daß er schon in frühester Jugend, zu einer Zeit, wo gewöhnliche Sterbliche nur ihre Windeln beschmutzen, den Sinn seiner Existenz erfaßt hatte und seine gewaltige Zukunft voraus-ahnte. Auch der A-Ismus, der sich heute zu einer bedeu-tenden Kunstrichtung ausgewachsen hat, war ihm damals schon bekannt, man setzte ihn auf einen Porzellannapf und die Sache erledigte sich von selbst. Als John drei Jahre alt war, begann er zum Erstaunen seiner Mitmenschen künst-lerisches Talent zu zeigen, indem er sich sein Gesicht mit Dreck oder Kot (es ist dies ein sehr dunkles Kapitel) bemalte. Die Leute kamen von weither, um sich das Talent des John, der mit lauter Stimme in echt amerikanischer Weise für sich Reklame machte, anzusehen, umdrängten ihn im Kreis wie ein seltenes Tier und äußerten ihre Verwunderung durch Kopfschütteln und Händeklatschen. Ein dickes Weib, das ganz vorn stehen wollte und in rücksichtsloser Weise vor-ging, fiel über einen Besen und brach den Hals. Diese Tatsache nahmen die Frauenvereinler, Temperenzler und

12 "Unser John" [*Our John*]. Printed page for *Dadaco: Dadaistischer Handatlas* (unpublished, planned for 1920). Cat. no. 171

Tubenstöße an ihrem Leib erfuhren. Sie müssen den Schrei der Bremsen in ihren Ohren fühlen, das Bellen der Hunde, das ferne Donnern der Hochbahn: die grandiose Sinfonie der Realität. Das gewöhnliche Bild, die gewöhnliche Skulptur ist ihnen zu abstrakt, zu geleckt, zu sehr geeignet, in Museen bei schmalzigen Eröffnungsfeiern als Beispiel guter Kunsttätigkeit zu dienen. Herr Meyer könnte noch zu seiner Gattin sagen: „Emma, hier ist Kunscht". Wie der Dadaist hat der Futurist ein unendlich feines Empfinden dafür, daß in jedem Kunstwerk schon eine Norm erreicht ist, aus der sich ein Haufe von Ignoranten ein Geseß machen könnte. Mit der Vollendung ist die progressive Tätigkeit des Geistes zu Ende; das Philistertum beginnt. Nur ganz selten gibt es überhaupt Künstler, die eine Sensibilität für dieses Phänomen haben. Den meisten erscheint es als eine Selbstverständlichkeit, überkommene Formen mit persönlichen Phantasien zu füllen, und das Gros der Banausen hält den, der besinnungslos mit 18 oder 20 Jahren ein einigermaßen geistiges Drama in die Welt seßt, für einen starken Künstler. Es sind im Grunde die konventionellen Instinkte, die der Bürger im Künstler sieht und anerkennt. Was ein Drama oder ein Roman ist, das ist ihm von Generationen, die künstlerische Ambitionen hatten, eingepaukt worden. Aber wenn jemand kommt und sucht nach dem Sinn dieser Formen, ob sie in dieser oder jener Zeit überhaupt einen Sinn haben, so ist der unfruchtbare Theoretiker da. Ein Dichter muß dumm sein, heißt es. Es scheint in der Tat so, — der Dadaist sträubt sich, ein Dichter zu sein. Wenn er es ist, hat ihn das Geschick übermannt.

Was den Dadaisten vom Futuristen zuerst unterscheidet, ist die einfache Tatsache, daß er der Jüngere ist. Er hat die gesamte Entwicklung, die schließlich die Entstehung des Futurismus veranlaßte, bewußt, anhand der Dokumente erlebt. Der Futurismus selbst steht vor ihm als ein abgeschlossenes Werk und ist ihm nicht mehr als das Kunstwerk, das mit seiner Konstituierung unter die bürgerlichen Begriffe fällt. Er verneint ihn, weil er besteht. Etwas muß mit ihm nicht in Ordnung sein, weil er besteht. Eine große Kunstrichtung, die so glänzend organisiert hat, daß der kleinste Krähwinkler Schönheitsesel seine Kinder mit dem Namen des Futuristen schreckt, ist über alle Maßen verdächtigt. Wie viel bürgerliche und sedimentäre Instinkte müssen sich hier betätigt haben. Der Dadaist, die Verkörperung der ewigen Progression des Geistes, das zentrifugale Element, das die Gedanken bis in sein Fleisch zu Ende denkt, hat mit dem Futurismus als Kunstrichtung nichts mehr zu tun. Er verlacht ihn, er hält ihn für gut genug, um ein Bonmot aus ihm zu machen.

Was den Dadaisten nicht zuletzt vom Futuristen unterscheidet, ist die unbestreitbare Tatsache, daß der Futurismus eine italienische Angelegenheit ist. Da ist man von den Bauten der Renaissance bedrängt, man stolpert über die

Dada in den Schulen

Dada-Vorführung auf Petra-Tageslichtapparat für Schulen

Apollo- und Ganymedstatuen, ist gefahrvoll bedinder überhaupt etwas neues zu schaffen, weil der Beschauer sogleich die Möglichkeit hat, klassifizierte Kunstwerke zum Vergleich heranzuziehen. Der Durchschnittsitaliener weiß, daß der Bel Canto, die schöne Linie der Prä- und Postraffaeliten einmal den Ruhm seines Vaterlandes gemacht habe. Er wird sich nicht davon abbringen lassen, den hier verkörperten Geist als etwas allein seligmachendes zu preisen, zumal überall die Türen der Museen für ihn geöffnet sind. Dagegen hat Marinetti Sturm gerannt; in seinem Herzen fand er die Renaissance, die er ständig totschlagen mußte, um Futurist zu sein. Er war in ständiger Polemik mit sich selbst, kam niemals zur ruhigen Übersicht seiner Machtmittel, weil er noch so und so viele Museen in Brand stecken mußte, weil ihm die Reliefs am Palazzo ducale oder der porta del populo in seine Träume grinste, weil er auf der Piazza del Herbe die Griechenjünglinge verfluchen mußte.

Von all diesen Dingen ist der Dadaist phantastisch weit entfernt. Da er das Leben mehr schäßt als die Kunst und den Problemen mißtraut, die einer Persönlichkeit dazu dienen, sich eine bestimmte Philosophie zu machen, hält er sich von jeder verbissenen Politik fern. Was geht ihn ein italienisches Spezialproblem an, es kommt ihm vor, als disputierten sich zwei Scholastiker.

Der Begriff der Bewegung, der bei den Futuristen irgendwie von der maschinellen Geschäftigkeit der Zeit abstrahiert war, ist von dem Dadaisten stark verallgemeinert worden. Es gibt Bilder, auf denen man ein Haus von allen Seiten sehen kann; der Begriff der Größe ist relativ, wir haben keinen Maßstab dafür, ob ein Kopf dünn oder dick ist, man vergleicht nur nach seinem eigenen. Skulpturen brauchen kein oben und unten zu haben, sie sind auch nichts anderes als Manifestationen der Fluktuation. Der Begriff der Bewegung überträgt sich von der Kunst aufs Leben und umgekehrt. Es gibt nirgendwo Ruhe. Wo Ruhe ist, hört die Progression des Geistes auf, der Sumpf, die Drecklache beginnt. Am Ende ist das Leben nichts anderes als das eilige Abrattern eines besseren Sensationsfilms. Aber die Bewegung ergreift vor allem das Gerümpel des sogenannten objektiven Geistes, wirft die moralischen Begriffe durcheinander, lehrt hinter die natürliche Zweiteilung der Dinge sehen, schafft einen überlegenen Standpunkt über Mann und Weib. Sie schafft die Tatsache der ironischen Einstellung, die einen weiteren Hauptartikel im Glaubensbekenntnis des Dadaisten bedeutet und ihn scharf von dem fast mit sozialistisch-dummen Propagationsmitteln arbeitenden Futurismus trennt. Was der Mangel an Ironie bedeutet, begreift man, wenn man sich die Futuristen als Freiwillige in diesen Krieg stürzen sieht, weil sie einmal im Gedanken an sich selbst den Kampf, und wäre es der Kampf mit Flugzeugen und Flammenwerfer über alles gestellt haben. Wieviel ehrliche

13 "Dada in den Schulen" [*Dada in School*]. Printed page for *Dadaco: Dadaistischer Handatlas* (unpublished, planned for 1920). Cat. no. 171

93

14   John Heartfield in front of the enlargement of his montage for Upton Sinclair's *Nach der Sintflut* [*The Millennium*].
Photomontage, 1927. Cat. no. 180

Jan Tschichold, 1928

The Malik· publishing company, established in the days of Dadaism, used photomontage mainly on its covers. Their author, John Heartfield, has created models of up-to-date dust jackets. He is the inventor of photomontage covers. His covers for Malik were the first of their kind.

Jan Tschichold, *Die neue Typographie. Ein Handbuch für zeitgemäß Schaffende*, p. 228. Berlin, 1928.

Lilly Becher, 1957

Today it is almost forgotten that he tested the artistic-political impact of photomontage on a wallflower that nobody took notice of, the dust jacket. Photomontage appeared for the first time on this slim, oblong, double page as a genre integrating the graphic, literary, and agitational means of expression into something new. The works, created mostly for the Malik publishing company in the twenties, were a bold experiment: Heartfield made the dust jacket "active," and let it "fight" for the author. It is hardly imaginable today what a fascinating contrast those miniature montages were to the usual, sober or whimsical book covers. Heartfield condensed.

Lilly Becher, "Beseelt von unserer Sprache: Zur Heartfield-Ausstellung, Deutsche Akademie der Künste, Berlin, September 1957," in Wieland Herzfelde, *John Heartfield*, (Dresden, [3]1986), pp. 345–47; here: pp. 345–46. Verlag der Kunst, Dresden, 1962, 1971.

Wieland Herzfelde, 1962

When our company began publishing novels in 1921, it required [. . .] particularly expressive dust jackets and book covers. They were meant to motivate not only the minority of leftist booksellers but also those of other persuasions to display in the windows our new publications as well as the reprints. The books had to be attractive at first sight and, at the same time, have an agitational effect. For we felt that even those who did not buy the book still should be influenced in accordance with its content by its very appearance alone. We even used the spines in a novel way. Even on the shelf the book should give food for thought and stimulate reading. The range of Heartfield's knowledge and advertising experience now proved their worth. He adapted himself at once to the new task: to transform his revolutionary technique into an advertising tool for rev-

olutionary literature. When his typocollages and photocollages from 1917 to 1920 are compared with the books' dust jackets, covers, and end papers – and also with his work for magazines and brochures of the following years – one can see immediately that he no longer cut up photos in order to paste them together rhythmically and with aggressive humor [. . .]

The whole appearance of our books changed. The impulse came from booksellers and readers who sent books or jackets back to us to have us exchange them for clean ones. And in fact, the white art paper or the high gloss (super-calendered) paper necessary to print photos in halftone became grubby in no time at all. It then occurred to us to varnish the jackets. That had not been done before, and our printers first had to go to some trouble to try it

out. And we had yet another idea – and continued to use it even when the varnishing process worked – to print photos on the spines, and eventually on the whole book cover, so as to leave as few blank spaces as possible to get soiled, while at the same time gaining additional space for advertising. If the photo was of an oblong format there were no difficulties, unless, as in the case of *Jimmie Higgins*, the same image was printed on both back and front. The idea of using two *different* pictures simultaneously was realized in 1923 for the new edition of the novel *100 %* [*100 %: The Story of a Patriot*]. (Attempts to attribute photomontage to Dadaism or *Neue Jugend* [*New*

(continued on page 98)

15   Upton Sinclair, *Jimmie Higgins*. Dust jacket, 1928 (36th–42nd thousand). Cat. no. 311

16   Oskar Maria Graf, *Frühzeit* [*The Early Time*]. Photomontage for cover design, 1922.
Cat. no. 76

Youth] are due to its confusion with collage, i.e., a haphazard pasting together, at best pleasant or shocking.)

John Heartfield, he alone, took the decisive step, much later, in 1928, with the new edition of the novel entitled *Drei Soldaten* [*Three Soldiers*]. The first edition, of 1922, had an illustration only on the front, a photo of three soldiers at the edge of a wood writing letters home from the front, with the American flag in the background. The new dust jacket replaced the star-spangled banner with a dark blue starry sky. That was more romantic and saved the printing in red. On the back of the jacket, hitherto blank, Heartfield juxtaposed the picture on the front with a photo in which three dead soldiers are lying on a road under a pale blue morning sky, under trees riddled with shrapnel. The effect was more than a simple comment on the subject: it carried an antithetical message. It expressed the realist nature of the book. Four years earlier, Heartfield had arranged "Väter und Söhne 1924" [*Ten Years After: Fathers and Sons 1924*] in a similar manner.

Later, when Heartfield made deliberate use of it, we called the outcome of this method dialectic photomontage.

Wieland Herzfelde, *John Heartfield*, (Dresden [3]1986), pp. 46–48. Verlag der Kunst, Dresden, 1962, 1971.

17   Upton Sinclair, *100%. Roman eines Patrioten* [*100%. The Story of a Patriot*]. Cover design, 1921. Cat. no. 166

Walter Benjamin, 1934

Let us recall Dadaism. The revolutionary strength of Dadaism lay in testing art for its authenticity. Still lifes were compiled from tickets, rolls of yarn, and cigarette butts that were merged with painterly elements. The whole lot was put into a frame. And then it was shown to the public: Look, your picture frame breaks the bounds of time; the tiniest authentic fragment of everyday life tells more than painting does. Just like the bloody fingerprint of a murderer on a book page tells more than the text. A good deal of this revolutionary substance made its escape into photomontage. You need to consider only the works of John Heartfield, whose technique turned the book cover into a political instrument.

Walter Benjamin, "Neue Sachlichkeit und Photographie," (1934) in *Gesammelte Schriften*, 7 vols., eds. R. Tiedemann and H. Schweppenhäuser, II/2, pp. 692–93. Suhrkamp Verlag, Frankfurt/Main, 1972–89.

18   Upton Sinclair, *100%. Roman eines Patrioten*. Dust jacket, 1928 (43rd–50th thousand).
Cat. no. 309

Rolf Sachsse, 1990

Unlike many avant-garde artists who tried their hand amateurishly at advertising in the twenties, [John Heartfield] was endowed with a comprehensive professionalism that saved him equally from academic formalism – of the Bauhaus kind, for instance [...] – and from economic failure. Thanks to Heartfield's work, the Malik publishing company was able to sell vast numbers of editions of its books. [...] Dust jackets – for these are at issue here, despite the often-used, misleading terms "book production" and "book design" [...] – are, according to contemporary usage, packaging design, with fixed rules of production and a high identificatory value for publishers and readers. [...]

Helmut Herzfeld's work as a designer in the area of industrial production became more professional, but he did not attain particular skills in the graphic arts – his illustrations were criticized as "dilettantish." Apart from Dada's own brand of precisionism [...] and a certain flirtation with the job designation *Monteur* [assemblyman], John Heartfield's work in the area of book lay-out, when defined in technical terms, appears as design using new technical devices linked with considerations of how to achieve the best possible results that are both aesthetically effective and economical. All calculatory problems and even a certain amount of outside funding taken into account, the Malik publishing company was, for its day, a solidly managed enterprise in which Heartfield's dust jacket work had a specific importance within the system of labor division, namely, as Tucholsky put it, to provide good-looking, well-fitting suits for books. [...]

Rolf Sachsse, "Mit das Beste auf dem Gebiet der Reklame-Fotomontage...," in exhibition catalogue *John Heartfield*, Altes Museum, Berlin, et al., pp. 266–73; here: pp. 266, 267. DuMont Buchverlag, Cologne, 1991.

19   *Eros: Das Buch der Leidenschaft und der Liebe* [*Eros: The Book of Love and Passion*]. Dust jacket, 1925.

Cat. no. 92

20a   John Dos Passos, *Drei Soldaten*
[*Three Soldiers*].
Dust jacket (second version), 1929
(11th–17th thousand). Cat. no. 314

20b   John Dos Passos, *Drei Soldaten*. Dust jacket (second version),
1929 (11th–17th thousand). Cat. no. 314

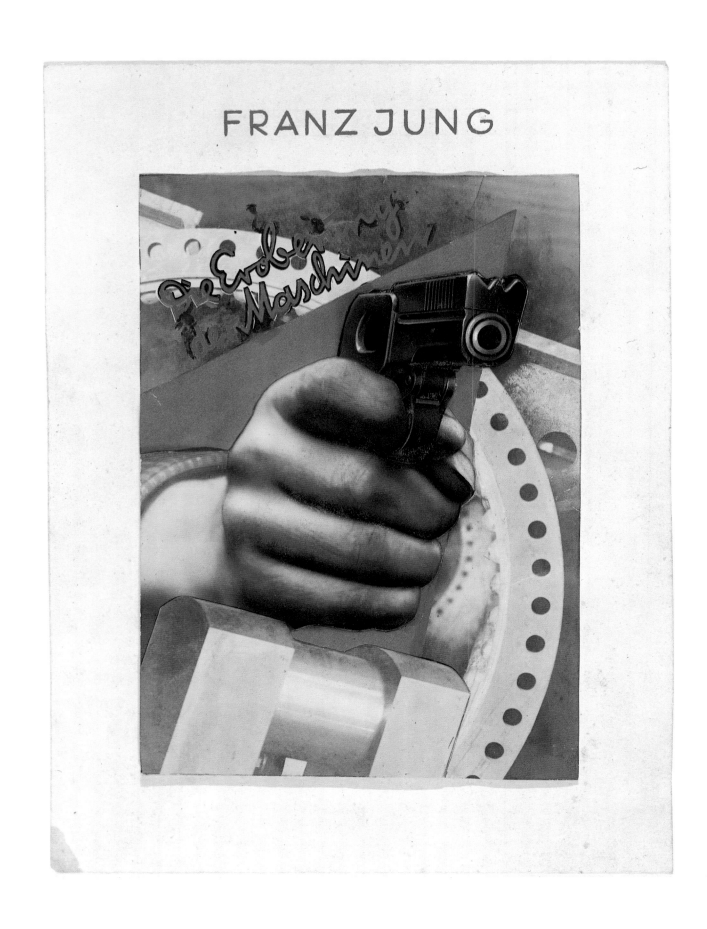

21   Franz Jung, *Die Eroberung der Maschinen* [*The Conquest of the Machines*].
Photomontage for cover design, 1923. Cat. no. 81

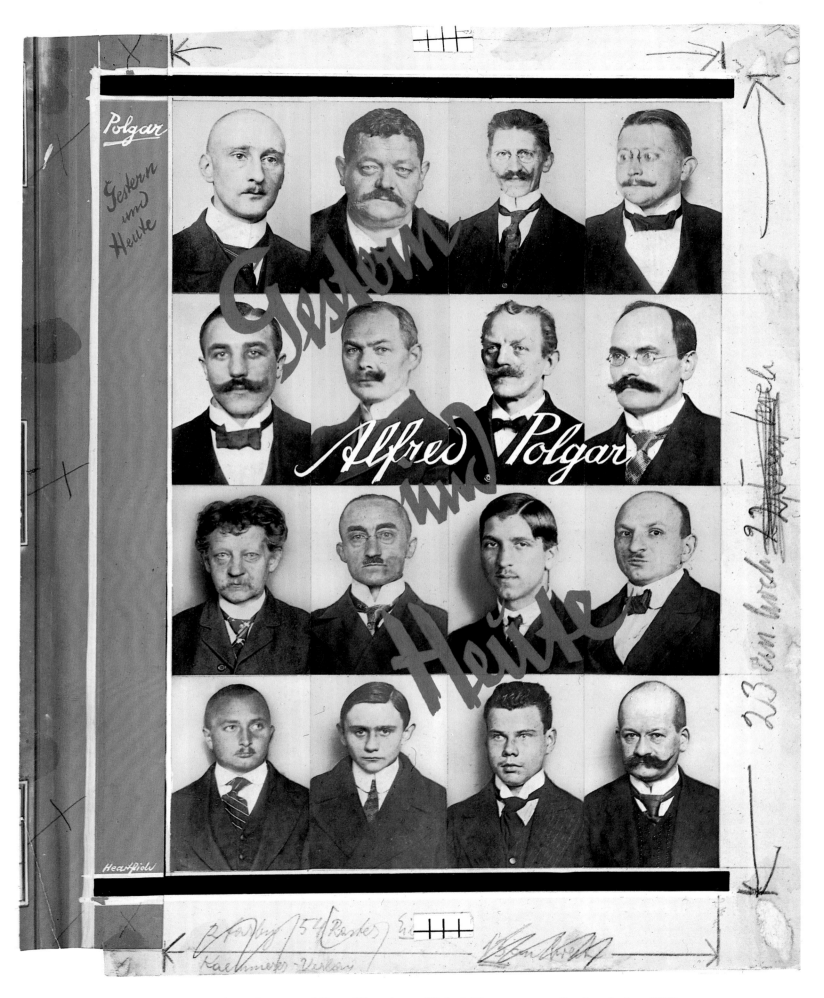

22　Alfred Polgar, *Gestern und Heute* [*Yesterday and Today*]. Photomontage for dust jacket, 1922.
Cat. no. 304

John Heartfield, 1967

In the 1924 almanac of the Malik publishing company (*Platz dem Arbeiter!*) [*Make Way for the Worker!*] there are two photos, one below the other, which illustrate very clearly what I have said so far about work with photos. After all, this isn't photomontage yet. [...] At the top, there is a picture showing a general, who has died behind the lines, being buried with [...] all that pomp and ceremony. The second one shows poor soldiers at the front being buried where grenades have burst, and then being covered over with lime. Yes, this picture is in the book, with a very effective caption. So, here are two juxtapositions, above and below [...]

From an interview with John Heartfield (1967), in Roland März, ed., *John Heartfield: Der Schnitt entlang der Zeit. Selbstzeugnisse – Erinnerungen – Interpretationen*, pp. 464–65. Verlag der Kunst, Dresden, 1981.

23a   *Platz dem Arbeiter!* [*Make Way for the Worker!*]. Cover design, 1924. Cat. no. 80

Wie ein in der Etappe gestorbener General begraben wurde

Wie die an der Front abgeschlachteten Proletarier verladen wurden

24   *Der Fall Sacco und Vanzetti* [*The Sacco and Vanzetti Case*]. Photomontage for magazine cover, 1927, Cat. no. 83

Hans Reimann, 1927

[…] he is one of the few in Germany who has grasped the importance of packaging. He knows that Odol remains nonsensical as long as nobody understands what Odol actually is [a German mouthwash]. And he knows that all depends on the *How*. He is not out to move mountains. But he makes dead books spring to life through his designs for dust jackets. And the fact that he is unequalled in this is evident not only from the circulation figures of hard-to-sell books, but also from his imitators. John Heartfield was the first who dared to use scissors to produce dust jackets, cleverly cutting up selected photos and then putting them together again to form a new totality.

How does he go about working on a jacket for Sinclair's *Wechsler* [*The Moneychangers*]? John takes the "center of the world." That's to say, not the Berlin Reichstag, but the Chicago Corn Exchange. He cuts out the center of that center, pastes it onto an ordinary stock listing from a daily newspaper, and varnishes the whole thing. Or, what about a jacket for Sinclair's *Nach der Sintflut* [*The Millennium*]? John takes three dozen pictures of rough seas, pastes them together, selects, retouches, enlivens them by rearranging them, enlarges them to ten times their size, and, finally, achieves the illusion of foaming waters crashing over skyscrapers he has taken from other photos. He then reduces it in size, and

there's the Flood. Or he composes a trefoil combining the pictures of a millionaire tycoon, a movie star, and Jesus of Nazareth. He carelessly festoons it with the book title in the scrawl of a shopboy. Or he cuts out three soldiers, paints as a background a mammoth star-spangled banner, and adds the cursory title, this time in an intellectual's handwriting.
Im Zwischendeck nach Südamerika [*In Steerage to South America*] by Wilhelm Herzog […] what jacket will make the strongest impression on the reader before he has even started to read? The bows of a huge ocean liner. Some script above, some script below, and two garish stripes at the end. Basta! –

25   Upton Sinclair, *Die Wechsler* [*The Moneychangers*]. Dust jacket, 1925. Cat. no. 167

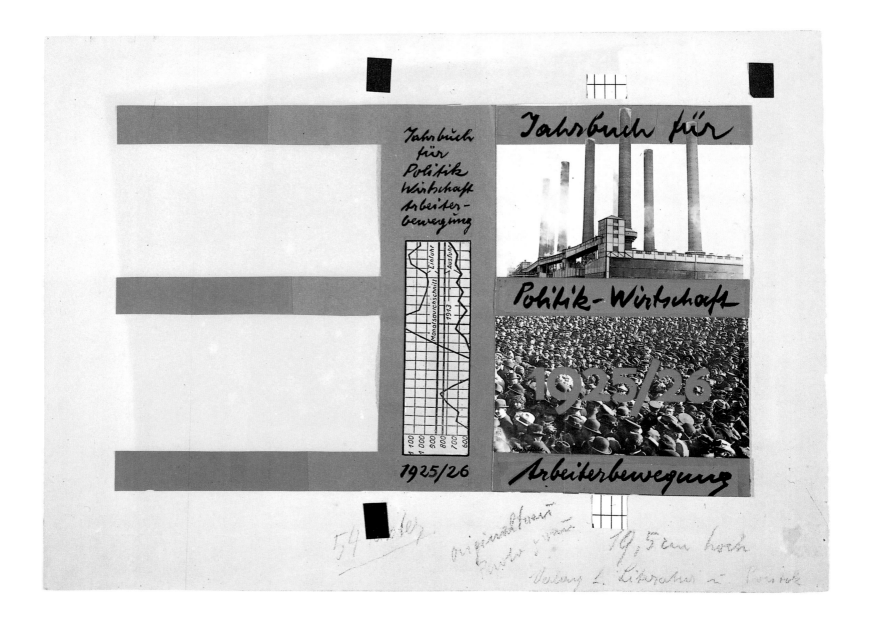

Franz Jung's *Arbeitsfriede* [*Industrial Peace*] is conveyed by Heartfield's poetic composition: a quiet gable-end view of single-family houses sketched against a cloudy evening sky. –

Oskar Maria Graf's *Frühzeit* [*The Early Time*] is adorned with the stern portrait of the Bavarian author, into which socialist spikes project from above and below, and appear to have been pulled away from his face. – Sinclair's *Samuel* [*The Seeker*] has a front cover that smacks of Charlie Chaplin and a back cover that shows nothing but depressingly endless railroad tracks. *König Kohle* [*King Coal*] by Upton Sinclair is symbolized by smokestacks and chimneys. Heartfield doesn't add anything to this but

a minimum of script. – *Der Sumpf* [*The Jungle*] really becomes a swamp. – Marietta Shaginyan's *Abenteuer einer Dame* [*Adventures of a Society Lady*]: a triangular vision of slippery asphalt with arc lamps. – Wittfogel's *Das erwachende China* [*China Awakening*] inspires the artist to create a kaleidoscope in blue and yellow. – And his most remarkable achievement is the cover to Jung's *Eroberung der Maschinen* [*The Conquest of the Machines*]: Here the unbearable tension of certain scenes of *Battleship Potemkin* is achieved with a Browning pistol, a fist, and a mystical confusion of machines into which is wedged a red triangle. This is the work of someone who has grasped the meaning of Futurism.

And Expressionism. And accumulation. For Heartfield's work is truly expressionist – with a practical background.

His dust jackets are disquieting, exciting, gentle, intriguing, and always extraordinary. If I were a publisher, I'd love to give him new assignments every day. He would have to design book covers, advertisements, posters, and advertising circulars for me, and I would benefit.

Hans Reimann, "John Heartfield," in *Das Stachelschwein* (Berlin, June 1927), pp. 38–40.

26   *Jahrbuch für Politik – Wirtschaft – Arbeiterbewegung 1925/26.* [*Almanach for Politics – Economics – Workers' Movement 1925/26*]. Photomontage for dust jacket, 1926. Cat. no. 125

27   Karl August Wittfogel, *Das erwachende China* [*China Awakening*]. Photomontage for dust jacket, 1926.
Cat. no. 132

Kurt Tucholsky, 1932

If I weren't Peter Panter, I'd like to be a dust jacket at the Malik publishing company. That John Heartfield is really a small wonder of the world. All the things that come into his head! What magical things he does! I've had one of his photomontages framed, and one wants to keep nearly all of them. The dust jacket of *Traumfabrik* [*Factory of Dreams*] by Ilya Ehrenburg looks like a gilded cookie box. Since German books as yet haven't worked their way up to a standard appearance like those of the French, it has to be said that they are best dressed at Malik's.

Kurt Tucholsky, *Gesammelte Werke*, III, p. 1004. Rowohlt Verlag, Reinbek, 1960.

28   Vsevolod Ivanov, *Der Buchstabe G* [*The Letter G*]. Dust jacket, 1930. Cat. no. 329

29　Ilya Ehrenburg, *Die Traumfabrik* [*Factory of Dreams*]. Dust jacket, 1931. Cat. no. 339

János Reismann (Wolf Reiss), 1972

Most of the books that had to be published quickly at the Malik publishing company were by Sinclair and Ehrenburg. To some extent, I was involved in this: for example, taking a photograph of a wooden board in perspective that would be used to put cut-out figures on, which Jonny had already prepared for the back cover of Ehrenburg's *Heiligste Güter. Roman der großen Interessen* [*Most Sacred Possessions*].

One morning, Jonny came with his pockets full of silver and copper coins and, of course, matches, because it had something to do with money and a crucifixion of Christ on rifle cartridges. So that wasn't any great problem. I remember how we had to arrange them all to Jonny's specifications, and then the whole thing was photographed. This was a staged dust jacket. The book hadn't been printed yet,

but it was at the publishing house. Then we realized that the book wasn't particularly interesting or well-written – but the jacket was very interesting.

From an interview with Gertrud Heartfield (1972), in Roland März, ed., *John Heartfield. Der Schnitt entlang der Zeit. Selbstzeugnisse – Erinnerungen – Interpretationen*, pp. 224–45. Verlag der Kunst, Dresden, 1981.

30   Ilya Ehrenburg, *Die heiligsten Güter* [*Most Sacred Possessions*]. Dust jacket, 1931.
Cat. no. 338

Hans Reimann, 1927

His worst works are illustrative drawings, his best are ads. As an illustrator, he is as much of a dilettant as Walter Mehring; as a commercial artist, he is as great as George Groß [*sic*]. And by that I mean his quite ordinary Malik advertisements, contrived simply with typographical tricks like those that frequently appear in magazines and publishers' ads. They are very successful; their smartness and eye-catching qualities are fascinating, they exude tranquility and an unforgettable attractiveness. The devices he employs to achieve this are of the greatest austerity. Occasionally, a single bold rule would suffice. John is capable of transforming a boring, stodgy advertisement put before him into a sublime delight through ingenious rearrangement. He has a sure eye for effective display.

Hans Reimann, "John Heartfield," in *Das Stachelschwein*, p. 38. (Berlin, June 1927).

31   Advertising leaflet for Ilya Ehrenburg's *Julio Jurenito*, 1929. Cat. no. 315

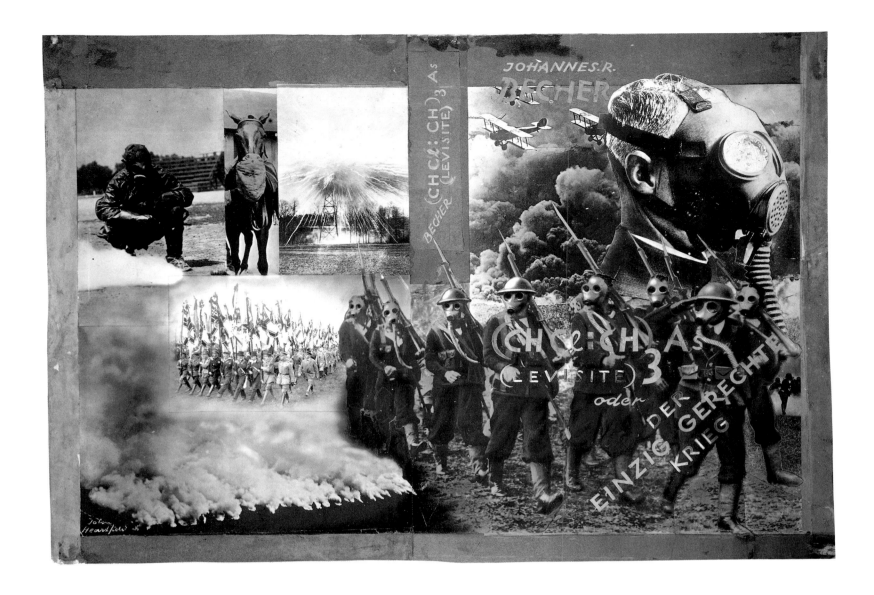

Wolf Reiss, 1934

Heartfield's work is a fierce struggle, repeated day after day, to realize his ideas and aims. "People really don't have any idea," he once said, "how difficult it is to be a *Photomonteur.*" [...]

Taking photos for Heartfield, based on meticulous pencil sketches and always under his personal supervision, often covered sessions lasting many, many hours. He strove for nuances which I could no longer even perceive. While they were being developed in the darkroom, he would also stand at the enlarger till the prints were ready. I often was so tired that I couldn't stand, couldn't think, only wanted to sleep—but he would run home with the photos still wet, dry them, cut them out, and assemble them under a heavy glass plate. He would sleep for two

hours, and from eight in the morning he would already sit with the retoucher for two, three, four, five hours, his nerves stretched to the breaking point: It was always possible that the retoucher might still botch things up. Even when the montage was ready, the relief didn't last long: There were new plans, new ideas. He browsed about again in the photo archives for hours and days on end to find out whether there were any photos (or at least a suitable head) available of Hermann Müller, Hugenberg, Röhm—whatever the case might be—which would fit into his concept. Everything else would take care of itself. Then, back to the photographers, all of whom he hated—including me—because they wouldn't perceive the nuances; from the photographer, to the retoucher,

whom he had "drilled" himself; in Berlin, the American method of retouching has developed primarily because of his demands. Of course, there were intermittent pauses of varying length, but the nervous tension—will everything work out as he has expected—never ceased. It is a tremendous responsibility, Heartfield is a revolutionary artist: An idea can never be striking enough, the formulation never precise enough, the montage never clear enough. Better go back again to the archives, to the photographers, to the retoucher.

Wolf Reiss, "Als ich mit John Heartfield zusammenarbeitete," in *Internationale Literatur*, pp. 186, 188. (German edition, Moscow, 5, 1934).

32   Johannes R. Becher, *(CH Cl:CH)₃ As (Levisite) oder Der einzig gerechte Krieg* [*Lewisit or The Only Just War*]. Photomontage for cover design, 1926. Cat. no. 130

33　Franz Carl Weiskopf, *Wer keine Wahl hat, hat die Qual* [*Who Has No Choice Has the Agony*].
Photomontage for dust jacket, 1929. Cat. no. 157

34   *An Alle! 10 Jahre Sowjet-Union 1917–1927* [*To Everybody! 10 Years of the Soviet Union 1917–1927*].
Photomontage for back cover of magazine, 1927. Cat. no. 68

35　　Fedor Panferov, *Die Genossenschaft der Habenichtse* [*The Cooperative of the Have-Nots*].
Photomontage for dust jacket, 1930. Cat. no. 333

36   Walter Müller, *Wenn wir 1918 . . .* [*If we in 1918 . . .*] Dust jacket, 1930. Cat. no. 331

37   Ludwig Turek, *Ein Prolet erzählt* [*A Worker Narrates*]. Dust jacket, 1930. Cat. no. 337

38   Michael Gold, *Juden ohne Geld* [*Jews Whithout Money*]. Dust jacket, 1931. Cat. no. 340

39   Upton Sinclair, *Der Sumpf* [*The Jungle*]. Dust jacket, 1924. Cat. no. 101

40   Upton Sinclair, *Die Metropole* [*The Metropolis*]. Dust jacket, 1925. Cat. no. 165

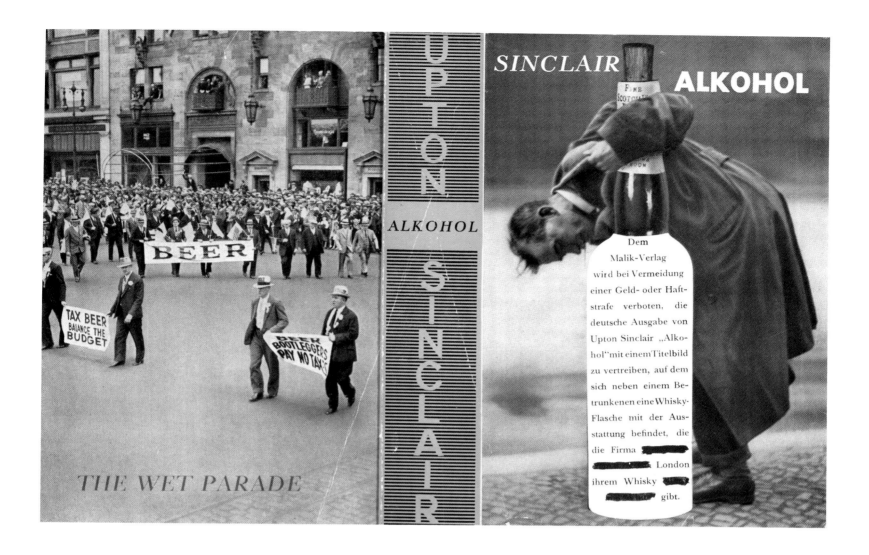

Mieczysław Berman, 1973

In 1932 or 1933 I saw John Heartfield's dust jacket for Upton Sinclair's *Alkohol* [*The Wet Parade*]. I saw a drunkard on his last legs, holding on to a bottle of alcohol as though it were a lamppost. There was a label "Scotch Whisky" on the bottle. It was pale green against a gray photographic background. Beautifully printed and varnished, with "Alkohol—Sinclair" in white characters on it. I stared at this jacket for maybe half an hour. This time I was even more surprised. What had the artist done? He had created a pungent satirical illustration rendered faintly lethal by the delicate green color. The Scotch whisky bottle had a particularly aggressive effect. Now that was graphic.

What does the artist give us with these [...] dust jackets? On the one hand [as for Fedor Gladkov's *Cement*] an impressive poster, an idealization and monumentalization of the Red Army, and on the other hand this wonderful illustration: this noxious atmosphere—alcoholism. There is a type of dust jacket by Jonny Heartfield that is done simply in one color: black. And that is black photography. Now and then these photographs come from the great works of Soviet cinematic art and have been used for the books of Soviet authors such as Maxim Gorki's *Märchen der Wirklichkeit* [*Tales of Reality*]. Heartfield selected a scene from a Soviet film: a fisherman by a river. Perhaps it's the Vol-

ga or the Oka. You only see a black silhouette of a person fishing that merges with the ground, and on this ground there is written in white: Maxim Gorki, *Märchen der Wirklichkeit*. The water and the horizon are light gray, endless and infinite; only the fishing rod cuts a line through the gray.

From an interview with Gertrud Heartfield, in Roland März, ed., *John Heartfield: Der Schnitt entlang der Zeit. Selbstzeugnisse – Erinnerungen – Interpretationen*, pp. 245–47; here: pp. 246–47. Dresden, 1981.

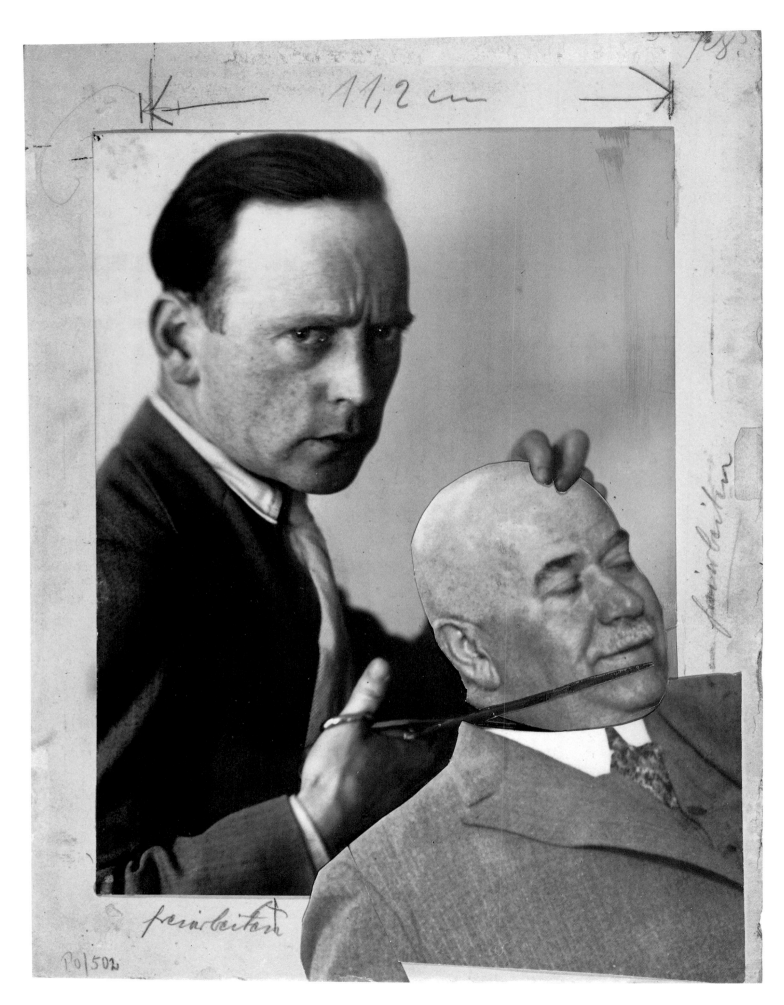

42 John Heartfield with Police Commissioner Zörgiebel. Photomontage for the *Arbeiter-Illustrierte-Zeitung*
[*Workers' Illustrated Newspaper*] (*AIZ*, Berlin), no. 37, 1929. Cat. no. 194

Wieland Herzfelde, 1971

In February 1919, we published a four-page illustrated periodical in news-paper format. At Grosz's suggestion, we called it *Jedermann sein eigner Fußball* [*Everybody His Own Football*], which was supposed to mean something like: Don't let yourself get kicked around, get moving yourself. Thus a new form of agitation began for us, one directly aimed at single political events. On the front page you see two unsigned photocollages, one depicting a football flying in the air, with arms and legs and a photo of my head on it; the other bears the heading "Contest! Who's the prettiest?" and six photo portraits of members of the Ebert/Scheidemann government set on the photograph of an open fan, as well as Noske, Ludendorff, Erzberger on the fan handle. On pages 2 to 4, also designed by Heartfield, there are illustrations by Grosz. [. . .] In the very same month, we published a similar periodical, *Die Pleite* [*The Bust*]. Each one of all six issues was confiscated every time (and each time after it was too late). [. . .] As in the case of all the issues of the *Pleite* and many Malik books, Grosz also did the front cover of this periodical. *Die Pleite* published a number of photos which through the addition of a cap-tion became a satirical contribution. [. . .]

The logical consequence was that in the summer of 1923, when the KPD [German Communist Party] founded the satirical weekly *Der Knüppel* [*The Club*], Heartfield and Grosz took charge of running it and procured the cooperation of many of their colleagues, including some from abroad. To be on the safe side, the contributors either did not sign their work or used pseudonyms. For example, my brother signed as Mött; Grosz, as Ehren-fried, Baldur, and Böff; the Bulgarian Angelushev, to whom, by the way, we owe the best drawing of Thälmann, used the name Fuck. The three of us occasionally designed posters and leaflets, too. In the *Knüppel*, as previ-ously in the *Pleite*, Heartfield frequently used photos, but he seldom com-bined them with collages. Joint collages of the kind stamped "Grosz-Heart-field mont." did not appear in the *Knüppel*, nor did "photomontages." The term was still unknown at the time. John, it is true, was nicknamed even during the war the *Monteur* [assemblyman] by his friends, not because of his working technique, but because he was in the habit of wearing overalls. He did not want to look like an artist, but he did not want to look like an advertising executive, either.

Wieland Herzfelde, "George Grosz, John Heartfield, Erwin Piscator, Dada und die Folgen—oder Die Macht der Freundschaft," in *Sinn und Form*, (23, 6 1971), pp. 1224–51. Aufbau Verlag, Berlin and Weimar, 1976, for id.; *Zur Sache*, Berlin/Weimar, 1976.

43a   George Grosz, "S. M." [*H*(is) *M*(ajesty)]. *Die Pleite* [*The Bust*], no. 7, July 1923, title page.

Cat. no. 176

Faschistenruf.

Zeichnung von John Heartfield

Voran die Ehrhardtleute.
ahu — ahu
Bahn frei der Roßbachmeute.
ahu — ahu
Platz Blond und Blau und Deutschen Eichen.
Wir fordern Blut und Leichen.
ahu.

> (Musik. Negertrommeln. Tanz der Wilden)
> Kilimantscharo. Tanganjika.
> Kilimantscharo. Tanganjika.

Hört ihr die Volksseele kochen?
ahu — ahu
Bewaffnet bis auf die Knochen.
ahu — ahu
Jeder sein eigner Klempnerladen.
So halten wir Paraden.
ahu.

> (Musik. Negertrommeln. Tanz der Wilden.)
> Kilimantscharo. Tanganjika.
> Kilimantscharo. Tanganjika.

Das Hakenkreuz im Schilde.
ahu — ahu
Die Hitlerschützengilde
ahu — ahu
Wir hassen Juden und Proleten
und werden sie zertreten.
ahu.

> (Musik. Negertrommeln. Tanz der Wilden.)
> Kilimantscharo. Tanganjika.
> Kilimantscharo. Tanganjika.

Die höchste Pflicht der Christen:
ahu — ahu
Tod allen Kommunisten.
ahu — ahu
Nur keinen einzigen vergessen.
Lieber lebendig fressen.
ahu.

> (Musik. Negertrommeln. Tanz der Wilden.)
> Kilimantscharo. Tanganjika.
> Kilimantscharo. Tanganjika.

Wir haben keine Sorgen.
ahu — ahu
Das Vaterland lohnts morgen.
ahu — ahu
Inzwischen wird die Not uns lindern
mit Gott Rauben und Plündern.
ahu.

> (Musik. Negertrommeln. Tanz der Wilden.)
> Kilimantscharo. Tanganjika.
> Kilimantscharo. Tanganjika.

Von Blut und Schnaps besoffen
ahu — ahu
sehn wir den Himmel offen.
ahu — ahu
Hoch lebe Willem, unser Kaiser!
Prost Rest! und schreit euch heiser.
ahu.

> (Musik. Negertrommeln. Tanz der Wilden.)
> Kilimantscharo. Tanganjika.
> Kilimantscharo. Tanganjika.

Oskar Kaneh

44   "Front Heil!." *Der Knüppel* [*The Club*], no. 4, June 1927, front page. Cat. no. 148

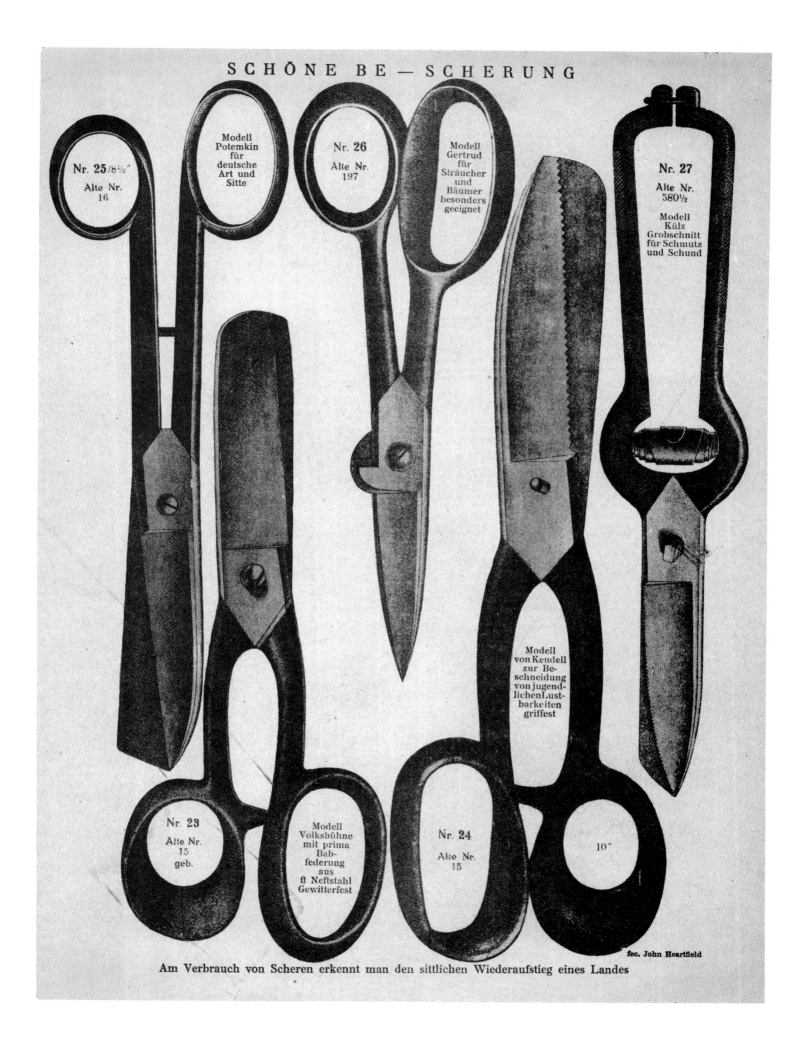

Am Verbrauch von Scheren erkennt man den sittlichen Wiederaufstieg eines Landes

45 "The Whole Shebang." *Der Knüppel*, no. 5, August 1927, unpag. Cat. no. 141

46a   "A Peace Cake and Its Ingredients." *Die Rote Granate* [*The Red Grenade*], August 1926, back cover.

Cat. no. 150

46b "A Peace Cake and Its Ingredients." Photomontage (1926), revised for a second version
for the *Arbeiterkalender* [*Workers' Calendar*], 1927. Cat. no. 181

47a   "Rationalization is on the March!." *Der Knüppel*, no. 2, February 1927, p. 5. Cat. no. 138

47b "Rationalization is on the March!." Photomontage for *Der Knüppel*, no. 2, February 1927, p. 5.
Cat. no. 138

48 *Die Arena*, no. 2, February/March 1927, front page. Cat. no. 91

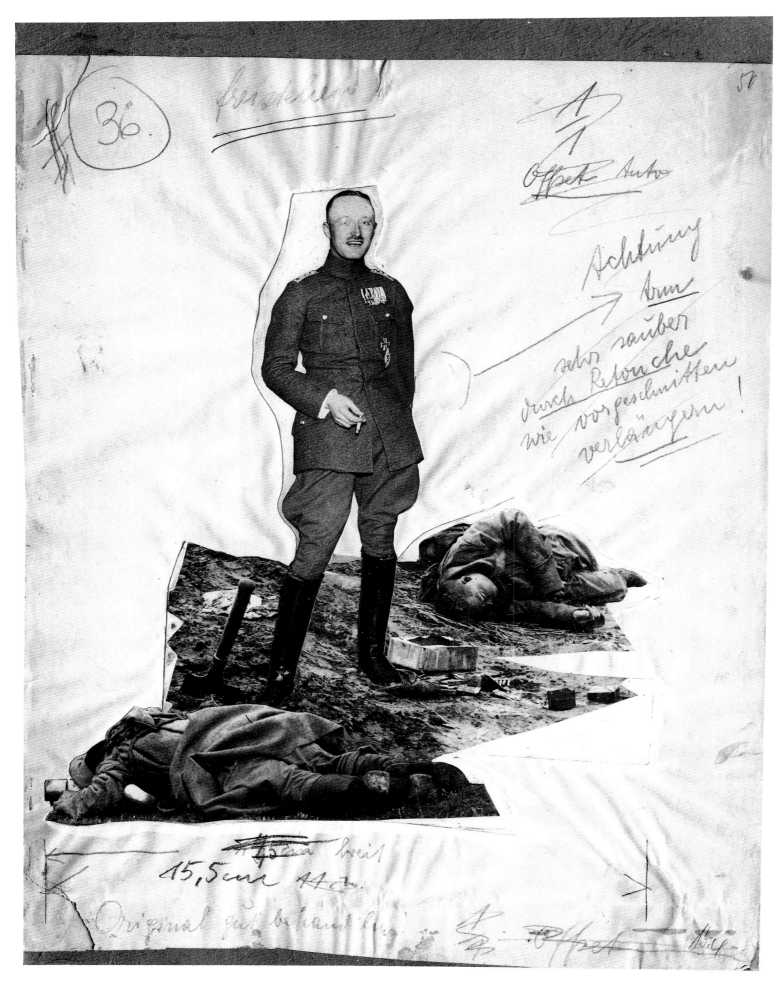

50   "Comrades! People! Property and Blood Have Been Sacrificed Incessantly for the last 5 Years..."
Photomontage for *Der Knüppel*, no. 6, June 1926, unpag. Cat. no. 179

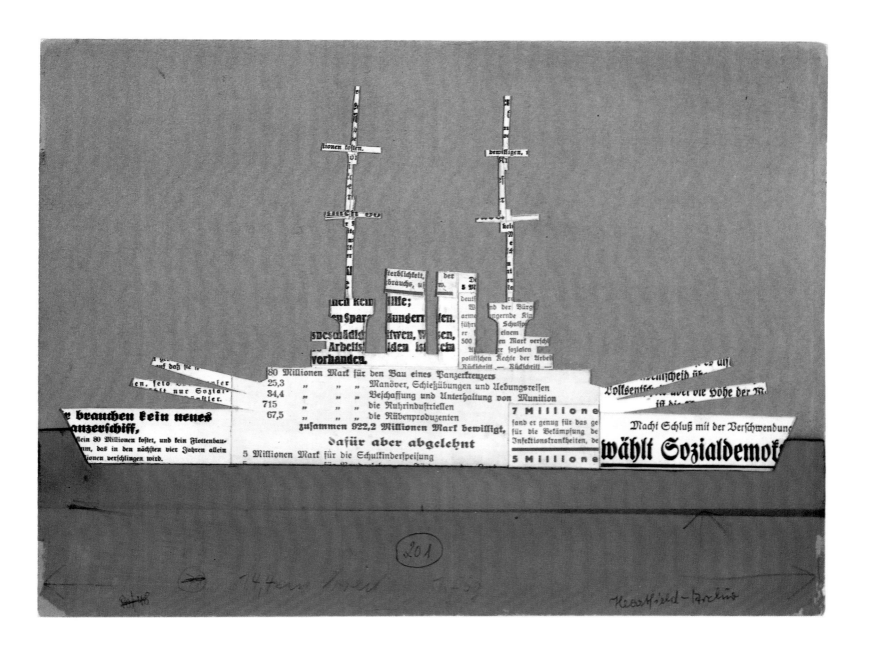

51   "Solution to the Ingenious Picture Puzzle." Montage for *Hurra! Der Panzerkreuzer A ist da!*
[*Hurray! The Armored Cruiser A is Here!*], special leaflet of the German Communist Party, 1928, p. 8.
Cat. no. 191

Hurra! DER PANZERKREUZER A ist da!

15 PF.

Reichskanzler Müller–Franken

SCHWERER ALS 9 MILLIONEN STIMMZETTEL!

52a   "Heavier than 9 Million Ballots!." *Hurra! Der Panzerkreuzer A ist da!*, 1928, front page.

Cat. no. 186

Soz. ialismus in Sicht!

Neuestes SPD.-Ministerlied
(Besonders zynisch und schnoddrig zu singen)

Achtzig Millionen,
Achtzig Millionen
Kostet so'n kleines Panzerschiff.
Achtzig Millionen
Achtzig Millionen — —
In den Steuersäckel ein leichter Griff.
Und es war stets so der Welten Lauf:
Den Säckel füllt der Prolet wieder auf.
Achtzig Millionen,
Achtzig Millionen — —
Ein treuer Hund folgt auf den Pfiff.
Achtzig Millionen,
Achtzig Millionen — —
'ne Kleinigkeit! — für ein Panzerschiff!

Achtzig Millionen,
Gott soll uns verschonen,
Für die Opfer aus großer Zeit?!
Achtzig Millionen
Den Trägern von Kronen!
Doch für die Krüppel der Kriege — —
Das führt zu weit!
Wir opferten schwerer für's Vaterland,
Verloren das letzte Quantum Verstand!
Achtzig Millionen
Für blaue Bohnen
Gaben und geben wir jederzeit!
Wir verschwenden Milliarden
Und nicht nur Millionen,
Gilt es des Bürgertums Herrlichkeit.

Achtzig Millionen,
Achtzig Millionen
Soll'n wir an bettelnde Kinder verschenken?
Achtzig Millionen — —
Man will uns entthronen:
Wir sollen der Witwen und Waisen ge-
denken!!
Neun Millionen, die uns gewählt,
Sind empört, daß wir im Mai
ihnen Märchen erzählt.
Na, neun Millionen,
Wir müssen betonen,
Sind eine kleine Minderheit
Von sechzig Millionen,
Die Deutschland bewohnen.
Unser Wirken ist der gesamten „Mensch-
heit" geweiht.

Achtzig Millionen
Für Bauten zum Wohnen?
Obdachlose, seid doch gescheit!
Achtzig Millionen,
Sie werden's uns lohnen.
Stell'n wir für „Höhere Zwecke" bereit.
Wir bewilligten schon einmal Kriegskredite,
Nahmen den Kindern die letzte Schnitte.
Achtzig Millionen
Für Panzer, Kanonen.
Verpulvern wir gern, wenn es endlich so
weit!
Milliarden, Billionen — —
Selbst unsere — — Pensionen!
Damit man uns vom Bolschewismus befreit.

John Heartfield.

Die Fahrt in den Sozialismus

Es waren noch nicht drei Jahre seit jenem denkwürdigen Volksentscheid über den Bau von Kriegsschiffen vergangen, da hatte die ganze SPD. mit ihren Plüschsofas auf einem Panzerkreuzer bequem Platz. „Seht ihr", sagte Scheidemann, wie gut, daß wir damals den Panzerkreuzer gebaut haben. Jetzt wissen wir wenigstens, wozu er gut ist." Und Bernstein brachte einen längeren Antrag ein, der auf deutsch ungefähr besagte, die SPD. solle mit der praktischen Verwirklichung nicht länger zögern und auf dem Panzerkreuzer ins Weltmeer hinaussteuern und sehen, ob sich nicht doch irgendwo der Sozialismus entdecken lasse. Und so geschah es. Die SPD. schiffte sich ein, was ihr nicht schwer fiel, und die Fahrt begann.

Schon das Leben an Bord hatte etwas von jenem Idealzustand, für den die Sozialdemokratie jahraus, jahrein das Martyrium einer Koalitionspolitik erlitten hatte. Hilferding, Crispien und Stampfer kochten täglich die Suppe, die die Mitglieder unter Aufsicht von Severing auszulöffeln hatten. Scheidemann war die ganze Zeit über beschäftigt, die Fahne nach dem Wind zu hängen, während Kautsky von der hohlen Warte, auf die er zu leben gewohnt war, Umschau nach dem Sozialismus halten mußte. Sie hatten Proviant für ein ganzes Jahr und als eiserne Ration die gesamten Zeitungsnummern des „Vorwärts" von seinem Erscheinen an. Außerdem hatten sie sich mit Parolen eingedeckt, die ausgegeben wurden, sowie sich Hunger bemerkbar machte, denn danach verging jedem sofort der Appetit. Endlich nahte der historische Augenblick, wo dem Kautsky zu rufen hatte: „Sozialismus in Sicht!" (siehe unser nebenstehendes Bild).

„Täuschst du dich auch nicht?" fragte Philipp vorsichtshalber, „ist es wirklich der, den wir suchen?" „Ja," rief Kautsky herunter. „Ich sehe ihn fast genau so, wie Marx ihn sich vorgestellt hat!" „Na, wir werden es ja erleben", meinten alle, und die Spannung stieg aufs höchste.

Wer aber beschreibt ihr Entsetzen, als sie beim Näherkommen entdecken mußten, daß sie sich in Sowjetrußland befanden. „Rettungsboote zu Wasser!" rief Philipp aufgeregt, „rette sich, wer kann!", und es dauerte nur wenige Augenblicke und das Schiff war von allen verlassen und schwamm melancholisch weiter der Küste zu. Die Sozialdemokraten aber ruderten mit aller Macht rückwärts und versuchten wieder den rettenden Hafen der demokratischen Republik zu erreichen, denn den Sozialismus hatten sie nicht gemeint.

Immer auf dem Boden der Tatsachen,
aber diesmal schwankt er mehr als sonst!

Scheidemann   Hilferding   Noske   Löbe   Müller

Photomontagen von John Heartfield

UNSERE BLAUEN JUNGENS

Wissell   Severing   Hilferding   Müller   Koch

Gruppenaufnahme der sozialdemokratischen Reichsminister auf der Parteikonferenz der SPD. Es ist begreiflich, daß bei diesem Anblick die Opposition umfiel

Panzerkreuzer-Sonate

(Melodie:
„Ich hab mein Herz in Heidelberg verloren...")

Am 20. im Maien
Und kurz noch nach der Wahl,
Da war von den Parteien
Der Sozi so sozial.
Ein Kriegsschiff? — Ausgeschlossen!
Doch die Steuer wird gesenkt.
Der Parteivorstand, der Parteivorstand
Ganz heimlich bei sich denkt:

Refrain:
Ist der Ministersessel erst erklettert,
Dann wird bewilligt, daß der Panzer klirrt.
Und wenn wir vorher noch so sehr gewettert,
Mein Gott, da hab'n wir eben uns geirrt.
Herr Künstler schlägt den Schaum in großen
              Bogen,
Der „Vorwärts" ist drei Tage radikal.
Doch schaukelt bald die Flotte auf den Wogen,
Und Noske, der wird Admiral.

Was schrei'n die Kommunisten?
Nach Osten fährt das Schiff!
Als ob sie gar nicht wüßten,
Daß es untauglich ist.
Ihm fehlt doch die Tonnage,
Doch türmen kann es fein.
Und so renken wir, und so renken wir,
Die Krise wieder ein.
Refrain:

Es dämmern uns im Herzen,
Wenn der November tagt,
Wie wir mit großen Schmerzen,
Den Kaiser weggejagt.
Und kehrst du einstmals wieder,
Wir seh'n den Irrtum ein,
Und dann singen wir, und dann singen wir,
Mit dir die Wacht am Rhein.
Refrain:

DA WUNDERN SICH SELBST DIE FLUNDERN

„Der schlägt aber mächtig Schaum"
„Den hat doch auch die SPD. gebaut"

Kreuzerglossen

Reichskanzler Müller-Frankens auffallende Aehnlichkeit mit Wilhelm II. steht außer Frage.
Wieso denn?
Nun, er zeigt eine besondere Vorliebe für Wilhelms Lieblingsdevise: „Deutschlands Zukunft liegt auf dem Wasser!"

Gut beobachtet!
Während der letzten Parteikonferenz der SPD. bemerkte ein Zuhörer im Hinblick auf die Opposition: „Die Blase hält nicht mehr zusammen. Es wird dauernd von Schiffen geredet."

Was will man mehr!
„Was ist der Unterschied zwischen Mai 1928 und August 1928?"
„Im Mai behaupteten die Kommunisten, die SPD. werde in der Regierung nur die Geschäfte des Bürgerblocks fortführen.
Richtig: denn im August behaupten sogar die Sozialdemokraten, daß sie den Panzerkreuzer nur auf Anordnung der alten Bürgerblockregierung bauen."

Größte Manövrierfähigkeit gesichert
Wie wir hören, sollen alle b e s o n d e r s leicht d r e h - u n d w e n d b a r e n Teile auf dem Panzerkreuzer A mit sozialdemokratischen Parolen versehen werden.

Sollmann will sich nicht scheiden lassen!
Sollmann kommt nun auf die Sitzungen des Parteiausschusses und der Reichstagsfraktion in Berlin zu sprechen und erklärt, alles was über diese Sitzungen in der bürgerlichen Presse zu lesen ist, ist aus den Fingern gesogen. Es ist keinem von uns eingefallen, etwa unseren Ministergenossen die Achtung zu versagen. Was müßten wir für schlechte Genossen sein! Wenn Sie sich wegen jedes Fehlers von Ihrer Frau scheiden ließen, wo kämen Sie da hin!
Sollmann vor den Kölner SPD.-Funktionären.

Auflösung des raffinierten Vexier-Pusselspieles

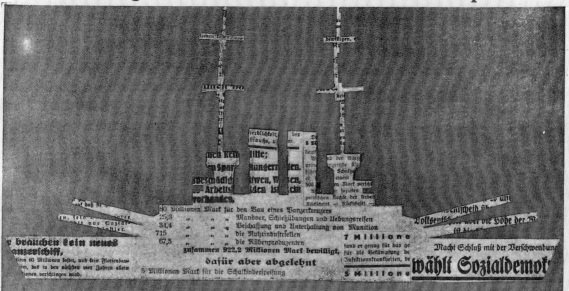

Zusammengeschnitten aus Original-Wahlflugblättern der SPD. von John Heartfield

aus den Wahlnummern der sozialdemokratischen Presse vom Mai 1928, auf die 9 Millionen Wähler hineingefallen sind

Schrittweise zum Sozialismus!

Rede zur Panzerkreuzerfrage nach der Referenteninstruktion der SPD.

Genossen und Genossinnen! Es soll nicht verkannt werden, daß der Panzerkreuzer die Parteireferenten — gewissermaßen — vor eine schwere Situation stellt. Aber wir haben schon schwierigere Kisten geschoben! Denkt doch bloß an die Wochen nach dem Kapp-Putsch, an die Reichswehrexekutive gegen Sachsen u. dgl. Es kommt nur darauf an, wie man es den Massen beibringt! Wir als verantwortungsbewußte Führer müssen — gewissermaßen — auch mal den Mut zur Unpopularität haben.

Wie liegen denn die Dinge, Genossen und Genossinnen? Welches sind jetzt unsere Aufgaben, wo sich der Mitglieder — gewissermaßen — eine Erregung bemächtigt hat? Wir müssen unbedingt nachweisen, daß sich unsere Regierungsmitglieder — einerseits — in einer gewissen Zwangslage befunden haben, — andererseits — aber auch, daß das neue Schiff — gewissermaßen — militärisch harmlos ist. Ich gebe sogar noch weiter und mache mich erbötig, unsere alten Parteifunktionäre zu überzeugen, daß der Kreuzerneubau absolut im Interesse der Arbeiter, des Friedens und des Sozialismus liegt! (Zwischenruf: Quadratur des Kreises!) Das scheint nur so, gewissermaßen, Genosse Seydewitz. Es kommt darauf an, wie man es macht! (Lebhaftes: Sehr richtig! — Neuer Zwischenruf: Was haben wir vor den Wahlen versprochen?) Darauf antworte ich: Mit Sentimentalitäten macht man heutzutage keine Staatspolitik! Verbrennt doch einfach eure alten Wahlredenmanuskripte! (Sehr gut!)

Also Genossen und Genossinnen! Wir müssen den Massen vor allem beibringen, daß wir — gewissermaßen — den Beschluß der Bürgerblockregierung durchführen mußten. Das klingt absurd, aber — gewissermaßen — nur auf den ersten Blick. Das ist durchaus parlamentarisch und demokratisch, Genossen. Es ist z. B. auch der Fall denkbar, daß nach uns mal wieder eine Bürgerregierung kommt. Angenommen nun, es liegt von uns aus ein noch nicht verwirklichter Beschluß vor — beispielsweise — Sozialisierung des Bergbaus vor. Wenn wir jetzt nicht den Panzerkreuzer bauen, würden doch die Bürgerlichen in diesem Fall die Sozialisierung auch nicht durchführen. — Ja, seht ihr, Genossen, als Staatsmann muß man eben an alles denken!

Schließlich stand die Frage doch so, ob der Panzerkreuzer von einer rein bürgerlichen, oder von einer Koalitionsregierung gebaut wird. Der Unterschied ist gar nicht so belanglos, wie es manchem Genossen erscheint. Dadurch, daß unsere Genossen sich daran beteiligten, wurden — gewissermaßen — die republikanischen Belange gewahrt. In der Offiziersmesse wird Eberts Bild neben Hindenburg und Prinz Heinrich hängen. So, Genossen und Genossinnen, wird der republikanische Gedanke — gewissermaßen — langsam, aber sicher, auch in der Marine verankert. Und dann noch eins! Bei Auslandsreisen wird der Panzerkreuzer A neben der schwarzweißroten Kriegsflagge auch ab und zu die Handelsflagge mit der schwarzrotgoldenen Gösch zeigen.

Mancher stellt sich etwas schwerfällig an. Nichts ist leichter, als zu beweisen, daß in einem kommenden Krieg Panzerschiffe nur altes Eisen sind. Den Ausschlag geben da U-Boote, Bombenflieger und Gastanks. Kein Kommunist kann uns nachweisen, daß wir für so etwas gestimmt haben. (Zuruf: Weil die Entente das verbietet!!) Auf diesen Zuruf, Genosse Levi, gebe ich nicht ein! (Lebhaftes: Sehr richtig!) (Neuer Zwischenruf: 80 Millionen für altes Eisen!) Darauf komme ich eben! Das ist ja das Großartige, daß uns das Schiff sozusagen keinen Pfennig kostet. Denn die Millionen müssen ja bei den anderen Posten des Wehretats wieder eingespart werden. In Wirklichkeit wird also durch dieses Schiff unsere Abrüstung — gewissermaßen — von hinten herum — begonnen, ohne daß unsere Militaristen das merken. Der neue Panzerkreuzer ist also — gewissermaßen — nur ein Ausfluß unserer pazifistischen Haltung. Wenn man das den Genossen nur richtig klar macht (Zuruf) und, wie Genosse Crispien ganz richtig bemerkt, an die Rote Armee und Flotte Sowjetrußlands erinnert, dann wird es auch kapiert.

Aber, Genossen und Genossinnen, die 80 Millionen sind keineswegs ins Wasser geworfen. Sie kommen indirekt

Wider das östliche Analphabetentum
oder die Kulturmission der Sozialdemokratie

Zeichnung von George Grosz

Crispien: „Wir werden den Russen schon das ABC und D beibringen!"

den Arbeitslosen der Werft- und Metallindustrie als produktive Erwerbslosenhilfe zugute. Wenn die Kommunisten trotzdem gegen den Kreuzer auftreten, so erhellt daraus, daß sie in Wirklichkeit für die Arbeitslosen gar nichts übrig haben! Auch ihr Antrag, das Geld für Kinderspeisung zu verwenden, ist nur Moskauer Demagogie. Die Arbeiter ziehen Arbeit „Wohltaten" vor, weil sie sich sagen:

„Nicht betteln, nicht bitten. Nur mutig gestritten!"

Wir können, angesichts der Massenarbeitslosigkeit — gewissermaßen — gar nicht genug Schiffe bauen. Das ist ein Stück praktische Gegenwartsarbeit, nur so kommen wir — gewissermaßen schrittweise — zum Sozialismus! Unter diesem Gesichtspunkt haben unsere Genossen in der Regierung zugestimmt.

Ich sehe an dem Kopfnicken der Genossin Toni Sender, daß sie das — gewissermaßen — auch einsieht. Also warum dann die ganze Aufregung, Genossen? Es soll mal einer kommen, der es besser macht. Die Kommunisten ganz gewiß nicht! Die pfeifen trotz allen Geschreis — gewissermaßen — schon auf dem letzten Loch. Erst dieser Tage ist wieder ein kommunistischer Gemeindevertreter zu uns übergetreten. Und in Moskau, da haben die Arbeiter trotz zehn Jahre Räteregiment noch nicht jeder eine Villa. Daran muß man immer wieder erinnern, das zieht bei unseren Genossen — gewissermaßen — immer noch am besten!

Im übrigen: laßt unsere Genossen ruhig ein bißchen toben, die Genossen Rosenfeld und Aufhäuser können ruhig ein paar scharfe Resolutionen fabrizieren. Das wird sogar ganz gut sein! Deshalb bleibt doch alles bei der Stange, und bis zu den nächsten Wahlen ist noch lange hin. Uns kriegt keiner wieder aus die Regierung! Uns kann — gewissermaßen — keiner es so dick geben, wie wir es vertragen können! Die verantwortlichen Genossen wissen schon, was sie zu tun haben. Also, Genossen, nur nicht ängstlich sein. Uns kann keiner (Lebhafter Beifall.) Karl Grünberg

Was kümmert's uns ...!

Was kümmert's uns, wenn Kinder Hunger leiden,
Mögen sie auf der Strecke bleiben!
Wir bauen Panzerkreuzer, Deutschland zum Gewinn
Und halten den Kanzlerposten in treudeutschem Sinn.

Was kümmert's uns, geht's gegen die Sowjetunion.
Wir streichen vom Etat nicht eine einzige Million.
Wir lassen uns nicht lumpen, wir halten stand:
Kämpfen mit Hindenburg für Kreuzer und Vaterland.

Was kümmert uns alles! Wir haben den Kriegsächtungspakt,
Wir haben in Brüssel schwarz-rot-gold geflaggt,
Wir haben uns die Parole gestellt:
„Deutschland wieder v o r a n in der Welt!"

Was kümmert's uns, daß der Pöbel gegen uns tobt.
Hauptsache, wir werden von den Nationalen gelobt.
Wir erringen, daß sei unser Schwur,
Mit Phosgen und Kreuzer — Deutschlands höchste Kultur.

Wir aber, wir Proleten, tragen im Blut
Lenins Vermächtnis als höchstes Gut!
Wir werden schützen mit starker Hand
Sowjetrußland — unser Vaterland!

P. Bartolain.

Herausgegeben vom Zentralkomitee der Kommunistischen Partei Deutschlands. — Verantwortlich für den gesamten Inhalt: Hugo Eberlein, M. d. L., Berlin. — Druck: „Peuvag" Papier-Erzeugungs- und Verwertungs-Akt.-Ges., Abteilung Friedrichstadt-Druckerei, Berlin C 25, Kleine Alexanderstraße 28.

52d "Solution to the Ingenious Picture Puzzle." *Hurra! Der Panzerkreuzer A ist da!*, 1928, p. 8.
Cat. no. 189

139

Alexander Abusch, 1976

In the case of *Die Rote Fahne* [*The Red Flag*], we said, "My dear Jonny, we've got to turn out one of the paper's [front] pages for next Sunday; it's got to be something really special." [...] We kept saying, "Five, the five, the five," and so on, "What can you say about it? Vote for List 5, the Communist Party [...] What can you say about it that's new?" And then one of us said, "The hand's got five fingers." And at once Jonny jumped up and said, "Yes, that's right. The hand's got five fingers!" And that was really all there was to it. The party achieved great success at the elections, not least with the help of that wonderful poster of Heartfield's. [...] But, of course, without *Die Rote Fahne*, without the Communist Party, without the huge mass movement, this would never have happened. But then again, it is true that without Heartfield somebody or other might have said, "The hand's got five fingers." And that would have been the end of it, and if Heartfield hadn't had the idea, nothing would have come of it. That's what makes the artist; that's life, and that's art and the connection between life and art.

From a conversation with Alexander Abusch, in Eckhard Siepmann, *Montage: John Heartfield: Vom Club Dada zur Arbeiter-Illustrierten-Zeitung*, pp. 123–24. Berlin, 1977.

Eckhard Siepmann, 1977

After the KPD [German Communist Party] had discontinued its satirical magazine, *Der Knüppel* [*The Club*], Heartfield published a series of photomontages on the front page of *Die Rote Fahne*. The appreciation thus expressed to him by the Party marked a stage in his artistic development. At the same time, it reflected the enthusiasm with which the revolutionary workers in the twenties began to acclaim his works.

[...] Abusch's claim that Heartfield's art found unanimous approval with the agitprop section of the Party probably would not hold up under closer inspection; by some accounts, Heartfield's patience was often tried in debates with the comrades in charge — as far as the aesthetic side of his work was concerned; at the same time, he emphasized repeatedly how decisive that political reorientation was for his later work.

Siepmann, *op. cit.*, p. 121.

53 "The Hand Has 5 Fingers . . ." *Die Rote Fahne* [*The Red Flag*], May 13, 1928, front page.
Cat. no. 192

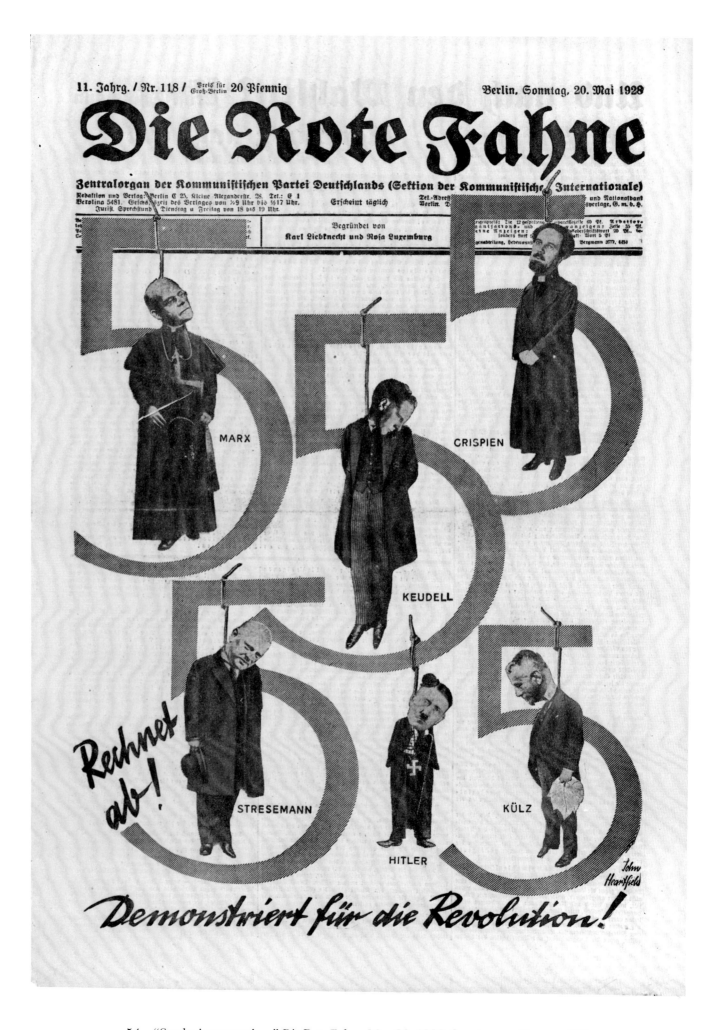

54   "Settle Accounts! . . ." *Die Rote Fahne*, May 20, 1928, front page. Cat. no. 183

55 "Strike at it! Subscribe!." *Die Rote Fahne*, October 14, 1928, front page. Cat. no. 185

56   "Be as Determined as These Three . . ." *Die Rote Fahne*, May 17, 1928, front page.
Cat. no. 182

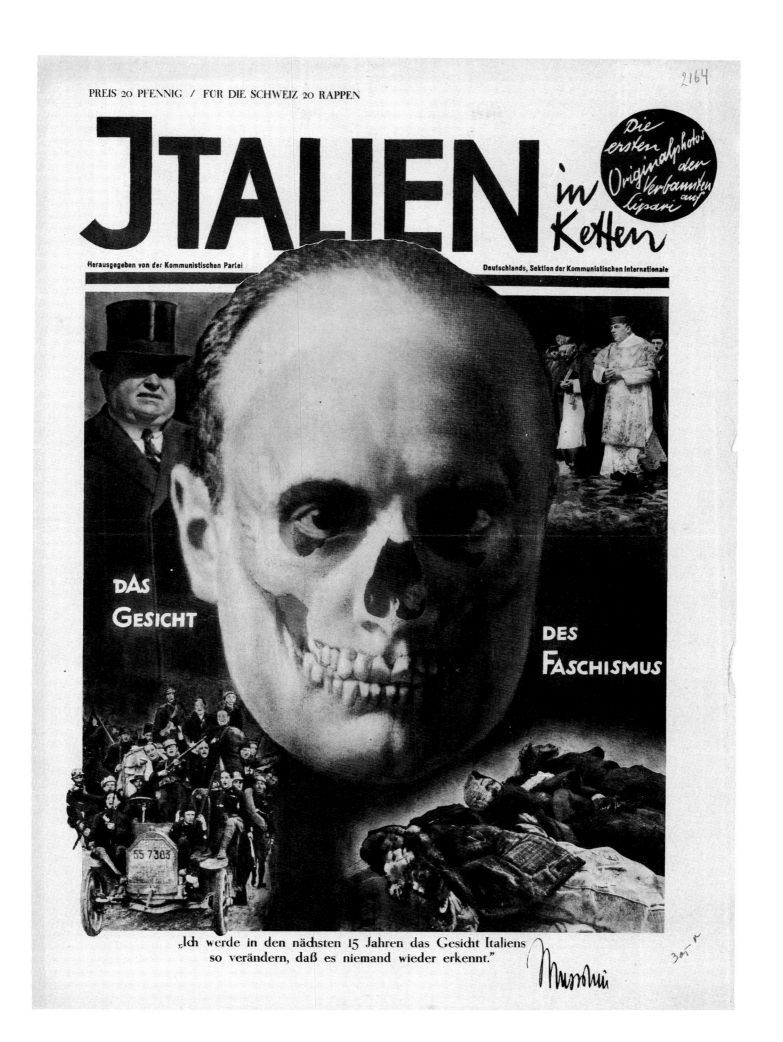

57   "The Face of Fascism." *Italien in Ketten* [*Italy in Chains*], 1928, front page. Cat. no. 105

58   "Fight with us!." Election poster, 1930. Cat. no. 225 (reprint)

59 "Capitalism is Robbing Them of Their Last Piece of Bread . . ." Election poster, 1932. Cat. no. 226

147

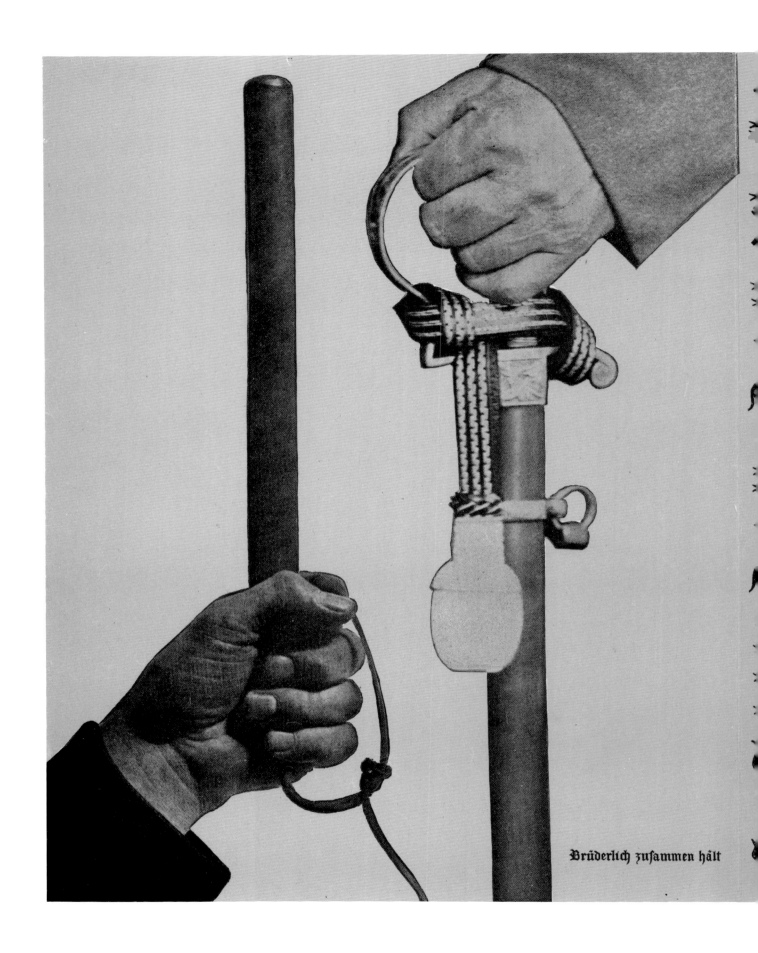

Brüderlich zusammen hält

60a Kurt Tucholsky, *Deutschland, Deutschland über alles*. Dust jacket, 1929. Cat. no. 316

Statistik

Wir sind ein armes Land. Ich, der gelernte Arbeiter mit Frau und drei Kindern, arbeite 50 Tage im Jahre nicht für mich —

über 2 Tage arbeite ich für die Reichswehr, und zwei weitere Tage im Jahre arbeite ich, damit wir eine schöne Polizei haben.

46

60b   Kurt Tucholsky, *Deutschland, Deutschland über alles*, 1929, p. 46. Cat. no. 318

Einen halben Tag muß ich für die Kirche arbeiten, der ich gar nicht mehr angehöre, und

47

eine Woche für die Beamten. für alle die vielen über-
flüssigen Beamten.

Dafür habe ich es dann mit der Kunst und Wissenschaft
leichter; das ist in 3 Stunden gemacht.

Wir sind ein armes Land!

Wir haben 28 807 988 Mark allein in Preußen für
Pferdezucht übrig und

48

60d   Kurt Tucholsky, *Deutschland, Deutschland über alles*, 1929, p. 48. Cat. no. 318

wenig zu essen,

aber 230 990 Mark für die Seelsorge in der Reichswehr und 2 164 000 Mark für die Umzüge unserer Botschafter und Gesandten, denn wenn die nicht umzögen, was hätten sie sonst zu tun? Und

49

ich, der Buchhalter, beziehe ein Jahresgehalt von 3600 Mark, und meine Frau gibt wöchentlich 40 Mark aus. Und 433 Wochen müßte ich arbeiten, um so viel zu erarbeiten, wie der Herr Tirpitz, der die deutsche Flotte danebenorganisiert hat, als Pension bekommt. Herr Schlachtenverlierer Ludendorff bekommt 17000 Mark,

50

60f Kurt Tucholsky, *Deutschland, Deutschland über alles*, 1929, p. 50. Cat. no. 318

denn wir zahlen an Pensionen für die alten Monarchisten im Jahr 206 931 960 Mark, denn wir habens ja — das heißt: eigentlich haben wirs nicht, aber was ist da zu tun, wenn wir doch einen neuen Panzerkreuzer haben müssen, der 80 Millionen Mark kostet! Und wenn die Offiziere morgens spazierenreiten müssen, dann kann man keine schönen Augenkliniken haben; wir brauchen unser Geld anderswo.

51

4*

61   "German Sports." Photomontage for Kurt Tucholsky's *Deutschland, Deutschland über alles*, 1929, p. 109.
Cat. no. 319

Axel Eggebrecht, 1929

What is shown in this book on Germany actually has to be brought to the attention of a lot of people no matter what: proletarian hovels, eerily desolate palace façades, hotel lounges, generals' faces, prisons, champagne glasses, letters, animals – there's no use in itemizing. These are only a few randomly tasted ingredients of a savory salad you will have to taste yourself in order to feel the true warmth in your stomach. And under, above, and below these pictures Tucholsky has placed his small and large pieces: *Panter* blows, *Tiger* bites, *Wrobel* vignettes. Even the honorable Herr Wendriner has been called in. And a few of those poems stir our souls so intensely that melancholy and resignation evaporate and we boil in hot anger and bitter rage. The title of this book is not intended altogether ironically, though. It has always been suspected that only disappointed love could be so constant and brutally hostile. This time, Tucholsky confesses at the end of it all his love for this country, in a curiously faint and moving way (m-o-v-i-n-g, people!). And that is possibly the most beautiful thing. – The book can be studied in detail just as well as it can be skimmed over. A hundred times we are forced to the ground by hate, brutality, banality, and shame, only to be revived again by trenchancy and serene assurance. Perhaps this is the only expedient way nowadays to propagate the will to change, to renew, to improve; in other words the will to revolutionize this dormant country. If this book were to turn out to be quite a big success, it might be realized that the dream of awakening is still very vivid in Germany.

Axel Eggebrecht, review of *Deutschland, Deutschland über alles*, in *Die literarische Welt*, (34, 1929), pp. 5–6.

62   "The Dormant Reichstag." Negative montage for Kurt Tucholsky's *Deutschland, Deutschland über alles*, 1929, p. 138.
Cat. no. 320

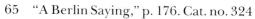

63–66 Photomontages for Kurt Tucholsky's *Deutschland, Deutschland über alles*, 1929

67   "Subjects." Photomontage for Kurt Tucholsky's *Deutschland, Deutschland über alles*, 1929, p. 152.
Cat. no. 325

68   "German Talking Film." Photomontage for Kurt Tucholsky's *Deutschland, Deutschland über alles*, 1929, p. 225.
Cat. no. 326

69   "Sticking Together Fraternally." Photomontage for Kurt Tucholsky's *Deutschland, Deutschland über alles*, 1929, back cover. Cat. no. 317

70   "Gale Force 1917." *Volks-Illustrierte* [*People's Illustrated*] (*VI*, Prague), September 29, 1937, unpag.

Cat. no. 289

Peter Gorsen, 1973

The image-text-montages and the so-called "picture poems," which earned the *AIZ* so much praise and fame even in the bourgeois history of the press, thus came from the need to dismantle the available material of the bourgeois photo agencies and to put it in another context related to the class perspective of the proletarian dictatorship and its sympathizers; it was more than simply due to a general aesthetic originality in inventing and fabricating layouts. The creative design – the "spectacular" proletarian newspaper aesthetic – ensued from the requirements of a reportaging intent on serving the suppressed needs of the working class for information, education, and entertainment. [...]

As in Heartfield's case, we are dealing with the conversion and ideologization of material (partly familiar from the bourgeois press as well) from the viewpoint of the suppressed, struggling proletariat. [...] The quoted news as factual material already commented upon, already assessed, is ruined and put to a different use, one that makes transparent the class antagonism that allowed diverse interpretations of the very same material.

Peter Gorsen, "'Das Auge des Arbeiters' – Anfänge der proletarischen Bildpresse," in *Ästhetik und Kommunikation*, pp. 11–13, 10, 1973.

Ernst Bloch, 1938

[...] in [the montage] there is a friction of pertinent moments, a flash is produced that illuminates whole situations; John Heartfield photographs an old model of a ship, uses ration cards for sails, the text reads: "Gale force 1917. Now we're sailing into the grand age." Brecht makes a montage from situations stretched to the extreme in his new play *Furcht und Elend des Dritten Reichs* (*99 Prozent*) [*The Private Life of the Master Race*]. He instructively highlights the trouble brewing, the nastiness and ticklish danger, the contradictions of the regime; the reader will make sense of it for himself. Those are the advantages of a descriptive depiction; it delves right into the depths of Nazi life, with fire tongs, as is appropriate here.

Ernst Bloch, "Der Nazi und das Unsägliche," in *Das Wort*, 9, 1938, p. 114; also in *Gesamtausgabe*, 11, *Politische Messungen, Pestzeit, Vormärz*, pp. 185–92; here: pp. 190–91. Suhrkamp Verlag, Frankfurt/Main, 1970.

71　"Little SA man, What Now?" *Arbeiter-Illustrierte-Zeitung* (*AIZ*, Berlin), December 25, 1932, p. 1227.
Cat. no. 221

DEUTSCHE NATURGESCHICHTE

DEUTSCHER TOTENKOPF-FALTER
(Acherontia atropos germanica) in seinen
drei Entwicklungsstufen: Raupe, Puppe, Falter

METAMORPHOSE

»Metamorphose«, (griechisch μορφή - Gestalt) bedeutet: 1. In der Mythologie: die Verwandlung von Menschen in Bäume, Tiere, Steine u. s. w. 2. In der Zoologie: die Entwicklung mancher Tiere über Larvenformen und Puppen, beispielsweise Raupe, Puppe, Schmetterling. 3. In der Geschichte der weimarer Republik: die geradlinige Folge EBERT — HINDENBURG — HITLER.

Fotomontage: John Heartfield

72 "German Natural History." *Arbeiter-Illustrierte-Zeitung* (*AIZ*, Prague), August 16, 1934, p. 536.
Cat. no. 266

Zum Krisen-Parteitag der SPD

Die Sozialdemokratie will nicht den Zusammenbruch des Kapitalismus. Sie will wie ein Arzt zu heilen und zu bessern versuchen. (Fritz Tarnow, Vorsitzender des Holzarbeiterverbandes)

FOTO-MONTAGE: JOHN HEARTFIELD

Die Tierärzte von Leipzig: „Selbstverständlich werden wir dem Tiger die Zähne ausbrechen, aber zunächst einmal müssen wir ihn gesundpflegen und herausfüttern."

73   "On the Crisis Party Congress of the SPD [German Social Democratic Party]."
Arbeiter-Illustrierte-Zeitung (AIZ, Berlin), no. 24, 1931, p. 477. Cat. no. 207

Fotomontage: John Heartfield // Umschlagbild des „Braunbuchs über Reichstagsbrand und Hitlerterror" // Das Gesicht Goerings ist einer Originalfotografie entnommen und wurde nicht retuschiert.

74 "Goering: The Executioner of the Third Reich." *Arbeiter-Illustrierte-Zeitung* (*AIZ*, Prague),
September 14, 1933, front page. Cat. no. 241

Weil er sich aufs Programm der NSDAP berief

Reichsminister Dr. Frick:
„Der Herr Reichskanzler hat eindeutig festgestellt, daß die Revolution abgeschlossen ist. Wer weiterhin noch von einer Fortsetzung der Revolution oder von einer zweiten Revolution redet, muß sich darüber klar sein, daß er sich damit gegen den Führer selbst auflehnt und entsprechend behandelt wird".

Dreizehnhundert rebellische SA-Leute sind im Konzentrationslager Wilsede in der Lüneburger Heide untergebracht. Bei einem gemeinsamen „Fluchtversuch aus dem Lager" wurden 13 SA-Männer von SS erschossen.

Bei Gleiwitz O/S schoß SS auf SA-Männer, die gemeinsam mit den Arbeitern streikten. Drei SA-Leute wurden getötet.

Fotomontage
John Heartfield

„Dir werden wir unsern »Sozialismus« im Konzentrationslager schon beibringen"

75   "Because He Relied on the Program of the NSDAP [National Socialist German Workers' Party]."
Arbeiter-Illustrierte-Zeitung (*AIZ*, Prague), July 20, 1933, p. 483. Cat. no. 234

76　"A New Man — Master of a New World." *Arbeiter-Illustrierte-Zeitung* (*AIZ*, Prague),
November 1, 1934, front page. Cat. no. 272

77 "Hurray, the Butter is All Gone!." *Arbeiter-Illustrierte-Zeitung* (*AIZ*, Prague), December 19, 1935, p. 816.
Cat. no. 279

Faschistische Ruhmesmale

Denkmal des Duce in Abessinien

Fotomontage: John Heartfield

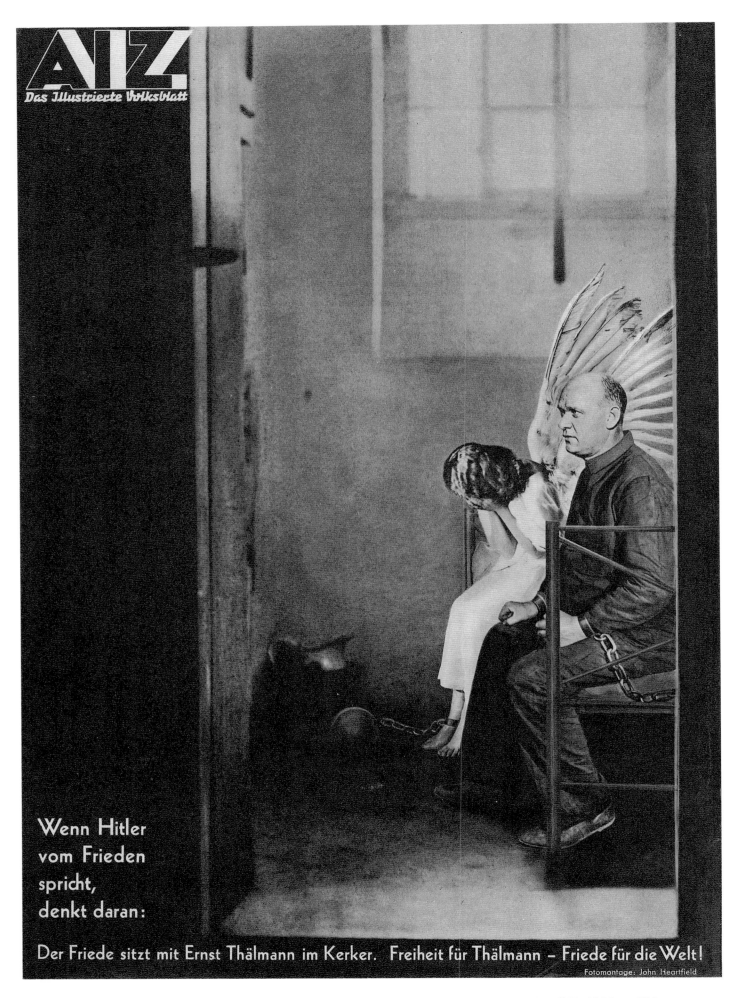

79 "When Hitler Talks of Peace . . ." *Arbeiter-Illustrierte-Zeitung* (*AIZ*, Prague), April 12, 1936, p. 256.
Cat. no. 281

Brauner Künstlertraum

„Der Berliner Bildhauer Georg Kolbe erhielt den ehrenhaften Auftrag, ein Denkmal des Generalissimus Franco zu schaffen. Gleichzeitig wurde er mit der Herstellung eines Beethovendenkmals für die Stadt Frankfurt am Main betraut."

Berliner Zeitungsmeldung

Selbstgespräch im Traum: „Franco und Beethoven, wie schaff' ich dies bloß? Am besten mach' ich wohl einen Kentauren, halb Tier, halb Mensch."

Montiert: John Heartfield.

Der friedfertige Raubfisch

„Ich verabscheue die kollektive Sicherheit! Ich lade die kleinen Fische einzeln ein, zweiseitige Verträge mit mir abzuschließen".

Fotomontage: John Heartfield

81 "The Peaceful Fish of Prey." *Volks-Illustrierte* (*VI*, Prague), May 12, 1937, p. 307.
Cat. no. 286

„In der Zeitschrift »Archiv für Biologie und Rassenforschung«, Berlin, ist ein Artikel unter dem Titel »Nutzen, welchen das Luftbombardement vom Standpunkt der rassischen Selektion und der Sozialhygiene bringt« erschienen. In dem Artikel heißt es u. a.: »Am meisten leiden unter Luftbombardements die stark bewohnten Teile der Städte. Da diese Gegenden zumeist vom Lumpenproletariat bewohnt sind, wird die Gesellschaft dadurch von diesen Elementen befreit. Schwere Bomben mit einem Gewicht von einer Tonne bringen nicht nur den Tod, sondern rufen auch sehr oft Irrsinn hervor. Menschen mit schwachen Nerven können derartige Erschütterungen nicht aushalten. Das gibt uns die Möglichkeit, Neurastheniker zu konstatieren. Dann bleibt nur noch übrig, solche Menschen zu sterilisieren. Dadurch wird die Reinheit der Rasse gesichert.«"
(Prager Abendzeitung, Nr. 118)

Tokio. (United Press.) Ein Sprecher der japanischen Marine, Vizeadmiral Noda, erklärte, daß die Marine mit den bisherigen Erfolgen des Bombardements auf Kanton sehr zufrieden sei. Die Bombardements würden fortgesetzt werden.

Das ist das Heil, das sie bringen!

Fotomontage: John Heartfield

82   "This is the Salvation They Bring!." *Volks-Illustrierte* (*VI*, Prague), June 29, 1938, unpag.
Cat. no. 293

Normalisierung

Der deutschen Kolonie in Österreich soll eine angemessene Möglichkeit zur gesellschaftlichen Betätigung gegeben werden.
Aus dem Abkommen zwischen Deutschland und Österreich über die Normalisierung der Beziehungen.

Dieses Zeichen ⌗ ist das
österreichische „Krukenkreuz"

„Diese kleine Differenz werden wir auch noch aus der Welt schaffen".

83   "Normalization." *Arbeiter-Illustrierte-Zeitung* (*AIZ*, Prague), July 29, 1936, p. 496.

Cat. no. 283

In Durango getötet durch faschistische Flieger: 12 Nonnen, 2 Priester. — In Durango zerstört durch dieselben Flieger: Kloster der Augustinerinnen, Jesuitenkirche, Kirche Santa Maria. — In Eibar getötet durch Junkersbomber: 112 katholische Männer, Frauen, Kinder und Geistliche. — In Amorebieta und Bilbao getötet durch Junkers- und Heinkelbomber: 480 katholische Männer, Frauen, Kinder und Geistliche. — In Guernica getötet durch nationalsozialistische Flieger Francos: 2000 Zivilpersonen, darunter die Mehrzahl Frauen und Kinder sowie mehrere Nonnen und Priester, alles katholische Basken. — In Guernica zerstört durch die gleichen Flieger: alle Kirchen bis auf eine einzige. — In Amorebieta zerstört durch Heinkelbomber: das abseits liegende, deutlich gekennzeichnete Augustinerkloster. — In Madrid zerstört seit Beginn der Belagerung: sieben Kirchen; beschädigt: fast alle. — In Almería zerstört durch die Schiffsgeschütze der deutschen Flotte: die Kathedrale, die Kirche des Heiligen Sebastian und das Hospiz. — In Durango getötet durch faschistische Flieger: 12 Nonnen, 2 Priester. — In Durango zerstört durch dieselben Flieger: Kloster der Augustinerinnen, Jesuitenkirche, Kirche Santa Maria. — In Eibar getötet durch Junkersbomber: 112 katholische Männer, Frauen, Kinder und Geistliche. — In Amorebieta und Bilbao getötet durch Junkers- und Heinkelbomber: 480 katholische Männer, Frauen, Kinder und Geistliche. — In Guernica getötet durch nationalsozialistische Flieger Francos: 2000 Zivilpersonen, darunter die Mehrzahl Frauen und Kinder sowie mehrere Nonnen und Priester, alles katholische Basken. — In Guernica zerstört durch die gleichen Flieger: alle Kirchen bis auf eine einzige. — In Amorebieta zerstört durch Heinkelbomber: das abseits liegende, deutlich gekennzeichnete Augustinerkloster. — In Madrid zerstört seit Beginn der Belagerung: sieben Kirchen; beschädigt: fast alle. — In Almería zerstört durch die Schiffsgeschütze der deutschen Flotte: die Kirche des Heiligen Sebastian und das Hospiz. — In Durango getötet durch faschistische Flieger: 12 Nonnen, 2 Priester. — In Durango zerstört durch dieselben Flieger: Kloster der Augustinerinnen, Jesuitenkirche, Kirche Santa Maria. — In Eibar getötet durch Junkersbomber: 112 katholische Männer, Frauen, Kinder und Geistliche. — In Amorebieta und Bilbao getötet durch Junkers- und Heinkelbomber: 480 katholische Männer, Frauen, Kinder und Geistliche. — In Guernica getötet durch nationalsozialistische Flieger Francos: 2000 Zivilpersonen, darunter die Mehrzahl Frauen und Kinder sowie mehrere Nonnen und Priester, alles katholische Basken. — In Guernica zerstört durch die gleichen Flieger: alle Kirchen bis auf eine einzige. — In Amorebieta zerstört durch Heinkelbomber: das abseits liegende, deutlich gekennzeichnete Augustinerkloster. — In Madrid zerstört seit Beginn der Belagerung: sieben Kirchen; beschädigt: fast alle. — In Almería zerstört durch die Schiffsgeschütze der deutschen Flotte: die Kathedrale, die Kirche des Heiligen Sebastian und das Hospiz. — In Durango...

Den katholischen Opfern des Faschismus zum Gedenken!
Allen katholischen Männern und Frauen zur Mahnung!

Christus-Marmorstatue von Balthasar Permoser (1651-1732)

Fotomontage: John Heartfield

84   "In Memory of the Catholic Victims of Fascism!. . ." *Volks-Illustrierte* (*VI*, Prague), June 9, 1937, p. 369.
Cat. no. 288

Illustration zu Grimms Märchen von der Katze und der Maus.

Es war einmal eine Katze und eine Maus, die beschlossen, fürderhin in eitel Freundschaft zu leben. Sie hatten als gemeinsamen Vorrat ein Töpfchen mit Schmalz angeschafft und hinter einem Haus verborgen. Eines Tages gelüstete es die Katze nach dem Schmalz und sie sagte: „Liebes Mäuslein, du mußt allein das Haus hüten, ich bin zu einer Kindstaufe eingeladen." Sie schlich zum Vorrat hin und schleckte die oberste Schmalzschicht ab. Als sie zurückkehrte, fragte die Maus: „Wie heißt das Kind?" — „Hautab," antwortete die Katze. Das Mäuslein entsetzte sich darob, doch ließ es sich nichts anmerken. Bald darauf mußte die Katze abermals zu einer Kindstaufe. Diesmal schleckte sie den Schmalztopf halb aus. „Wie heißt das Kind?" fragte die Maus wieder. „Halbaus", antwortete die Katze. Das Mäuslein entsetzte sich, aber es ließ alles beim alten bewenden. Die Katze gelüstete es aber auch noch nach dem Rest und sie nahm wieder einmal Urlaub unter dem Vorwand, daß sie ein drittesmal Pate stehen müsse. Diesmal leckte sie den Topf ganz aus. Als das Mäuslein sie wieder nach dem Namen des Kindes fragte, erwiderte sie: „Ganzaus!" — „O weh, was sind das für schreckliche Namen! Mir wird ganz angst und bange!" jammerte das Mäuslein. Da fuhr die Katze sie an: „Unterschreib mir einen Schein, daß ich auch mit dir Ganzaus machen kann, oder . . . ich freß dich, mein liebes Mäuslein!" Und wenn es nicht gestorben wär, so lebte es noch heute. Und wer's nicht glaubt, der zahlt einen harten Taler.

85 "Illustration for Grimm's Fairy Tale of the Cat and the Mouse." *Volks-Illustrierte* (*VI*, Prague), March 2, 1938, unpag. Cat. no. 291

86   ". . . The More Pictures They Remove, the More Visible Reality Becomes!."
Arbeiter-Illustrierte-Zeitung (*AIZ*, Prague), May 3, 1934, p. 288. Cat. no. 259

87   "The Most Gigantic Lying Mouth of All Times . . ." (obliterated by the censor).
Volks-Illustrierte (*VI*, Prague), October 5, 1938, unpag. Cat. no. 295

Bernd Kuhnert, 1976

To realize an idea for a picture, he had scissors, the tonal value of photographs, paint for retouching, and printing technology at his disposal. What resulted were original montages with an exciting, aggressive content and a technical mastery in the handling of the material means. He worked with the gray tones of a photograph just as a painter uses paint. Each tonal value is related to, and functionally depends on, the content.

All the montages were made to be printed. Therefore, the pasted original had to be retouched in order to be ready for printing. For example, the mouth and the lines of cheeks and eyes had to be accentuated by retouching, so that facial expressions would not become shallow in the course of the printing process. Dark areas were reworked with the air brush so that they would not appear too deep. Unequal tonal values among the various assembled photo fragments had to be balanced, and pasted edges made invisible by air brushing. Then the montage was ready and could be printed. Often, two per week were produced.

Very beautiful original montages emerged from this method of working. The assembled fragments consisted of brownish mat-sheen photographic paper in varied tonal gradations; to these were added mat air brush paint in varied tones: light gray to ochre, delicate blue to sepia and Chinese white, in order to separate or accentuate lines.

These tones were not employed for aesthetic reasons; they were determined by the technical process of printing.

Bernd Kuhnert, "Die Tonwerte bei Heartfield-Montagen," in Eckhard Siepmann, *Montage: John Heartfield. Vom Club Dada zur Arbeiter-Illustrierten-Zeitung*, p. 283. Berlin, 1977.

DER SINN VON GENF

Wo das Kapital lebt,
kann der Friede nicht leben!

A·I·Z

ERSCHEINT WÖCHENTLICH EINMAL — PREIS 20 PFG.,
Kc. 1,60, 30 GR., 30 SCHWEIZER RP. — V. b. b. —
— JAHRGANG XI — NR. 48 — 27. 11. 1932

In Genf, der Stadt des Völkerbundes, wurde mit
Maschinengewehren in die gegen den Faschismus
demonstrierenden Arbeitermassen geschossen.
15 Tote, über 60 Verwundete blieben auf dem Platze.
(Ausführliche Bildreportage unseres
Sonderberichterstatters auf den Innenseiten.)

Montage: JOHN·HEARTFIELD

88a   "The Meaning of Geneva." *Arbeiter-Illustrierte-Zeitung* (*AIZ*, Berlin), November 27, 1932, front page.

Cat. no. 219

88b   "The Meaning of Geneva." Photomontage for the *Arbeiter-Illustrierte-Zeitung* (*AIZ*, Berlin),
November 27, 1932, front page. Cat. no. 220

Zum Brandstifter-Prozess in Leipzig

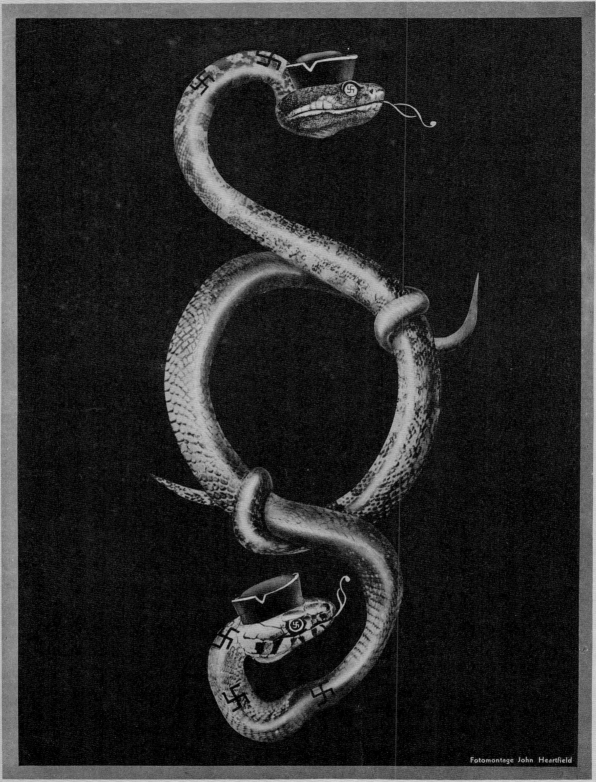

Sie winden sich und drehen sich und nennen sich deutsche Richter

89a   "... They Twist and Turn and Call Themselves German Judges." *Arbeiter-Illustrierte-Zeitung* (*AIZ*, Prague),

October 19, 1933, p. 691. Cat. no. 244

89b "... They Twist and Turn and Call Themselves German Judges." Photomontage for the *Arbeiter-Illustrierte-Zeitung*
(*AIZ*, Prague), October 19, 1933, p. 691. Cat. no. 245

NEUER LEHRSTUHL AN DEN DEUTSCHEN UNIVERSITÄTEN

VÖLKISCHE TIEFENSCHAU

Ein Professor Vitlawopsky von der Universität Heidelberg hat festgestellt, daß das menschliche Hühnerauge, allerdings nur das germanische, befähigt ist, in die Zukunft zu schauen. Hitler hat sogleich nach Bekanntwerden der Entdeckung des genialen Forschers die Überführung von 1300 Hühneraugenoperateuren ins Konzentrationslager angeordnet.

Original-Aufnahme aus dem teutonischen Busch von John Heartfield.

90a "New Chair at the German Universities." *Arbeiter-Illustrierte-Zeitung* (*AIZ*, Prague), August 31, 1933, p. 579. Cat. no. 239

186

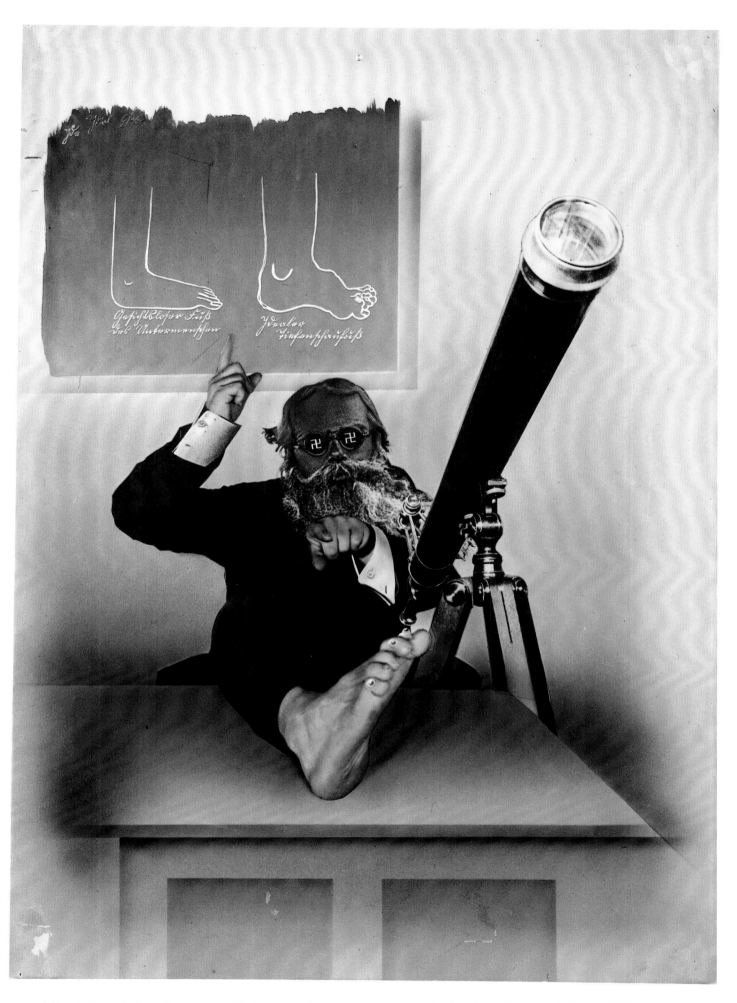

90b　"New Chair at the German Universities." Photomontage for the *Arbeiter-Illustrierte-Zeitung* (*AIZ*, Prague),
August 31, 1933, p. 579. Cat. no. 240

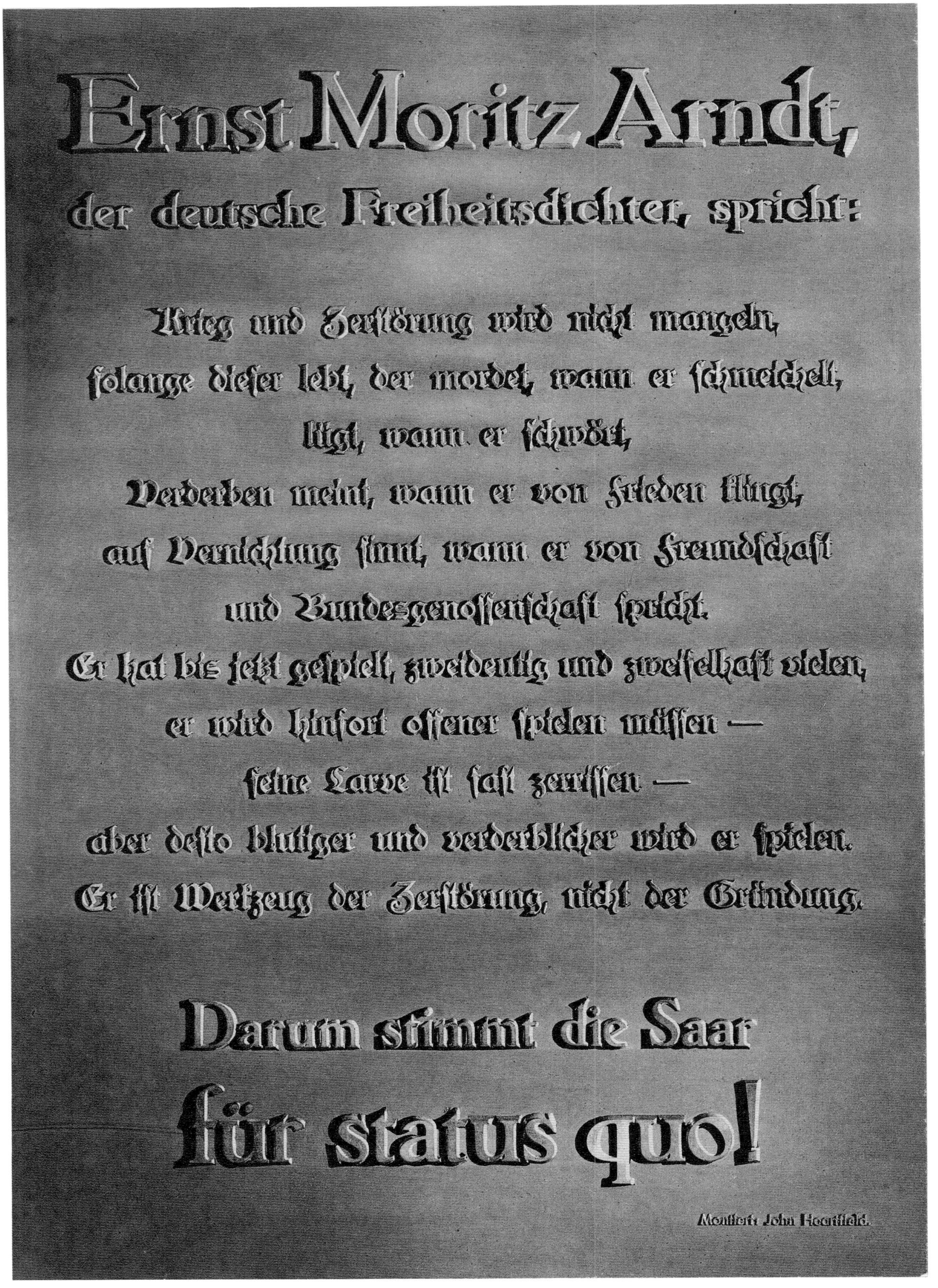

Ernst Moritz Arndt,
der deutsche Freiheitsdichter, spricht:

Krieg und Zerstörung wird nicht mangeln,
solange dieser lebt, der mordet, wann er schmeichelt,
lügt, wann er schwört,
Verderben meint, wann er von Frieden klingt,
auf Vernichtung sinnt, wann er von Freundschaft
und Bundesgenossenschaft spricht.
Er hat bis jetzt gespielt, zweideutig und zweifelhaft vielen,
er wird hinfort offener spielen müssen —
seine Larve ist fast zerrissen —
aber desto blutiger und verderblicher wird er spielen.
Er ist Werkzeug der Zerstörung, nicht der Gründung.

Darum stimmt die Saar
für status quo!

Montfort John Heartfield.

91a   "Ernst Moritz Arndt, the German Freedom Poet, Speaks…" *Arbeiter-Illustrierte-Zeitung* (*AIZ*, Prague),
188   January 17, 1935, p. 48. Cat. no. 277

91b "Ernst Moritz Arndt, the German Freedom Poet, Speaks . . ." Montage for the *Arbeiter-Illustrierte-Zeitung*
(*AIZ*, Prague), January 17, 1935, p. 48. Cat. no. 278

189

Hurra, Hurra! Der Brüning-Weihnachtsmann ist da!

Er hat uns Not verordnet
und Lohnabbau diktiert,
den Krankenschein besteuert,
dafür das Heer verteuert.
Er hat sich nicht geniert
Kriegsopfern, Blinden, Kindern
das Brot vom Mund zu reißen.
Um es den Großagrariern
und Schiebern nachzuschmeißen.
Auch Stillgeld ist ein Luxus,
das Trinken überhaupt.
Wir brauchen Panzerkreuzer.
Wer hungert — wird beraubt!
Ein deutscher Mann ist niemals
                    arbeitslos:
Die 4 Millionen sind vom Feind
                    bestochen,
sonst hätten sie sich längst verkrochen
und unsre arme Wirtschaft wär' sie los.
Das hat sogar die SPD begriffen
drum stellte sie sich Mann für Mann
zum Schutz der Notverordnung an.
(So folgt der Hund, wenn ihm
                    sein Herr gepfiffen.)
Herr Hitler rüstet unterdes zum
                    Wotansfeste
Sein Christbaumschmuck ist
                    anerkannt der beste
(Man kann zum Fest der Liebe
                    sich im Hängen üben!)
Wie jeder Papst fischt Adolf auch im
                    Trüben.

Es schließen Brüning, Hitler, Braun
(das war den Brüdern zuzutraun)
Burgfrieden unterm Weihnachtsbaum
auf daß die Dividenden steigen.

Doch aus ist dieser schöne Traum
wenn die Proleten zeigen,
daß sie zu kämpfen lernten . .
Wer Hakenkreuze sät, wird
                    rote Fäuste ernten!

Montiert: JOHN HEARTFIELD

Der Hitler-Christbaumschmuck ist keine böswillige Erfindung
Die Nationalsozialisten handeln tatsächlich damit

92a   "Hurray, Hurray! The Brüning Santa Claus is Here!." *Arbeiter-Illustrierte-Zeitung*
(*AIZ*, Berlin), no. 51, 1930, p. 1003. Cat. no. 202

92b "Hurray, Hurray! The Brüning Santa Claus is Here!." Photomontage for the *Arbeiter-Illustrierte-Zeitung* (*AIZ*, Berlin), no. 51, 1930, p. 1003. Cat. no. 203

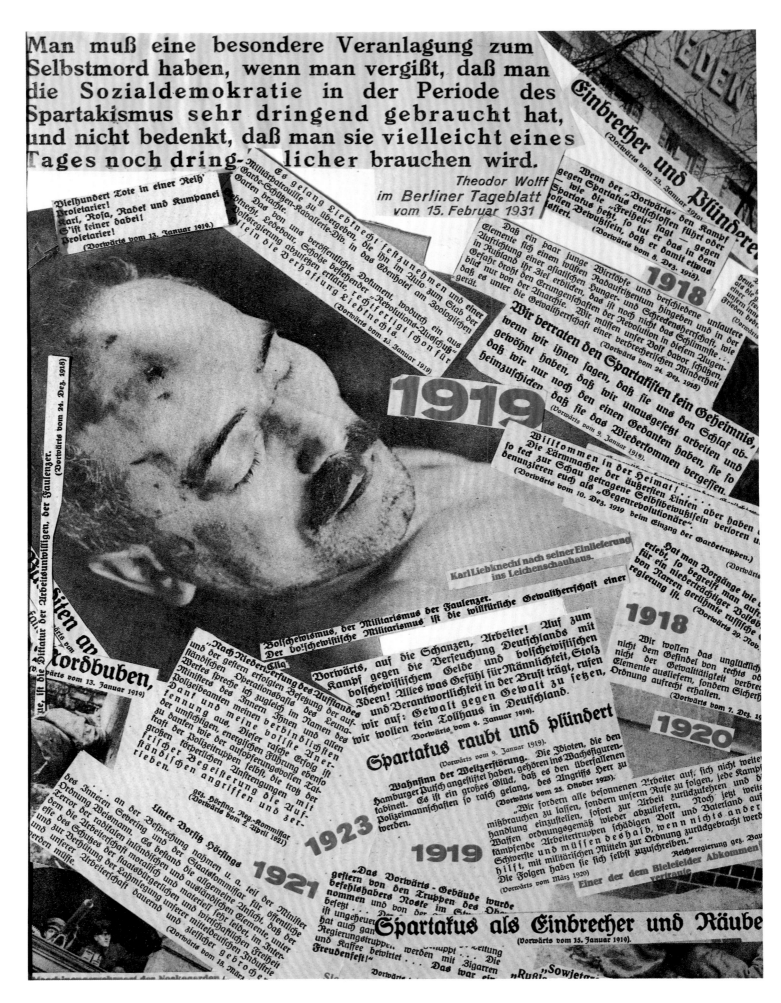

Man muß eine besondere Veranlagung zum Selbstmord haben, wenn man vergißt, daß man die Sozialdemokratie in der Periode des Spartakismus sehr dringend gebraucht hat, und nicht bedenkt, daß man sie vielleicht eines Tages noch dring- licher brauchen wird.

Theodor Wolff im Berliner Tageblatt vom 15. Februar 1931

93 "One Has to Have a Particular Predisposition to Suicide . . ." Montage for the *Arbeiter-Illustrierte-Zeitung* (*AIZ*, Berlin), no. 13, 1931, p. 253. Cat. no. 206

Louis Aragon, 1935

In no time, the poetic *ban* was replaced by the social *ban,* or, more precisely, under the pressure of events, in the struggle in which the artist now found himself involved, the two had merged: *the poetry of the Revolution was the only poetry there was any more.* These were passionate years, with the Revolution suppressed in one place, triumphant in another, when in the same way, at the extreme cutting edge of art, Mayakovsky emerged in Russia and Heartfield in Germany. And these two, under the dictatorship of the proletariat, under the dictatorship of Capital, proceeding from poetry at its most incomprehensible, from the ultimate in art for the few, achieved the most brilliant contemporary illustration of what an art for the masses could be, that magnificent and bafflingly discredited thing. [...]

Nowadays John Heartfield knows to salute beauty. And if, in the photomontages of recent years – the von Schacht with the huge detachable collar, the cow jointing itself with a knife, the anti-Semitic dialogue of two wading birds – if in these the visitor to the exhibition at the Maison de la Culture detects the old shadow of Dada, let him pause by the dove spiked on a bayonet in front of the League of Nations palace, by that Nazi Christmas tree with its branches twisted into swastikas, and what he will detect there will not be the legacy of Dada alone, but of painting through the centuries. There are still lifes by Heartfield, such as those where the scales tilt under the weight of a revolver, or von Papen's briefcase, or the scaffolding of Hitlerian playing cards, which remind me irresistibly of Chardin. Here, quite simply, with scissors and paste, the artist has surpassed the best that modern art had tried to do, with the Cubists, on that lost road of the mystery of everyday life. Simple objects, like Cézanne's apples and Picasso's guitar in their time. But here there is also *meaning,* and meaning has not disfigured beauty. Nowadays John Heartfield knows to salute beauty.

Louis Aragon, "John Heartfield et la beauté revolutionnaire," lecture given on May 2, 1935, at the Maison de la Culture, Paris; in *Les Collages,* pp. 85, 88–89. Hermann, Editeurs des Sciences et des Arts, Paris, 1965.

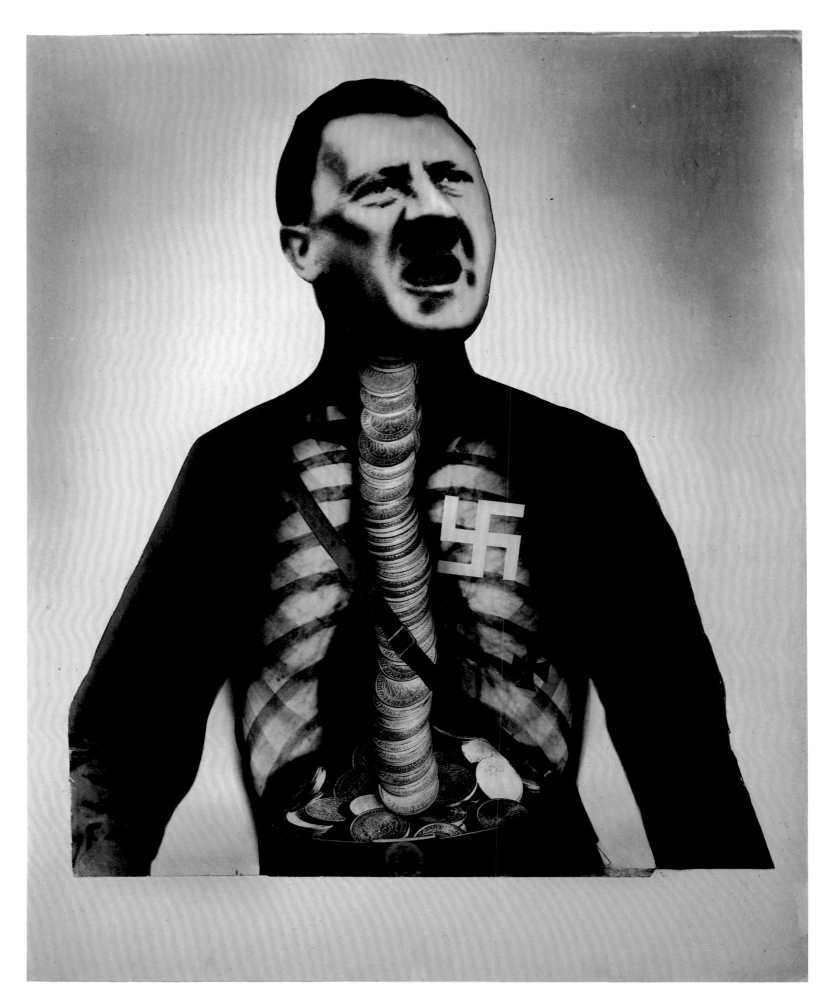

94 "Adolf, the Superman: Swallows Gold and Spouts Junk." Photomontage for the *Arbeiter-Illustrierte-Zeitung* (*AIZ*, Berlin), July 17, 1932, p. 675. Cat. no. 213

95   "Six Million Communist Votes." Photomontage for the *Arbeiter-Illustrierte-Zeitung* (*AIZ*, Berlin),
November 20, 1932, front page. Cat. no. 218

96　"The Judgment of the World: What the Court Withheld is Written in His Face."
Montage for the *Arbeiter-Illustrierte-Zeitung* (*AIZ*, Prague), December 28, 1933, p. 851. Cat. no. 249

97 "War." Photomontage for the *Arbeiter-Illustrierte-Zeitung* (*AIZ*, Prague), July 27, 1933, p. 499.
Cat. no. 237

98   "The Old Slogan in the 'New' Reich: Blood and Iron." Photomontage for the *Arbeiter-Illustrierte-Zeitung*
(*AIZ*, Prague), March 8, 1934, p. 147. Cat. no. 253

99 "Choir of the Arms Industry: 'A Mighty Fortress is Our Geneva'." Photomontage for the *Arbeiter-Illustrierte-Zeitung*
(*AIZ*, Prague), April 12, 1934, p. 240. Cat. no. 257

100 "Dialogue at the Berlin Zoo." Photomontage for the *Arbeiter-Illustrierte-Zeitung*
(*AIZ*, Prague), June 7, 1934, p. 368. Cat. no. 264

101 "As in the Middle Ages . . . So in the Third Reich." Photomontage for the *Arbeiter-Illustrierte-Zeitung*
(*AIZ*, Prague), May 31, 1934, p. 352. Cat. no. 262

102 "Every War Victim His Own Cross of Honor!." Photomontage for the *Arbeiter-Illustrierte-Zeitung* (*AIZ*, Prague),
September 27, 1934, p. 632. Cat. no. 271

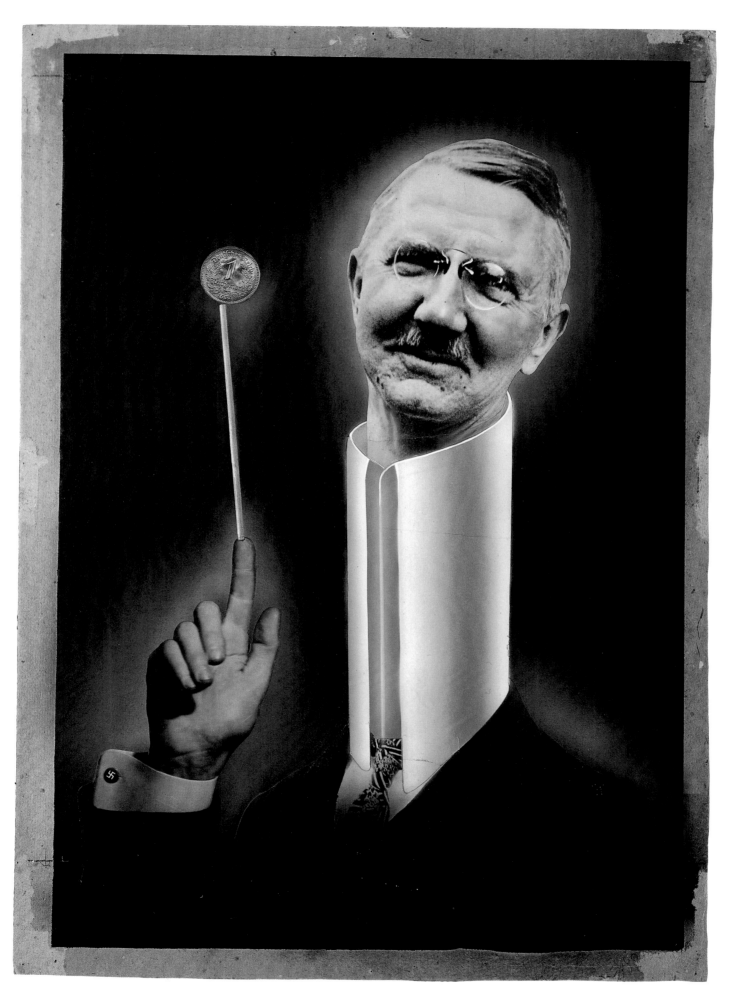

103   "Hjalmar or The Growing Deficit." Photomontage for the *Arbeiter-Illustrierte-Zeitung* (*AIZ*, Prague),
April 5, 1934, p. 224. Cat. no. 255

104 "The Three Magi from Sorrowland." Photomontage for the *Arbeiter-Illustrierte-Zeitung* (*AIZ*, Prague),
January 3, 1935, p. 16. Cat. no. 276

105   "The Thousand Year Reich." Photomontage for the *Arbeiter-Illustrierte-Zeitung* (*AIZ*, Prague),
September 20, 1934, p. 616. Cat. no. 269

Mac Donald - Socialism
Macdonald = Sozialismus

2156

Peschawar vom Feind entsetzt.
Die Lage beffert fich. Die Afridis fliehen. Ihr Wider-
ftand war nur fchwer zu brechen. Erft das Eingreifen von
80 Flugzeugen, die 5000 Bomben abwarfen
entfchied den Sieg.   Vorwärts Nr. 265
                                            10. Juni 1930.

NACH INDIEN
TO JNDIA

"Die fortschreitende Verwirklichung der Selbstverwaltung der Indier"
"The progressive realisation of Indian Self-government"

Montage: JOHN HEARTFIELD

„Ich kann doch nicht untätig zusehen, daß noch ein weiteres Sechstel der Erde dem Kapitalismus verloren geht"
"I really cannot remain inactive while capitalism is being threatened with the loss of another sixth of the world"

543

106   "MacDonald-Socialism." *Arbeiter-Illustrierte-Zeitung* (*AIZ*, Berlin), no. 28, 1930, p. 543.
Cat. no. 198

Oskar Maria Graf, 1938

He did not have any prototypes, for who before him had come up with the idea of arranging various photos in order to make a work of art out of them? He did not even have a tradition to build upon. No intellectual or artistic teacher had influenced him, no Chodowiecki, no Gavarni or Daumier. And what is more, Heartfield did not even possess the sharp intellect that is indeed less expected of painters but to a high degree is a must for artists who are critical of society. No, our dear Jonny had only one thing: a heavy heart that reacted with immense intensity to every adverse, unjust, sinister, and degrading manifestation of our community. This tortured, crushed heart alone was his guide.

Thus the overwhelming simplicity of his aggressive photomontages; thus the inimitable obviousness and the moving veracity in his graphic work. [...] It is explicitly clear to the executioners back home what an invaluable weapon Heartfield's montage is. They know what kind of adversary they have in the small, unassuming Jonny. They hate him like hardly any other, and woe if they catch hold of him.

The unbearable events are the driving force of his art. Like every genuine artist, Heartfield is at once a fanatical moralist and a Don Quixote. He wants to change people and the system, but he also knows deep down inside that such an undertaking is very often akin to fighting windmills. Thus his almost venomous self-derision, his nagging embarrassment when someone praises him or his work; thus his incorruptible, often grandiose irony, his gallows humor that sometimes comes thick and fast in the striking gravity of his artistic efforts. [...]

Like no one else, Heartfield shows what is concealed behind things and appearances. He has turned photomontage into an extremely effective photo lampoon. [...] His works move and activate millions of well-mannered people, and even the most indolent of hearts detects in those works what ghastly evil threatens us all.

Heartfield is not just a great artist; he is an artist who is absolutely indispensable.

Oskar Maria Graf, "John Heartfield: Der Photomonteur und seine Kunst," in *Deutsche Volkszeitung* (Paris, November 20, 1938).

107　"The Destruction of Berlin." *Illustrierte Rote Post* [*Illustrated Red Post*], no. 39, September 1932, front page.
Cat. no. 222

TODESKONJUNKTUR

Die Rüstungs-Industrie betet:

„Je mehr Chinesen ihr Leben verhauchen,
umso kräftiger unsre Schlote rauchen:
Tausend tote Chinesen
decken schon unsre Spesen.
Hunderttausend tote Chinesen
und wir werden genesen.
Zehn Millionen tote Chinesen
könnten uns von der Krise erlösen.

Oh, Herr! Steh bei uns Herrn der Erde,
daß das Feuer im Osten größer werde!"

Schneider-Creuzot
Armstrong
Vickers
Bethlehem Steel
Skoda

Montage:
JOHN
HEARTFIELD

75

**Werktätige! Kämpft gegen die imperialistische Kriegspolitik!
Wählt zur Betriebsrätewahl: Einheitsliste!**

108   "Prospects for the Death Business." *Arbeiter-Illustrierte-Zeitung* (*AIZ*, Berlin), January 22, 1933, p. 75.
Cat. no. 228

109 "The Summit of Their Economic Wisdom." *Volks-Illustrierte* (*VI*, Prague), April 28, 1937, p. 269.
Cat. no. 285

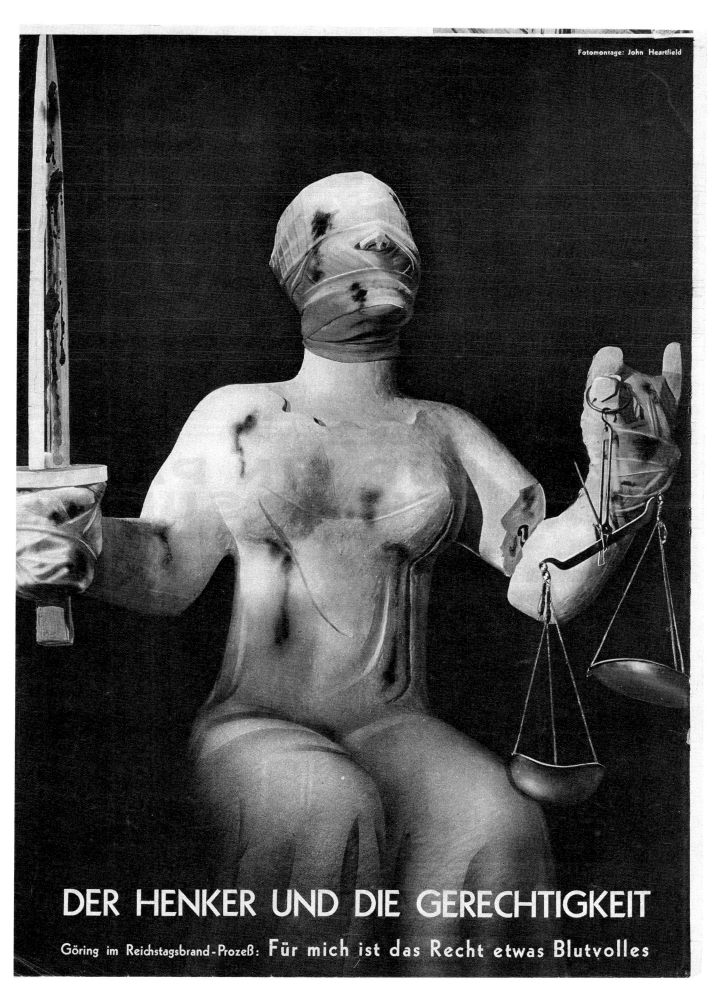

Fotomontage: John Heartfield

DER HENKER UND DIE GERECHTIGKEIT

Göring im Reichstagsbrand-Prozeß: **Für mich ist das Recht etwas Blutvolles**

110   "The Executioner and Justice." *Arbeiter-Illustrierte-Zeitung* (*AIZ*, Prague), November 30, 1933, p. 787.
Cat. no. 248

Mahnung

Heute noch seht ihr im Film den Krieg in anderen Ländern.
Doch wisset: wenn ihr nicht einig euch wehrt, mordet er morgen auch euch!

Fotomontage: John Heartfield

111 "Warning." *Volks-Illustrierte* (*VI*, Prague), October 13, 1937, unpag. Cat. no. 290

MADRID 1936

¡NO PASARAN! ¡PASAREMOS!
Sie kommen nicht durch! Wir kommen durch!

Fotomontage: John Heartfield

112 "Madrid 1936." *Volks-Illustrierte* (*VI*, Prague), November 25, 1936, p. 240. Cat. no. 284

Der Fuchs und der Igel.
Eine Tierfabel nach Lafontaine

Es sprach der Fuchs zum Igel klein:
„Vertrau mir, zieh die Stacheln ein,
Nie hätt ich dich gebissen!
Du störst den Frieden ohne Not,
Ich fühle mich direkt bedroht,
Ich wollt' dich ja nur – küssen!"

Fotomontage: John Heartfield

113   "The Fox and the Hedgehog." *Volks-Illustrierte* (*VI*, Prague), June 15, 1938, unpag.
Cat. no. 296

114 "Sudeten Germans, You'll Be the First Hit!." *Volks-Illustrierte* (*VI*, Prague), September 14, 1938, unpag.

Cat. no. 297

KAISER ADOLF: The Man Against Europe

115   "Kaiser Adolf: The Man Against Europe." *Picture Post*, September 23, 1939, front page.

Cat. no. 299

John Heartfield, 1967

I came to England, where I was supposed to work for *Picture Post*. Some of my work had already been published in *Liliput,* too, and in *Picture Post.* And [...] then [...] I got a contract with the Labour Party [i. e., the trade union newspaper *Reynolds News* – R. M.], and something went wrong because all of a sudden there were altogether different captions than I had made and so forth, so that I ran the risk that all of a sudden quite another Heartfield was in the world; that's when I had to stop. That was really hard. But we did quite a lot of work. Really, quite a lot of work, to hold all the emigrants together in the "Free German League of Culture" [...] and so on.

From an interview with John Heartfield (1967), in Roland März, ed. *John Heartfield: Der Schnitt entlang der Zeit. Selbstzeugnisse – Erinnerungen – Interpretationen,* pp. 464–69; here: p. 468. Dresden, 1981.

Gertrud Heartfield, 1977

It was January 1943 when he got an offer from Lindsay Drummond to work at his newly established publishing company. He was supposed to supervise the printing there, design dust jackets and, where necessary, illustrate books, too.

[...] that was a liberal bourgeois publishing company. He worked there until the end of 1949 and then went for a short while to Penguin Publishing Co. before we returned to Germany. Johnny knew that he couldn't design jackets in the way he had done in Germany for Malik and other progressive publishers; therefore he studied very attentively the English book production. He had developed a completely new method for his English book designs; he profited quite a lot from the books that were published at Drummond.

From an interview with Gertrud Heartfield, in Eckhard Siepmann, *Montage: John Heartfield. Vom Club Dada zur Arbeiter-Illustrierten-Zeitung,* pp. 222, 224. Berlin, 1977.

116 Aleksandr Pokryshkin, *Red Air Ace*. Photomontage for brochure cover, 1945.

Cat. no. 354

117 Roger Motz, *La Belgique Invaincue*. Photomontage for dust jacket, ca. 1942. Cat. no. 345

118   Ilya Ehrenburg, *The Russians Reply to Lady Gibb*. Photomontage for brochure cover, 1945.
Cat. no. 350

119   J. J. Lynx, ed., *The Future of the Jews.* Design for dust jacket, 1945. Cat. no. 352

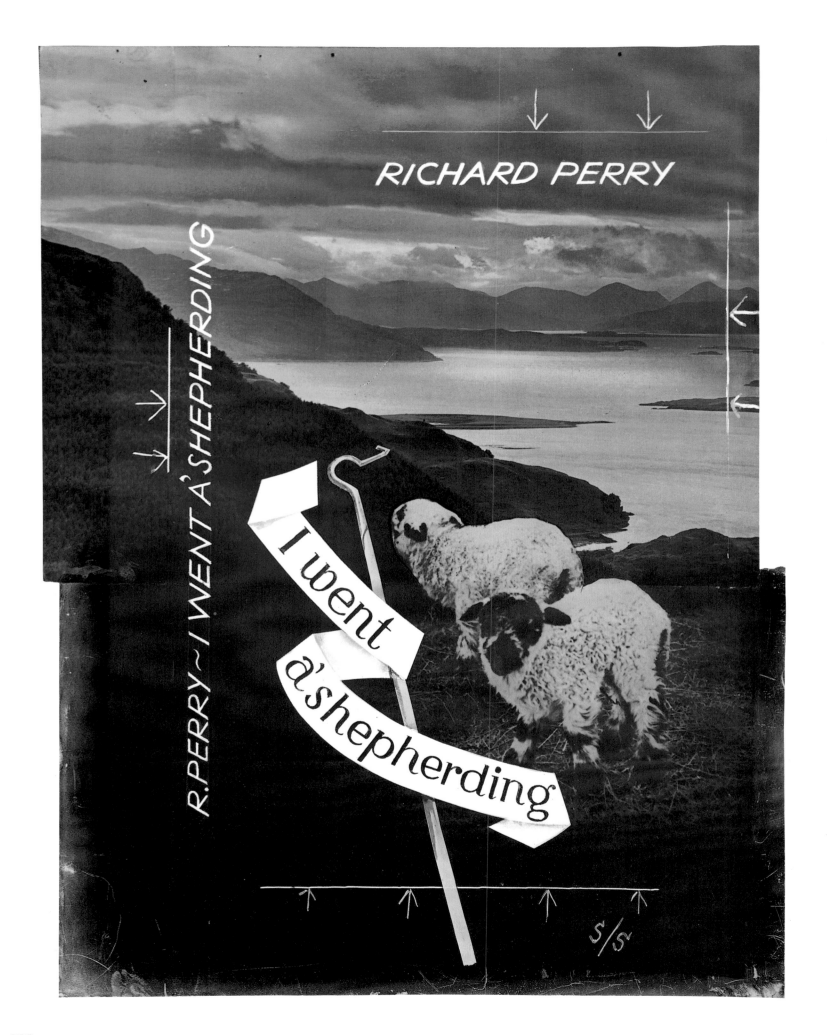

120   Richard Perry, *I Went A'Shepherding*. Photomontage for dust jacket, 1944. Cat. no. 349

121   Bert Stiles, *Serenade to the Big Bird*. Design for dust jacket, 1947. Cat. no. 357

JEWS DRIVEN LIKE CATTLE

STRIPPED OF ALL
POSSESSIONS

"Thousands of Jews from the
Corridor, Gdynia, Poznan, Katowice
and other Polish towns, as well as
from Czecho-Slovakia and Austria,
have already been transported like
cattle to this reservation."

122 "Reservations." Photomontage for *Reynolds News*, December 1939. Cat. no. 298

123 "Five Minutes to Twelve." Photomontage, 1942. Cat. no. 300

124 "And yet it moves!." Photomontage for brochure cover, 1943. Cat. no. 346

125   Pavel Troyanovsky, *The Last Days of Berlin*. Photomontage for brochure back cover, 1945.
Cat. no. 355

126a   Gerhart Hauptmann, *Die Weber* [*The Weavers*]. Stage set design "Villa Dreißiger" for
the production at the Grosses Schauspielhaus (Berlin), 1921. Cat. no. 360

126b   Gerhart Hauptmann, *Die Weber*. Stage set design "Spring Landscape" for the production at the Grosses Schauspielhaus (Berlin), 1921. Cat. no. 361

Hugo Fetting, 1977

With varying lengths of interruptions, John Heartfield's work for the stage covers a period of almost half a century. [...]

When Heartfield made his entrance as a stage and costume designer in the fifties, this engagement was nothing more than the reawakening and reshaping of an old affiliation that had never been lost nor ceased, namely, the affiliation between Heartfield and the theatre. From then on until the sixties, he collaborated on several productions of the Deutsches Theater and the Kammerspiele as well as on a production of the Berliner Ensemble. [...]

Heartfield's sense and understanding of the theatre never let him forget that human beings are the focus of everything that happens on the stage. That is why it is useless to look for the sensational, the forced original in his décor. To him, the message was always more important than the effect. Content and substance of the play always remained essential for him. To translate it into the idiom of stage design, to make it visible and perceptible, was his priority. To this end he employed all the possibilities and effects of the theatre and exploited stage technology to its full capacity. [...] Heartfield's stage designs were austere where abundance was not missed, and lavish where austerity would have detracted. He stylized where realism would have been extravagant, and parodied where wit necessitated it. He gave priority to the character of the play over artistic invention. His décor always testified to both his acute power of observation and to the breadth of his imagination, which never induced him to become lost in the frivolous, the picturesque, the merely illustrative. The sense of the whole remained dominant, without neglecting the characteristic detail in the process. Irrespective of the extent to which he used backdrops, scenery, machinery, and props, in his stage settings Heartfield made the environment visible without distracting attention from the action on stage. In uniting space and actors, groups and plane, he made the stage design a part of the action. As a stage designer, Heartfield was and remained a partner of the author, the director, and the actors. [...]

Hugo Fetting, "Heartfield an den Reinhardt-Bühnen" (1977), in Roland März, ed., *John Heartfield: Der Schnitt entlang der Zeit. Selbstzeugnisse — Erinnerungen — Interpretationen*, pp. 208–20; here: pp. 209, 218–19. Verlag der Kunst, Dresden, 1981.

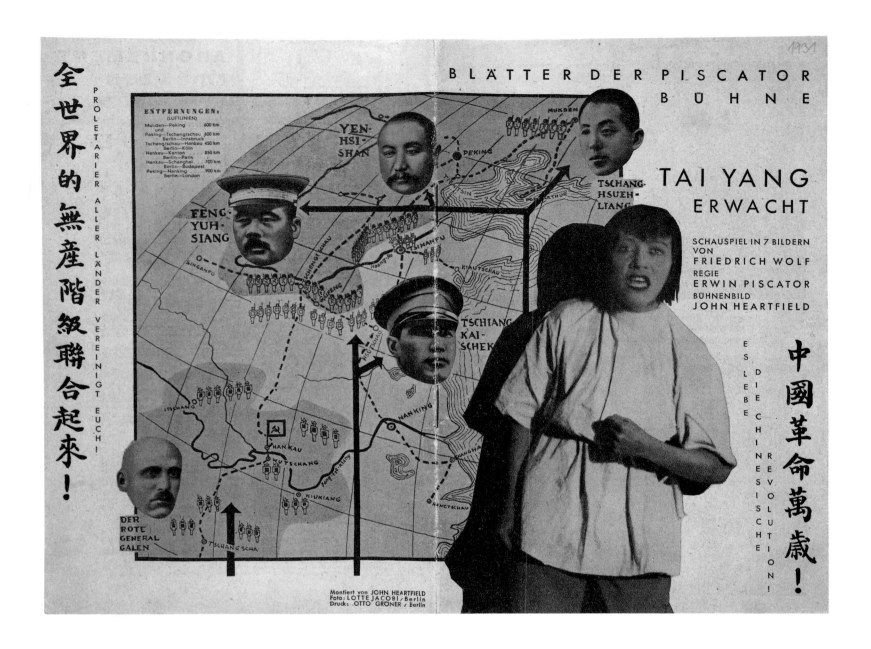

Bernhard Diebold, 1931

Everything plays a part at the Wallner-Theater. Everybody in the auditorium, too, is roaring, with the screaming posters in Chinese and Roman characters hanging from the boxseats: Down with the imperialists! Down with the white terror! Long live the Chinese revolution! At this Piscator evening, this poster onslaught takes the place of the miserable film that usually provides an emotional overture. Almost without noticing it, in the orchestra seats you are already in the middle of the drama's exposition. No curtain there to create the aesthetic distance between art and life, either. The musicians step onto the open stage, one after another, in the illuminated theatre, and wait for the actors, who gradually appear, dressed as Europeans in ready-made suits; then they put on their Chinese clothes and paint Chinese eyes on their Berlin faces—now they are ready and dressed to enact China's misery. [...] In this way, Piscator makes it plain for all to see: that China's misfortune is only a costume, as it were, for Europe's misfortune. The yellow grease paint is merely symbolic. The yellow tribulations are the same as the black-red-gold tribulations. A proletarian cry: We are all human beings and Chinese!

Frankfurter Zeitung, January 18, 1931.

127　Friedrich Wolf, *Tai Yang erwacht* [*Tai Yang Awakens*]. Playbill covers for the *Blätter der Piscator-Bühne* [*Magazine of the Piscator Theatre*], 1931. Ex. cat.

128   Nikolai Pogodin, *My Friend*. Stage photograph from the performance at the Moscow
Theatre of the Revolution, with a photomontage as backdrop, 1931. Cat. no. 363

129　Bertolt Brecht, *Die Mutter* [*The Mother*]. Poster for the production at the Deutsches Theater (Berlin), 1951.
Cat. no. 385

The Slide Projections for *Die Mutter* by Brecht, 1952

The slide projections for *Die Mutter* [*The Mother*] were expansive, very picturesque, with the contrast between light and dark strongly emphasized. They graphically reflected the atmosphere of the oppressive living conditions the workers had to endure in tsarist Russia: The factory towers menacingly over the little room in which Pelagea Vlasova's life takes place; the jail holds the imprisoned son in inescapable confinement; the street in which the workers are demonstrating is hemmed in by tall, narrow façades and seems to be endless. During three particular performances of the chorus the background slides were to be crosscut by photographic projections: "The Vlasovas of All Countries," "The Great Revolutionaries," "The Great Warmongers." In order to make them fully visible, Pelagea Vlasova's room was rigged out in transparent material (*Bizella* and gauze), which let the slide projections shimmer through. In the last scene, which is set on the eve of the great October Revolution, we sought to follow up the group of revolutionaries with other groups sketched in the projections.

Although we kept perspective foreshortening meticulously to scale, the intended effect failed to materialize. We only found the solution when we added a moving projection, a film, to the static slide on the panoramic screen. The projection screen fluttered down from above like a flag, and then the film was projected back through an aperture in the panoramic screen. Showing scenes from the October Revolution and the liberation of China, it intellectually furthered the action on stage into the present.

Theaterarbeit: 6 Aufführungen des Berliner Ensembles, p. 165. Dresden, 1952.

130   Bertolt Brecht, *Die Mutter*. Stage photograph with photo projections of the production at the Deutsches Theater (Berlin), 1951. Cat. no. 364

131   Bertolt Brecht, *Die Mutter*. Projection screen (reconstruction) for the production at the
Deutsches Theater (Berlin), 1951. Cat. no. 365

132a   Bertolt Brecht, *Die Mutter*. Projection design for the production at the
           Deutsches Theater (Berlin), 1951. Cat. no. 367

132b   Bertolt Brecht, *Die Mutter*. Projection design for the production at the
           Deutsches Theater (Berlin), 1951. Cat. no. 366

133 Arno Holz, *Sozialaristokraten* [*Social Aristocrats*]. Poster for the production at the
Deutsches Theater-Kammerspiele (Berlin), 1955. Cat. no. 388

134   Arno Holz, *Sozialaristokraten*. Curtain for the production at the
Deutsches Theater-Kammerspiele (Berlin), 1955. Cat. no. 370

135   Arno Holz, *Sozialaristokraten*. Stage photograph "Fiebig's Study" of the production at
the Deutsches Theater-Kammerspiele (Berlin), 1955. Cat. no. 371

Ilse-Maria Dorfstecher, 1990

After a very long break [...] Heartfield's most productive phase in theatre work in the GDR [German Democratic Republic] began with O'Casey's play *Harfe und Gewehr* [*The Shadow of a Gunman*], produced in 1954 under the direction of Rudolf Wessely; *Sozialaristokraten* [*Social Aristocrats*] by Holz, directed by Ernst Kahler in 1955; and Irwin Shaw's *Brooklyn-Ballade*, produced in 1956 under the direction of Wolfgang Hein [...].

The large number of surviving sketches and finished studies, the costume designs that occasionally include very precise specifications of the dress code that corresponds to the social reality of the respective character, give reason to suppose that Heartfield tremendously enjoyed this kind of work. Moreover, there are a number of historical studies he made for the Irish play preserved in his estate—references to and extracts from history books and depictions of old tools from various regions. [...].

With David Berg's *Mutter Riba* [*Mother Riba*], produced in 1955, Heartfield used new means that were most unusual for the GDR of the fifties. As a stage designer oriented to drama, he was not concerned with mere effect. Instead, his intention was to characterize the American milieu, from a distance, with attributes such as colorful, gaudy, brash, arrogant—attributes that come to mind when looking at the studies for the stage sets. Today, the display window of the supermarket gives the impression of a precursory overture to pop art. He brought with him from England the social and optical experiences for such depictions from the world of advertising, illustrated magazines and comics. Similar to the English pop artists later, he assembled collages of the total consumer's dream from packages and comic strip figures. [...]

In Heartfield's best works, the density of the milieu did not have the effect of heading for a new naturalism; rather, it always bore streaks of criticism on the one hand and of craftsmanship on the other.

Taking into account the spotlight and the sometimes brightly colored costumes, one can understand that a different artistic temperament, one similar to Piscator's, would have been needed to capitalize on these points. Thus, when he replied in his letter of September 9, 1956, to the sixty-fifth birthday greeting sent to him by Piscator, who had then left the United States to return to the Federal Republic of Germany, Heartfield's wish was tinged with a bit of melancholy: "Yes, I'd like to have a birthday present from you too, and it would be for me to do the décor for a play you would stage here in Berlin with us. And it would have to be a very bold construction, of the kind that can be done only with you, because no other director would so much as consider it."

Ilse-Maria Dorfstecher, "John Heartfield als Bühnenbildner 1951 bis 1966," in exhibition catalogue *John Heartfield*, Berlin, Altes Museum, et al., pp. 379–85; here: pp. 383–84. DuMont Buchverlag, Cologne, 1991.

136   Arno Holz, *Sozialaristokraten*. Stage set design "Fiebig's Study" of the production at the Deutsches Theater-Kammerspiele (Berlin), 1955. Cat. no. 372

137　Arno Holz, *Sozialaristokraten*. Costume design "Fiebig" for the production at the
Deutsches Theater-Kammerspiele (Berlin), 1955. Cat. no. 374

138   David Berg, *Mother Riba*. Stage photograph "Fashion Salon" of the production at the
Deutsches Theater-Kammerspiele (Berlin), 1955. Ex. cat.

Günther Rücker, 1990

At the beginning of the Korean war, a New York textile merchant from the Jewish milieu buys ladies' skirts at a cheap price. But ladies' slacks have become the fashion. His last great hope for profit falls to pieces. His son is killed in Korea. His father-in-law, a true big-time wholesaler, doesn't see why he should help the bankrupt, especially since the family tie with his daughter has ceased to exist. The wife of this small-time dealer collects signatures against the bomb; her husband thinks she's *meshuga*. His life has lost all meaning. No ladies' slacks, no son, no wife. The milieu recalls Gold's *Juden ohne Geld* [*Jews without Money*], now transplanted to the fifties. Common people, a small market, a candy-colored, rosy-pink office. Heart-

field put all the scenes of the action on a revolving stage. Loads of details. He constructed a model and asked me if there was anything I'd like to have changed. But I wasn't familiar with the milieu at all. Elisabeth Hauptmann, the translator, knew it very well; she had spent her period of emigration in the United States. Both principal actors had returned from emigration in Britain. I was very young and learned more from them than I could have given them as a director. The whole thing was a very modest success.

As with all his works, Heartfield was a bundle of energy. He had turned his hand to stage design because photomontage had come to an end; but also because it had been denounced and discredited in a man-

ner quite inconceivable today. What mystifies me to the present day is the fact that it never occurred to me to ask John Heartfield about his stage design work of the twenties and thirties. The young generation didn't have any historical awareness of the period prior to 1933. Nevertheless, right from the start my own relationship to John Heartfield was that of a somewhat younger brother to the older one. The *AIZ Photomonteur* in my perception absorbed the stage designer. As a child, I had regarded the former almost as a mythical figure in art and politics; the latter was an unknown quantity for me.

139   David Berg, *Mother Riba*. Stage set design "Tailors' Workshop 'Ajax-Röcke' [*Ajax Skirts*]" for the production at the Deutsches Theater-Kammerspiele (Berlin), 1955.   Cat. no. 383

140a,b David Berg, *Mother Riba*. Stage set design "Supermarket" and detail study
"Store Sign" for the production at the Deutsches Theater-Kammerspiele (Berlin), 1955.
Cat. nos. 382, 380

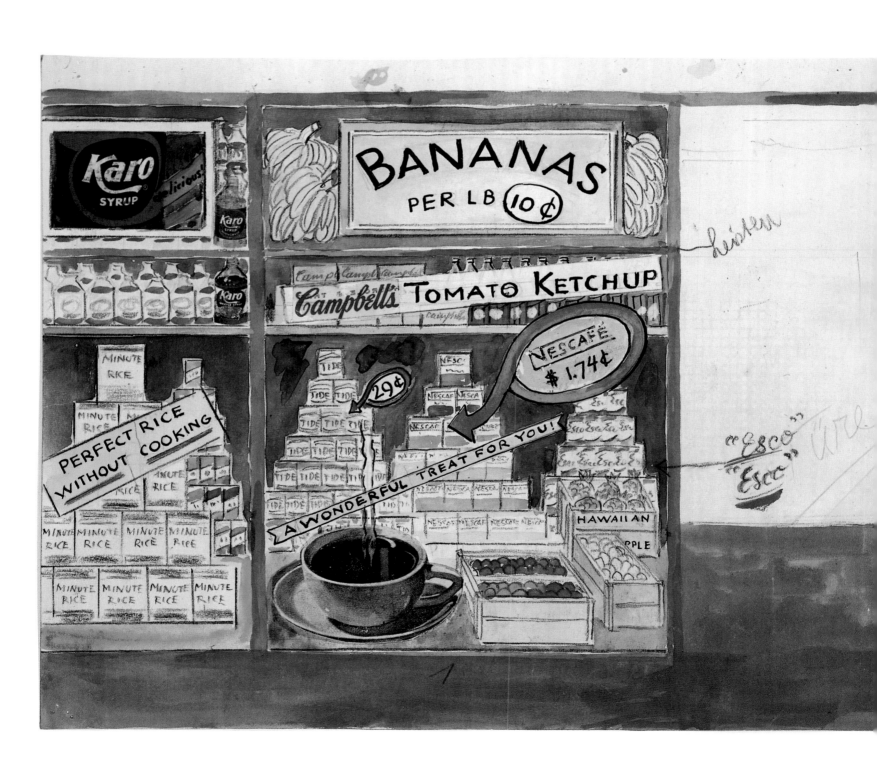

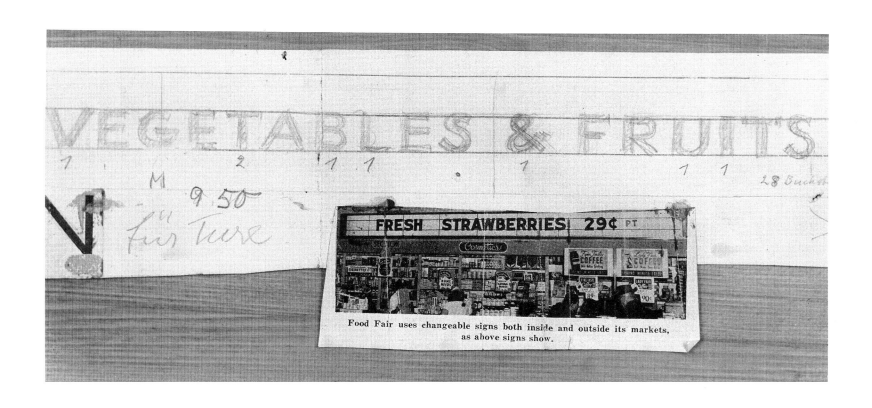

141   David Berg, *Mother Riba*. Production at the Deutsches Theater-Kammerspiele (Berlin), 1955.
Typographical design for storefront with photo of a supermarket pasted on it. Cat. no. 381

142   David Berg, *Mother Riba*. Stage photograph "Supermarket" of the production at the
Deutsches Theater-Kammerspiele (Berlin), 1955. Cat. no. 379

143   "Advertising Construction for the USSR in Front of the Railroad Station in Leipzig."
Design for the Leipzig Fair, 1927. Cat. no. 223

On signs held by figures:
V UPOMÍNKU na UMĚNÍ POPŮ tohoto krátce žijícího zmetka babičky DADA

IN MEMORIAM POP ART dieser Fehlgeburt der Grossmutter DADA

Peter Pachnicke, 1990

Fine or decorative arts, legitimate or illegitimate, High or Low – Heartfield did not think, feel, or work in such dichotomies. He took every job equally seriously, be it an ad, a dust jacket, an advertising media, a poster, a newspaper, a stage design, an exhibition. For every element of bourgeois daily life was to be revolutionized aesthetically as well, was to receive a face and body in which people would be able to see, hear, taste, smell, and touch the new with their own eyes, ears, mouths, noses, and hands. In this respect, he was not only a critic of bourgeois society; he also considered himself a designer of a communist utopia, unfolding his montage thinking on the surface, on the object, within space and in the action. As a consequence, his subject matter maneuvered constantly in the contradiction between satire exposing imperialism and pathos idealizing socialism.

144   John Heartfielde and Wieland Herzfelde at the Heartfield Exhibition
in Prague, 1964

145　Johannes R. Becher, *Winterschlacht* [*Winter Campaign*]. Poster for the production at the Berliner Ensemble (Berlin), 1954. Cat. no. 386

146   Vladimir Mayakovsky, *Lenin Poem* [*Vladimir Ilich Lenin*]. Poster for the production at the
Volksbühne (Berlin), 1966. Cat. no. 390

AN MEINE LANDSLEUTE

IHR, die ihr überlebtet in gestorbenen Städten,
Habt doch nun endlich mit euch selbst Erbarmen!
Zieht nun in neue Kriege nicht, ihr Armen,
Als ob die alten nicht gelanget hätten:
Ich bitt euch, habet mit euch selbst Erbarmen!

Ihr Männer, greift zur Kelle, nicht zum Messer!
Ihr säßet unter Dächern schließlich jetzt,
Hättet ihr auf das Messer nicht gesetzt,
Und unter Dächern sitzt es sich doch besser.
Ich bitt euch, greift zur Kelle, nicht zum Messer!

Ihr Kinder, daß sie euch mit Krieg verschonen,
Müßt ihr um Einsicht eure Eltern bitten.
Sagt laut, ihr wollt nicht in Ruinen wohnen
Und nicht das leiden, was sie selber litten:
Ihr Kinder, daß sie euch mit Krieg verschonen!

Ihr Mütter, da es euch anheimgegeben,
Den Krieg zu dulden oder nicht zu dulden,
Ich bitt euch, lasset eure Kinder leben!
Daß sie euch die Geburt und nicht den Tod dann schulden:
Ihr Mütter, lasset eure Kinder leben!

BERTOLT BRECHT

VEB Offizin Haag-Drugulin in Leipzig III/18/58

147   Bertolt Brecht, "An meine Landsleute" [*To My Countrymen*]. Typographical sheet, 1950.

Cat. no. 391

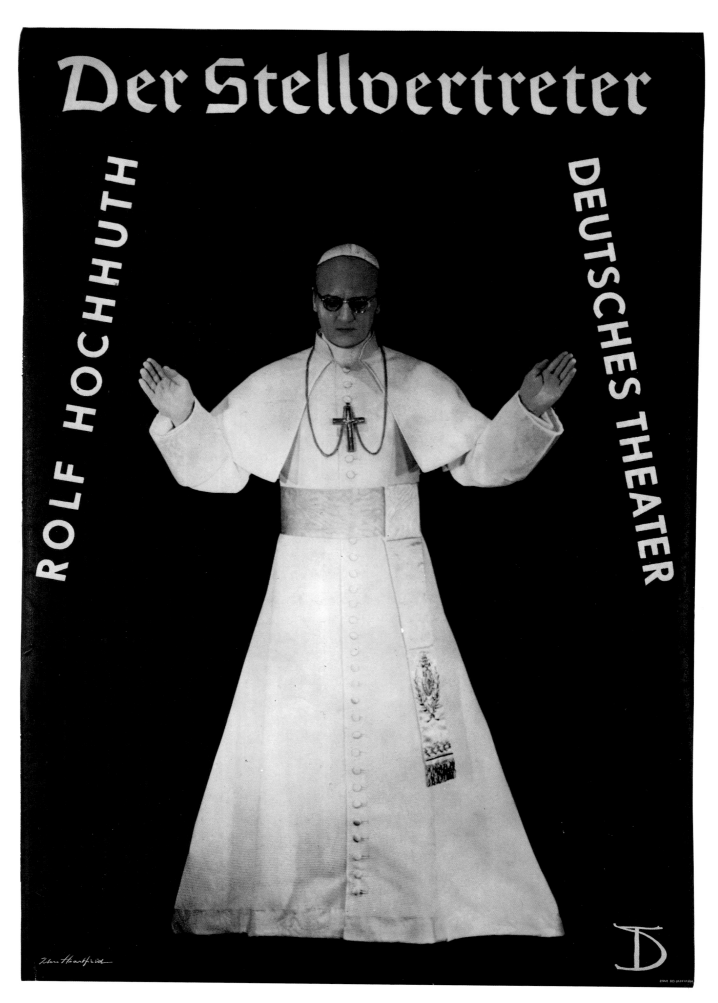

148   Rolf Hochhuth, *Der Stellvertreter* [*The Deputy*]. Poster for the production at the
Deutsches Theater (Berlin), 1966. Cat. no. 389

TRAVELS IN ETHIOPIA

BY
DAVID BUXTON

149   David Buxton, *Travels in Ethiopia*. Dust jacket, 1949. Cat. no. 358

Werner Klemke, 1990

In its very simplicity, the Brecht edition is consummate typography. The classical simplicity is of course in the English tradition, but from it he created something very much his own. In his work, Heartfield was meticulously precise. He was the most exacting person I have ever met; it had to be just right, and he insisted that one should examine the dust jacket with him to see if it worked. I often told him, "That's enough! Nobody will notice afterward." But he insisted. The jacket was laid out on the floor, and you had to get up on a chair with him. And there we would stand examining it from above to see if some detail was right. He would climb down again and again to move it slightly here and shift it there until he was quite satisfied. Of course, I understood him, but other people thought it very strange. I remember a discussion on the *Sozialaristokraten* [*Social Aristocrats*] poster. On that occasion, he didn't bring a finished design, to be sure, but only his folder containing the separate elements. He had the poster in his head, but in practice he began to construct it from the various pieces before our eyes, which often took hours. He knew what he wanted; what interested him was if and how the poster would appeal to the public at large. And then, when he was ready, he refused to fix down the pieces, but took the poster apart again and carried the parts away with him to have another go at it.

Poster, book cover, stage design – he didn't come with preparatory drawings but simply with illustrations of the objects, to show, for instance, to the stage hands what a sap ought to look like in *Sozialaristokraten*. He knew exactly what the inside of an attic looked like, or a parlor. I once said to him, "To me you're truly a modern artist, because—like an engineer—you work with nothing but prefabricated readymade parts."

From a conversation with Peter Pachnicke.

150   Bertolt Brecht, *Stücke XII* [*Plays XII*]. Dust jacket, 1959. Cat. no. 359

*Wenn wir es
alle nicht wollen,*

wird es nie sein!

John Heartfield

152   "Never Again!" Poster, 1960. After a photomontage for the *Arbeiter-Illustrierte-Zeitung* (*AIZ*, Berlin),
November 27, 1932 [Pl. 88b]. Ex. cat.

Hubertus Gassner

Heartfield's Moscow Apprenticeship 1931–1932

Heartfield's significance in modern art is undoubtedly due first and foremost to his achievements in the field of photomontage. He produced work of essential importance, making photomontage publishable and magazines well illustrated at least in Western Europe. He is to be credited not only for an expansion of the genre's function – carrying it beyond the bounds of original artistic montage to the harsher reality of the mass media – but also for the development of its own aesthetic quality. Heartfield earned for the initially often clumsy and awkward genre of photomontage an equal position among the other visual media.

In addition to describing Heartfield's operative concept, this essay will also examine the montage methods applied in his works. Heartfield's stay in Moscow in 1931/32 coincided with vehement debates held there on the so-called "creative method" in art, and these were far more intense than among German left-wing artists. Heartfield's photomontages were not merely the subject of these debates. The decisions made in the Soviet Union, and subsequently in Germany, regarding the "creative method" of revolutionary proletarian art had repercussions on his work.

We shall examine the question of whether this "Soviet year" had an influence on Heartfield and how he himself influenced the development of Soviet photomontage as an art form with the works produced there. Before we look at these mutual influences more closely, we should shed some light on the nature of his mission to the Soviet Union. Attendant circumstances and his trip's duration suggest that this was not just a private pleasure trip nor a conventional exchange of artists between two countries. Just before Heartfield's arrival in Moscow in April 1931, an interview with the "demon reporter" Egon Erwin Kisch was published in the Soviet art journal *Brigada khudozhnikov* [*Artists' Brigade*], entitled "Your Opinion on Heartfield, Comrade Kisch?"

While the Russian interviewer referred to Heartfield as "a practitioner of proletarian and revolutionary art who is little known in Russia," Kisch, on the other hand, called him one of "the most famous contemporary artists." The invention of photomontage, he claimed, could be attributed to him as much as the development of modern American book production. Although the bourgeoisie tried to lay claim to him, he rejected all financially attractive offers and remained loyal to the working class and its creative activity. Although according to Kisch, Heartfield adopted his working method from Dadaism, he used it to serve the "class struggle" by visually contrasting social conflicts and thus pointing out the "revolutionary necessity." By asserting Heartfield's bias, Kisch dismissed the Russian interviewer's trick question as to whether "John Heartfield's art originated in Dadaism." For at the beginning of the thirties, Dadaism was regarded in the Soviet Union as the epitome of bourgeois decadent art. The question clearly insinuates that the Dadaist origin of photomontage might cast shadows over its current manifestations, exposing it to formalist suspicions. In response to the rhetorical question whether Heartfield intended to visit the Soviet Union, Kisch answered: "I've heard that he wants to visit Moscow soon as a specialist for the reorganization of the Museum of the Revolution. His arrival is obviously arousing a great deal of interest in the Soviet Union, the enormous construction of which he has contrasted, in thousands of his works, to the collapse of the capitalist society."[1]

The interview was accompanied by a self-portrait of Heartfield brandishing a pair of scissors as he is about to sever the head of Berlin's police commissioner Zörgiebel from his body, thus visually equating this photomontage work with that of a revolutionary (cf. Pl. 42). The following montages illustrate the contrasting method referred to by Kisch: from the *Arbeiter-Illustrierte-Zeitung* (*AIZ*, of March 12, 1930), depicting a pregnant proletarian woman with her soldier-son killed in action in the background ["Forced to Deliver Human Material. Courage! The State Needs the Unemployed and Soldiers!"] (Pl. p. 297); and a picture of Reichstag stalls under the chairmanship of a National Socialist steel helmet, a capitalist top hat, and a bishop's mitre ["The Dead Parliament"] (*AIZ*, October 8, 1930).

Although still unknown in the Soviet Union, according to *Brigada khudozhnikov*, Heartfield was nevertheless the first Western artist granted a one-man exhibition in Moscow by the All-Russian Cooperative of Artists (Vsekokhudozhnik). The cooperative, founded in 1928, organized above all study trips for Soviet artist brigades to the country's large construction sites (Magnitogorsk, Kuzbass, Dnieprostroi, etc.) and touring exhibitions for workers of *raions* (regions) and peasants of *sovkhozy* and *kolkhozy*. In that spirit, Heartfield used the six months between his arrival in April and the opening of his exhibition in November to do practical work and teach. He spent several weeks with an artists' brigade at the Baku oil fields, collecting shots and ideas for a photographic report, published in the Soviet magazine *USSR im Bau* [*The USSR in Construction*] (No. 12, 1931). He gave courses on montage for soldiers and officers of the Red Army, as well as for photomontage artists and printers at the Graphic Institute. Numerous discussions were held at his exhibition; he also gave lectures at a number of institutions. In 1931, the magazine *Za proletarskoe iskusstvo* [*Proletarian Art*] reported on his plans: "Comrade Heartfield intends to carry out important tasks in Moscow on behalf of the Neuer Deutscher Verlag. He has to prepare two books about the Red Army and about the first and second Five-Year Plan. He also has to make arrangements for the Viennese exhibition *Wir bauen den Sozialismus* [*We are Building Socialism*]. Furthermore, Comrade Heartfield is working on the exhibition *The Imperialist War and the February Revolution* at the Museum of the Revolution. Also, he will be arranging an exhibition of his works at one of Moscow's largest factories. On June 24, Comrade Heartfield will give a lecture at the Polytechnical Institute on photomontage as a weapon in the class struggle. At this lecture, many of his photomontages will be exhibited. At the Graphic Institute, Heartfield will talk about his creative method of photomontage, its emergence, organization, development, and potential."[2]

The solo exhibition, however, did not take place at workplaces as initially planned. Instead, the Cooperative of Artists offered Heartfield its new exhibition premise on Kuznetsky Most in the city center. A leaflet issued by VOKS (All-Union Society for Cultural Relations Abroad) reported that the "artist's posters, book jackets and designs for newspapers, exceptionally acute in their composition and comprehensive in their political subject matter," were shown at the exhibition. "The exhibition closed with a discussion about Heartfield's creations, emphasizing the value of the artist's work for our correct path in applying photomontage to polygraphy."[3]

This short evaluation sums up the discussions among Russian artists and art critics on the form and function of photomontage, quoting Heartfield's works as examples, or counterexamples, to those of the Russian Constructivists. But we should also recall the intellectual climate, since Heartfield arrived during the heated controversies about poster design and polygraphy used for mass agitation and propaganda in the Soviet Union. The discussions had been initiated in February 1931 by the resolution of the Central Committee of the Communist Party regarding poster agitation and propaganda, i.e., two months before the arrival of the German *Monteur* in Moscow. In the following months, the party resolution triggered many disputes among Soviet artists, art critics, editors, and organizers of propaganda work; and as a result, the country's entire poster production was concentrated in the State Press for Art (IZOGIS). A copy of the

John Heartfield, "The Dead Parliament." *Arbeiter-Illustrierte-Zeitung* (*AIZ*, Berlin), no. 42, 1930, p. 823

257

Central Committee's resolution, accompanied by an editorial commentary, was published in the issue of *Brigada khudozhnikov* preceding the one featuring the Kisch interview. The commentary to paragraph 1, in which an "unjustifiably negligent attitude toward poster production on the part of the various publishers" and the "publication of a significant percentage of anti-Soviet posters and pictures" were ascertained, stated: "The poster and the mass-produced picture penetrate all spheres of everyday life and are a visual medium for the ideological re-education of the masses."[4]

The demand for an image able to "expose and assess reality" became the leitmotif of poster criticism as asserted in the party resolution. The search for such methods focused attention on Heartfield's photomontages, making them appear exemplary in the minds of many poster critics.

On April 5, 1931, the first meeting of the Workers' Council was held at the State Press, where posters produced by the Press were presented to male and female workers for appraisal. Of the twenty-two posters, only two met with the reviewers' unqualified approval: the graphic poster by Aleksandr Deineka, "We Must Become Specialists Ourselves," and the photomontage poster by Gustav Klutsis, "The USSR is the Shock Brigade of the World's Proletariat." The two designers were among the most prominent members of the artists' association OKTYABR [October] – Deineka primarily as a painter and draftsman, and Klutsis as the leading photomontage artist in the Soviet Union.

Heartfield had already become acquainted with the graphic production of the OKTYABR group prior to his departure from Berlin. Founded in 1928, the group united all distinguished Constructivists of the Soviet Union, including the architects Moisei Ginzburg and Aleksandr Vesnin, Vsevolod Meierkhold representing theatre, Vladimir Mayakovsky and Sergei Tretyakov representing literature, Sergei Eisenstein and Dziga Vertov for film, Aleksandr Rodchenko and B. Ignatovich for photography, El Lissitzky and Gustav Klutsis for poster and exhibition design, and many more. In 1931 the association had some five hundred members and was thus a major rival of the Association of Artists of Revolutionary Russia (AKhRR), a group of realist painters.

After OKTYABR had successfully staged its first exhibition in Moscow in May 1930, the second followed in October of the same year in Berlin. The invitation had been issued by the Association of Revolutionary Artists of Germany (ARBKD), with which Heartfield was affiliated. By inviting the Russian Constructivists, the German ARBKD intended to protest against the mainly genre and landscape paintings of the AKhRR previously shown in Berlin. Their quaintly packaged "petit bourgeois ideology" was to be countered and criticized by a new exhibition showing "ideologically more consistent, clearly revolutionary proletarian art in the USSR."[5] Thus, the most recent debates on revolutionary art between the Russian Realists and Constructivists were transferred to the secondary arena of Berlin and were heatedly discussed among artists and critics.

The OKTYABR exhibition in Berlin concentrated on architecture, photography, and graphics – areas in which the Russian Constructivists were leading at the time. In the section devoted to print design, particularly the photomontage artists, first and foremost Gustav Klutsis, were represented with their posters, book jackets, illustrations for magazines and books, newspaper montages, and wall news sheets. The works exhibited by Elkin, El Lissitzky, Klutsis, Kulagina, Gutnov, Pinus, Rodchenko, Sedelnikov, Senkin, Stenberg, Tagirov, and Telingater demonstrated to the artists of the ARBKD and the German audience the high level and success with which the Russian Constructivists had applied photomontage not only to the field of art but also to everyday mass publications. Heartfield was not only affected by all these activities as a confidant of the

ARBKD; he also participated actively, thanks to his acquaintance with the Russian artist and graphic designer A. Gutnov. Gutnov had studied at the Arts and Crafts School of Berlin at the end of the twenties and was one of the founding members of the OKTYABR group. In the Reichstag election campaign for September 14, 1930, Gutnov spoke on behalf of the KPD [German Communist Party] in Berlin and Magdeburg; together with Heartfield, he also organized propaganda for the party. For example, they tied two sheep to the Brandenburg Gate for a week, bearing a poster that claimed: "We Are Voting National Socialist."[6] Their forecast unfortunately proved to be right. One of the first pieces of work Heartfield created in 1930 for the *AIZ* shows a large fish, draped with top hat, swastika, and dollar bill, devouring a smaller fish upon which is written: "WITH GOD FOR HITLER AND CAPITAL" (*AIZ*, September 14, 1930). The subtitle "And I Voted for the Fish!" and the motto "6 Million Nazi Voters: Fodder for a Big Mouth" are juxtaposed to elucidate fact and comment. As secretary of the group, Gutnov was instrumental in preparing and organizing the Berlin OKTYABR exhibition, selecting a large part of the material and designing the catalogue. He spoke with German artists and members of OKTYABR at the opening and at two discussion evenings held in Berlin.

Five days after the Reichstag elections, in an interview with Alfred Durus (Alfréd Kéményi), art critic of the *Rote Fahne* [*Red Flag*], Gutnov commented on the current tasks of artists from the viewpoint of the OKTYABR group. Gutnov described a "new type of artist" who has left his studio for the factories: "The artist has become an industrial worker who works with other industrial workers in a factory. [...] The artist must work either industrially-collectively or as an agitator and propagandist. In the OKTYABR group, only six artists still work in studios, 240 artists are already out in factories and plants."[7] He continued that the artists have exchanged their easels for the tools of architects, exhibition and poster designers, and typographers, and they have instead worked in designers', technicians', and workers' collectives rather than as inspired individualists; or they are designing rooms and events at workers' clubs, and parades, together with the workers. The creation of works of art by the new type of artist involves "the participation of his factory's collective, e.g., in designing and planning a club with the critical involvement of the workers." According to Gutnov, the new "revolutionary proletarian" art was not produced by these new artists alone, but foremost and "above all by the artistically independent strata of the proletariat itself, through the work of the worker-draftsman, the worker-photographer, through the activity of the agitprop groups (TRAM), etc."[8]

As Alfred Durus notes in the interview, the revolutionary-minded members of the German ARBKD, since the end of the twenties, had modeled themselves on the image of the transformed artist. With his photomontages and typographical designs for the revolutionary press and book publications, Heartfield gave impetus to workers' independent creativity. In this respect, he can be regarded as a pioneer among German artists and can be considered close to the OKTYABR Constructivists not only regarding the technical production through photomontage and mass reproduction, but also with respect to his criticism (rooted in Dadaism) of individualist and self-serving artists.

It was the writer Sergei Tretyakov, Heartfield's friend and first biographer, who, during his stay in Berlin between January and April 1931, applied the term "operativism" to that new type of artist, which had initially been introduced by Gutnov and the OKTYABR group. In his lectures to German intellectuals on January 21 ("The Writer and the Socialist Village") and on April 19 ("The New Type of Writer"), Tretyakov repeated once again Gutnov's principal arguments, supporting them with his own practical experiences as an "operative writer."

Just as Gutnov pleaded on behalf of artists, Tretyakov, in reference to writers, propagated a double strategy: participation in material production, or at least in life in a wider sense, and "deprofessionalization of literature." In comparison with the old creative method, he explained the *differentia specifica* of the new type of artist as follows: "To put it simply: to invent an important theme is novelistic belles-lettres; to discover an important theme is reportage; to contribute constructively to an important theme is operativism." For the other side of the coin, aesthetic mass activity, Tretyakov predicts: "Writing will cease to be an unusual individual skill and will become part of communal education. The writer loses his guild-professional isolation by integrating himself into the economic process. He parts with the fetishes of individual handicraft by joining the operative collective brigades."[9]

Tretyakov's lectures caused more of a sensation in Germany than did the OKTYABR exhibition and the appearance of Gutnov: after all, they called into question the previous practices of literary creativity more acutely than the new genres of visual and product design, demanding of the artist not only a different style or genre – literary reportage, say, as a supplement to the novel or poem – but a completely new conduct of life.

Western intellectuals throughout the entire political spectrum raised objections to this conversion of art to "operativism": from the principal objections of Ezra Pound, Gottfried Benn, and Ludwig Marcuse to the involvement of art in practical life, to the position of the extreme Left in the circle around Johannes Becher, who dismissed Tretyakov's comments as "nonsense about the end of literature," and Georg Lukács, who blamed the "operative" writer for "distorting the truth" by rejecting totality and confining the world view to empirical facts.[10]

Heartfield, like hardly any other German artist, adopted Tretyakov's device – "I call operative the participation in the life of the subject matter itself" – and focused since 1930 above all on mass-produced magazines, in addition to book and poster designs.

If Walter Benjamin – in support of Tretyakov's remarks on "operativism" and the deprofessionalization of the writer – foresaw the newspaper as that paradoxical "theatre of the unbridled debasement of the word where its salvation is being prepared,"[11] then the possibility of saving not only the word but also the image, especially the photographic image, can be asserted. Even the blinding flood of pictures in the mass media (the salvation strategy) might be contained by the "operative" photographers and photomontage artists; i. e., whenever the images evolve from participating contemplation and are addressed to a specific, interested readership, or when the readers even design their illustrated newspapers and wall news sheets themselves.

In his speech at the Moscow Graphic Institute, Heartfield also examined the obligation of the revolutionary photomontage artist to use the new visual media in an "operative" way to instruct the masses to be independently active: "We must enlist photomontage as an instrument in the class struggle, always and wherever it can be used: in schools, in factories, in scientific institutions. In the hands of people who know how to handle it, this medium can become a genuine weapon of struggle, of study, and of construction."[12]

Sergei Tretyakov, who published parts of this speech in his 1936 monograph on the artist, considered photomontage to be the most suitable visual medium for deprofessionalizing art because of its technical production method: "Photomontage became the art of direct daily activity by the millions building socialism. It is truly a mass art, which does not require of its practitioners the specialized skills of the painter and the graphic artist – these are replaced by a pair of scissors – but gives free range to a combining ability; taste and wit are the specific talents of the photomontage artists. [...] If the army of photomontage creators were counted, it would probably number tens of thousands."[13]

Tretyakov describes how Heartfield explained the methods of photomontage to members of the Red Army in Moscow and how he worked with them. Furthermore, in Kharkov, one of the capital cities of the Ukraine, and in other towns, he taught and demonstrated the art of expressive, powerful montage, in particular for the wall news sheets that were widespread throughout the country, and also for the printed press. The masterly spareness and striking features of Heartfield's best works ensured "that they very quickly penetrated the ranks of the workers. They are copied and imitated and variations are made on them,"[14] for the workers' own photomontages.

Tretyakov himself produced his two most convincing works of literary "operativism" in the form of reports entitled *The Challenge,* about a writer in a *kolkhoz,* and *Chinese Testament: The Autobiography of Den Shi Khua as Told to Tretyakov.* In his foreword to the "bio-interview" with the Chinese student, he comments as follows on the "operative" method: "The book *Den Shi Khua* was created by two people: Den Shi Khua himself supplied the raw factual material, and I shaped it without distortion." This cooperation with the writer was necessary since the student had not yet mastered the "difficult art [...] of examining his own life in detail." The writer's role, therefore, alternated between that of "examining magistrate, confidant, interviewer, interlocutor, and psychoanalyst."

In both reports, the author did not hesitate to raise his own manner of writing to the status of literature. Tretyakov showed how he "operated" as an artist in the *kolkhoz* and in the interview. The methods of recording facts were made as apparent to the reader as the methods of their montage were made comprehensible. In both narratives, "deindividualization" and "deprofessionalization" of art were examined: this certainly did not mean neglect, or levelling of artistic techniques, or indifference to aesthetic form. Rather, "operative" art had to convert authentic factual material into an artistic form, which, in addition to an aesthetic experience, also provided insights into real life conflicts and their causes in order to arouse the desire in persons affected to change this life process. This required a highly qualified specialist: for the literary recording of facts à la Tretyakov, as for the photographic recording à la Heartfield, and, not least, for the processing and montage of these facts into an "operative" report and photomontage.

Heartfield was obsessed with his profession as hardly any other montage artist — a fact that by no means contradicted his approval of an "operative" artist's activities. János Reismann, Heartfield's photographer, testified to this obsession in his reports: "Heartfield's work is a struggle, repeated day after day, to realize his ideas and aims," wrote Reismann in 1934 in the Moscow-based magazine *International Literature.* "'People really don't have any idea,' he once said, 'how difficult it is to be a *Photomonteur.*' This is true but with the reservation that it is difficult to be a *Photomonteur* like Heartfield. [...] The shots that I took for Heartfield based on exact pencil sketches and always according to his personal instructions often took hours, many hours. He insisted on nuances that I was no longer capable of seeing."[15]

The book jackets Heartfield designed for publications produced above all by his brother Wieland Herzfelde's Malik-Verlag included those for Tretyakov's *The Challenge* [*Feld-Herren*] (1913) and for *Chinese Testament* [*Den Shi Khua*] (1932). Heartfield later wrote to Olga Tretyakova, wife of the writer, about the report from China: "[...] my brother Wieland and I both tried to give the book a characteristic jacket. Tretyakov helped us by sending us the photographs he had taken himself in Peking." Heartfield went on to say that the author was "sur-

John Heartfield, dust jacket (front and spine) for the *Illustrierte Geschichte der Russischen Revolution* [*Illustrated History of the Russian Revolution*], Berlin 1928

John Heartfield, dust jacket (front) for the *Illustrierte Geschichte der Deutschen Revolution* [*Illustrated History of the German Revolution*], Berlin 1929

prised and very pleased that we chose for the dust jacket the photo that shows the Chinese student whose life the book describes, standing in front of all those Chinese posters with slogans. We really had no idea that the Chinese in the photo is actually Den Khua."[16]

Tretyakov was not only a virtuoso writer and fine pianist but was a passionate photographer as well. For example, he illustrated the Russian editions of *The Challenge* with his own photographs and prepared his own independent photo essays. From his sojourn in the *kolkhoz*, he brought back 4,000 photographs. As a photographer-cum-writer and a photomontage artist-cum-author, he was in a position to judge Heartfield's photomontage work with particular expertise – something he did with the passion of the initiate in his analytical Heartfield monograph of 1936. The excerpt from Heartfield's letter, however, not only reports about the writer as photographer. It also documents the fact that Heartfield knew the two Tretyakov books, published by the Malik-Verlag not just superficially but he had studied them thoroughly – at least the "bio-interview" of the Chinese – and was thus thoroughly familiar with Tretyakov's "operative" method. The unanimous agreement on the need for a new type of artist was one of the foundations on which the friendships between Heartfield and Tretyakov, Heartfield and Gutnov were based.

When Heartfield arrived in Moscow, in April 1931, the artistic controversies conducted there since the end of 1930 with increasing vehemence were intensifying. For the fine arts, the aforementioned Central Committee resolution of February 1931 on poster agitation marked a decisive turning point. The debates were raised from the level of a group feud and theoretical discussion among critics and artists to an officially regulated party issue.

The party resolution placed the Department of Spatial Arts at the Institute for Literature, Fine Arts and Linguistics of the Communist Academy under an obligation to participate actively in the improvement of poster production. On April 13 and May 4, the first major discussion about poster production of the state press (IZOGIS) took place at the Academy, with photomontage posters as a prominent issue. Although participants agreed on the fundamental significance of the montage technique, they failed to reach a mutual decision about guidelines for its further development.[17] A subsequent meeting of the department was therefore called, where only the problems of photomontage were to be discussed. The paper on the fundamental principles given by Gustav Klutsis on June 7 was followed by a discussion on October 8 with department members and other artists. In his lecture, Klutsis repeated and expanded on the explanations in his Berlin catalogue text. He also mentioned Heartfield, referring to him as "a member of our shock brigade."[18]

During his stay in Moscow, Heartfield presented a number of his works at the photomontage show of June 1931, organized by the OKTYABR group at the Gorky Park exhibition pavilion on the occasion of Klutsis's lecture. Three of his book jackets could be seen on a display stand next to others by Klutsis and his pupil Pinus; these had been commissioned in 1929 by Willy Münzenberg's Neuer Deutscher Verlag: *Illustrierte Geschichte der Deutschen Revolution* [*Illustrated History of the German Revolution*], *Illustrierte Geschichte der Russischen Revolution* [*Illustrated History of the Russian Revolution*], and *Illustrierte Geschichte des Bürgerkrieges in Russland 1917–1921* [*Illustrated History of the Civil War in Russia 1917–1921*]. Heartfield was also represented with his *AIZ* photomontage "Das tote Parlament" ["The Dead Parliament"] (Fig. p. 257) in the IZOFRONT anthology, *The Art Front: The Class Struggle at the Front of the Spatial Arts*, published by OKTYABR in 1931.

Heartfield's cooperation with OKTYABR comes as no surprise – after all, he had received his invitation to the Soviet Union from the International Office of Revolutionary Artists, headed by the two OKTYABR members Alfred Kurella and Béla Uitz. In his lecture, Klutsis pleaded for the international amalgamation of all politically active photomontage groups, and that aim was affirmed with the invitation to Heartfield. Klutsis's relationship to Heartfield was amicable; they spent time together in Moscow. The two leading figures of political photomontage also met in Batumi, in the Georgian Caucasus, in the summer of 1931. Together with photomontage artists Senkin and Elkin, Klutsis had been sent to Georgia for August and September by Sovnarkom (Council of the People's Commissars), to study and document the progress of industrialization in Tiflis, Sukhumi, Batumi, and in the Donbas. At the same time, Heartfield visited the Georgian capital of Tiflis, the Baku oil fields, and also Batumi on the Black Sea, with an expedition brigade on behalf of the most distinguished Soviet photographic magazine, *USSR im Bau* [*The USSR in Construction*], which was published in several languages. From this expedition, they brought back hundreds of photographs, from which Heartfield then assembled the 1931 December issue of *USSR im Bau* (Fig. p. 273).

John Heartfield, dust jacket (front) for the *Illustrierte Geschichte des Bürgerkrieges in Russland 1917–1921* [*Illustrated History of the Civil War in Russia 1917–1921*], Berlin 1929

A photomontage poster by Klutsis, similarly propagating the early fulfillment of the first Five-Year Plan and depicting crane constructions looming into a red sky in dynamic obliquity, could have provided the inspiration for Heartfield's surprisingly Constructivist-oriented cover design. Other works by Heartfield also show similiarities with those of Klutsis; nevertheless, differences between the artistic methods remain obvious.

The tendency toward visual fusion, with smooth transitions, of montage elements into a homogeneous image is generally characteristic of Heartfield's photomontages. In that aspect his work is distinct from the harder cuts, more pronounced contrasts in shape, color, and texture [*Faktur*], sharper edges, and more abrupt transitions between parts favored by Klutsis and other Russian Constructivists. The distinction becomes apparent in the different adaptations of the same motif. The silhouette of Lenin, which Heartfield framed with an airplane wing above the roofs of a new Moscow housing development, and which was assembled for the ninth issue (1931) of *The USSR in Construction* on the subject of Moscow's reconstruction (Pl. p. 279), is also used by Klutsis in a photomontage poster design created around 1928/30. Here, the Lenin figure stands on a huge blast furnace, which towers above the crowd of workers in the lower area of the picture and actually encircles them. Again, the compositional layout is more artificial, and features more formal construction elements and a more contrasting, open, less pictorial montage form than in the Heartfield counterpart. The German's montages have their roots in Dadaist collages, in which a somewhat unstructured, incongruous conglomeration of photographic parts and quotations from the media and business confronts this world with a critically distorting mirror, wanting to expose, through exaggeration, its feigned and freewheeling activity. As a result of his work with books, Heartfield's photomontages since 1923 became increasingly sparse – after all, the cover motif had to be registered and understood in passing, as it were, if it was to have a strong promotional and agitational effect. Precisely this spare use of means, together with an obvious message and visual impact – which prompted Adolf Behne to call Heartfield's photomontages "photography plus dynamite" – also consolidated his reputation in the Soviet Union as a master of his art.

The photomontages of the Russian Constructivists, on the other hand, evolved from their strict, nonobjective form. For the first time in 1919, and thus parallel to Heartfield's first montages, Klutsis inserted photographic elements into such

Exhibition of the OKTYABR group, exhibition pavilion in Gorki Park, Moscow, June 1931
Left display panel, middle: dust jackets by Gustav Klutsis
Left display panel, right: dust jackets by John Heartfield

John Heartfield and Gustav Klutsis in Moscow, 1931

boldly linear structures created by means of texturing [*Faktur*], thus making use – as the artist later repeatedly stressed – of their double function as enrichment of the pictorial texture [*Faktur*] and as means of representation.

While the representational function of these fragments became more prominent among the Russian Constructivists in the course of the twenties; while the small-scale fragmentation of photographs gave way, in some cases, to larger sections; and while the constructive-linear elements of images were less emphasized than at the beginning, the artists never denied (at least, not until the controversies of 1931 on the correct method of pictorial composition) that Constructivism was their point of departure. Contrasting pictorial elements (monochromatic color planes, independent linear shapes, photographic elements, numerals, and letters) in order to evoke tension-laden textures [*Fakturen*] continued to be preferred to homogenized material that presented an illusionistic reality. Cleverly constructed juxtapositions of extreme angles and distances corresponded to an accentuation of tactile values. On the whole, the referential character of the image, and thus the reference – for the beholder – to an artificially contrived, qualifiable aspect of the depiction, suggested the power of photography.

In Heartfield's works, comparable compositional methods became prominent above all in the second half of the twenties, even though his formal and technical montage practices still were based on scenic or literary subjects. While the Russian Constructivists based the process of creating images on spatial and tactile perception, Heartfield's photomontages generally relied on human gesture and speech.

Irrespective of the close parallels, these obvious differences contributed to the fact that from late summer 1931 Heartfield's works were juxtaposed to those of the OKTYABR photomontage artists in the Soviet press, Soviet art magazines, and in public discussions, as the preferred alternative. The November issue (1931) of *Brigada khudozhnikov* drew a comparison between two of Klutsis's photomontages and a work by Heartfield. His book jacket for the *Illustrierte Geschichte der Russischen Revolution,* shown at the OKTYABR exhibition, was praised as exemplary for "unusual simplicity, exactness, and unambiguity" of its composition. It was written that Heartfield had set a precedent by making use of "only fundamental and essential" photographic elements and visual means to achieve "a condensed expression of the concept."

Gustav Klutsis, poster design, 1928/30

Compared to this economy of perception and concentration of means, Klutsis's photomontages, in the opinion of the commentator, were cluttered with details and were incoherent in their overall shape. While the postcard published in 1928 on the occasion of the Moscow Spartaciade was "inundated with mechanistically assembled material" and while the postures of the illustrated javelin thrower failed to correspond to the image of a Soviet athlete, the domination of man by the technical environment in the industrialization poster of 1931 was also criticized. The towering construction "literally [descends] upon the group of shock brigade workers."

In Klutsis's works, the artistic use of contrasts, scale, perspective, views, shape, and color – photomontage's principal means of mobilizing "social energy" in the beholder – are censured by the critic as a mechanistic and overladen arrangement of material: "The construction and the people are not conceived as being *organically in harmony with each other.*"[19] In this way, formal criticism became ideological criticism: because the Constructivist photomontage did not organically unite the illustrated building construction and portraits of shock brigade workers, Klutsis had made the political mistake of failing to comprehend and represent the working class and technology as an organic entity. The contrast between the horizontally arranged row of heads and the vertically looming scaffolding inferred a deliberate juxtaposition by the artist of man and technology. Ultimately, this could only mean that Klutsis doubted that the development of Soviet industry corresponded to the will and interest of the workers and was solely carried out for their benefit. Art criticism immediately turned into political criticism, so that a "formal mistake" could be interpreted automatically as political incorrectness.

Even if the criticized poster is not one of Klutsis's most convincing works, in this context, we are interested less in its formal quality than in its criticism. What had happened since the summer of that year when the Constructivist posters of the OKTYABR artists were still classified *grosso modo* as exemplary in public discussions?

The pictorial comparison between Heartfield and Klutsis had appeared in *Brigada khudozhnikov* as a commentary to the minutes of a discussion that had taken place on October 8 at the Institute for Literature, Fine Arts and Linguistics of the Communist Academy in Moscow. At this event, the above-mentioned lecture, given by Klutsis in June, was discussed. In the discussion, too, Klutsis was criticized for his representation of the shock brigade workers even by those who in principle acknowledged the importance of photomontage in contemporary poster production. He was accused of depicting the exemplary worker in an "impersonal manner," instead of portraying him as an emotionally moving character to identify with, one who would "mobilize the masses." Furthermore, the photomontages of Klutsis and the other Russian Constructivists were criticized in the discussion for having, in contrast to Heartfield, only insufficiently or not at all, represented the class enemy. Finally, the art critic Ivan Matsa (János Mácza) – like Klutsis, a leading member of the OKTYABR group – noted that when designing a composition, attention should be paid less to the formal contrasts described by Klutsis than to "the exactitude of the depicted subject [. . .] which is created by means of montage, and to the clarity and exactitude of the composition itself."[20]

For the last two points of criticism, Heartfield's photomontages were called upon at the event since they depicted and exposed the class enemy and fulfilled the demand for visual exactitude and clarity to a high degree. Tagirov in particular, a friend of Gutnov and also a member of OKTYABR, cited Heartfield's montages as exemplary works: "All Heartfield's posters possess a great political value whereas Klutsis, irrespective of the fact that his posters are better, only touches the surface of individual phenomena. This is a superficial political attitude." Tagirov's general evaluation was followed by practical suggestions: "We have to show German agitational art; Heartfield must visit us at the Graphic Institute every year, even if just for one or two months, and inform us of his experience with photomontage. It is absolutely essential that we profit from his experience."[21]

In his riposte, Klutsis vigorously opposed Heartfield's instruction to Soviet photomontage artists: "Personally, I am quite familiar with Heartfield's work and value it highly, but I believe we can learn very little from him. The enthusiasm Comrade Tagirov expresses with regard to the German artist Heartfield is characteristic of that group of workers who incorporated the principles of photomontage quite mechanically into their own graphic work and who want to introduce here this Western method just as mechanically. What Heartfield says about the imperialist war doesn't say anything about photomontage itself."[22]

This retort shows that, although the Russian Constructivist cherished Heartfield as a politically committed artist, Heartfield's methods were alien to him, if not to

Gustav Klutsis, poster *We Will Fulfill the Five-Year Plan in Four Years*, 1930

Page from *Brigada khudozhnikov* (Moscow), October 1931
Top left: Gustav Klutsis, postcard for the Spartaciade in Moscow, 1928
Top right: John Heartfield, dust jacket (front) for the *Illustrierte Geschichte der Russischen Revolution*, Berlin 1928
Bottom: Gustav Klutsis, poster *Work in the USSR is a Matter of Honor, Glory and Heroism*, 1931

Gustav Klutsis, postcard for the Spartaciade in Moscow, 1928

Gustav Klutsis, postcard for the Spartaciade in Moscow, 1928

be dismissed outright, and he spoke out against adapting them as guiding principles for Soviet artists. His demand "not [to] forget the exact composition" makes it clear that Klutsis found Heartfield's photomontages to be lacking in the polymorphic contrasting methods and open constructions developed by Constructivists, and that he rejected the organic arrangement of visual elements with their smooth transitions. Heartfield's rhetorical visual language relying on allegories, and his creative process frequently originating in a play on words were also alien to Constructivist photomontage. The Russian works focused not on pictorial wit and its intelligibility to the observer, but on the emotionally infectious, rousing effect of dynamic spatial structures and contrapuntally assembled photographic details. Yet, Klutsis's objection, and with it that of the OKTYABR Constructivists, did not withstand the campaign against their position. The discussion about the methodical procedures of photomontage, which reached its peak in autumn 1931, was only part of a more extensive attack on the last bastions of the Russian avant-garde. The critical comparison of Heartfield and Klutsis in *Brigada khudozhnikov,* carried out at the expense of the Constructivists, had summarized the key points. In public condemnations, Constructivist exhibits were accused of technicist formalism, of mechanistic methods, of anti-art functionalism, and of a "left-wing" aestheticism inspired by the West.

The attacks became so intense that the Constructivists were finally forced to undergo public self-criticism and to abandon their old convictions. In autumn 1931, still before the discussion of his lecture at the Communist Academy, Klutsis, together with the photomontage artists Elkin, Kulagina, Pinus, Senkin, and others, disassociated themselves from the OKTYABR group and requested permission to join the Russian Association of Proletarian Artists (RAPKh), founded in May of that year. RAPKh in particular, affiliated with the writers' organization RAPP (Russian Association of Proletarian Writers), intensified the ideological drumfire both against "right-wing deviants" (the old realistic painters) and the "left-wing deviants" of the avant-garde, while they themselves usurped representing the true party line and the class interests of the proletariat.

In this war of extermination against OKTYABR, the Russian Society of Proletarian Photo Journalists (ROPF), which was sympathetic with RAPKh, played an equally aggressive role. ROPF had been set up in September 1931; among its most active founding members were Max Alpert and Arkady Shaikhet, the two photographers with whom Heartfield had returned from his photographic excursion to Baku and Georgia shortly before.

The photo showing Heartfield among the Soviet artists was taken in Batumi. In this relaxed atmosphere on the Black Sea coast, the German appears to have acted as a kind of pacifying figure for the rival factions. He has put his left arm amicably around the painter Fedor Bogorodsky, while the right arm rests on Gustav Klutsis's leg. The realistic painter Bogorodsky, one of the leading representatives of the Association of Artists of Revolutionary Russia (AKhRR), already behaves like a traditionalist, in his Bavarian-style clothes. The OKTYABR trio, however, is no less stylized: as avant-garde collective, Klutsis, Senkin, and Elkin have all shaved their heads and donned sports clothes, emphasizing the functionally minded and efficiently operating Constructivists of the age of technology. The mutual aversion between Klutsis and Bogorodsky is just as imperceptible in this situation as the bitter rivalry for artistic leadership between the Constructivist group and the state-supported association of realists.

The group is joined on the right by Max Alpert and Arkady Shaikhet. As photo reporters for *The USSR in Construction,* they formed part of Heartfield's four-man expedition brigade. The famous photo reportage about the life-style of the working-class Filipov family in Moscow, which appeared in the *AIZ* in 1931, was also made by Alpert and Shaikhet. The authenticity of this report was called into question by the Social Democratic press. As counterevidence, the *AIZ* published a photo showing Heartfield with the Filipov family in Moscow, with the following caption: "The role of the SPD [German Social Democratic Party] is becoming clearer every day: it is the left wing of fascism. How else would it be possible for it to fight the Soviet Union – where socialism is creating a new world – with a new campaign of lies every day? Our picture reveals such a lie; it shows the well-known artist John Heartfield with the Filipov family in Moscow, which the SPD press had simply declared nonexistent. [...]"

Even if there is no proof that Heartfield participated in the ideological campaign against the OKTYABR artists – from which Soviet avant-garde art has still not recovered today – he clearly moved closer to the newly founded ROPF after his return from the photo expedition in late summer 1931, thus automatically distancing himself from his former OKTYABR comrades.

An official meeting with Heartfield and the members of ROPF took place in December.[23] Likewise, *Proletarskoe foto* [*Proletarian Photography*] also opened its pages to him. In the years 1931/32, this photo magazine became the platform for attacks by ROPF photographers against the Constructivists of the OKTYABR group. In its founding declaration, printed in the September issue of *Proletarskoe foto,* ROPF already led a general attack against OKTYABR, employing then common terms of abuse: "[...] bitter fire must be opened against the 'leftists,' who are basically new petit bourgeois aesthetes. The work of the leftists is inspired by Western decadence as represented by the modern bourgeois photographers, particularly Moholy-Nagy and his imitators. [...] In the conditions prevailing in the Soviet Union, the imitation of Western fashion, the renunciation of in-depth dialectical-materialistic analysis of the phenomena around us in favor of a mechanical gliding over the surface, will lead to a deviation from the course that proletarian photography should follow in the period of socialist construction."[24] Claiming that their work "exposes the nature of phenomena according to the methods of dialectical materialism," the ROPF photographers and photomontage artists at the same time declared that the "exposure of the mock revolutionary character" of OKTYABR artists is one of "the most important tasks in the overall plan of the struggle for the creative method of proletarian photography."[25]

This controversy about the artistic means was distorted into a class struggle under the pressure of the party leadership. The political exposure and destruction of dissenters became a topmost priority. The battle for the true line, however, remained shadow-boxing until the catchword of dialectical materialism as a creative method was explained in more concrete terms. It was here that Heartfield's photomontages came to the rescue. In them, the critics of the Constructivists considered the "creative method" to be most perfectly realized.

In view of this role of Heartfield's montages, as important arguments in the discussions of the time about the dialectical-materialistic method – which had been stipulated as mandatory but had not yet been shown in practice – it is reasonable to assume that the exhibition of his complete works, showing about 300 on November 20, had been consciously planned by the organizers as a contribution to the discussion, or even more: as a touchstone for future developments. All reviews emphasized the exemplary and helpful character of the undertaking. The German language magazine, *Sowjetkultur im Aufbau* [*Soviet Culture in Construction*], wrote: "The exhibition of works by the German artist John Heartfield working in the field of photomontage aroused particular interest in Moscow. The unusual sharpness and expressive design of the posters,

Gustav Klutsis, dust jacket for N. Bobrov's *The Day-to-Day Life of an Aviation Man,* Moscow 1930

From left to right: Heartfield, Alpert, Kiselovsky, un-identified, unidentified, Shaikhet. On the Black Sea coast near Batumi, August 1931

From left to right: Klutsis, Heartfield, Bogorodsky, El-kin, Senkin, Alpert, Shaikhet. Batumi, 1931

book jackets, and other works by Heartfield that were exhibited not only stirred interest among artists in the Soviet Union but also among the broad masses of the public. Like the exhibition itself, Heartfield's working methods have been commented on in depth in the Soviet press. The exhibition ended with a discussion about Heartfield's creative activity, in which the works of this artist, who has succeeded in following *the right course* in the application of photomontage to polygraphy, were recognized as most valuable."[26]

Even a more unsuspicious witness, the Bauhaus member Lou Scheper, who was staying in Moscow with her husband (Bauhaus master Hinnerk Scheper), shared this assessment of Heartfield's exemplary role in the Soviet discussion. In the December issue of the *Moskauer Rundschau* [*Moscow Review*], Lou Scheper announced, "A Contemporary Exhibition" of Heartfield's works. Alongside his works' technical virtuosity and effectiveness, the reviewer highlighted their wealth of ideas. "Not a single work – be it a poster, book cover, endpaper, illustration, or whatever – lacks a witty, political punch line; nowhere is the impact achieved by coarse, nonartistic means, yet everywhere these means clearly serve the effect. [...] Often it is a very simple, though always an intellectual idea that [brings about] the political mass impact." Scheper concluded that Heartfield's works were of significance to Soviet photomontage artists first and foremost because of the method applied in them of giving shape to ideas.[27]

In the magazine *Sovietskoe iskusstvo* [*Soviet Art*], on the other hand, Heartfield's "artistic images" were unfavorably compared to the "most naive, meaningless formalism" of the Constructivist photomontage artists, who did nothing more than "take a pile of photographs, cut them apart, paste them onto a sheet of paper, [and] arrange the composition into the 'diagonal,' 'vertical,' or 'horizontal.'" According to the reviewer, the German artist, however, in the exhibition succeeded to show "the face of the bourgeois world and the heroic struggle of the brotherly communist parties with such wealth and perfection" that his work should become a "means of international mass education."[28]

In *Proletarskoe foto,* the unofficial platform of ROPF, a richly illustrated, introductory editorial appeared under the title "FOR THE PROLETARIAN CREATIVE METHOD OF PHOTOMONTAGE – JOHN HEARTFIELD, A PROGRESSIVE INTERNATIONAL PHOTOMONTAGE ARTIST," together with several essays on Heartfield's work, which had already been printed elsewhere: in addition to the above-mentioned interview with Egon Erwin Kisch (under the new title "The Greatest Contemporary Artist"), an article by Sergei Tretyakov, in which the writer presented a summary of Heartfield's life, annotations to some of his montages, and examples of his reception among the Russian and German working class. Sections of this article were later included in Tretyakov's more extensive portrait of the artist (*People of a Funeral Pyre,* 1936) and in his monograph on Heartfield (1936).

Another contribution to this collection of articles comes from V. Kostin, who had been president of the youth association of OKTYABR until shortly before; he too had been forced emotionally, and even physically, by RAPKh to renounce Constructivism and to leave the association.[29] Kostin then called Heartfield – in a polemical turn against the claims repeatedly expressed by Klutsis – the "founder of photomontage" and "its best artist." He also repeated, *ex negativo,* the accusation of the overly elaborate and formalist aestheticism of Constructivist montages: by emphasizing the simple means that lent Heartfield's works their "extraordinary power and conviction" and guaranteed "a lively resonance and popularity among the masses." "With genuine proletarian hatred," the German photomontage artist exposed "all the motivating forces behind capitalist growth and prosperity," i.e., exploitation, unemployment, and colonialism.

The fourth contribution, that of L. Mezhericher, editor of *Proletarskoe foto*, emphasized the exemplary function of the Heartfield exhibition more candidly than either the two writers who sympathized with Constructivism or the former OKTYABR member Kostin. According to this article, Heartfield's works surpassed "by far everything previously" achieved by Soviet artists in the field of photomontage so that "without hesitation [we can] advise our photographers, poster artists, and illustrators to learn from our German comrade." Although Heartfield mastered "perfectly the form into which he transforms the initial photographic material," he would "at no time and no point [become] a formalist. Every kind of aestheticism is alien to him." One reprimand was directly addressed to Constructivist photomontage artists: "There are still a few among our artists who want to learn something from the bourgeoisie. In particular, the decadent urban photography and photomontage of the modern West (Moholy-Nagy, Aenne Biermann, Man Ray, and others) fill the hearts of some of our formalists with such sweet sorrow. We would rather apprentice them to Heartfield."[30]

Mezhericher recommended organizing mass excursions to the exhibition especially for worker-photo-correspondents. As a matter of fact, Heartfield gave daily guided tours of his exhibition to workers, peasants, and intellectuals, with Tretyakov serving as interpreter most of the time.[31] Like Lou Scheper in her review, Mezhericher also emphasized primarily the content of Heartfield's photomontages. The formal arrangement of the material avoided any kind of formalism because it always rested on a striking underlying visual concept, which in turn was based on a political proposition. "The political forcefulness and combative expediency of Heartfield's works lead him toward an extreme sparseness, toward a *superior union of idea and form* [...] *in all his works, form evolves from an idea.*"[32]

With his observation that the idea in Heartfield's works always retained "the dominant role," the reviewer tried to bring photomontages into accord with the methodical postulate set forth at the Kharkov conference in 1931 as a mandatory directive for the "dialectical-materialistic creative method" in art. Commenting on the main paper by L. Averbakh (the chairman of RAPP), Alfred Kurella explained to German readers the "exact definition of the term of proletarian literature," which was to be mandatory for the visual arts as well. It was "not the class background and not the mere intention" that made a proletarian artist. The "class character" of a work of art would be "determined on the basis of an analysis of the *ideas* expressed objectively in the work of art in question and, consequently, whom this work of art would serve objectively in the class struggle of its time."

Thus the idea of a work of art, whatever that might be in individual cases, became one of the cornerstones of the "dialectical-materialistic creative method." Heartfield conformed to these directives when he declared, in a lecture at the Moscow Graphic Institute, that the bourgeoisie had "no talented artists" and no "great, good art [...] because it *lacks* powerful *ideas*." In the Soviet Union, by contrast, "a new society is being built on the foundation of powerful, new ideas. A genuine art as well is developing on this foundation of socialist construction and work. And these ideas are not only powerful, and not only new: They are the *only ideas* that are *powerful* and the only ones that are *new*."[33]

Other characteristics of the "dialectical-materialistic creative method" are named in the introductory article to the four essays published in *Proletarskoe foto*. The author first noted that the work of each and every artist consisted of "*reconstructing* reality *from the point of view of class*," a reconstruction based on ideas, which had to include generalizing facts; for a mere listing or stringing together

Heartfield exhibition in Moscow, November 20 – December 10, 1931

John Heartfield, "Red Unity Will Make You Free!" (*AIZ*, Berlin), August 24, 1932, cover page

Brigade K. G. Koretsky, poster *This is Our Last and Decisive Blow,* 1932

of facts would not show their interrelation nor the conflict-laden fabric of reality. Photography in itself was ill-suited for such a generalization, undertaken from the class viewpoint. Its mechanical production of documentary images was also the cause of its weakness: the clinging to detail, to the single object or partial view. But photomontage could liberate the photographer from his dependence on facts; its technique and that of photography can produce a generalized statement. Like any other artist, the photomontage artist has to modify natural proportions and "reorganize the accidental correlations." "The *essential* and the *typical*" have to be liberated from the "secondary and the particular" so that the artist can "shape his intentions based on reality." His aims should express his *Weltanschauung* and the "pursuits of his social environment."

The "*generalization*" of reality according to the party line, and finding the "typical" in a situation or person on the basis of a preconceived "idea," were thought to be the most important techniques of the "dialectical-materialistic creative method" in photography, photomontage, and poster design. The "reconstruction" of visible reality by assembling its photographically fixed facts was supposed to make visible the "essence" behind the "phenomena." In the author's opinion, it was here that montage had the advantage over painting and drawing since the documentary nature of the individual photographs, artificially assembled and ideally programmed, gave power to facts: "What is special about these illustrations is that the *formal components* retain photography's *suggestion of reality*, but *in its generalized form overcomes* photography's *constraint*, its limitation to reconstruct." Aiming toward generalization and typification, photography should first and foremost preserve its idea-content, and should approximate more "great synthetic art."[34]

What this claim meant for photomontage in particular and for art in general can be illustrated with the author's example in *Proletarskoe foto*: To depict a blast furnace together with a figure of a worker towering above it – in order to show a "symbol of the proletariat's creative power" and thus generalize the portrait of the worker into that of a "ruler" over the "gigantic achievements of socialist technology" – could be achieved by photography only with difficulty, while posing no problem to photomontage.

Contrasting proportions and forms to activate vision, a technique championed by Constructivists like Klutsis, was then reduced to a crude practice serving to symbolize idealization and monumentalization. The assembled "reconstruction" of reality, by changing actual proportions, conformed to the "idea" that the working class was the owner and ruler of industrial construction, as propagated by the Central Committee of the Communist Party. In his important speech at the economic conference of June 23, 1931, Stalin reformulated the relationship of technology and the labor force. While since 1928, from the outset of the first Five-Year Plan, the general watchword had been "technology determines everything," human labor was now assigned priority. Stalin spoke explicitly of a new phase of socialist development, which necessitated "new methods" of leadership. "Indeed, the production plan is the active and practical work of millions of people. The reality of our production plan is those millions of workers creating a new life. The reality of our program are living people, we ourselves."[35]

From this general, "humanistically" embellished maxim, Stalin drew six directives for the new leadership methods, for example: introducing a strict wage hierarchy instead of collective wages; replacing collective plant management with individually responsible one-man control; increasing the number of old bourgeois specialists who supported industrialization; and training a technical working-class intelligentsia. In adminstration of art, the consequences of Stalin's directives became noticeable with some delay, but then with great impact. Stalin's emphasis on "*active* people" as the decisive productive force in industrial development required artists not just to dominate the "merely technical." The technique and composition of photomontage were now considered unacceptable by party-line critics. What was demanded was the organic fusion of photo fragments and color forms into an illusionistic unity without internal fractures. Blurring of hard cuts and edges between photo particles, toning down textural, compositional, and color contrasts within a montage would in this way assimilate the mode of depiction to its subject matter, to the Stalinist world of life and labor. The above-mentioned criticism in *Brigada khudozhnikov* of the two photomontages by Klutsis (Figs. p. 265) showed clearly the transmission of party directives to the visual arts. The lack of "*organic harmony*" between the shock brigade workers and the technology depicted were criticized, as much as the abrupt transitions and disproportions in the montage structures. This criticism was expanded in another article by Kostin on "Photomontage and the Mechanistic Errors of OKTYABR," published in 1932. Here, too, the author referred to Heartfield's works as examples of the components' organic correlation. The montages formed an "*artistic, living image*" ("*obraz*") that had a logical, but not a "schematic" construction, as in the case of the Constructivists.[36] But while in this comparison Heartfield's sparseness and ability to fuse the montage structure were still cited as positive counterexample to the Constructivist misuse of visual elements, criticism hit him a bit later, too.

The art critic Evgeny Kronman (Eugen Kronmann), who at the time (1932) had sharply criticized Tatlin for his supposed "descent into technique," discerned in Heartfield's photomontages as well a lack of the "human" factor and a fatal tendency toward "things." "Heartfield's recent work, in the twelfth issue of the photo magazine *USSR im Bau,* which he designed, upsets us very much. That issue features the oil industry in the Soviet Union. [. . .] Yet, in this magazine, the new builders, the shock brigade workers, are missing." The "most important element" making up socialist production had been "hidden by machines and drilling rigs." With all respect to the "superior technical perfection" of the photographs and the "most ingenious perspectives," there was no "example of the new quality of socialist work in the entire issue, an offense against the cause of glory, honor, and heroism."[37]

The threat resounding in this criticism of Heartfield's "petit bourgeois intellectualism" was reframed in more conciliatory terms when the critic informed the artist that "the stay in the Soviet Union [would] be a critical test for him. He will have to increase his knowledge of theoretical Marxism and work hard on himself," if he wanted to overcome "leftist formalism" and learn and apply the "dialectical-materialistic" method. "Heartfield's working method is not always dialectical; to acquire it, the artist has a lot of work ahead of him."[38]

Kronman did not impart to the reprimanded *Monteur* what exactly was the "dialectical-materialistic creative method" he had missed; he only listed what it was not, namely, neither "mechanistic," "schematic," "formalist," nor "of things." Instead, and in line with the party watchword, the critic knew all the better what was to be demanded of art: "portraying the new man, the shock brigade worker." Measured by this stipulation, however, Heartfield had been "from early on incapable of portraying the positive side of the program of the proletarian struggle. Virtually all of his political photomontages emphasize the negative characteristics of the enemy. [. . .]"[39] The new humanity in the economy demagogically proclaimed by Stalin required of the artist a "humanistic" depiction of mankind. The positive figure of the new Soviet man, the hero of honor and glory, was to take the place of the exposed and derided class enemy.

In view of Heartfield's work published before 1932, this reprimand appears as

Bezbozhnik [*The Atheist*], no. 7, July 1934, cover page. Use of a photomontage by Heartfield for the Geneva Disarmament Conference (cf. Pl. 99)

exaggerated as Kostin's remark, of the previous year, claiming that in addition to exploitation, colonial slavery, and the "decaying foundation of capitalist society" Heartfield's montages also showed, "in the background of this dying world," the resolutely advancing "ranks in the millions of working class masses," from whose mouths the "song of the *komsomoltsy* [...] cheerfully resounds."[40]

In this period, when Stalinism was firmly established, the objective, fair opinion had no place. The fact of the matter is that Heartfield evidently took the criticism to heart when leaving the Soviet Union and tried to incorporate a few heroic masters of technology in his montages (Pl. 76). In this effort, though, he managed to achieve a barely convincing representation of the "new man." The dramatic arrangement is not well brought together with the documentary quality of the photographs.

The metaphor of the clenched fist and the arm with countless faces and fists in it is more convincing in the medium of photomontage – an expressive image of the joining of many people in anti-fascist unity (Fig. p. 274). Heartfield evidently borrowed here from Klutsis, whose well-known photomontage poster with the many voters' hands, outstreched and floating in the same direction (Fig. p. 275), demonstrates as strikingly the accord of the individual with the collective will. Drama in photomontages can be convincing only where it is shown as having been constructed. Only in this way can dramatic messages appeal, without professing to be a reflection of reality, which is in itself dramatic and allegedly perfect. Only when the constructed image of reality does not conceal that it has been produced, only then can the viewer discern that he, too, can produce reality, that is to say, change it. By contrast, the official demand directed to Constructivists for a "synthetic montage" (Mezhericher) is an attempt to get around the documentary quality of photographic material and the picture composition based on a fictitious "living artistic image" (Kostin), so that the depiction might reflect the unity of man and technology, the individual and society, the masses and the party leadership that has already been achieved.

Apart from Tretyakov, probably the most penetrating appreciation in the Soviet Union of Heartfield's achievement was the exhibition review written by the art scholar Aleksei Fedorov-Davydov, then director of Moscow's Tretyakov Gallery and theorist of the OKTYABR group. Still, he too followed the ritual of politicized art criticism conditioned by the times, rebuking "formalist errors in principle ... by leading masters of Soviet photomontage," "exaggerated ideas about the potential of photomontage, artificial differences to painting, and at the same time an inadequate ability to exploit fully the actual potential of photomontage."[41] Like his colleagues, he too took the "discussion of Heartfield's creative method [...] as the point of departure for the treatment of more general questions on photomontage as a special genre of the visual arts." Fedorov-Davydov, in accord with other critics, considered photomontage a "fine opportunity for a dialectical depiction of phenomena."[42]

As the only one among the advocates of the "dialectical creative method" in the visual arts, he offered at least a definition of its method of depiction – to "expose the universal in detail, in all its real concreteness, in its political and social topicality." "This depiction conveys in a kind of snapshot a dialectical notion of a process, of a movement, and of the unity of opposites, and, finally, it passes judgment, exposing the true nature and essential correlations."[43] While Heartfield's "creative method [might not be] fully dialectical, that is, proletarian," because there are "moments of formalism and mechanism" in his photomontages, nevertheless they come very close to the "dialectical method of depicting reality." By tearing objects and phenomena "out of the familiar, as it were 'real,' context, and putting them in a new, 'nonreal' one," Heartfield could have them enter into unfamiliar relationships that were more truthful than the "accidental 'real' relationships." By their juxtaposition, things or events can be shown in a situation that "reveals the real in the present."

Fedorov-Davydov regarded as the most successful examples of such a confrontation the montage of a model armored cruiser in the hands of Social Democrat Chancellor Hermann Müller (Pl. 52a), the juxtaposition of a nocturnal view of Boston with the photograph of an electric chair on the front and back covers of Upton Sinclair's novel *Boston* (Fig. p. 275), and the combination of a steel helmet with a Rhine landscape (Fig. p. 40). In the critic's opinion, the particular strength of these montages lay in their instant intelligibility which, more than the "instantaneous registration by the viewer," "sets off a complicated chain of logical associations, compelling [him] to ponder for a long while."[44]

Fedorov-Davydov considered Heartfield's montages to be dialectical images: In the collision of visual and verbal quotations from seemingly divergent spheres of reality, they uncovered their buried, yet essential kinship. This kind of juxtaposition, however, is not, as with the Constructivists, a matter of visual contrasts; quite to the contrary, Heartfield's montages for the most part evoked the illusion of a unified pictorial space in order to show the unity of opposites of things and events.

Fedorov-Davydov also enlisted the Hegelian dialectic of individual and general unity in order to demonstrate the dialectical method in Heartfield's creative work. As "Müller's smile and the armored cruiser [symbolize] hypocrisy and compromise," so "in the individual and the particular [...] universality" is represented. This analysis of the "dialectical creative method" poses the question whether Heartfield, as his interpreter suspected, intended to symbolize the *general* hypocrisy of social democracy with his combination of the improbable, or whether he did not have a very *specific political incident* and a very *concrete target* in mind for his montage.

Fedorov-Davydov's analysis shows the attempt to make photomontage an art and place it beside painting as an equal. Yet the argument is not so much concerned with elevating the *Photomonteur* onto Parnassus. The bestowal of a higher honor was rather intended to separate photomontage from its concrete life practice, to divert it from being specific to being universal. Art was to create an image of, rather than intervene in, reality. This retrogression of photomontage's methods and techniques, suited for mass use, into a "high" art striving for generalizations served to defuse it as a medium of self-articulation by the masses in everyday life and in the political field. At the same time, by making the shock brigade worker and the "Soviet intelligentsia" into types of the "new man," a medium of communication was snatched out of the hands of the individual. The production of images was to be raised to an artistic level that was no longer accessible to the masses as producers but only as consumers of a false picture of themselves.

The criteria laid down for graphic production at the beginning of the thirties in the context of the Stalinization of Soviet society were applied unconditionally by Soviet critics as prerogatives for revolutionary proletarian art in capitalist countries. Consequently, it was deprived of its critical function, cherished until then. Kostin's, Kronmann's, and Fedorov-Davydov's call for depicting the positive side of reality as well (which photomontage achieved first and foremost through the unity of opposites) shows both this regressive change of paradigms in the production and use of the new visual medium and of the mechanical application of a false illusion of heroism.

As evidence of formalist traces and a mechanistic worldview even in the case of Heartfield, Fedorov-Davydov pointed out that he "is much stronger in satire, in

Gustav Klutsis retouching the photomontage panel
The Party is the Head of the Working Class, ca. 1936

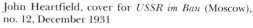

John Heartfield, cover for *USSR im Bau* (Moscow), no. 12, December 1931

273

15 JAHRE SOWJET-UNION

Wir schwören: „In der Stunde der Gefahr lassen wir
unser sozialistisches Vaterland nicht im Stich"

John Heartfield, "15 Years of the Soviet Union"
(*AIZ*, Berlin), October 30, 1932, p. 1035

John Heartfield, "Every Fist Becomes One Clenched
Fist" (*AIZ*, Prague), October 4, 1934, cover page

protest, in the depiction of the negative than in the *depiction of the positive*. We look in vain for the classical ideals of the proletariat in his works. The 'spirit of destruction' is not shown here as a 'spirit of creation.' But this, after all, is antithetical *unity*, i.e., the dialectical depiction of the revolutionary proletariat."[45]

In this spirit, *unity* rather than the earlier emphasis on *opposites* was increasingly evoked at the end of 1931. In 1932, when Stalin finally declared the class struggle and the establishment of socialism in the Soviet Union complete, unity of individual, no longer opposed, forms was decreed in art, as well as a necessary method of work. The "positive" became the all-dominating value and conveyed the image of a society harmoniously and enthusiastically pursuing its construction. Only outside this island of bliss did evil reign. Evil appeared incorporated in the military aggressor against the workers' paradise, and was exposed and attacked through caricature.

In 1932, images composed of discontinuities and opposites were completely banned from Soviet art and photomontage. It gave way to the painterly polished delusion, welded into uniformity, of a reality inspired by one single will and striving toward a common goal. The photomontage of the former Constructivists, too, was forced to assimilate itself to painting, sometimes with a distortion beyond recognition of its technical methods and processes in order to decorate reality in detail with harmonious forms and luminous colors. The brush of the retoucher replaced the scissors. Documenting facts was as unthinkable as was their montage assemblage in order to gain insights about far-reaching changes. Moreover, every form of montage was now suspected by Soviet critics of not conforming to the official methods and was immediately condemned as "formalist and mechanistic." By the time these invectives were aimed in Heartfield's direction, he had already left the country.

While until 1931 Heartfield's methods of organizing material, despite all individuality, showed similarities to those of the Russian Constructivists, after his return from the Soviet Union in 1932, he used literature much more in his montages. The increasing importance of text and figures of speech as a point of departure for his pictorial idea can be traced back, among other reasons, to the discussion in the Soviet Union; later in Germany, Georg Lukács demanded a psychologically motivated description of society in a work of art.

The introduction of the terms "essence" and "appearance" into the political-aesthetic discussion, and the corresponding restriction of the creative method to a reflection of "essence" in the "appearances," brought about once again a separation of the image from reality at the beginning of the thirties. The consequent reduction of empirical reality to mere surface led in the thirties not only to criticism and condemnation of the open montage forms but also to criticism and renunciation of the working methods of an intervening art, whose impact on the viewer depended on these very methods of organizing the material. The consumer of images was deprived of his competence as producer once more, and his expropriation in the field of media went hand in hand with his political inaction. This new change of paradigms in art was marked by the establishment, in the Soviet Union, of Stalinism, and in Germany, of fascism.

Certain observations made in 1932 by Alfred Durus, art critic of the German Communist Party, illustrate how decisions made in the Soviet Union on the correct production of art found their way into German party groups and associations. Although Heartfield always called himself a *Monteur* in order to stress the technical and proletarian quality of his art, as opposed to conventional artistic activity, Durus, in a review of a photomontage exhibition of the Bund revolutionärer bildender Künstler Deutschlands [Association of Revolutionary

Visual Artists of Germany] (BRBKD), spoke out against the derivation of photomontage from the "new industrial technology." "We must fight this mechanistic bourgeois concept, this overemphasis of the technical side of photomontage. Photomontage is not a crane, it is not a railway coach, and the *Photomonteur* is not an engineer." Rather than this allegedly "bourgeois" notion of photomontage, it meant "for us" "a potentially exhaustive (total) visual recording of social reality, an *epochal artistic medium*."[46]

This juxtaposition of "mechanistic bourgeois" photomontage and "total-visual" recording of reality can only be understood as a reaction to the discussions about the "dialectical-materialistic method of creation" conducted in the Soviet Union and applied to Germany. Durus tried to defend photomontage's existence under the postulate of this method, to protect it against the accusations of being mechanistic and artless.

In his choice of words and juxtaposition of terms, Durus was explicitly referring to the controversy over the "creative method" of proletarian revolutionary art and, above all, literature, conducted in 1931/32 in the *Linkskurve* [*Left Turn*], organ of the Bund proletarischer revolutionärer Schriftsteller [Association of Proletarian Revolutionary Writers] (BPRS), affiliated with the BRBKD. In the May issue of 1932, the chairman of this association, the poet Johannes R. Becher, took issue with Heartfield, seeking to play down his importance for the workers' movement. Tretyakov had written about the "Visual Arts" in the April issue of the left-wing Münzenberg Press *Magazin für Alle* [*Magazine for Everybody*], referring, as he had already done in his article in *Proletarskoe foto,* to Heartfield's popularity among German workers: "Every worker, every young Communist, every pioneer in Germany is just as familiar with Heartfield's montages as he is with the poetry of Weinert and the songs of Hanns Eisler." Becher contradicted this assessment as he would not have "our successes" in revolutionary proletarian literature and art linked with the names listed by Tretyakov.[47] Together with Eisler, Ottwalt, and Tretyakov, Heartfield belonged to those left-wing bourgeois artists who were allied with Brecht. These artists, concealing or openly displaying their hostility, formed a counterpoint to the group around Becher within the sphere of left-wing intellectuals. From Georg Lukács in particular, who in the summer of 1931 had been sent to Berlin by Moscow to support the BPRS leadership against so-called "leftist" deviations, the Becher faction received some theoretical support. Lukács voiced his opinions on matters concerning the creative method primarily in the *Linkskurve.* There he applied the criteria of the Soviet discussion so unconditionally to the quite different artistic and socio-economic situation in Germany that the writer Ernst Ottwalt, an ally of Brecht and Tretyakov, felt compelled to retort, "that we cannot blindly take over the Soviet Union's literary-political problems into our literary-political situation. The conditions against which we are struggling and under which we are forced to produce are different."[48]

Although the methical and political controversies between left-wing artists in the Weimar Republic were fought out, in contrast to the Soviet Union, primarily in literary circles, their consequences did not fail to leave their mark on the visual arts. The condemnation of reportage and montage forms as a mechanistic "experiment in form," initiated by Lukács in the 1931 November issue of the *Linkskurve* with a sharp criticism of Willi Bredel's working-class novel, had consequences also on the official party appreciation of Heartfield's photomontages. Later on, Bredel wrote to him in a somewhat aesopian-style: "Our development is dialectically so complicated that your novel form of artistic expression was considered formalism. In truth, it is the very opposite. [. . .]"[49]

Gustav Klutsis, poster design *We Will Fulfill the Plan of Great Works,* 1931

John Heartfield, dust jacket for Upton Sinclair's *Boston,* Berlin 1929

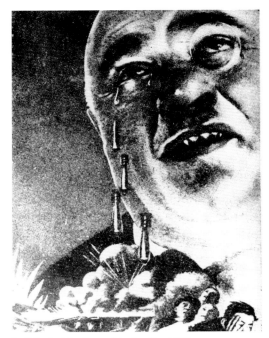

B. Klinch, *The Tears of the Pacifist*, 1932

In his 1932 criticism of Ottwalt's factual novel about the German justice system, which also contained a critical dig at Tretyakov's bio-interview *Chinese Testament* published shortly before, Lukács insisted above all on the necessity to give artistic shape to the "totality" of "living interrelations between living people and thus, indirectly, between them and the society in which they live and with which they fight out their conflicts."[50] This demand, already familiar from the Russian discussions, moved Durus to the above-mentioned statement that photomontage was an "*epochal artistic means*" for the "(total) visual recording of social reality," since it is capable of "uncovering social *relationships and reciprocities, transitions and opposites*," and sharpens the viewer's "awareness of the essence of social conditions."[51]

Yet Lukács would not suffer such objections, voiced by other writers as well, to his criticism of reportage and montage forms put forward with all the vehemence of official party sanction. He insisted on his assertion that the proletarian revolutionary artist can "focus constantly on the driving forces of the overall process only if he chooses dialectical materialism as the basis of his creative method." The writer, however, "in petit bourgeois opposition to capitalist society, is incapable of taking as his point of departure that overall process and its driving forces, which he does not understand. His aim is to expose details."[52]

Yet this very exposure of details – with a few exceptions – was what was at stake in Heartfield's newspaper photomontages from 1930 on: reacting directly to daily events, they unmasked with satirical means the political phraseology of the bourgeois parties. The catalogue of errors, drawn up by Lukács in accordance with Soviet critics of formalism, reads like a description of the techniques employed by Heartfield, particularly in his works for the *AIZ* from 1930 on:[53]

1) The criticized *restriction of a depiction to "single, isolated facts (or, at best, conglomerates of facts), divorced from the vivid contradictory unity of the overall process"* is in fact indispensable for achieving concreteness and effectiveness in the relevant photomontages of topical events. Their often polemically narrowed bias is aggressively onesided and deliberately abstains from qualifying the unmasking process by considering all aspects.

2) *According to Lukács, "'experimenting' with subject matter" leads to "arranging the material irrespective of content and composition; it merely answers to the author's abstract political [...] intent." Like montage as a whole, its "central character" is no longer the socially conditioned totality of "individual fate," but merely an illustration of factual subject matter.* And indeed, Heartfield's figures are character masks, marionettes, wild beasts, victims, heroes, and class warriors: champions of an idea but not people with individual fates. Nor does the photographic portrait make an individual out of the symbolic figure. Its actions are obviously motivated by the author's intention and are mostly so alienated that they make the viewer perceive the unknown element in the known.

John Heartfield, "And Hitler's Offers of Peace are Followed 'Immediately' by his Doves of Peace" (*AIZ*, Prague), April 5, 1936, cover page

3) *According to Lukács, the "irrelevance of the method of depiction regarding the depicted" results from abstraction and "overemphasis of the content" out of proportion to the experiences of the individual heroes: "The method of depiction has no relation whatever to the depicted."* But it is precisely this incongruity, the grotesque inconsistency, that produces one of the essential shock-effects of alienation in Heartfield's visual-verbal rhetoric. The physiognomy, attitude, or action of the depicted contradicts its own explanation or, rather, makes apparent the involuntarily self-exposing double-entendre. To reveal the truth hidden in the rhetorical image, Heartfield illustrates visually the verbal metaphor as

well as the paradoxical relations between words and images. It is this very "encounter of incompatible elements in the montage that provokes our perceptive faculties,"[54] especially when the probability of the photographic detail and the inserted text is in contrast to improbable combinations.

4) *"The subjective factor neglected in the process of giving shape to the work appears in it as the author's unshaped subjectivity, as moralizing commentary, and as superfluous, accidental characterization of figures not organically related to the action."* Lukács's point seems to refer directly to the emblematical structure of Heartfield's *AIZ* montages, as the text inserted in them does assume an important structural function. In terms of media, the writing is indeed extrinsinc to the image; at the same time, it is indispensable because without the commentary the image frequently would not only be incomplete but also incomprehensible. Thus, although the text has an "inorganic," albeit essential, relation to the image in photomontage, with an effect similar to Brecht's *Intervall* interrupting the spectators' illusions, that connection is by no means incidental, or even superfluous, as Lukács insinuated. It is precisely in the contrapuntal or paradoxical relation that text and image arrange themselves into a unity of mutual references.

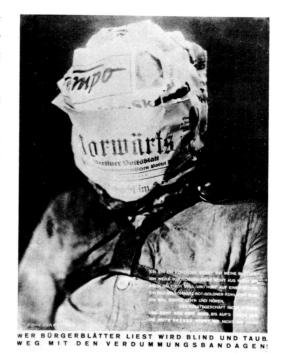

John Heartfield, "Those Who Read the Bourgeois Press..." (*AIZ*, Berlin), no. 6, 1930, p. 103

When in 1931 and 1932 Georg Lukács, on instructions from Moscow, tried to establish norms for the "creative method" within the circle of revolutionary proletarian and left-wing bourgeois writers, he did not mention Heartfield's name, so that the latter need not feel affected by the harsh criticism passed on the writers concerned. Yet the books of the authors that Lukács attacked – besides Tretyakov and Ottwalt, mainly Ilya Ehrenburg, Vera Inber, Marietta Shaginyan, Vsevolod Ivanov, and Mikhail Sholokhov, as well as Upton Sinclair and John Dos Passos – were without exception published by Wieland Herzfelde's Malik-Verlag, and were designed by John Heartfield. Thus the general judgment of documentary literature and its methods of montage amounted to an indirect, but fundamental criticism of the company's publishing policy, even though some Malik books were respected by Lukács.[55]

It was not until the "Expressionism debate" in the second half of the thirties, when the disputes of 1931 and 1932 recommenced with a wider circle of German writers and artists in exile participating, that Lukács turned his attention directly to Heartfield. In a passage criticizing the montage method, Lukács designated photomontage as the source of literary montage. Although ascribing little importance to it, he acknowledged its legitimacy as a minor genre: "While montage, in its original form as photomontage, can make a striking and sometimes powerfully agitatorial impact, it actually draws its effectiveness from the unexpected combination of quite different, isolated bits of reality torn from their context. Fine photomontage has the effect of a good joke. But when this one-way connection – justified and effective for the individual joke – claims the right to shape reality, [...] relation, [...] totality, [...] then the result is bound to be utter monotony."[56]

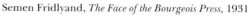

Semen Fridlyand, *The Face of the Bourgeois Press*, 1931

Just how poorly Lukács thought of the joke as a method in art may be inferred from his criticism, made some years before, of the Russian writer Vsevolod Ivanov. Lukács inveighed against *Der Buchstabe G* [*The Letter G*], a collection of stories with an excellent cover design by Heartfield (Pl. 28), on the grounds that the stories had a "disjointed, isolated, grotesque, anecdotal character." Ironic depiction, however, "in order to be more than superficial ridicule of grotesque superficial phenomena," presupposed "a very intimate understanding of the motivations."[57] Elsewhere, there is a further qualification to the effect that irony had ceased to be the "means of expression for this world."[58]

John Heartfield and Sergei Tretyakov in Moscow, 1931

Other Soviet authors came to the defense of Heartfield's degradation to the status of superficial farceur. In 1936, two years before Lukács's disparagement of photomontage in the German-language periodical *Das Wort* [*The Word*], Tretyakov published his monograph on John Heartfield. In total contradiction to Lukács's belittling reference to the structural analogy of photomontage and jokes, Tretyakov judged this affinity positively: "Let those comrades who have mastered the art of photomontage pay close attention to the frequency with which Heartfield's compositions spring from a joke, a witticism, a proverb, or a metaphor."[59] Tretyakov gives as an example the visual realization, frequently used by Heartfield, of a verbal metaphor: for instance, when the debilitated Reichstag is "entombed" with a gigantic coffin lid, or when Hitler's propaganda speeches are "seen through" with an X-ray of his chest (Pl. 94).

Tretyakov is the first of Heartfield's interpreters to examine more closely his method of image-text combination. He declares that the verbal foundation and commentary of Heartfield's visual rhetoric is decisive in all photomontage – an obvious opinion of a writer: "[...] where a photograph, under the impact of text, reports not just on the fact it enshrines but also on the social trend expressed by this fact, then we have a photomontage. Where it is impossible to detach photograph from text without damaging the meaning, then we have a photomontage."[60] This paramount significance of the text as integral and necessary component of the pictorial montage was from the start not at all peculiar to Heartfield's works. The verbal formulation, as adage or proverb, metaphor, political slogan, or cliché, did not assume its central role as a "visual trigger" and "visual key" until after Heartfield's return from the Soviet Union. The increasing importance of the text also coincided with the participation of his brother, the writer and publisher Wieland Herzfelde, in the creative process. "Many of the montage texts come from him," as Tretyakov wrote in 1936.[61]

The growing "textualization" of Heartfield's photomontages after 1931 could probably be attributed to a number of factors. The context of their publication, the journalistic medium, the newspaper for which Heartfield did montage work especially from 1932 on, were without doubt responsible for that tendency, as were the demands of the "dialectical-materialistic method" for a "total" recording of social reality with all its correlations and contradictions. As this all-embracing depiction of reality can only be achieved in philosophy or history,[62] hardly in literature, and certainly not in the visual arts, the text frequently had to support the image to fulfill that inappropriate task asked of it.

Heartfield not only used text to generalize or photographically document facts, but also to make the message explicit. A picture in itself seldom has a perceptive impact. In Tretyakov's words: "Sometimes, in a complex montage, Heartfield inserts several texts, hedging, as it were, the path followed by his caricature to ensure that it reaches its target."[63]

This increased complexity of the image was often achieved at the expense of the picture's quality. The narrative arrangement of photo fragments and words occasionally began to dominate the picture. The visual obviousness was sacrificed to the narrative element. The pithiness of his montages, so highly praised in 1931/32, was later often lost in complicated interrelations between text and image. When writing overtakes the visual in montage, the viewer has to become a reader. At least that is how a reviewer of Tretyakov's monograph on Heartfield correctly saw it: "Therefore, Heartfield's montages must not merely be looked at, but must be read. The various details assembled for this or that reason become legible signs. And, by reading attentively, the viewer comprehends

PP. 279–286. The USSR in Construction, monthly, Nr. 9 (Moscow, September 1931). Cat. no. 205.

THE USSR IN CONSTRUCTION

Photographs by John Hartfield (Moscow).

YESTERDAY AND..

O–DAY

After four days of work, Moscow workmen have a well organised rest. The workman spends his free time in the library of the Park of Culture and Rest.

Or else he takes the air, stretched out on a garden chair.

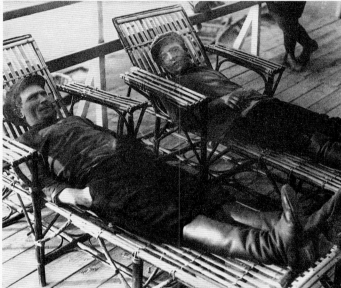

He can also take exercise in the park gymnasium.

Nowhere are children taken care of as they are in USSR. Two sets of figures prove it. Under the tsarist regime the death rate among infants was 27%, it is now 12%.

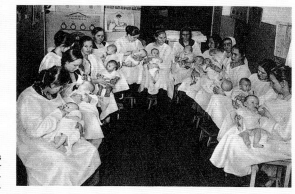

Women workers nursing their babies at the day nursery of the former „Tsindelevka" factory, in the interval which they get for that purpose.

Children taking a sun bath in the children's solarium at the Park of Culture and Rest.

In the children's homes the children have their play out of doors.

Handicraft in bread making is dying out. Moscow has four bread factories.

Mechanised bread making produces from 100 000 to 250 000 kilos of bread per day.

Cooking kettles in the № 1 Kitchen-Factory in the Leningrad road.

Large kitchen-factories liberate women from kitchen work and set them free to work in factories and offices.

Enormous dining-rooms, like this one at „AMO" works, are rightly called plant sections for purposes of nutrition.

The former jostle and tostle of markets places
is replaced by regular rows of booths and stalls.

Workmen and employees get their food products
and articles of general necessity in closed sto-
res, attached to enterprises.

The demonstration of the workers' children at the setting to work of the reconstructed plant AMO.

USSR IN CONSTRUCTION

A MONTHLY ILLUSTRATED MAGAZINE

PUBLISHED IN RUSSIAN, ENGLISH, GERMAN AND FRENCH

№ 9 WERE DONE BY THE PHOTO REPORTERS:

Alpert, Blohin, Gliazer, Gruntal, Zaduraeff, Ignatovich. Carmen, Kudoyaroff, Langman, Mikulina, Ozersky, Petrussoff, Rodchenko, Samsonoff, „Soyuzphoto", Tuless, Friedland, Halip, Schaikhet, Sterenberg, Chemko, Yablonovsky

Lay-out by R. OSTROVSKY and I. URAZOV   Text by A. LITVAK and J. SUDACHKOFF

Editorial Board: M. Gorky, A. Goltsman, G. Grinko, T. Enukidze, I. Ionoff, M. Kalmanovich, M. Koltsoff, F. Konar, P. Krasnoff, G. Piatakoff (editor in-chief), S. Uritsky, A. Halatoff

SUBSCRIPTION RATES FOR 1931: one year — $ 5.00; six months — $ 2.5; three months — $ 1.25

Subscriptions accepted by: USSR: „Mezhdunarodnaya Kniga", 18 Kuznetsky Most, Moscow; USA: „Amkniga" Corporation, 19 West, 27th street, New-York City; England: „Kniga", Ltd., Bush House, Aldwych, London, W. C. 2; Germany: „Kniga", — Buch - und Lehrmittelgesellschaft m. b. H., Ritterstrasse 61IV, Berlin SW 68

Editorial Offices: Malaya Nikitskaya, 6, Moscow, USSR. The State Publishing Union of RSFSR
IZOGIS № 2434. Glavlit № B-3883

Paper and printing by Goznak. Printed in USSR (Russia). Moscow, 1931

whose blood is dripping from the axe blades [...]"[64] (Pl. 98). The "hedging" and targeting of such associations aroused in the viewer obviously seemed necessary to the *Monteur,* when the seizure of power by the Nazis made them the favorite target of his critical satire. Now, more than ever, it was imperative to call names and lash out at atrocities.

One important aspect of Heartfield's method had escaped Tretyakov, with all his authoritatively written and sharply discerning analysis. János Reismann, very familiar with the artist's craft and working method, emphasized in the Moscow magazine *Das Wort* the function of ideological criticism of Heartfield's montage method, i.e., the exposure of Nazi propaganda with its own means. The *Monteur* cut up, enlarged, reduced, and assembled the enemy's verbal and photographic material "so as to reveal their real content, which was deliberately distorted. It is only in this way that he brings to light the real truth in complete accordance with the photograph's subject matter, which is sometimes hard or impossible to grasp. Thus he reveals, in a manner comprehensible to everyone, the substance, or the essence, however distorted, of the message contained in the original photograph. The masters of the Third Reich enjoyed being photographed, the more often the better, in poses of sham folksiness, of fake amiability. [...] Heartfield would take such a photograph, let it pass through his witch's kitchen, and conjure up a finished, easily understandable 'portrait,' in which lies and hypocrisy are exposed, and the true meaning and significance of the original, now properly transmitted, stand out undisturbed."[65]

In the Soviet Union, it had to be left to a foreigner to refer explicitly to montages' ideological function. Around 1936, the Soviet reception of such a reference would have been risky – it could have been understood all too easily as an invitation to a similar critical analysis of the equally affected and theatrical representations of Soviet reality. Tretyakov, therefore, presented his friend, the *Photomonteur,* not so much as a critic of ideology, but rather as an epic artist who not only created an "art dealing with reality" but also an art "able to change that reality." "The epic quality," Tretyakov wrote in 1936, "lies in the fact that for every contingency we seek explanations in what is stable and regular."[66]

Two years before, Walter Benjamin, with direct reference to Brecht but also with Heartfield and the "operative" Tretyakov of earlier times in mind, had defined the epic artist as one who "is less concerned with filling the public with feelings, even seditious ones, than with alienating it in an enduring manner, through thinking, from the conditions in which it lives. It may be noted, by the way, that there is no better start for thinking than laughter. And, in particular, the convulsion of the diaphragm usually provides better opportunities for thought than convulsion of the soul. Epic theatre is lavish only in occasions for laughter."[67]

On one side, epic as the search for the stable and regular, on the other, as a method of alienation from the status quo: Tretyakov defined the epic under the Stalinist, Benjamin under the Nazi, regime. But, faced with this diabolical constellation of power, neither an exaggerated affirmative art nor an art reflecting laughter could be liberating. Tretyakov and Klutsis were arrested and shot by Stalin's henchmen in 1938; fleeing from the Nazis, Benjamin committed suicide in 1940. Heartfield survived the reign of terror in exile, first in Prague and then in England, from where he returned to the German Democratic Republic in 1950. As we know, the accusations against formalism in photomontage, discussed in this essay for the period of the thirties, were still prevalent during his lifetime, so that even in his last years the *Monteur* was denied an adequate sphere of activity for his revolutionary art.

1. "Ihre Meinung zu Heartfield, Genosse Kisch?" in *Brigada khudozhnikov*, 4 (1931), p. 25; in the translation by Gertrud Heartfield (1980, Berlin, Heartfield Archive, Collection of Newspaper Cuttings), in *John Heartfield: Der Schnitt entlang der Zeit. Selbstzeugnisse – Erinnerungen – Interpretationen*, Roland März, ed. (Dresden, 1981), pp. 275–76.
    In the Russian original there is, so to speak, a last-minute notice in the margin: "Heartfield arrived in Moscow at the time that this issue was going to print." This confirms April as the date of his arrival.
2. *Za proletarskoe iskusstvo*, 8 (1931).
3. "News on Soviet Art," typescript of VOKS (All-Union Society for Cultural Relations Abroad), Central State Archive of the October Revolution.
4. "Was bedeutet der Beschluss des Leninschen Führungsorgans und wie soll er erfüllt werden?" Resolution of the Central Committee of the Communist Party on poster agitation and propaganda, in *Brigada khudozhnikov*, 2/3 (1931), pp. 1–3; in the German translation in *Zwischen Revolutionskunst und Sozialistischem Realismus: Dokumente und Kommentare*, Hubertus Gassner and Eckhart Gillen, eds. (Cologne, 1979), p. 434.
5. Alfred Durus (Alfréd Keményi), "Diskussionsabend der ARBKD [Association of Revolutionary Artists of Germany]: Kunst in der USSR. ARBKD beschließt eine neue Ausstellung sowjetrussischer Kunst," in *Die Rote Fahne*, 179 (1930); facsimile of the article in the exhibition catalogue *Revolution und Realismus: Revolutionäre Kunst in Deutschland 1917 bis 1933*, Nationalgalerie Berlin (Berlin [GDR], 1979), p. 29.
6. Information given verbatim to the author by Gutnov.
7. A. I. Gutnov and F. Tagirov, "Zur bevorstehenden Sowjetrussischen Ausstellung der Gruppe OKTYABR: Der Künstler wird Industriearbeiter." Interviews with two members of OKTYABR in *Die Rote Fahne* (September 19, 1930); in *Zwischen Revolutionskunst und Sozialistischem Realismus* (see footnote 4), pp. 189ff.
8. Ibid.
9. Sergei Tretyakov, "Der Schriftsteller und das sozialistische Dorf," in idem, *Die Arbeit des Schriftstellers: Aufsätze – Reportagen – Portraits* (Reinbek, 1972), pp. 120ff. With regard to Tretyakov's stay in Berlin see Fritz Mierau, "Tretyakow in Berlin," in *Berliner Begegnungen: Ausländische Künstler in Berlin 1918–1933* (Berlin, 1987), pp. 206–11.
10. The replies of Siegfried Kracauer, Ludwig Marcuse, Gottfried Benn, and Ezra Pound can be found in *Russen in Berlin 1918–1933: Eine kulturelle Begegnung*, Fritz Mierau, ed. (Berlin, 1988), pp. 544–65; for J. Becher and G. Lukács see Fritz Mierau, *Erfindung und Korrektur: Tretjakows Ästhetik der Operativität* (Berlin [GDR], 1976), pp. 29ff.
11. Walter Benjamin, "The Author as Producer" (1934); idem, *Reflections. Essays, Aphorisms, Autobiographical Writings* (New York/London 1978), p. 225. Translated by Edmund Jephcott.
12. John Heartfield, speech at the Moscow Graphic Institute (1931), in Eckhard Siepmann, *Montage: John Heartfield. Vom Club Dada zur Arbeiter-Illustrierten-Zeitung* (Berlin, 1977), p. 175.
13. Sergei Tretyakov and Solomon Telingater, *John Heartfield. A Monograph* (Moscow, 1936), p. 79. Translated from the Russian by Keith Hammond.
14. Ibid., p. 173.
15. János Reismann (Wolf Reiss), "Als ich mit John Heartfield zusammenarbeitete," in *Internationale Literatur* (Moscow), 5, 1934, pp. 186–88; reprinted in *John Heartfield* (see footnote 1), pp. 188–91, here: pp. 189–90.
16. John Heartfield, letter from September 29, 1962 to Olga Tretyakova, in *John Heartfield* (see footnote 1), p. 321.
17. Refer to the discussion on poster production of IZOGIS, April 13 – May 4, 1931.
18. Gustav Klutsis, "Die Fotomontage als neues Problem der Agitationskunst," in *Literatura i iskusstvo*, 9/10 (Moscow, 1930), pp. 86–95.
19. *Brigada khudozhnikov*, 5/6 (1931).
20. I. Matsa (János Mácza), in *Literatura i iskusstvo* (see footnote 18), p. 97.
21. F. Tagirov, ibid., pp. 98f.
22. Gustav Klutsis, ibid., p. 98.
23. Cf. *Proletarskoe foto*, 1 (January 1932), p. 41. The "creative method" of photography was discussed at the "grand evening" of the ROPF on December 2, 1931. As mentioned in the report, "the well-known German photomonteur D. Heartfield" would also be giving a lecture.
24. Declaration of the initiative group ROPF in *Proletarskoe foto*, 2 (October 1931); in the German translation in Rosalinde Sartori and Henning Rogge, *Sowjetische Fotographie 1928–1932* (Munich, 1975), p. 79.
25. S. Fridlyand, in *Proletarskoe foto*, 1 (September 1931); in Sartori and Rogge (see footnote 24), p. 80.
26. *Sowjetkultur im Aufbau*, 2/3 (1932), p. 58.
27. Lou Scheper, "Eine zeitgemässe Ausstellung," in *Moskauer Rundschau* (December 13, 1931).
28. A. Alf, "Masken des Feindes. Wege eines proletarischen Künstlers," in *Sovetskoe iskusstvo*, 61 (Moscow, November 30, 1931); in *John Heartfield* (see footnote 1), p. 277.
29. Cf. "V. Kostin about his errors: letter to the editor," in *Za proletarskoe iskusstvo*, 3, (1932), p. 17; in *Zwischen Revolutionskunst* (see footnote 4), pp. 405ff.
30. L. Mezhericher, "Die Arbeiten von Heartfield – Beispiel einer auf die Klasse gerichteten Meisterschaft," in *Proletarskoe foto*, 3 (1932), p. 19.
31. Cf. János Reismann, in *John Heartfield* (see footnote 1), p. 286.
32. L. Mezhericher (see footnote 30), p. 19.
33. Heartfield, speech at the Moscow Graphic Institute (see footnote 12), p. 175.
34. "L. P.," in *Proletarskoe foto*, 3 (1932), p. 14.
35. I. V. Stalin, speech made on June 23, 1931, in *15 Eiserne Schritte: Die Sowjetunion in den Jahren des Aufbaus 1917–1932*, V. A. Kurella, L. Mezhericher et al., eds., with a cover design by Heartfield (Berlin, 1932), pp. 258–66.
36. V. Kostin, "Die Fotomontage und die mechanistischen Fehler des OKTYABR," in *Za proletarskoe iskusstvo*, 7/8 (1932), pp. 18ff.
37. Evgeny Kronman (Eugen Kronmann), "John Heartfield," in *Marxistisch-Leninistische Kunstwissenschaft*, 5/6 (Moscow, 1932), pp. 176–83; in the German translation of Wieland Herzfelde, *John Heartfield*, 2nd ed. (Dresden, 1971 [1962]), pp. 343f.

38. Ibid.

39. Ibid.

40. V. Kostin, "Die Sprache des Klassenhasses," in *Proletarskoe foto*, 3 (1932), p. 21.

41. Aleksei Fedorov-Davydov, "Kämpferische Kunst: John Heartfield, ein proletarischer Künstler," in *Brigada khudozhnikov*, 1 (1932), pp. 35 ff.; in *John Heartfield* (see footnote 1), pp. 277–84; here p. 278.

42. Ibid., p. 279. For this and other passages of the text (footnotes 43, 45), my translation, which has been examined against the original, conforms only partially with the German copy cited in footnote 41.

43. Ibid., (but see footnote 42).

44. Ibid., p. 280.

45. Ibid., p. 282 (but see footnote 42).

46. Alfred Durus (Alfréd Kéményi), "Photomontage und Buchgraphik. Zur 3. Ausstellung des Bundes revolutionärer Künstler," in *Die Rote Fahne*, 17 (1932); in *John Heartfield* (see footnote 1), pp. 178–79.

47. Johannes R. Becher, "Kühnheit und Begeisterung," in *Die Linkskurve*, 5 (1932), p. 2. In his definitive treatise, Becher was explicitly referring to the discussion in the Soviet Union when he noted: "In this essay certain formulations from the Russian literary discussions – which also apply to us – have been partially adopted verbatim." With respect to the disputes between the official party faction represented by Becher and the left-wing bourgeois artists, refer, for instance, to the account given by Christel Hoffmann, in *Berliner Begegnungen* (see footnote 9), p. 146.

48. Ernst Ottwalt, "'Tatsachenroman' und Formexperiment: Eine Entgegnung an Georg Lukács," in *Die Linkskurve*, 10 (1932).

49. Willi Bredel, laudatory article (1961) on the occasion of Heartfield's 70th birthday in *John Heartfield* (see footnote 1), p. 453. Heartfield also reported that contrary to the way various members of the *AIZ* staff would like to claim in retrospect, collaboration did not run so smoothly with the *AIZ*, whose editor-in-chief from 1927 to 1933 was the wife of Johannes R. Becher (!), Lilly Becher. In an interview from 1967, Heartfield reported that the *AIZ* editorial staff resisted continuing the regular collaboration. This affiliation "wasn't all that easy either, but in that case the working class helped me; that is the workers themselves. [...] The workers wrote, 'Why doesn't Heartfield do something, couldn't you people get him to do something?' There were so many, that's the truth [...] and people would ask, 'Couldn't you do another one for us?' And I'd say, 'Could I? Of course, I will.' And then it happened that I was making a montage for the Workers' Illustrated and then later, when I was living as an emigré in Prague, weekly, almost weekly [...]" (cited after *John Heartfield* [see footnote 1], p. 468).
This conflict with the editorial staff evidently occurred after Heartfield's return from the Soviet Union, because after his arrival in Berlin at first no photomontages by him appeared in the *AIZ* for about three months, although in 1930, when the party aesthetes had not yet pronounced their verdict on the montage form, his monthly collaboration at the *AIZ* had been announced. When the May issue with his first photomontage for the year 1932 was confiscated, a number of left-wing bourgeois intellectuals, including Brecht, signed a petition, but not Becher nor Lukács. Photomontages by Heartfield appeared once again in the *AIZ* only after the Central Committee of the Russian Communist Party had resolved on April 23, 1932, to dissolve RAPP, RAPKh, ROPF, and all the other writers' and artists' groups and to collaborate closely with sympathizers and bourgeois artists.

50. Georg Lukács, "Reportage oder Gestaltung?," in *Die Linkskurve*, 8 (1932), p. 28.

51. Durus, "Photomontage und Buchgraphik" (see footnote 46), pp. 178, 179.

52. Lukács (see footnote 50).

53. When not otherwise indicated, all the following quotations have been taken from Lukács's treatise "Reportage oder Gestaltung?" (see footnote 50).

54. Hilmar Frank, "Visuelle Rhetorik: Zur Theorie der Fotomontage," in Siepmann, *Montage: John Heartfield* (see footnote 12), pp. 230–33; here: p. 232.

55. Just how important the authors, who had been reprimanded by Lukács, were for Heartfield's own artistic development is substantiated by a comment made during his period of emigration in England: "[...] a positive period of intensive development, diffusion, adoption of new influences – from the 'proletcult' to Russian experimentalists such as Tatlin or Mayakovsky, and in particular such writers as Ehrenburg up to the gradual *shift in emphasis:* Had the revolution brought the good tidings of *'We are not alone,'* the lesson that Ehrenburg and other Russians taught was: *Not* how, *but* what." Transcript of an interview with Heartfield recorded by Francis D. Klingender in 1944, in *John Heartfield* [see footnote 1], pp. 48–64; here: p. 59.

56. Georg Lukács, "Es geht um den Realismus," in *Das Wort*, 6 (1938); reprinted in *Die Expressionismusdebatte. Materialien zu einer materialistischen Realismuskonzeption*, Hans-Jürgen Schmitt, ed. (Frankfurt am Main, 1973), p. 211.

57. Georg Lukács, "Neue russische Belletristik," in *Moskauer Rundschau*, 22 (April 26, 1931).

58. Ibid.

59. Tretyakov, *John Heartfield* (see footnote 13), p. 77.

60. Ibid., pp. 67–68.

61. Ibid.

62. For Lukács's historical, philosophically oriented concept of literature developed in the contemporary Russian context, see Laszlo Sziklai, *Georg Lukács und seine Zeit: 1930–1945* (Vienna, Cologne and Graz, 1986), pp. 100 ff.

63. Tretyakov, *John Heartfield* (see footnote 13), p. 67.

64. I. Dukor, "Heartfield," in *Literaturnaya gazeta*, 21 (Moscow, 1937), in *John Heartfield* (see footnote 1), p. 319.

65. János Reismann (Wolf Reiss), "John Heartfield", in *Das Wort*, 7 (Moscow, 1937); in *John Heartfield* (see footnote 1), p. 317.

66. Sergei Tretyakov, *Menschen eines Scheiterhaufens* (Moscow, 1936); in the German translation in idem, *Gesichter der Avantgarde*, Fritz Mierau, ed. (Berlin and Weimar, 1985), p. 134.

67. Benjamin, "The Author as Producer" (see footnote 11), p. 236.

"The Meaning of the Hitler Salute." Photomontage for the *Arbeiter-Illustrierte-Zeitung*
(*AIZ*, Berlin), October 16, 1932, p. 985. Cat. no. 216

Sergei Tretyakov, 1936

"Montage Elements"

A photomontage by the Dadaist Heartfield consisted of a large number of small details. But over time Heartfield's language became increasingly laconic, his photomontages were constructed more and more sparingly, greater expressiveness being achieved by fewer elements.

His most perfect works are those which involve no more than two elements. We should not forget that a photomontage is not necessarily a montage of photographs. No – it may be a photo and a photo, a photo and text, a photo and paint, a photo and a drawing.

He himself said: "Often it is enough to touch a photograph with a tiny spot of color to turn it into a photomontage, a work of art of a special kind."

Sergei Tretyakov/Solomon Telingater, *John Heartfield: A Monograph*, Moscow, 1936, see also for the following quotations. Translated from the Russian by Keith Hammond.

"Photo-Words"

Simplicity and the ability to present an important idea in a few "photo-words" represent the quality of Heartfield's work. [...] An example: a struggle was being waged against Hitler, who was winning over the broad masses by demagogic means, profiting from his "disinterested" policies.

Heartfield possessed a large number of photographs of Hitler making speeches. He selected one showing Hitler with his palm flung upward in the fascist salute. However, the artist looked for an alternative meaning to this movement. A movement can reveal the true person: a civilian often reveals himself by a dashing click of the heels, in which even the untutored ear can distinguish the ring of a colonel's spurs. A bomb could be put into Hitler's upturned hand, the bomb he intended to throw into the powder keg of Europe. The figure of some parasite could be placed on this hand for display – someone like Horst Wessel, for instance, one of those whom fascism was elevating from the putrid sewers of contemporary bourgeois decay to the role of heroes.

But this did not satisfy Heartfield. He looked for a peg in Hitler's maxims.

Hitler was fond of saying: "Millions stand behind me." The artist began to play with words – what millions? Millions of people? Or millions of marks, perhaps? Whose millions of marks? Those of the bankers financing Hitler, who, in their hands, was not a great dictator but merely a medium-sized puppet. And so the outlines of the photomontage took shape: money is put in the outstretched hand by a figure which is really huge. Hitler's gesture is reinterpreted and he is assigned both his correct social significance and his correct social stature.

Untitled ["The Last Green"]. Photo-colormontage, early 1920s. Cat. no. 175

through the pen of George Grosz. In addition to showing the entire repulsiveness of the over-fed rentier, the drawing lends a peculiar quality of paradox to the whole montage. The paintings are reproduced photographically and have about them a feeling of the real (although they are only representations). Their owner is presented unrealistically, through caricature. He is a spectre, a transitory monster, this lord of slave-objects.

The montage forming the jacket's back is beside the one on the front and shows the artist Liebermann before a portrait of Hindenburg, giving a concrete example of the general principle expressed by the front cover.

This photograph is difficult for us to understand without explanation. But the German intellectual (at whom the jacket was principally aimed) knew that Liebermann was a living embodiment of the downfall of so-called "independent" art. A man of great talent, who long maintained a highly independent and principled stand, Liebermann was eventually bought by the bourgeoisie and made into a highly-paid manufacturer of portraits of bankers, generals, and princes.

Thus, on the two sides of the jacket the production of works of art and their consumption in a capitalist society are shown. Incidentally, we should qualify the above by noting that Liebermann, as president of the German Academy of Arts, found the courage to resist the Nazis, who went through German art with an Aryan comb; and he refused to cooperate with them.

"Photo and Color"

Heartfield takes an ordinary working-class room, a window looking onto a blank wall, a small plant in the window, and he touches the leaf of the plant with a pale green color – the entire photograph instantly acquires a particular meaning. Firstly, the gray tint of the photograph becomes the color gray. The pale green spot of the leaf is, as it were, stifled by the terrible gray atmosphere. The green leaf is the only living thing, but it is extremely stunted, as things born in prison cells are. From this springs the concept informing the picture – that a worker's apartment in a capitalist country is a prison cell.

If Heartfield had made the leaf bright green, the entire scene might have taken on an entirely different meaning.

The transparency of the green was consciously chosen to emphasize the morbid, sickly, and anemic elements in the photograph.

"Photo and Photo"

But, of course, those montages, in which one photograph is combined with another with the maximum simplicity, are Heartfield's principal strength.

Some of his compositions are very elaborate – entire photo-poems, which do not reveal their meaning immediately and contain quite complex ideas. These are, for the most part, book jackets.

This is how Heartfield put together a dust jacket for Sinclair's *Mammonart*, a book describing the transformation of art in a capitalist society into the slave and whore of the bourgeoisie. Against a background of outstanding works of world art – paintings by Rembrandt, Hals, and Degas, and an Egyptian sculpture of Queen Nefertiti – lounges their owner, a bourgeois, who possesses them and savors them.

To emphasize the contrast between the splendid pictures and the man, he is represented, not by a photograph, but

Upton Sinclair, *Die goldne Kette* [*Mammonart*]. Dust jacket, 1928.
Cat. no. 395

Text is very essential to Heartfield's montages. Sometimes, in a complex montage, Heartfield inserts several texts, hedging, as it were, the path followed by his caricature to ensure that it reaches its target.

The interaction of photo and text is especially evident in his renowned election poster of an open hand. The number 5 of the communist electoral list is burned by all possible means into the consciousness of those to whom the poster is addressed. It is shouted by the number 5 and repeated by the word five and the open palm. But even here the most important thing – to remind the reader once again – is that the starting point of the photomontage is a reinterpretation of the photograph. The five fingers are not simply a representation of the number five, but they have a double meaning – the number of the list and a hand preparing to seize the enemy. The second meaning is emphasized by the slogan, and Heartfield even modified the photograph of the hand itself in the interests of expressiveness, lengthening the fingers where necessary and deflecting the thumb more acutely to one side.

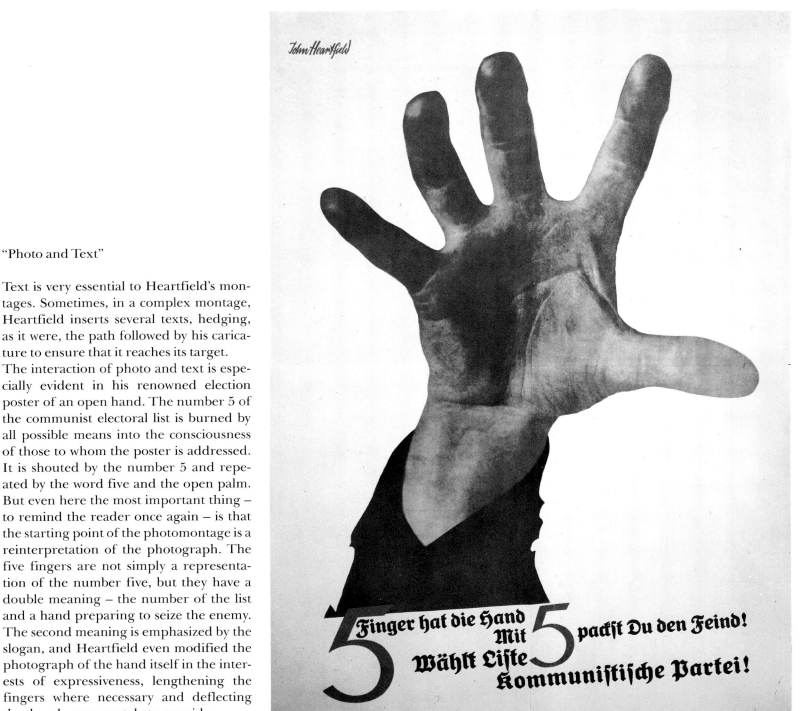

"Stagings"

In some of Heartfield's photographs the element of montage precedes the taking of the photograph – these are stagings.

"The Hand Has 5 Fingers..." Election poster of the KPD [Communist Party of Germany], May 1928. Cat. no. 134

"O Christmas Tree in Germany, How Crooked Are Your Branches!" Staged montage for the
Arbeiter-Illustrierte-Zeitung (*AIZ*, Prague), December 27, 1934, p. 848. Cat. no. 401

Upton
Sinclair

Upton Sinclair

Nach
der
Sintflut

Nach der Sintflut

"Spatial and Temporal Distance"

The relative size of the objects in a photomontage plays an important semantic role. [...] In the photomontage "The Torrent Sweeps Away the Skyscrapers," a normal-sized breaking wave beside vastly diminished skyscrapers does not belittle the skyscrapers, but produces the feeling of a gigantic wave, symbolizing the force sweeping away the bourgeois world.

On the other hand, in "The Factory of Cannon Fodder" and several similar works there are no paradoxical contrasts of scale or unexpected juxtapositions. On the contrary.

Two parts of a montage: a tired pregnant woman and the corpse of a dead soldier. The corpse is seen in perspective and forms the background of the picture. The transition from this background to the large-scale foreground is quite consciously masked in every way to preserve the realistic perspective.

Thus the corpse, placed in physical perspective, is also a corpse emerging unexpectedly in the social perspective.

The distended stomach of the pregnant worker, and the dead soldier lying in the distance, are dialectically one and the same essence. The distance at which the soldier lies is temporal, not spatial.

This is the most dialectical, the most economical of all Heartfield's works. Perhaps for that reason it does not require any caption. [...]

In the photomontages that have been mentioned, Heartfield first of all creates the illusion of real space while at the same time correcting the deficiencies of photography and presenting the background more sharply and on a larger scale than is within the ability of the camera. As a result, what is singled out in perspective is given the necessary significance, emphasis, and direction.

Upton Sinclair, *Nach der Sintflut* [*The Millennium*]. Dust jacket, 1925. Cat. no. 116

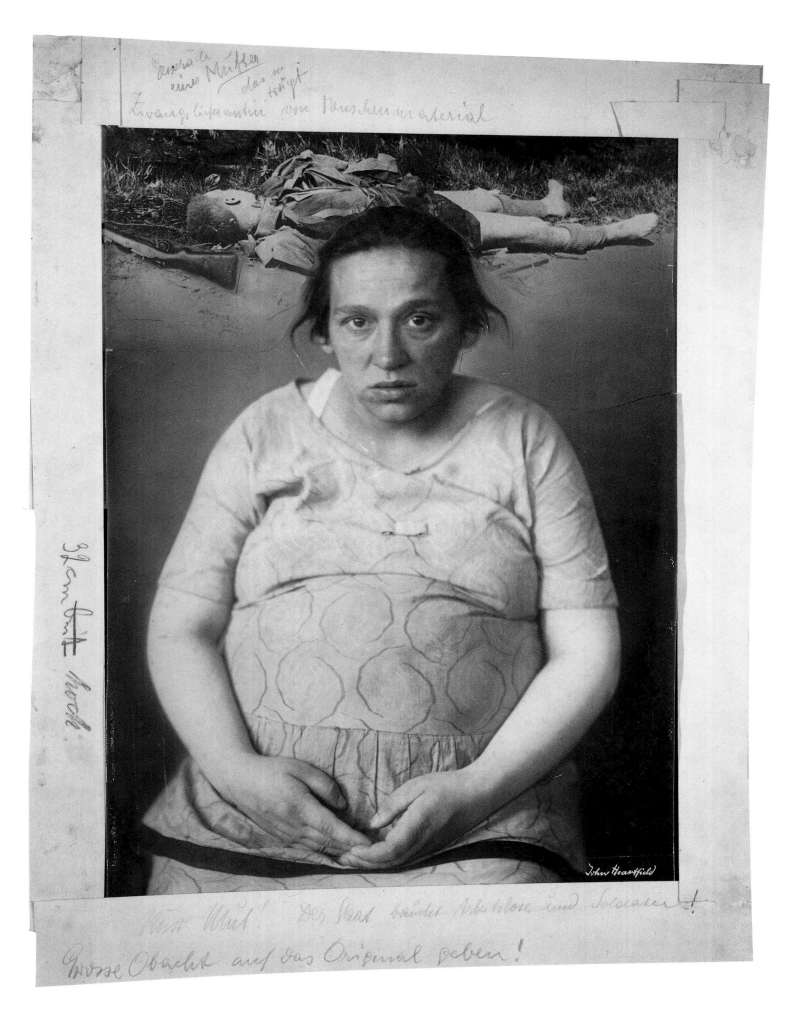

"Forced to Deliver Human Material." Photomontage for the *Arbeiter-Illustrierte Zeitung*
(*AIZ*, Berlin), no. 10, 1930, p. 183. Cat. no. 196

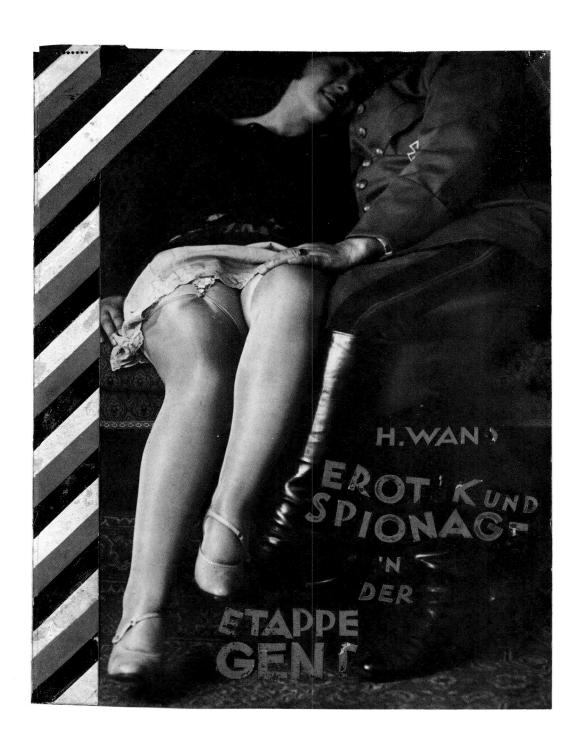

"Censorship Changes Images"

By giving the Communist Party so sharp a propaganda weapon, Heartfield, in creating his montages, naturally attracted the tireless attention of the censors, who were ever ready to halt his militant activity. He was obliged to devote a great deal of ingenuity to defending his rights. [...]

On [one] occasion the jacket of a book on eroticism and espionage came under attack. The cover depicted a lounging, highly-decorated colonel stroking the leg of a woman who is sprawling on his knees. The face of the colonel was deliberately left obscure to prevent the censors from turning their attention to an individual. The public prosecutor, finding the activity of the colonel's hand obscene, demanded that this piece of indecency be removed. Eroticism, of course, was not at fault. In bourgeois Germany hundreds of utterly licentious pornographic books were published and not a single prosecutor was disturbed. The truth was that the erotic scene discredited that sacred cow of the bourgeoisie, the German officer, whom the book also exposed as careless with military secrets.

Heartfield responded by introducing a third person into the picture, that of the prosecutor himself, trimming with enormous scissors a sheet of paper covering the culpable spot. From the prosecutor's lips issue the words: "This needs looking into." The second version evoked a still more furious ban. Heartfield then removed the prosecutor, cut out the corresponding place in the photograph, and stuck over it the exact text of the court's decision. The addition of this "fig leaf" gave the photograph a genuine ambiguity.

Heinrich Wandt, *Erotik und Spionage in der Etappe Gent* [*Eroticism and Espionage at Ghent Base*]. Photomontage for dust jacket (first version), 1928. Cat. no. 87

Heinrich Wandt, *Erotik und Spionage in der Etappe Gent*. Photomontage for dust jacket (third version), 1928, Cat. no. 313

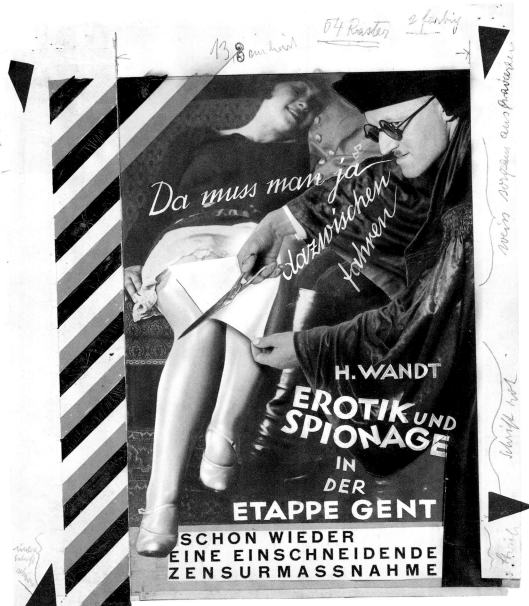

Heinrich Wandt, *Erotik und Spionage in der Etappe Gent.*
Dust jacket (second version), 1928. Cat. no. 88

Petra Albrecht/Michael Krejsa

Biographical Chronology

1891

June 19, birth of Helmut Herzfeld in Berlin-Schmargendorf. His father, Franz Herzfeld (pseudonym Franz Held, 1862–1908), was a socialist writer. His mother, Alice, née Stolzenberg (1867–1911), was a textile worker and political activist.

1899

Helmut, his brother Wieland, and his sisters are abandoned by their parents.

Helmut took his younger brother Wieland (Wieland Herzfelde, writer, publisher, director of the Malik-Verlag [Malik Publishing Company]) and his sister Lotte by the hand, followed by his frightened older sister Hertha, and brought them to "Uncle Ignaz" [Varn-schein], the Protestant mayor of Aigen near Salzburg, where the family had previously lived. He decided to look after the poor orphans, and had all four of them baptized in the Protestant church. He did his best to look after them, but could not cope, and distributed them among various guardians. Helmut, the eldest, was sent to a monastery. And before helping with the mass every morning, he prayed secretly that God would forgive him, a baptized Protestant, for having to participate in a Catholic service.[1]

Hellmuth Bachmann, 1942

1905

After finishing elementary school, starts an apprenticeship in a bookshop in Wiesbaden.

1908

Studies at the Königliche-Bayerische Kunstgewerbeschule [Royal Bavarian Arts and Crafts School] in Munich. Is influenced by the commercial designers Albert Weisgerber and Ludwig Hohlwein.

Alice Herzfeld with daughter Hertha and son Helmut. Berlin, ca. 1894

The Varnschein Family with foster children (*from left to right*) Ignaz Varnschein, unidentified, Wieland, unidentified, Charlotte, Klara Varnschein, Hertha, unidentified. Aigen near Salzburg, ca. 1901

Franz Held

Alice Herzfeld

1912

Works as a commercial artist for the Druckerei Gebrüder Bauer, a printing company in Mannheim. Designs his first book jacket for the *Selected Works* of his father, Franz Held.

By the time Helmuth turned fourteen, he had already painted several beautiful landscapes in oil. "Uncle Ignaz" wrote to the children's real uncle, who lived in Berlin and who managed their father's inheritance – around 60000 marks per child – asking for his permission to let the talented Helmuth study. By "studying," the Austrian Uncle Ignaz meant attending secondary school; however, the uncle in Berlin meant university. He considered it far too early, and, as the child's guardian, replied with a forceful "no." Helmuth moved to Wiesbaden to begin an apprenticeship in a bookshop and from there to

various other apprenticeships, none of which he finished. He finally managed to be sent to Munich a few years later, where he completed a basic course and was admitted to the Malerakademie [Artists' Academy]. There he worked enthusiastically and on a ridiculously meagre monthly allowance — his uncle sent him 50 marks a month from his money. He studied all the things he needed to know as a graphic designer and artist, was happy, optimistic, and always surrounded by friends.[2]

Hellmuth Bachmann, 1942

1913

Moves to Berlin where he studies at the Kunst- und Handwerkerschule [Arts and Crafts School] under Ernst Neumann.

1914

In September, is conscripted into military service (the Kaiser-Franz-Josef Regiment).

1915

Destroys earlier paintings (mainly landscapes). Due to a feigned nervous breakdown, is released from military service as "capable of working." Friendship with George Grosz.

1916

Changes name to John Heartfield in protest against the nationalistic slogan "Gott strafe England!" [May God Punish England!].

At Christmas, it was 1914 — they assured us the war would be over — they sent us to the post office in Grunewald [district of Berlin]. We had to act as postmen and deliver the Lokalanzeiger, *that detested war-mongering newspaper, and letters to the priggish inhabitants of the Grunewald district. Do you know what I did? I walked to the nearest gutter and threw the letters and everything into it. One day, I told the art critic Alfred Kerr in London: "That's how I handled your mail too." [...] But it wasn't just an outburst of temper that made me do something as decisive as translating my name into English. It was rather my response to Hans Lissauer's hate-filled song "Gott strafe England!" But that wasn't the only protest against the war. With my help, my brother Wieland founded the publishing company* Neue Jugend [New Youth]. *The first printed issue was number 7. [...] I started working with photos in* Neue Jugend, *which I published at that time in particularly large formats. In Moscow, I told [Sergei] Tretyakov of earlier works that I had produced with other people, which put me on the right course toward inventing photomontage — if that's what you want to call it. We had often made postcards in that fashion [...] as soldiers. [...]*

As far as George Grosz's comment is concerned [that he and Heartfield had invented photomontage in Grosz's studio at five o'clock one May morning], I would say that we made many pasted pictures together. I also worked with him in other ways in our publishing company, the company belonging to my brother and myself, producing work such as the Kleine Grosz Mappe [Small Grosz Portfolio] *and* Das Gesicht der herrschenden Klasse [The Face of the Ruling Class]. *I also ordered and collected drawings from him for the* Die Pleite [The Bust] *and* Der Knüppel [The Club] *of which I was editor.[3]*

John Heartfield, 1966

Helmut in Wiesbaden, ca. 1906

1917

With his brother Wieland, starts the Malik-Verlag. Works as film set designer for the Grünbaum brothers, and as director of the Military Educational Film Service (later called UFA). Marries Helene Balzer.

1918

Becomes a member of the Berlin Club Dada. Birth of son Tom. On December 30, joins the German Communist Party (KPD), together with his brother Wieland, George Grosz, and Erwin Piscator.

At that time, we became Dadaists. Naturally, this was almost a nihilistic attitude on the part of us artists. It couldn't have been anything else, because most of us were from the middle class and didn't have the connections to the working class that we should have had. To begin with, we argued vehemently, especially with our artist friends, in a Dadaist way. But not only with them, but also with visitors at our Dada events.
[...] the Dadaists fought fiercely against the barbaric state that Germany had flung itself into and in which it remained as a result of the war. [...] It was our decided opinion that a Dadaist was and had to be a radical opponent of exploitation and that was what we always planned.[4]

John Heartfield, 1966

Heartfield at the UFA. Berlin 1919

1919

Is dismissed from UFA because he called for a strike after the murder of Karl Liebknecht and Rosa Luxemburg. Becomes coeditor of a satirical periodical *Jedermann sein eigner Fußball* [*Everybody His Own Football*], which is banned after the first edition. Together with Wieland Herzfelde and George Grosz, founds the political and satirical magazine *Die Pleite*.

The Herzfeld Family (*from left to right*): Helene (née Balzer), Tom, and Helmut Herzfeld. Photo from the *Dada Almanach*. Berlin 1920

Letter from John Heartfield (Berlin) to Otto Dix, dated June 9, 1923. Nuremberg, German National Museum, Archive for Visual Art, Estate of Otto Dix

DER MALIK-VERLAG / BERLIN-HALENSEE

BANK-KONTO: CARSCH, SIMON & Co., BERLIN   KURFÜRSTENDAMM 76
POSTSCHECKKONTO: BERLIN 56702   Fernruf: Kurfürst CO 67-69.   FERNRUF: STEINPLATZ 4495

VII/IV.301   jetzt: BERLIN W 9, KÖTHENERSTR. 38   (360) B23   DEN 9.6.1923

Herrn Otto Dix

Lieber Kamerad Dix!

George Grosz und ich geben wieder die Pleite heraus, die Dir ja bekannt ist. Nun lässt George Grosz Dich durch mich herzlichst bitten, doch an derselben mitzuarbeiten. Die Zeichnungen werden photolitographisch reproduziert auf die Grösse 25x36 cm. Wir wünschen insbesondere schon für die 1.Nummer ein Blatt von Dir. Da aber am Freitag der laufenden Woche schon Redaktionsschluss der 1.Nummer sein muss, bitten wir Dich, umgehend ein Blatt für uns zu zeichnen und es per Express eingeschrieben an John Heartfield, Der Malik-Verlag, Berlin W.9., Köthener Strasse 38., zu senden.

Als Thema kannst Du ein satyrisches Blatt, der Spiesser in der heutigen Zeit, der Spiesser und die Revolution, oder noch besser Niederkartätschung von streikenden Arbeitern durch Reichswehr und Fascisten oder Hungerkravalle und, im Gegensatz, fressende Bürger, uns zeichnen. Das wird von uns gebraucht. Doch solltest Du etwas anderes Passendes auf Lager haben, so geht auch dies. Evtl. auch ein Blatt einer Prostituierten, wie Du bei J.B.Neumann eines einer Dirne (mit Schleier) ausgestellt hattest. Also wir sind nicht eng. Hungerkrawall wäre natürlich am aktuellsten. Für prompte Rücksendung Deiner gesandten Arbeiten stehen wir unbedingt sein. Unsere Mittel sind gering, aber über Bezahlung werden wir mit Dir wohl einig werden.

Wir hoffen, dass Du uns sicher unterstützt und uns umgehend ein Blatt sendest, das spätestens Freitag in Berlin ist. Wir freuen uns sehr darauf, danken Dir und begrüssen Dich herzlichst

in alter Kameradschaft

mit besten Grüssen von George Grosz

Dein John Heartfield

Boxing match with (*from left to right*) Erwin Piscator, George Grosz, Wieland Herzfelde, and John Heartfield. Berlin, ca. 1924

1920

Heartfield and Grosz write an article entitled "Der Kunstlump" ["Art Rogue"], which triggers heated discussions about the significance of proletarian art. June 30 – August 25: *Erste Internationale Dada-Messe* at the gallery of Dr. Otto Burchard, Berlin, organized by Grosz, Hausmann, and Heartfield. Produces set designs for Piscator's *Proletarisches Theater* [*Proletarian Theatre*] in Berlin. Birth of daughter Eva. Friendship with Otto Dix.

1921–22

Designs book jackets, typography, and layouts for the Malik-Verlag, the Verlag für Literatur und Politik, and the Neuer Deutscher Verlag. Becomes a set designer at the Rheinhardtbühne in Berlin. Works mainly for the KPD: as editor and designer of the satirical periodical *Der Knüppel* (1923–1927) and of the KPD's periodical *Die Rote Fahne* [*The Red Flag*].

1924–27

First encounter and friendship with Bertolt Brecht. On the tenth anniversary of the outbreak of the war, exhibits his first contemporary photomontage, "After Ten Years – Fathers and Sons," in the window of the Malik bookshop in Berlin. Founds the Rote Gruppe [Red Group] in Berlin with George Grosz, Rudolf Schlichter, and Erwin Piscator. Makes title pages and layouts for the sports paper *Die Arena* [*The Arena*]. From 1927, becomes a set designer for the Piscator theatre (Theater am Nollendorfplatz). Marries Barbara Friedmann.

Opening of the First International Dada Fair, Berlin 1920
From left to right: Raoul Hausmann, Hannah Höch, Otto Burchard, Johannes Baader, Wieland und Margarete Herzfelde, Otto Schmalhausen, George Grosz und John Heartfield
Under the ceiling: "Heartfield-Schlichter mont.", "Prussian Archangel."
Photo: Berlin, Bildarchiv Preussischer Kulturbesitz

305

John Heartfield in judge's robe. Berlin, ca. 1928

1928

Makes posters including "The Hand Has 5 Fingers," and photomontages for the periodical *Italien in Ketten* [*Italy in Chains*] and for the title pages of *Rote Fahne*.

1929

At the International Werkbund exhibition FILM UND FOTO, Stuttgart 1929, has room 3, covering approximately 10 × 10 meters of space. The exhibition catalogue contains no checklist of his works, probably because they are too numerous to include. Finds one phrase by Vincent van Gogh so important that he has it mounted on the wall in large letters: "A FEELING FOR OBJECTS AS SUCH IS MORE IMPORTANT THAN A FEELING FOR PAINTING." One hundred and ten frames with newspaper and magazine pages, book covers, and posters are displayed on the walls as well as four display cases showing book jackets and covers from the Malik-Verlag, Berlin, and from the Verlag für Literatur und Politik, Vienna/Berlin.[5]

Once, he just used an enormous hand, ready to grab something, as an election poster, as usual with an urgent message [The Hand Has Five Fingers – Beat the Enemy with "5" –

Vote List 5]. In the next few days, he received fantastic offers from three major German industrial firms asking him to become their advertising director; some had a concealed reference to the fact that he would be able to practice his political art – which would never make him a rich man anyway – far more effectively in his free time and without financial worries. He turned down the offers. He wanted to have free rein in his political and ideological struggle, to encourage others in this struggle.[6]

Hellmuth Bachmann, 1942

In 1929, the publishing company Neuer Deutscher Verlag was able to persuade Kurt Tucholsky to write texts to select photos and photomontages by John Heartfield. Tucholsky carried out this task with great reservation. He mistrusted the militant and orthodox world of the Communist Party. Nevertheless, together with John Heartfield, I called on him again and again and eventually we managed to persuade him to agree. The Communist press celebrated Deutschland, Deutschland über alles *as a courageous book. In an advertising letter, the publisher declared "that although it is not a Communist book, it will help to soften up the sections of the population we want to attract to our movement." The* Börsenblatt für den Deutschen Buchhandel *refused to advertise the book on the grounds that the cover montage was by Heartfield [. . .].[7]*

Babette Gross, 1967

International Werkbund Exhibition FILM UND FOTO, Stuttgart 1929, Heartfield Room

John Heartfield dancing a fox-trot with the Russian photoreporter Max Alpert. Batumi 1931

John Heartfield at the exhibition *Revolutionary Art of the West* at the Museum for New Western Art (Pushkin Museum), before his work "The Hand Has 5 Fingers." Moscow 1932

1930

Works on a regular basis for the *Arbeiter-Illustrierte-Zeitung (AIZ)* [*Workers' Illustrated Newspaper*], published by the Münzenberg-Konzern. Becomes acquainted with Vladimir Mayakovsky and Ilya Ehrenburg in Berlin.

1931–32

(April 1931 – January 1932) trip to the USSR: lectures, gives lessons, and travels to Baku, Batumi, and Odessa on behalf of the newspaper *USSR in Construction*. Exhibits around 300 of his works in Moscow. Friendship with Sergei Tretyakov; becomes acquainted with Aleksandr Rodchenko. Returns to Berlin.

1933

After the start of the fascist dictatorship in Germany, flees to Czechoslovakia and continues working for the *AIZ* (1936–1938, published as *Volksillustrierte Zeitung* [*People's Illustrated Newspaper*]) and the Malik-Verlag in Prague.

On Good Friday, 1933, the SS broke at night into my apartment, where I happened to be in the process of packing up my works of art. I managed to escape arrest by jumping from the balcony of my apartment, which was located on the ground floor. At the urging of the Party, I emigrated by walking across the Sudeten Mountains to Czechoslovakia on Easter. In early November 1934, I was expatriated by Hitler's government.[8]

John Heartfield, 1951

He is not a member of a party. Wants to remain in Prague on a permanent basis and make a new life for himself together with his brother. The above-mentioned is married and has two children. The children are in Holland, his wife is still working in Germany. In Berlin, he lived in the Potsdamer Straße (1)18 and worked as a free-lance graphic designer. He was attacked on the night of April 16 by Storm Troopers of the German National Socialists and was mistreated (teeth knocked out). The above-named is of Jewish faith (now nondenominational). He was forced to leave Germany because he was always in danger of being attacked. He wants to bring his familiy to Prague when he has the travel documents. He has been urged to apply for approval to stay without a passport.[9]

1933

1934

Takes part in an international caricature exhibition at the Prague art society Mánes, which causes diplomatic friction between Czechoslovakia and Germany. His friend Mikhail Koltsov tries to help the threatened artist move to Moscow, but Heartfield refuses the offer.

Dear Heartfield,
The largest, leading satirical periodical Krokodil *[Crocodile] (with a circulation of 300,000) has now been taken over by the Pravda press. As of May 1, I will be its editor. The magazine will be improved and will become a world-famous satirical magazine. I attach great importance to your continued, regular work. The best thing would be for you to move to Moscow — where everything necessary will be arranged for you and your family — so that you can work for* Krokodil, AIZ, *etc., in peace.*
If you are unable to come immediately, then I want to ask you to start work right away from Prague. I would like to feature whole-page montages once or twice a month. Topics:

fascism, danger of war, labor, exploitation, proletarian resistance ... but no personal depictions, e. g., Göring, Hitler.

I hope to hear from you very soon and trust that the first montage will arrive here in the near future. You can see the format from the copy of the newspaper that is being sent to you by the same mail. To avoid any misunderstandings, payment will be made in Soviet currency.
I hope you are in good health.
With best regards,
Mikhail Koltsov[10]

Mikhail Koltsov, 1934

From left to right: Wieland Herzfelde, John Heart-field, and Kurt Kersten. Prague 1934. (Kurt Kersten, writer and publicist, close confidant and associate of Willi Münzenberg)

Dear Comrade Heartfield,

I have recently been informed that you think that I and a number of others are working against you (among others named, Alexander Keil, i. e., Sándor Ék). I assume that your comments on this matter have been considerably magnified by gossip. I believe that it would not be correct to pass over your assumption in silence. I have to note objectively that you are quite wrong. We (not only myself but also [Heinrich] Vogeler and Keil) have always spoken of your work and of you with the greatest respect and have always opposed the gossip spread around by mediocre "geniuses," such as [Gustav] Klutsis. This is not to our benefit but it is our natural revolutionary duty. Unfortunately, foolish attacks by the otherwise outstanding [Erich] Weinert against you, Piscator, and George Grosz have ended up in the same issue of International Literature *[3, (1935)] as my featured article about you.*

How Weinert's autobiography could be published without deleting the relevant sections still today remains a mystery to me. I can only put it down to exhaustion on the part of [Karl] Schmückle. We want to talk sincerely and as comrades. How can I work against you when I do my utmost to defend your work in the local press (articles I have written about your montages will soon appear in the English edition of International Literature *and in* Iskusstvo*). I have to admit that it was mainly the anti-fascist energy in your works, rather than any aesthetic or even "personal" considerations, that compelled me to do this. But can one separate work from the person? – Dear Heartfield, I believe things are difficult enough for us as it is; we really should not make life harder for each other. I for my part have the misfortune of having to work with artists who are in the theoretical front of the fine arts. I am really fed up with it. And I have the even greater misfortune of having to finish quickly a book about "German revolutionary artists" by June 15. [...] I call this a misfortune because obtaining the essential material involves almost insurmountable difficulties. [...] I would be very grateful if you could send me a detailed autobiography: a detailed description of your origins (to clarify how you absorbed the material of satire biologically with your mother's milk) – the Chaplinesque tragicomic material of the conditions of your emigration, etc. [...].*

In friendship and with rev[olutionary] greetings,
[Alfred] Durus[11]

Alfred Durus, 1935

From left to right: John Heartfield, Vladimir Hnizdo (Heartfield's retoucher), Fritz Erpenbeck (writer and journalist), at the printing company of M. Schulz, supervising a layout of the *AIZ*. Prague, ca. 1936

1935

Stays in Paris from March to August. The exhibition *150 photomontages* (Maison de la Culture) takes place there in April/May. Becomes acquainted with Walter Benjamin. Designs book jackets for Willi Münzenberg's *Editions du Carrefour,* including *Das braune Netz* [*The Brown Net*].

1936

Participates in the international photo exhibition at the art society Mánes, Prague. Sergei Tretyakov publishes first monograph about Heartfield in Moscow.

From left to right: Gustav Regler (publicist and associate of Münzenberg), John Heartfield, Tristan Tzara (Rumanian writer and Dadaist) at the Heartfield exhibition *150 photomontages politiques et satiriques d'actualité.* Paris 1935

Oskar Kokoschka and John Heartfield. Paris 1935

John Heartfield with his son Tom, who lived in Prague from 1936–38. Prague, ca. 1937

From left to right: Wieland Herzfelde, Gertrud Herzfelde, unidentified, George Herzfelde (son of Wieland Herzfelde) when departing for the U.S.A. London, April 1939

From left to right: George Herzfelde, John Heartfield, Wieland Herzfelde. London 1939

1937

Becomes a member of the Prague Oskar Kokoschka League. Participates in the exhibtion *50 Years Mánes.* Because Germany threatens to break off diplomatic relations with Czechoslovakia, some of Heartfield's works are removed from the exhibition.

1938

Flees from Prague to England (December 6) before the imminent occupation of Czechoslovakia by fascist Germany. Exhibits in New York at the Pat Henry Club.

1939

Becomes involved in the Artists' International Association (AIA) and the Free German League of Culture [Freier Deutscher Kulturbund]. In April, says farewell to his brother Wieland, who is refused a Residence permit for England. Exhibition *One Man's War against Hitler* at the Arcade Gallery, London.

1940

Is interned as enemy alien (category C); severely ill. Becomes acquainted with German emigré Gertrud Fietz.

1941

The League of Culture honors Heartfield's fiftieth birthday with an exhibition of his book jackets and photomontages.

Dear Friends,
With reference to your notification regarding the [Czech Refugee] Trust Fund's intention to carry out a general evacuation from London, I urge you to help me to stay in London. Although my state of health – and the difficulties it causes – has so far prevented me from finding paid employment, I still hope to be able to find work that I am physically capable of doing in the near future. However, I am convinced that I will only be able to do this in London and that such prospects only exist here. As you know, I published a number of my photomontages as free-lance work in London newspapers (Lilliput, Picture Post, Reynolds News) *prior to my internment, but I was unable to find a paid position. The present lack of space in newspapers has now made this possibility even more difficult. Nevertheless, this does not mean that I will not be able to work for a newspaper again.*
[. . .] I am now taking part in a training course that is organized by the Free German League of Culture, which helps people find work as an inspector in the metal industry.
I also give lectures on art, for example on April 26, on "What Peasant Breugel [sic] Has to Say to Us." In addition, I am organizing an exhibition of my works on the occasion of my fiftieth birthday – in about two months – which will involve lectures about my "photomontage" working method. I am able to find the necessary material for my work only in London libraries, such as in the British Museum, the Victoria and Albert Museum, and the Courtauld Institute. I am still being treated at the Maida Vale Hospital. I have been living in my present apartment for over two years now, and have been given all the care and attention that I need.
For all these reasons, I ask you to refrain from evacuating me.
Yours sincerely, John Heartfield (Helmut Herzfeld No. 393)[12]

John Heartfield, 1941

John Heartfield during his period of internment at the camps in Lutton, Huyton, and York, England. Summer 1940

Attendance list of the painters' section of the Free German League of Culture, dated January 13, 1942. Second signature from the top: John Heartfield. Heinz Worner Archiv, Berlin

1942–45

Is involved in events organized by the League of Culture and participates in its exhibition *Allies Inside (Nazi) Germany* in London (1942). Designs books for English publishers, such as Lindsay Drummond Ltd., Dennis Dobson Ltd., and Penguin Books Ltd. (until 1950). Is given permission to work as a free-lance cartoonist (1943). Konrad Farner publishes *John Heartfield. Photomontagen zur Zeitgeschichte* [*John Heartfield. Photomontages on Contemporary History*] *(Zürich, 1945).*

Dear old John,
[. . .] It was good to hear from you and to know that you are still alive and busy, as in the old days as a "Monteur" – remember? – when you always had paper and newspapers sticking out of your pockets, just as one would expect a photomontage artist to look. And many thanks, too, for remembering my fiftieth birthday. [. . .] At a time when friendships are so rare and everyone has to look after themselves, I was deeply touched by your friendship. It is good that our friendship has not been destroyed by political moths. Sometimes I feel very depressed when I look at the emigré newspapers and see how the various groups are fighting

Panel 6 of the exhibition *Allies Inside Germany* (July 3-August 26, 1942) with the photomontage "Five Minutes Before Twelve," created by John Heartfield for this event. Documentation: Heinz Worner; graphic design: René Graetz. Heinz Worner Archiv, Berlin

Gertrud Fietz and John Heartfield. Probably in Blackwater, 1947

each other. It is somehow my fate or perhaps my nature that I must remain a "lone wolf" (sorry, that sounds a bit romantic but you know what I mean). [...] I am glad that the horrific nightmare of the Hitler régime is coming to an end. What the future will bring us (apart from death) nobody knows. [...] I am more skeptical than optimistic. [...] Wiel[and] Herzfelde showed me a beautiful collection of your photomontages [...] what a shame that modern magazines don't print photomontages. Nevertheless, I often thought there were better opportunities for them in the U.S.A. than in rather conservative England. It's a shame that your talents are not properly recognized in Europe. [...] Wiel is not really as fat as [Stefan] Heym described him, let's say he is a little plump, although as always full of vigor. [...] He is proud of his new Aurora-Verlag [Aurora Publishing Company]; it's like 30 years ago: the entire company in one room [...][13]

George Grosz, 1945

1946

Has an exhibition in Amsterdam, *Sturmzeichen. John Heartfields Warnungen vor Krieg und Faschismus* [*Signs of Storm. John Heartfield's Warnings of War and Fascism*], participates in the exhibition *Kämpfende Kunst* [*Combative Art*] in Basel.

1947–48

Still in London, Heartfield is offered an appointment as professor of satirical graphics, at the department of applied arts, at the Humboldt University in East Berlin. An injury to his spine, caused by an accident, and the question, "Do I have to become a professor?" are initial reasons for him to remain in England.

To the
Central Administration for National Education, Berlin
Attn.: Herr President [Paul] Wandel
Re.: Johnny Heartfield

The above-named is well known as a staunch anti-fascist. As a result of his artistic achievements in photomontage, as well as to culture and politics, he has made a name for himself well beyond the borders of Germany. He has greatly developed the art of photomontage. Due to persecution by the Nazis, he was forced to leave Germany and emigrated first to Czechoslovakia and later to England, where he still lives. He has continued his work in exile. Since the end of the war, exhibitions of his photomontages have been staged in America, France, Switzerland, Czechoslovakia, and in the Soviet Union. His work has been generally well received by the press, especially by the French poet Louis Aragon. Heartfield is still sprightly and artistically active. He wishes to return to Germany. We can support this wish most sincerely.

With a socialist greeting!
Socialist Unity Party of Germany.
Central Secretariat. Department: Personnel Policy
Müller[14]

1947

1949

After Wieland Herzfelde's return to Leipzig from the U.S.A., intensive efforts are made for John Heartfield's return to Germany. Bertolt Brecht intercedes for the "new arts" (poster and photomontage) in the new cultural scene. After the founding of the German Democratic Republic (October 7, 1949), Herzfelde makes arrangements for his brother's participation in the *II. Deutsche Kunstausstellung* [*Second German Art Exhibition*] in Dresden. Cultural-political problems (formalism) cast their shadows.

Dearest John,

[...] I've been wooried that you're still not as well as you should be. Hopefully, your traveling plans [return to the Soviet Occupied Zone] will be realized all the same. Try to make it in the spring. [...]

Your works at the exhibition [Second German Art Exhibition *in Dresden, September 10–31, 1949] are well insured. I'm sure that everything will be returned to me intact. I was at the opening. Your works and Böff's [George Grosz's] made a very strong impact. There has also been a turn in the evaluation of Böff. I haven't heard of any attacks in* The Voice of Germany *[Deutschlands Stimme]; there was only one in* Neues Deutschland *[central organ of the Socialist Unity Party in the GDR]. Is it possible that you made a mistake? [...]*

Greetings to both of you from the two of us.

Your Wieland[15]

Wieland Herzfelde, 1949

Dear Herr [Georg?] Böhm,

Many thanks for your letter of October 7 [Founding day of the GDR!] of this year. You may well understand that it is difficult for me to make a decision from so far away. When I return home, I wish, of course, to use my artistic skills where they have the most beneficial impact for the cause. It is clear to me that I can only find this out with your kind help, that of the Ministry of Education and of my friends in Germany, for this decision cannot be made without knowing what the needs are over there.

I would not hesitate to take a teaching position in graphic art at the Art Academy in Dresden, but I would prefer such a position in Leipzig, should there be a possibility. Due to bad health, I do not wish to think of Berlin. [...]

With best wishes I remain

Very sincerely yours,

[John Heartfield][16]

John Heartfield, 1949

1950

In view of the Cold War between East and West and the "abnormal circumstances caused by Germany's division,"[17] efforts for Heartfield's return become more complicated. East German officials are especially suspicious of emigrés who want to return so "late" from exile in the West. Heartfield manages to return to Leipzig with Gertrud Fietz on August 31, 1950. The brothers collaborate on work for GDR theatres and publishing companies in their "Werkstatt: H & H."

1951

As a result of a resolution passed on August 24 by the Socialist Unity Party of Germany and its Central Party Control Commission, all "Western emigrants," including the Herzfelde brothers, are suspected of "treasonable connections" to Western secret service agencies. Direct and indirect contacts with the director of the International Relief Action Committee for Victims of the Nazi Regime, the American Noel Field, provide enough pretext to overlook Heartfield. Also for security reasons, Heartfield is not admitted to the Socialist Unity Party of Germany because of his contact with staff members [Bill Carrey, Helene Radó, and Herta Tempi] of the USC [Unitarian Service Committee] set up in London by Noel Field.[18]

He suffers his first heart attack. George Grosz visits Heartfield in an East Berlin hospital. The Heartfield exhibition, which has been announced for the 60th birthday of the future Minister of Culture Johannes R. Becher, is canceled.

Johnnie talked uninhibitedly about his difficulties; because absolute openness was a duty when it came to anything concerned with the party, he reported to Comrade Joos [of the Socialist Unity Party of Germany, which worked with the Ministry for State Security] that he did not know the agent Noel Field; but he did know his brother [Hermann Field], the dentist, who once put two fillings in his teeth. Until the dentist's complete innocence has been proven, Heartfield was sure that his case was temporarily suspended. Wieland made no comments about his brother's words, born of hope and confidence. [...][19]

Stefan Heym, 1990

My dear [Wilhelm] Sternfeld,
[...] It's possible you may have learned that I almost died last year. I collapsed in the train from Leipzig to Berlin. I had a heart attack. I'm feeling better now. [...]
I've found out from [Johannes R.] Becher how very well you've acted about the PEN Club matter [the setting up in London of the PEN Club of German authors abroad]. Of course, I'm very glad to hear this. It is clear such good composure is important. Is there an attempt to split German literature as well, perhaps even the German language?! The longing of most Germans, even in West Germany, for unity is so great, that everyone who works against it, in whatever field it may be, is considered its foe and a foe of every advancement that is hostile to progressive literature. [...]

Wieland Herzfelde and John Heartfield. Berlin, ca. 1952

Now, back to me. Be assured that where we are neither thin nor fat capitalists are eaten for breakfast or for supper. That happens often enough where you are and elsewhere. [...] We've got other cares and problems. Can peace be maintained, can splendid things be accomplished here? And I believe we can maintain peace. Our main problem is to do everything aimed in that direction. Since I, as you well know, am an old pacifist, you can imagine how important maintenance of peace is to me. That's everybody's main objective here. I suppose that's so among you old friends. Your stand for the unity of the Pen Club is a point in favor for it a[nd] for you. On this note of peace, I greet you a[nd] your wife, the old friends a[nd] acquaintances of London with all the best. [...]

Most cordially John Heartfield. Write again soon.[20]

John Heartfield, 1952

1952

Marries Gertrud Fietz. Works on Nikolai Pogodin's play *Glockenspiel des Kreml* [*The Chimes of the Kremlin*] (Berliner Ensemble) with artists Wolfgang Langhoff and Betty Loewen, who are also menaced by party decisions. Suffers second heart attack in Leipzig; stays in hospital until May 1953.

1953/54

Revival of several works for Berlin theatres (Kammerspiele, Berliner Ensemble, etc.). Stefan Heym calls for public recognition of Heartfield's artistic work.

"Tell me, do you know what's become of John Heartfield?" This question, which sounds like the beginning of a detective story, is quite justified. It is almost as if one of the greatest and most original artists of our time had disappeared without a trace, disappeared without a trace in our midst, in the GDR! [...]

John Heartfield is well-known abroad. His works have been exhibited in the Soviet Union and in America with tremendous success. Not so in the GDR. Why? Are there perhaps people who believe Heartfield's montages have to do with "formalism" because spines made from gold coins do not exist? Is that the reason why he is not encouraged to continue with his photomontages?

I believe that John Heartfield, considering his work and the magnitude of his art, deserves a place in the Academy. [...]

And finally, I believe it would be well and good if one of those bodies that have to do with bestowing national awards seriously considered John Heartfield.

As a rule, national awards are given for books, plays, and films. But here lies a whole life's work before us. Here is an artist who has proved all his life what he can do and where he stands. [...][21]

Stefan Heym, 1954

1956

Changes in the U.S.S.R. after Stalin's death (1953) bring about half-hearted revocations of decisions in the GDR with respect to party measures, expulsions, and discrimination for reasons of "behavior hostile or damaging to the party" on the part of former "Western emigrés." The political recognition of the Herzfelde brothers follows such admissions of "immoderacy." In October, Heartfield is elected a full member of the Deutsche Akademie der Künste, [East] Berlin. His party membership is regarded as uninterrupted.

The application of Comrade Helmut Herzfeld (John Heartfield) for the restitution of his party membership is approved. Membership in the Party of the Working Class [Communist Party of Germany and Socialist Unity Party] is considered to be uninterrupted as of December 12, 1918.
Grounds:
In view of today's standpoint, the decision of March 13, 1951 is no longer valid. Even as a nonparty member, Comrade Heartfield has been active according to the spirit of the party since his return from emigration in 1950.[22]

1957

The first comprehensive Heartfield exhibition in the GDR *John Heartfield und die Kunst der Fotomontage* [*John Heartfield and the Art of Photomontage*] takes place at the Akademie der Künste. Moves from Leipzig to Berlin. Trip to China. Receives National Award Second Class. In Moscow, some of his works (which were exhibited at the Moscow Exhibition of 1931) are returned to him.

1958–59

Participates in several exhibitions in the GDR and in Switzerland. First film, *John Heartfield, ein Künstler des Volkes* [*John Heartfield, an Artist of the People*] (DEFA).

When we came to the GDR, and the brothers tried to continue working together on an artistic basis, it was impracticable. The years of emigration, with diverse kinds of experiences on both sides in different countries, had formed different people. [. . .] Johnny was very unhappy and desperate about the situation, but he couldn't change it. He had become another person. [. . .]
And then there was Johnnie's illness – his two heart attacks and the times spent in the hospital. [. . .]
But then, thanks to the strenuous efforts of his friends Brecht, [Bodo]Uhse, and [Stephan] Hermlin, John was elected to the Academy. From then on, he had a life of his own. Things began to pick up with his exhibitions. [. . .][23]

Gertrud Heartfield, 1972

John Heartfield and Olga Tretyakova, wife of the author of the first Heartfield monograph, Sergei Tretyakov, a victim of the Stalinist political purges in 1939. Moscow 1958

Gertrud and John Heartfield. Berlin 1967

John Heartfield's apartment in Berlin, photographed after his death in 1968

1960–61

Is awarded title of professor and given other honors.

1962

Comprehensive Heartfield monograph by Wieland Herzfelde is published by the Verlag der Kunst, Dresden. Heartfield participates in the *V. Deutsche Kunstausstellung* [*Fifth German Art Exhibition*].

1964–65

Legalization of the pseudonym "John Heartfield." Exhibitions in Warsaw, East Berlin, Prague, Budapest, Rome, etc.

1966–67

John Heartfield at the Gertrauden Cemetery. Güstrow 1962

Exhibitions *Der Punkt auf's I* [*The Dot on the I*] in West Berlin; *Der Malik-Verlag* in East Berlin; *Wartet nur balde...* [*Just you wait...*] in Frankfurt am Main; and in other West European cities such as Stockholm and London.

1968

After a severe illness, John Heartfield dies in East Berlin on April 26. According to his will, an archive of his entire work is to be established at the Akademie der Künste zu Berlin [Address: Heartfield-Archiv, Robert-Koch-Platz 10, O-1040 Berlin].

Hardly anybody nowadays will deny that Heartfield was a great artist – although I think there are only a few who could say why. That has always been a very difficult question. The fact that John Heartfield put all of his skill, based upon the great European tradition, in the service of daily politics isn't a difficult question, it's an interesting one. At a particular historical moment, there was for him no cause more important than socialism. After he realized this, the objective for him was easy – but hard to make. [...] Seen from a distance,

Heartfield was a simple person; at close range, a complicated person – or better still – a person with an immense span. He was a wise man and a child. An awful, hairsplitting pedant and a very successful artist. He was someone who loved and someone who hated. [. . .] The world and our lives seem very complicated. Heartfield made them transparent. His brother lent him a hand. His wife made it possible. [. . .][24]

Werner Klemke, 1968

1. Hellmuth Bachmann [probably Barbara Herzfeld]. "John Heartfield: Zu seinem 50. Geburtstag am 19. Juni 1942," in *Argentinisches Tageblatt* (Buenos Aires), 54, 167, p. 10.
2. Ibid.
3. Radio interview, Berlin 1966. Heartfield-Archiv, Akademie der Künste zu Berlin.
4. Ibid.
5. Elisabeth Patzwall, *Rekonstruktion des Heartfield-Raumes aus der Internationalen Werkbundausstellung* FILM UND FOTO *1929 in Stuttgart,* brochure for the John Heartfield exhibition (Berlin, 1991), p. 6.
6. Hellmuth Bachmann, *John Heartfield* (see footnote 1).
7. Babette Gross, *Willi Münzenberg. Eine politische Biographie* (Stuttgart, 1967), p. 226.
8. Curriculum vitae. Leipzig, 1951. Heartfield-Archiv, Akademie der Künste zu Berlin.
9. Document to determine Heartfield's identification, dated April 25, 1933. State Central Archives of Prague. Prague Police Headquarters 1931–1940. Sign. H 1723/6. Translated from Czech.
10. Letter from the writer Mikhail Koltsov (Moscow) to John Heartfield (Prague), dated April 27, 1934. Heartfield-Archiv, Akademie der Künste zu Berlin.
11. Letter from the art critic Alfred Durus [i. e., Alfréd Kéményi] (Moscow) to John Heartfield (Prague), dated February 25, 1935. See also Hubertus Gassner's contribution in this catalogue.
12. Letter from John Heartfield (London) to the Czech Refugee Trust Fund, Thomas Mann Group (London), dated April 1, 1941. Die Deutsche Bibliothek, German Exile Archive 1933–1945, Frankfurt/Main, Estate of Wilhelm Sternfeld, sign. EB 75/177.
13. Letter from George Grosz (New York) to John Heartfield (London), dated April 4, 1945, in George Grosz, *Briefe 1913–1959,* ed. Herbert Knust (Reinbek, 1979), pp. 348–49. (This letter was not sent)
14. Letter of the Central Secretariat of the Socialist Unity Party of Germany. Department of Cadre Policy (Berlin) to Paul Wandel, President of the Central Administration for National Education (Berlin), dated October 16, 1947. BArchP, R-2, Akten-Nr. 1090, Bl. 207 [Federal Archives, Potsdam Departments. Sign. R 2, file no. 1090, sheet 207.]
15. Letter from Wieland Herzfelde (Leipzig) to John Heartfield (London), dated September 21, 1949. Heartfield-Archiv, Akademie der Künste zu Berlin.
16. Letter from John Heartfield (London) to [Georg?] Böhm. German Administration for National Education in the Soviet Occupied Zones (Berlin), dated November 6, 1949. Heartfield-Archiv, Akademie der Künste zu Berlin.
17. Letter from Wieland Herzfelde (Leipzig) to John Heartfield (London), dated May 30, 1950. Heartfield-Archiv, Akademie der Künste zu Berlin.
18. Document of application for Heartfield's readmission to the party, dated March 19, 1951. Institut für Geschichte der Arbeiterbewegung, Berlin, Zentrales Parteiarchiv (ZPA). Sign. 2/4/457.
19. Stefan Heym, *Nachruf* (Berlin, 1990), pp. 544–45. See also Georg Hermann Hodos, *Schauprozesse: Stalinistische Säuberungen in Osteuropa 1948–54* (Berlin, 1990), pp. 57–65.
20. Letter to John Heartfield (Leipzig) to the writer Wilhelm Sternfeld (London), dated September 22, 1952. Die Deutsche Bibliothek, German Exile Archive 1933–1945, Frankfurt/Main, Estate of Wilhelm Sternfeld, sign. EB 75/177.
21. Stefan Heym, "Offen gesagt," in *Berliner Zeitung,* 10, 135, June 13, 1954, p. 2.
22. Document of application for Heartfield's readmission to the party dated March 19, 1951. Institut für Geschichte der Arbeiterbewegung, Berlin, Zentrales Parteiarchiv (ZPA). Sign. 2/4/457.
23. Letter from Gertrud Heartfield (East Berlin) to Heinz Schnabel, director of the Akademie der Künste of the GDR (East Berlin), undated [1972]. Akademie der Künste zu Berlin, Zentrales Akademie Archiv.
24. Werner Klemke, "Trauerrede zu Heartfields Beisetzung am 30. 4. 1968," in *Mitteilungen der Deutschen Akademie der Künste zu Berlin,* 6, 4, 1968, pp. 2–3.

Checklist of Exhibited Works

Explanatory Note

The checklist corresponds, with some exceptions, to the original exhibition in Germany, but not all the works listed are shown at every venue. Almost all works from the German exhibition are shown in Great Britain and Ireland. Roman type designates works that are exhibited in American museums. An asterisk * denotes works exhibited *only* in America; a diamond ◆ to those that are shown *only* in Great Britain and Ireland. The checklist begins with reproduced works from the First International Dada Fair (Erste Internationale Dada-Messe), held in Berlin in 1920. Helen Adkins has recreated a section of the room and has compiled nos. 1–60. Next are the works of the "Heartfield Room" from the International Werkbund exhibition FILM UND FOTO held in Stuttgart in 1929. This room has now been reconstructed for the first time by Elisabeth Patzwall (nos. 61–172); indicated are works shown as reproductions, since the originals' whereabouts are unknown. Numbers 173–407 include designs (such as photomontages or drawings) for newspapers and magazines, book jackets, posters, and works for the theatre, and their later imprints, or reproductions. Elisabeth Patzwall compiled catalogue entries of nos. 61–407 on the basis of her catalogue raisonné, completed in 1990 and as yet unpublished. All works are the property of the John Heartfield-Archiv at the Akademie der Künste zu Berlin, to whose holdings the inventory numbers refer.

All dimensions, in inches and centimeters, are sheet-size unless otherwise indicated. The following abbreviations are used:

AIZ   Arbeiter-Illustrierte-Zeitung [Workers'
           Illustrated Newspaper]
sig.   signed
unsig.   unsigned
inv. no.   inventory number
l.   left
no.   number
t.   top
n.d.   not dated
unpag.   unpaginated
r.   right
b.   bottom
VI   Volks-Illustrierte [People's Illustrated]
*   shown only in New York, San Francisco,
           Los Angeles
◆   shown only in London, Dublin, Edin-
           burgh

1–60   Dada Room Reconstruction, 1920

This condensed compilation of selected works shown in 1920 at the First International Dada Fair in the gallery of Dr. Otto Burchard in Berlin, is based on the research which in 1988 led to a historical reconstruction of the first room (see exhibition catalogue *Stationen der Moderne*, Berlinische Galerie, Berlin 1988). The selection of works and the Dadaist installations attempt to illustrate the essential points of the fair and Heartfield's and his circle of friends' share in it. Only reproductions, reconstructions and prints in facsimile are shown. The Dadaists themselves did not put any value on the "genuine work of art"; in 1920 they presented originals and reproductions side by side. In their own words, the main concern was the "duty to make current affairs, their date and locations the content of their pictures, which is the reason why they [...] consider illustrated newspaper and press editorials as the source of their production." The identification of authors and titles is based on

information from the exhibition catalogue of 1920. The typographic posters, now all lost, did not figure in the original checklist. They are most likely the fruit of active evening discussions among the organizers: *Dadasopher* Raoul Hausmann, *Monteurdada* John Heartfield, and *Marshall* G. Grosz.

Here again I must express my deepest thanks to all who collaborated on the historical reconstruction of *Stationen der Moderne*, especially Ariel Alvarez, Michael Sellmann, Henryk Weiffenbach, and Hanns-Rudolf von Wild.

Helen Adkins

Dada Room Reconstruction, 1920

Wall 1

1   John Heartfield
    Dada photo: Portrait of the Dadasopher Raoul Haus-
    mann
    1920/1988
    Black-and-white photograph, retouched
    Pasted letters: "Down with Art"
    ["Nieder die Kunst"], black ink on paper
    42" × 34¼" [105 × 86 cm]
    George Grosz, Raoul Hausmann, John Heartfield
    Two typographic posters
    Letterpress, black ink on paper
    "It's Time You Opened Up Your Mind!"
    ["Sperren Sie endlich Ihren Kopf auf!"]
    1920/1988
    15 ¼" × 34 ½" [38 × 86 cm]
    "Clear it for the Claims of our Times!"
    ["Machen Sie ihn frei für die Forderungen der Zeit!"]
    1920/1988
    11½" × 34½" [29 × 86 cm]
    Reconstruction: Michael Sellmann and Henryk Weif-
    fenbach (photograph); Michael Sellmann (posters)

2   Raoul Hausmann
    "Optophonetic Poem"
    ["Optophonetisches Gedicht (kp'erioUM)"]
    1919
    Reproduction in "Dadaco" dimensions
    12¾" × 9½" [32 × 24 cm]
    ("Dadaco" prototype: private collection)

3   Raoul Hausmann
    "Synthetic Cino of Painting"
    ["Synthetisches Cino der Malerei"]
    1918
    Reproduction in "Dadaco" dimensions
    12¾" × 9 ½" [32 × 24 cm]
    (Original montage: private collection)

Wall 2

4   John Heartfield
    Dada photo: Portrait of the Monteurdada John
    Heartfield
    1920/1988
    Black-and-white photograph, retouched; pasted let-
    ters: "Dada (is) great" ["Dada (ist) groß"], red ink on
    paper, "and John Heartfield is its prophet" ["und
    John Heartfield ist sein Prophet"], black ink on paper
    54" × 34½" [135 × 86 cm]
    George Grosz, Raoul Hausmann, John Heartfield
    Two typographic posters
    Letterpress, red ink on paper
    "Down with Art"
    ["Nieder die Kunst"]
    8" × 34½" [20 × 86 cm]
    "Down with Bourgeois Spirituality"
    ["Nieder die bürgerliche Geistigkeit"]
    12" × 34½" [30 × 86 cm]
    Reconstruction: Michael Sellmann and Henryk Weif-
    fenbach (photograph); Michael Sellmann (posters)

5   George Grosz
    "The Guilty One Remains Unknown"
    ["Der Schuldige bleibt unerkannt"]
    1919
    Reproduction
    20¼" × 14¼" [50.7 × 35.5 cm]
    (Original collage: Chicago, The Art Institute of
    Chicago)

6   Raoul Hausmann, John Heartfield
    "Dadaco. Dada Handatlas"
    ["Dadaco. Dadaistischer Handatlas"]
    1920
    "Dada in School"
    ["Dada in den Schulen"]
    Reproduction
    12¾" × 9½" [32 × 24 cm]
    (Original: Milan, coll. Arturo Schwarz)

7   Raoul Hausmann, John Heartfield
    "Dadaco. Dada Handatlas"
    1920
    "Our John"
    ["Unser John"]
    Reproduction
    12¾" × 9½" [32 × 24 cm]
    (Original: Milan, coll. Arturo Schwarz)

8   Raoul Hausmann, John Heartfield
    "Dadaco. Dada Handatlas"
    1920
    "For the Cement Workers!"
    ["die Zementarbeiter ein!"]
    Reproduction
    12¾" × 9½" [32 × 24 cm]
    (Original: Milan, coll. Arturo Schwarz)

9   Dada photo: Heartfield-Hausmann
    1920
    Reproduction
    6¾" × 5" [17 × 12.5 cm]
    (Whereabouts of original unknown)

10 George Grosz, Raoul Hausmann, John Heartfield
    Typographic poster
    "Wiertz: One day all artistic painting will be sup-
    planted and replaced by photography"
    ["Wiertz: Dereinst wird die Photographie die gesamte
    Malkunst verdrängen und ersetzen"]
    1920/1988
    Letterpress, black ink on green paper; pasted photo-
    graph (self-portrait of John Heartfield)
    24" × 32" [60 × 80 cm]
    Reconstruction: Michael Sellmann

11 John Heartfield
    Printed sheet for the "Small Grosz Portfolio"
    ["Kleine Grosz-Mappe"]
    June 1917
    Malik-Verlag (4 pages)
    Reproduction (all pages)
    11¼" × 8½" [28.1 × 21.5 cm]
    (Originals: Berlin, Berlinische Galerie; Berlin,
    Heartfield-Archiv, Akademie der Künste zu Berlin)

Wall 3

12 Max Ernst
    "Stamen and Marseillaise of the Dada Arp"
    ["Staubgefäße und Marseillaise des Dada Arp"]
    1919
    Reproduction
    12" × 10" [30.2 × 25 cm]
    (Original: Private collection)

13 Hannah Höch
Two Dada dolls
1916/1988
Cloth, cardboard, beads
Height: ca. 24" [60 cm]
Reconstruction: Isabel Kork and Barbara Kugel
(Originals: Berlin, Berlinische Galerie, Hannah-
Höch-Archiv)

14 George Grosz, Raoul Hausmann, John Heartfield
"The dada 3"
["Der dada 3"]
April 1920
Malik-Verlag (16 pages)
Reproduction
9¼" × 6¼" [23.2 × 15.7 cm]
(Original: Berlin, Heartfield-Archiv, Akademie der
Künste zu Berlin)

15 John Heartfield
New Youth, weekly issue
[Neue Jugend Wochenausgabe] no. 2
June 1917
Malik-Verlag (4 pages)
Reproduction
25½" × 19¾" [64 × 49.5 cm]

Wall 4

16 John Heartfield
*Dada photo: Portrait of the Propagandada Marshal
G. Grosz*
1920/1988
Black-and-white photograph, retouched
42" × 32" [105 × 80 cm]
George Grosz, Raoul Hausmann, John Heartfield
Two typographic posters
Letterpress, black ink on paper
"Dada is the Wilful Decomposition"
["Dada ist die willentliche Zersetzung"]
13½" × 32" [34 × 80 cm]
"of the Bourgeois World of Concepts"
["der bürgerlichen Begriffswelt"]
7¼" × 32" [18 × 80 cm]
Reconstruction: Michael Sellmann and Henryk Weif-
fenbach (photograph); Michael Sellmann (posters)

17 George Grosz, Raoul Hausmann, John Heartfield
Typographic poster
"Dada is on the Side of the Revolutionary Proletariat"
["Dada steht auf Seiten des revolutionären Pro-
letariats"]
1920/1988
Letterpress, red ink on paper
24" × 30" [60 × 75 cm]
Reconstruction: Michael Sellmann

18 *"Grosz-Heartfield"*
Cover of the political portfolio "God with Us!"
["Gott mit uns!"] by George Grosz
1920
Malik-Verlag (portfolio of nine lithographs)
Reproduction
19¾" × 13" [49.2 × 32.8 cm]
(Original: Berlin, Heartfield-Archiv, Akademie der
Künste zu Berlin)

19 John Heartfield
Cover for "Germany Must Go Under"
["Deutschland muß untergehen"] by Richard
Huelsenbeck
1920
Malik-Verlag (13 pages)
Reproduction
9¼" × 6¼" [23 × 15.5 cm]

(Original: Berlin, Heartfield-Archiv, Akademie der
Künste zu Berlin)

20 John Heartfield
"Life and Times in Universal City at 12.05 Noon"
["Leben und Treiben in Universal City, 12 Uhr 5
mittags"]
1919
Reproduction
ca. 22¾" × 28½" [ca. 57 × 71 cm]
(Whereabouts of original unknown)
As no. 15
Reprint, 1967 (last page)
22½" × 18" [56 × 45 cm]
Original dimensions: 25½" × 19¾" [64 × 49.5 cm]

21 George Grosz, Raoul Hausmann, John Heartfield
Typographic poster "Dada is Political"
["Dada ist politisch"]
1920/1988
Letterpress, red ink on paper
22" × 32" [55 × 80 cm]
Reconstruction: Michael Sellmann

Wall 5

22 George Grosz
"Mr. Krause"
["Herr Krause"]
Reproduction
22" × 12¾" [55 × 32 cm]
(Whereabouts of original unknown)

23 Hannah Höch
*"Cut with the Kitchen Knife Dada Through the Last
Weimar-Beerbelly-Culture Epoch of Germany"*
["Schnitt mit dem Küchenmesser Dada durch die letzte
Weimarer Bierbauchkulturepoche Deutschlands"]
1919
Reproduction
45½" × 36" [114 × 90 cm]
(Original: Berlin, Staatliche Museen Preussischer
Kulturbesitz, Nationalgalerie)

24 Raoul Hausmann
"The Racketeerers"
["Die Schieberger"]
1920
Reproduction
12½" × 9¼" [31.5 × 23 cm]
(Whereabouts of original unknown)

25 Raoul Hausmann
"The Art Critic"
["Der Kunstreporter"]
1919
Reproduction
12¾" × 10¼" [31.7 × 25,4 cm]
(Original: London, The Trustees of the Tate Gallery)

Wall 6

26 Johannes Alberts
*"A. Preiss †, the First True Unforgettable Super-
Music-Dada in his Scene 'dadaist wooden puppet
dance'"*
["A. Preiss †, der erste wahre unvergeßliche Obermusikdada in seiner Szene 'dadaistischer Holzpuppentanz'"]
1919
Reproduction
12¼" × 5½" [30.5 × 14 cm]
(Whereabouts of original unknown)

27 Raoul Hausmann
"Tatlin Lives at Home"

["Tatlin lebt zu Hause"]
1920
Reproduction
16½" × 11¼" [41 × 28 cm]
(Original lost in 1967)

28 Raoul Hausmann
"An Old Masterpiece"
["Ein altes Meisterwerk"]
1920/1988
7½" × 9½" [19 × 23.5 cm]
Reconstruction: Michael Sellmann

Wall 7

29 George Grosz, Raoul Hausmann, John Heartfield
Typographic poster
"Dada is Against the Expressionist Art Swindle"
["Dada ist gegen den Kunstschwindel der Expressio-
nisten"]
1920/1988
Letterpress, black ink on paper
26" × 30" [65 × 75 cm]
Reconstruction: Michael Sellmann

30 *"Grosz-Heartfield mont."*
"Dada-merika"
1919
ca. 25½" × 19½" [ca. 64 × 48.5 cm]
(Whereabouts of original unknown)

31 Raoul Hausmann
"Portrait of a Butler (Dr. Anselm Ruest)"
["Portrait eines Dienstmannes (Dr. Anselm Ruest)"]
1919
Reproduction
10½" × 8½" [26.5 × 21 cm]
(Original: private collection)

32 Raoul Hausmann, John Heartfield
"Dadaco. Dada Handatlas"
["Dadaco. Dadaistischer Handatlas"]
"Caravan"
["Karawane"]
1920
Reproduction
12¾" × 9½" [32 × 24 cm]
(Original: Milan, coll. Arturo Schwarz)

33 Raoul Hausmann, John Heartfield
"Dadaco. Dada Handatlas"
"Citizen Faces"
["Hausmann – bürger Deetse"]
1920
Reproduction
12¾" × 9½" [32 × 24 cm]
(Original: Milan, coll. Arturo Schwarz)

34 Raoul Hausmann, John Heartfield
"Dadaco. Dada Handatlas"
"anlogo blago bung"
1920
Reproduction
12¾" × 9½" [32 × 24 cm]
(Original: Milan, coll. Arturo Schwarz)

35 Raoul Hausmann, John Heartfield
"Dadaco. Dada Handatlas"
"Meliorism"
["Meliorismus"]
1920
Reproduction
12¾" × 9½" [32 × 24 cm]
(Original: Milan, coll. Arturo Schwarz)

36 Francis Picabia
"ROUND EYE, Bushman Drawing"
["OEIL ROND, Buschmannzeichnung"] 1920

Reproduction
16″ × 12½″ [40 × 31 cm]
(Whereabouts of original unknown)

37 Johannes Baader
"Gutenberg Commemoration Sheet"
["Gutenberggedenkblatt"]
1920
Reproduction
14″ × 19½″ [35 × 49 cm]
(Original: Paris, Musée National d'Art Moderne,
Centre Georges Pompidou)

38 John Heartfield
Cover for "Fantastic Prayers" ["Phantastische
Gebete"] by Richard Huelsenbeck
1920
Malik-Verlag (31 pages)
Reproduction
10½″ × 7¼″ [26 × 18 cm]
(Original: Zürich, Kunsthaus Zürich)

39 George Grosz
"Contempt of a Masterpiece by Botticelli"
["Mißachtung eines Meisterwerkes von Botticelli"]
1920/1988
7″ × 10¾″ [17.5 × 27 cm]
Reconstruction: Michael Sellmann

40 George Grosz, Raoul Hausmann, John Heartfield
Typographic poster
"Everyone Can Dada"
["Dada kann jeder"]
1920/1988
Letterpress, black and red ink on paper
22″ × 24″ [55 × 60 cm]
Reconstruction: Michael Sellmann

41 Francis Picabia
"Brilliant Muscles"
["Muscles Brillants"]
1919
Reproduction
9″ × 7¼″ [22.8 × 18 cm]
(Whereabouts of original unknown)

42 Otto Schmalhausen
"High School Course in Dada"
1920
Reproduction
4¾″ × 6½″ [11.9 × 15.4 cm]
(Original: Berlin, Berlinische Galerie, Hannah-
Höch-Archiv)

43 George Grosz
"The 'Convict' Monteur John Heartfield after Franz
Jung's Attempt to Put Him on His Feet"
["Der 'Sträfling' Monteur John Heartfield nach
Franz Jungs Versuch ihn auf die Beine zu stellen"]
1920
Reproduction
16¾″ × 12¼″ [41.9 × 30.5 cm]
(Original: New York, The Museum of Modern Art)

44 John Heartfield
Cover for "Dada Triumphs!"
["Dada siegt!"] by Richard Huelsenbeck
1920
Malik-Verlag (40 pages)
Reproduction
8¾″ × 5¼″ [22 × 13 cm]
(Original: Berlin, Heartfield-Archiv, Akademie der
Künste zu Berlin)

45 George Grosz
"Portrait of the Kurfürstendamm Poet, Wieland
Herzfelde"

["Portrait des Dichters vom Kurfürstendamm Wieland Herzfelde"]
1920
Reproduction
11¾″ × 9¼″ [29.5 × 23 cm]
(Whereabouts of original unknown)

46 George Grosz, Raoul Hausmann, John Heartfield
Typographic poster
"I Can Live without Food and Drink, but not without
DADA. Marshal G. Grosz. – I cannot either. John
Heartfield. – Neither can I. Raoul Hausmann"
["Ich kann ohne Essen und Trinken leben, aber nicht
ohne DADA. Marschall G. Grosz. – Ich auch nicht.
John Heartfield. – Auch ich nicht. Raoul Haus-
mann"]
1920/1988
Letterpress, black and red ink on green paper
20″ × 28″ [50 × 70 cm]
Reconstruction: Michael Sellmann

47 John Heartfield
New Youth, weekly issue, no. 1
May 1917
Malik-Verlag (4 pages)
Reproduction
25½″ × 19¾″ [64 × 49.5 cm]

48 Rudolf Schlichter
"Phenomenon Works"
["Phänomen-Werke"]
1920
Reproduction
24¾″ × 18¾″ [61.7 × 46.6 cm]
(Original: private collection)

49 George Grosz, Raoul Hausmann, John Heartfield
Typographic poster
"Dada is the Opposite of Life Alienation"
["Dada ist das Gegenteil von Lebensfremdheit"]
1920/1988
Letterpress, black ink on paper
12¾″ × 16″ [32 × 40 cm]
Reconstruction: Michael Sellmann

50 George Grosz, Raoul Hausmann, John Heartfield
Typographic poster
"Dilettantes, Rise up Against Art"
["Dilettanten erhebt Euch gegen die Kunst"]
1920/1988
Letterpress, black and red ink on paper
26″ × 32″ [65 × 80 cm]
Reconstruction: Michael Sellmann

51 Otto Dix
"45 % Employable!"
["45 % erwerbsfähig!"]
1920
Reproduction
66″ × 98″ [165 × 245 cm]
(Original destroyed around 1938)

52 George Grosz
"A Victim of Society"
["Ein Opfer der Gesellschaft"]
1919
Reproduction
19½″ × 15¾″ [49 × 39.5 cm]
(Original: Paris, Musée National d'Art Moderne,
Centre Georges Pompidou)

53 George Grosz
"Gallery of German Male Beauty, Prize Question
'Who is the most Beautiful'?"
["Galerie deutscher Mannesschönheit, Preisfrage
'Wer ist der Schönste?'"]
1919

Reproduction
11″ × 14½″ [27.5 × 36 cm]
(Whereabouts of original unknown)

54 George Grosz, Raoul Hausmann, John Heartfield
Typographic poster
"Take Dada Seriously, It's Well Worth While!"
["Nehmen Sie Dada ernst, es lohnt sich!"]
1920/1988
Letterpress, black ink on orange-colored paper
22″ × 28″ [55 × 70 cm]
Reconstruction: Michael Sellmann

Wall 8

55 George Grosz
"Germany, a Winter's Tale"
["Deutschland, ein Wintermärchen"]
1917
Reproduction
ca. 86″ × 52¾″ [ca. 215 × 132 cm]
(Whereabouts of original unknown)

Wall 9

56 Georg Scholz
"Farmer's Portrait"
["Bauernbild"]
1920
Reproduction
39¼″ × 28″ [98 × 70 cm]
(Original: Wuppertal, Von-der-Heydt-Museum)

57 The Dadaist Walter Serner
Photograph (reproduction)
1920
8½″ × 7″ [21.2 × 17.2 cm]
(Whereabouts of original unknown; negative: Heidelberg, Walter-Serner-Archiv)

58 George Grosz, Raoul Hausmann, John Heartfield
Typographic poster "Art is Dead. Long live Tatlin's
New Machine Art"
["Die Kunst ist tot. Es lebe die neue Maschinenkunst
Tatlins"]
1920/1988
Letterpress, black ink on orange-colored paper
24″ × 32″ [60 × 80 cm]
Reconstruction: Michael Sellmann

In the Room

59 "Grosz-Heartfield mont."
"The Greedy Bourgeois Heartfield Turned Wild
(Electro-mech. Tatlin sculpture)"
["Der wildgewordene Spiesser Heartfield (Elek-
tromech. Tatlin-Plastik)"]
1920/1988
Tailor's dummy, revolver, door-bell, knife, fork, 'C',
'27', dentures (plaster), Order of the Black Eagle horse
blanket embroidery), Osram light bulb, (1988 Osram
reconstruction of the 1920 model), Iron Cross Stand
35½″ × 17¾″ [90 × 45 cm]; height of figure: 51″
[130 cm]
Reconstruction: Michael Sellmann
Berlin, Berlinische Galerie

60 "Heartfield-Schlichter mont."
"Prussian Archangel (ceiling sculpture)"
["Preussischer Erzengel (Deckenplastik)"]
1920/1988
Pig's head made of papier-mâché, officer's uniform,
body-girdle "Vom Himmel hoch, da komm ich her"
["From heaven on high I come"], notice: "For a total
understanding of this work of art one has to drill daily
for twelve hours on the Tempelhoferfeld, equipped
with a fully-packed knapsack and armed for heavy

322

marching order" ["*Um dieses Kunstwerk vollkommen zu begreifen, exerziere man täglich zwölf Stunden mit vollgepacktem Affen und feldmarschmässig ausgerüstet auf dem Tempelhoferfeld"*]
Height: ca. 72" [*ca. 180 cm*]
Reconstruction: Isabel Kork, Michael Sellmann
Berlin, Berlinische Galerie

61–172   Reconstruction of the Heartfield Room at the Werkbund exhibition FILM UND FOTO, Stuttgart, 1929

The catalogue of the original FILM UND FOTO exhibition does not contain a list of the Heartfield works, probably because such a list would have gone beyond the scope of the catalogue. Here it is now possible, sixty years later, to document precisely Heartfield's extensive contribution to the Werkbund exhibition.

Elisabeth Patzwall

Wall A

61   "First International Dada Fair"
["Erste Internationale Dada-Messe"]
Berlin 1920
Front page of catalogue
12½" × 15½" [31.2 × 38.5 cm]
unsig. reprint
Ill. p. 85

62   New Youth, weekly issue, no. 2
Prospectus for the "Small Grosz Portfolio"
Malik-Verlag, Berlin-Südende, June 1917
Front page
25½" × 20½" [64 × 51.5 cm]
unsig.
Reprint (reduced in size)
Ill. pp. 73–76

63   Like no. 61
2nd and 4th pages
Reproductions
Ill. pp. 86, 88

64   "The dada 3"
["Der dada 3"]
Malik-Verlag, Dada Section, Berlin 1920
Front page (2 ×), 8th and 9th inside pages each
9¼" × 6¼" [23.2 × 15.7 cm]
Front page sig., b. l.: "John Heartfield mont."
Inv. nos 4877, 1459
Ill. pp. 77–80

65   *above: "Dada-merika"*
Collage, 1919
10½" × 7½" [26 × 19 cm]
inscr. b. l.: "Dada-merika/Grosz Heartfield mont."
Reproduction
(Whereabouts of original unknown)
Ill. p. 67

66   *below:*
Like no. 64
2nd and 3rd inside pages
each 10½" × 7½" [23.2 × 15.7 cm]
sig. in imprint: "Technical printing layout: John Heartfield"
Inv. no. 4877

67   *"Down! Down! Down!"*
["Nieder! Nieder! Nieder!"]
Poster (?), mid-1920's
Reproduction
(Whereabouts of original unknown)

68   "To Everybody! 10 Years of the Soviet Union 1917–1927"

["An Alle! 10 Jahre Sowjet-Union 1917–1927"]
Vereinigung Internationaler Verlagsanstalten, Berlin 1927
Design for back cover of magazine
Photomontage with red paper
19¾" × 15¾" [49.6 × 39.2 cm]
unsig.
Inv. no. 876
Ill. p. 116

69   W. I. Lenin
"Speech About the Revolution of 1905"
["Rede über die Revolution von 1905"]
Verlag für Literatur und Politik, Wien 1925
Design for dust jacket
Photomontage with text
11" × 7" [27.5 × 17.8 cm]
unsig.
Inv. no. 1424

70   "Illustrated History of the Russian Revolution"
["Illustrierte Geschichte der Russischen Revolution"]
Neuer Deutscher Verlag, Berlin 1927
Front page of prospectus
11½" × 9" [29 × 22.5 cm]
sig., b. l.: "Heartfield"
Inv. no. 1562

71   "Vote List 5. May 1928. Slogan: Vote Communist!"
["Wählt List 5. Mai 1928. Kampfruf: Wählt Kommunisten!"]
The Female Warrior [Die Kämpferin], Berlin, nos. 4/5, 1928
Front page
12¾" × 9½" [31.9 × 23.7 cm]
unsig.
Inv. no. 2392
(Whereabouts of original unknown)

72   *"Life and Times in Universal City at 12:05 Noon"*
["Leben und Treiben in Universal City, 12 Uhr 5 mittags"]
Collage, 1919
Reproduction
(Whereabouts of original unknown)
Ill. p. 68

73   Upton Sinclair
"Jimmie Higgins"
Gustav Kiepenheuer Verlag, Potsdam 1923
(11th–15th thousand)
Design for title page and back cover
Photomontage with red paper, text
7¾" × 6¾" [19.4 × 17 cm]
sig., b. l.: "Heartfield"
Inv. no. 592

74   *Vladimir Mayakovsky*
"150 Millions"
["150 Millionen"]
Malik-Verlag, Berlin 1924
Malik-Bücherei, Bd. 5
Book cover design
Reproduction
(Whereabouts of original unknown)

75   *Upton Sinclair*
"100 %"
Malik-Verlag, Berlin 1921
Rote Roman-Serie, Bd. 2
Book cover design, 1st version
Reproduction
(Whereabouts of original unknown)

76   Oskar Maria Graf
"The Early Time"
["Frühzeit"]
Malik-Verlag, Berlin 1922
Rote Roman-Serie, Bd. 5
Book cover design
Photomontage with red paper and text
9" × 6¼" [22.5 × 15.5 cm]
unsig.
Inv. no. 566
Ill. p. 97

77   *Maxim Gorki*
"Fairy Tale of Reality"
["Märchen der Wirklichkeit"]
Malik-Verlag, Berlin 1928
Dust jacket
7½" × 5" [19 × 12.5 cm]
unsig.
Inv. no. 5167

78   *Upton Sinclair*
"Samuel the Seeker"
["Samuel der Suchende"]
Malik-Verlag, Berlin 1924
Dust jacket
7½" × 11" [19 × 27.7 cm]
unsig.
Inv. no. 1584

79   Franz Jung, ed.
"Jack London. A Poet of the Working Class"
["Jack London. Ein Dichter der Arbeiterklasse"]
Verlag für Literatur und Politik, Wien 1924
Book cover design
Photomontage with red paper and cut-out script
10¼" × 7¾" [25.8 × 19.3 cm]
sig., b. l.: "Heartfield"
Inv. no. 567

80   *"Make Way for the Worker! First Almanac" (of the Malik-Verlag)*
["Platz dem Arbeiter! Erstes Jahrbuch" (des Malik-Verlages)]
Malik-Verlag, Berlin 1924
Paperback
9½" × 12½" [23.5 × 31.5 cm]
unsig.
Inv. no. 5167 (reprint)
Ill. p. 104

81   Franz Jung
"The Conquest of the Machines"
["Die Eroberung der Maschinen"]
Malik-Verlag, Berlin 1923
Book cover design
Photomontage with text
9" × 6½" [22.2 × 16.5 cm]
unsig.
Inv. no. 564
Ill. p. 102

82   Maxim Gorki
"The Ninth of January"
["Der 9. Januar"]
Malik-Verlag, Berlin 1926
Malik-Bücherei, Bd. 20
Book cover design
Photomontage with text
7¾" × 10½" [19.2 × 26.1 cm]
unsig.
Inv. no. 4500

83   "The Sacco and Vanzetti Case"
["Der Fall Sacco und Vanzetti"]

Vereinigung Internationaler Verlagsanstalten, Berlin 1927
Booklet cover design
Photomontage with text
9½" × 6¼" [23.7 × 15.5 cm]
sig., b. l.: "Heartfield"
Inv. no. 595
Ill. p. 106

84 *Wilhelm Uhde*
"Fortuna's Friendships"
["Die Freundschaften Fortunas"]
Rudolf-Kaemmerer-Verlag, Dresden 1927
Book cover
7¾" × 5" [19.5 × 12.5 cm]
unsig.
Reproduction

85 *Franz Jung*
"Peace on the Labor Front"
["Arbeitsfriede"]
Malik-Verlag, Berlin 1922
Rote Roman-Serie, Bd. 4
Dust jacket
7¾" × 5" [19.1 × 12.7 cm]
unsig.
Reproduction

86 "Mammonart"
["Die Goldne Kette"]
Malik-Verlag, Berlin 1928
Design for dust jacket, front
Photomontage with red paper and the reproduction of a drawing by George Grosz
13¾" × 9¼" [34.2 × 23 cm]
unsig.
Inv. no. 1761

87 *Heinrich Wandt*
"Eroticism and Espionage at Ghent Base"
["Erotik und Spionage in der Etappe Gent"]
Agis-Verlag, Wien/Berlin 1928
Design for dust jacket, 1st version
Photomontage
8¼" × 7" [20.9 × 17.8 cm]
unsig.
Inv. no. 2234
(Back cover as reproduction)
Ill. p. 298

88 *Like no. 87*
Dust jacket, 2nd version
(after censorship)
7½" × 11" [18.6 × 27.5 cm]
unsig.
Reproduction
Ill. p. 299

89 *Richard Huelsenbeck*
"Africa in Sight"
["Afrika in Sicht"]
Wolfgang-Jess-Verlag, Dresden 1928
Book cover
8" × 11½" [20.3 × 28.8 cm]
Front page sig., b. l.: "John Heartfield"
Reproduction

90 *The Arena. The Sports Magazine*
[Die Arena. Das Sportmagazin]
Arena-Verlag, Berlin, Heft 1, January 1927
Design for front page
Photomontage with red paper
10" × 7½" [25.2 × 18.5 cm]
sig., b. l.: "Heartfield"
Inv. no. 1425
Ill. p. 133

91 The Arena. The Sports Magazine
Arena-Verlag, Berlin, Heft 2, February/March 1927
Front page
10" × 6¾" [24.5 × 17 cm]
Ill. p. 132

92 *"Eros. The Book of Love and Passion"*
["Eros. Das Buch der Leidenschaft und der Liebe"]
Rudolf-Kaemmerer-Verlag, Berlin 1925
Dust jacket
9" × 12" [22.3 × 30 cm]
Title page sig., b. l.: „Heartfield"
Reproduction
Ill. p. 100

93 *John Pepper*
"General Strike and General Treason in England"
["Der Generalstreik und der Generalverrat in England"]
Verlag Carl Hoym Nachf., Hamburg/Berlin 1925
Book cover design

94 *Aleksandr Fadeyev*
"The 19"
["Die 19"]
Verlag für Literatur und Politik, Wien/Berlin 1928
Dust jacket
8" × 11½" [19.8 × 28.8 cm]
Back cover sig., b. l.: "Heartfield"
Inv. no. 1695
(Whereabouts of original design unknown)

95 The New Russia. Magazine for culture, Commerce and Literature
[Das Neue Russland. Zeitschrift für Kultur, Wirtschaft und Literatur]
Neuer Deutscher Verlag, Berlin, Heft 3/4, May 1927
Design for front page
Photomontage with colored papers, text in cutout and painted script
9¾" × 7¼" [24.6 × 18.4 cm]
sig., b. l.: "Heartfield"
Inv. no. 1100

96 *The New Russia*
Berlin, no. 1/2, March 1927
Front page
Reproduction

97 *The New Russia*
Berlin, no. 5/6, July 1927
Front page
Reproduction

98 *The New Russia*
Berlin, no. 3/4, May 1927
Front page
Reproduction

99 *Upton Sinclair*
"King Coal"
["König Kohle"]
Malik-Verlag, Berlin 1925
Design for dust jacket
Photo-text montage
8" × 11½" [19.8 × 29 cm]
unsig.
Inv. no. 597

100 *"Rasputin, the Romanovs, the War and the People Who Revolted Against Them"*
["Rasputin, die Romanows, der Krieg und das Volk, das gegen sie aufstand"]
Blätter der Piscatorbühne (Publications of the Piscator Theatre), Berlin, no. 1, January 1928
Design for program cover
Photomontage with colored paper
10" × 7" [25 × 17.2 cm]
sig., b. l.: "Heartfield"
Inv. no. 586

101 Upton Sinclair
"The Jungle"
["Der Sumpf"]
Malik-Verlag, Berlin 1924
Book cover
7½" × 11¼" [19 × 28.3 cm]
(Whereabouts of original design unknown)
Back, sig., b. l.: "Heartfield"
Inv. no. 1621
Ill. p. 120

Wall B

102 *"To Everybody! 10 Years of the Soviet Union 1917–1927"*
Vereinigung Internationaler Verlagsanstalten, Berlin 1927
P. 1, 8
14¾" × 10¾" [each 37 × 27 cms]
Sig. in imprint: "Overall layout: John Heartfield"
Inv. no. 902

103 *"⅙ of the Earth is Ours! Economic and Political Facts in Pictures from the Soviet Union"*
["⅙ der Erde unser! Wirtschaftliche und politische Tatsachen in Bildern aus der Sowjetunion"]
Verlag Die Einheit, Berlin 1928
Outside page
12½" × 16" [31 × 40 cm]
Front page sig., b. l.: "Heartfield"
Inv. no. 1213

104 *Like no. 102*
P. 14
Inv. no. 3871
P. 15
Reproduction

105 "Italy in Chains"
["Italien in Ketten"]
Vereinigung Internationaler Verlagsanstalten, Berlin 1928
Front page: "The Face of Fascism"
15¼" × 10¾" [38 × 27 cm]
sig. in imprint: "Pictorial layout and typography: John Heartfield"
Inv. no. 3869
Ill. p. 145

106 *Like no. 105*
PP. 4,5: "Mussolini Will Establish 'Order'!"
["Mussolini schafft 'Ordnung!'"]
15¼" × 21½" [38 × 54 cm]
Inv. no. 3869

107 *"Class Warfare Against Coalition! Red Front in Red Berlin!"*
["Klassenkampf gegen Koalition! Rot Front im Roten Berlin!"]
The Red Flag [Die Rote Fahne] Berlin, no. 124, May 27, 1928
Front page
18¾" × 12¾" [47 × 32 cm]
sig., b. l.: "John Heartfield"
Inv. no. 655

108 *"Not a Man, Not a Penny for Imperialist War Armaments! All Out for the Peoples' Referendum!"*
["Keinen Mann, keinen Pfennig den imperialistischen Kriegsrüstungen! Heraus zum Volksbegehren!"]

The Red Flag, Berlin, no. 239, October 10, 1928
Front page
18¾″ × 12¾″ [47 × 32 cm]
sig., t. r.: "Heartfield"
Inv. no. 659

109 *"Strike at it! Subscribe!"*
["Schlagt zu! Zeichnet Euch ein!"]
The Red Flag, Berlin, no. 243, October 14, 1928
Front page
18¾″ × 12¾″ [47 × 32 cm]
sig., t. r.: "Heartfield"
Inv. no. 4692

110 *"We Nearly Made It!"*
["So weit waren wir schon!"]
The Club [Der Knüppel], Berlin, no. 3, March 1926
3rd page
ca. 18¾″ × 12¾″ [ca. 33 × 27 cm]
unsig.
Inv. no. 3910

111 *"13 Years of Murder"*
["13 Jahre Mord"]
Vereinigung Internationaler Verlagsanstalten, Berlin 1927
Front page, p. 10; pp. 6,7
10½″ × 7½″ [26 × 18.5 cm]
Sig. in imprint: "Overall layout, John Heartfield"
Inv. no. 4130, 1211

112 *Erich Wollenberg*
"As a Red Soldier at the Gates of Munich"
["Als Rotarmist vor München"]
Internationaler Arbeiter-Verlag, Berlin 1929
Book cover design
Photomontage with red paper, text
10″ × 13¾″ [25.2 × 34.6 cm]
unsig.
Inv. no. 575

113 *Like no. 112*
Book cover
7½″ × 5″ [18.5 × 12.5 cm]
unsig.
Reproduction

114 *"How a Photomontage is Made"*
["Wie eine Fotomontage entsteht"]
(with the montage for Upton Sinclair's "The Millennium")
Reconstruction
(Whereabouts of original unknown)

115 *Upton Sinclair*
"The Millennium"
(originally a reproduction of no. 114, retouched)
Reconstruction
(Whereabouts of original unknown)

116 Upton Sinclair
"The Millennium"
Malik-Verlag, Berlin 1925
Dust jacket
7½″ × 11¼″ [19 × 28 cm]
unsig.
Inv. no. 762
Ill. p. 298

117 "To Everybody! 10 Years of the Soviet Union 1917–1927"
Vereinigung Internationaler Verlagsanstalten, Berlin 1927
Front page
14¾″ × 12¾″ [37 × 27 cm]
sig., b. l.: "Heartfield"
Inv. no. 687

118 *"Illustrated History of the Civil War in Russia 1917–1927"*
["Illustrierte Geschichte des Bürgerkriegs in Russland 1917–1927"]
Neuer Deutscher Verlag, Berlin 1928
Design for dust jacket
Photomontage with red paper, painted text (front) and type (back)
10″ × 7½″ [25.2 × 18.6 cm] (front)
13¼″ × 10¼″ [33 × 25.8 cm] (back)
sig., b. r.: "Heartfield"
Inv. no. 1098

119 *Like no. 118*
Dust jacket
11½″ × 17½″ [28.7 × 43.7 cm]
sig., b. r.: "Heartfield"
Inv. no. 1657

120 *"Song of the Red Sailors"*
["Song der Roten Matrosen"]
Design for Canons Against the War [Kanonen gegen den Krieg]
Berlin 1928
4th page
Photomontage with pen-and-ink writing
19¼″ × 22½″ [48.2 × 56.2 cm]
unsig.
Inv. no. 505

121 Fedor Gladkov
"Cement"
["Zement"]
Verlag für Literatur und Politik, Wien/Berlin 1927
Pictorial layout
3″ × 4″ [7.7 × 9.8 cm]
Inv. no. 563
Photographic enlargement
7¼″ × 5¼″ [18 × 13 cm]
Inv. no. 1848
Retouched photo
7¼″ × 5″ [18 × 12.8 cm]
Inv. no. 1849
Dust jacket
8″ × 17″ [20 × 42.6 cm]
sig., b. l.: "John Heartfield"
Inv. no. 1608

122 "Two Kinds of Armaments"
["… Zweierlei Rüstungen"]
Design for Canons Against the War, Berlin 1928, 3rd page
Photomontage with gray paper
19¼″ × 25½″ [48.3 × 64 cm]
unsig.
Inv. no. 525

123 "O Christmas Tree, O Christmas Tree, Your Branches Should Teach Us Something"
["O Tannenbaum, O Tannenbaum, dein Kleid soll uns was lehren"]
The Female Warrior, Berlin, no. 12, 1928
Cover
9″ × 7¾″ [22.2 × 19.4 cm]
unsig.
Inv. no. 1750

Wall C

124 "Red Front"
["Rot Front"]
1927
Montage detail, proof print
10″ × 6¾″ [25 × 16.7 cm]
unsig.

Inv. no. 1672
Ill. p. 36

125 "Almanac for Politics – Commerce – Workers' Movement 1925/26"
["Jahrbuch für Poltik – Wirtschaft – Arbeiterbewegung 1925/26"]
Verlag Carl Hoym Nachf., Hamburg/Berlin 1926
Design for dust jacket
Photomontage with red paper and painted text
7½″ × 12″ [19 × 30 cm]
Front page sig., b. l.: "Heartfield"
Inv. no. 570
Ill. p. 108

126 *"Illustrated History of the German Revolution"*
["Illustrierte Geschichte der Deutschen Revolution"]
Internationaler Arbeiter-Verlag, Berlin 1929
Dust jacket
11½″ × 8½″ [29 × 21 cm]
unsig.
Reproduction

127 "Illustrated History of the Russian Revolution"
["Illustrierte Geschichte der Russischen Revolution"]
Neuer Deutscher Verlag, Berlin 1928
Dust jacket
11½″ × 8¾″ [28.7 × 21.7 cm]
sig., b. r.: "John Heartfield"
Inv. no. 3048

128 *Title and date unknown*
(Two hands smashing a crucifix)
possibly design for dust jacket
Reproduction after an exhibition photo of 1929
(Whereabouts of original unknown)

129 *Nikolai Bucharin*
"Problems of the Chinese Revolution"
["Probleme der chinesischen Revolution"]
Verlag Carl Hoym Nachf., Hamburg/Berlin 1927
Book cover
8½″ × 5¾″ [21.1 × 14.5 cm]
sig., b. l.: "Heartfield"
Reproduction

130 Johannes R. Becher
"(CH Cl:CH)₃ As (Lewisite) or The Only Just War"
["(CH Cl:CH)₃ As (Levisite) oder Der einzig gerechte Krieg"]
Agis-Verlag, Wien/Berlin 1926
Book cover design
Photomontage with colored paper
12½″ × 18¼″ [31.5 × 45.5 cm]
sig., b. l.: "John Heartfield"
Inv. no. 1494
Ill. p. 114

131 *"Murder of Our Brothers in China! Outcry in Europe Against China's Hangmen!"*
["Mord an unseren Brüdern im Osten! Sturm in Europa gegen die Henker Chinas!"]
Poster, 1927
25½″ × 19″ [63.8 × 47.5 cm]
sig., b. l.: "Heartfield"
Reproduction

132 Karl August Wittfogel
"China Awakening"
["Das erwachende China"]
Agis-Verlag, Wien 1926
Design for dust jacket
Photomontage with colored paper

14¾″ × 20½″ [37 × 51.5 cm]
sig., b. l.: "Heartfield"
Inv. no. 581
Ill. p. 109

133 "Proletarians of All Nations, Unite!"
["Proletarier aller Länder vereinigt Euch!"]
Cover for the German Communist Party magazine
(KPD), May 1927
Reproduction
(Whereabouts of original unknown)

134 "The Hand has 5 Fingers – With 5 You Seize
the Enemy – Vote List 5 – Communist Party!"
["5 Finger hat die Hand –
Mit 5 packst Du den Feind! Wählt Liste 5
Kommunistische Partei!"]
Election poster of the German Communist
Party (KPD), May 1928
25¼″ × 19¼″ [63 × 48 cm] and 34¼″ × 23½″
[85.5 × 59 cm]
sig., t. l.: "John Heartfield"
Reproductions
Ill. p. 294

135 Canons Against The War. War Is Casting Its
Shadow in Front!
[Kanonen gegen den Krieg. Der Krieg wirft
seinen Schatten voraus!]
Special issue of the German Communist Party
magazine
Design for front page
Photomontage
25¼″ × 19¼″ [63.2 × 48.2 cm]
sig., b. r.: "John Heartfield"
Inv. no. 422

136 Traugott Lehmann
"The White Plague"
["Die weiße Pest"]
Vereinigung Internationaler Verlagsanstal-
ten, Berlin 1926
Book cover design
Photomontage with black and white paper
19¼″ × 14½″ [48.2 × 36.4 cm]
sig., b. l.: "Heartfield"
Inv. no. 501

137 Hurray! The Armored Cruiser A is Here!
[Hurra! Der Panzerkreuzer A ist da!]
Special issue of the German Communist Party
magazine, Berlin 1928
Design for front page
Photomontage with text
24½″ × 19¼″ [61 × 48 cm]
sig., b. r.: "Heartfield"
Inv. no. 445

138 "Workers' Drawings and Poems from the Fac-
tories. Rationalization is on the March!"
["Arbeiterzeichnungen und Gedichte aus den
Betrieben. Die Rationalisierung marschiert!"]
The Club, Berlin, no. 2, February 1927
p. 5

above left:
design for p. 5
Photomontage with opaque color
12¾″ × 9½″ [32 × 24 cm]
unsig.
Inv. no. 865
Ill. p. 131

below right:
p. 5
12¾″ × 9½″ [32 × 24 cm]

sig., b. r.: "John Heartfield fec."
Inv. no. 3928
Ill. p. 130

top right/bottom left:
Günter Reimann
"The German Economic Miracle"
["Das deutsche Wirtschaftswunder"]
Vereinigung Internationaler Verlagsanstal-
ten, Berlin 1926
Book cover
9¼″ × 6¼″ [23 × 15.7 cm]
sig., b. l.: "Heartfield"
Reproductions

139 Traugott Lehmann
"The White Plague"
["Die weiße Pest"]
Vereinigung Internationaler Verlagsanstalten, Ber-
lin 1926
Design for dust jacket, back
Reproduction
(Whereabouts of original unknown)

Wall D

140 "Foundations of the New World. America,
You're Better Off . . .!"
["Grundlagen der neuen Welt. Amerika, du
hast es besser . . .!"]
Publications of the Piscator Theatre, Berlin,
March 1928
Design for pp. 8/9
Photomontage, retouched
12¾″ × 18½″ [32 × 46 cm]
unsig.
P. 8/9
9¼″ × 12½″ [23 × 31 cm]
unsig.
Inv. no. 513

141 top:
"The Whole Shebang"
["Schöne Be-Scherung"]
The Club, Berlin, no. 5, August 1927
penultimate page
12¾″ × 9½″ [32 × 24 cm]
sig., b. r.: "fec. John Heartfield"
Inv. no. 676
Ill. p. 127

bottom left:
"Religious Socialism"
["Religiöser Sozialismus"]
The Club, Berlin, no. 4, June 1927, page 5
9″ × 8½″ [22.2 × 21.5 cm]
Inscription, b. r.: based on an idea from a film still of
Harold Lloyd's "The Freshman". By John Heartfield
Inv. no. 677

bottom right:
Design for page 5
Motion picture still, retouched
8¾″ × 8¼″ [22 × 20.5 cm]
unsig.
Inv. no. 2064

142 Top:
"Unatoned Murders"
["Ungesühnte Mordverbrechen"]
The Club, Berlin, no. 8, November 1926, without p.
no.
ca. 4¾″ × 9½″ [ca. 12 × 24 cm]
unsig.
Inv. no. 1543

middle:
"Dress Rehearsal of the Funeral Procession for the
Reichstag"
["Generalprobe zum Leichenbegängnis des Deut-
schen Reichstages"]
The Club, Berlin, no. 7, July 1926
Page 2 (middle)
ca. 7½″ × 9½″ [ca. 19 × 24 cm]
unsig.
Inv. no. 3918

bottom:
"Off with the Sorrow's Mask!"
["Weg mit der Sorgenmaske!"]
Advertisement for "Dr. League-of-Nations Health
Salts"
The Club, Berlin, no. 4, April 1926
Page 3 (detail)
ca. 3½″ × 9½″ [ca. 9 × 24 cm]
unsig.
Inv. no. 3911

bottom right:
Advertisement design
Photomontage, retouched
5″ × 6¼″ [12.2 × 15.4 cm]
sig., b. l.: "Heartfield"
Inv. no. 866

143 Top:
"A Republican Minister of the Interior, or Czarist
unto Death"
["Ein republikanischer Innenminister oder Zaren-
treu bis übers Grab"]
Der Gummiknüppel (The Billy Club), Berlin,
October 1926
Page 3
Retouched photo of design
9″ × 8″ [22.4 × 20.1 cm (picture)]
and
Design for p. 3 above
Photomontage
5½″ × 8″ [13.5 × 20.2 cm (picture)]
Inv. no. 872

bottom:
Detail of p. 3 above
ca. 4½″ × 5½″ [ca. 11 × 14 cm]
sig., t. r.: "fec. John Heartfield"
Inv. no. 873

144 "For His Silence"
["Für sein Schweigen"]
"America! You're Better Off!"
Publications of the Piscator Theatre, Berlin, March
1928
Page 10
9½″ × 6¼″ [23 × 15.5 cm]
sig., b. l.: "Heartfield"
Inv. no. 3283

145 "America, You're Better Off!"
Publications of the Piscator Theatre, Berlin,
March 1928
Front page design
Photomontage with painted text
12¾″ × 9½″ [32 × 24 cm]
sig., b. l.: "Heartfield"
Inv. no. 500

146 Untitled
(Industrial magnate with monocle and top hat)
Design for book cover or dust jacket for the Verlag für
Literatur und Politik, Vienna and Berlin, ca. 1928
Photomontage with red paper
8¾″ × 6½″ [22.1 × 15.5 cm]
unsig.
(Whereabouts of original unknown)

147 *"Kautski: Socialism in Sight!"*
["Kautski: Sozialismus in Sicht!"]
Photomontage, 1928
Reproduction based on exhibition photo of 1929
(Whereabouts of original unknown)

148 "Front Heil"
The Club, special issue: "The Plumbing Shop"
["Der Klempnerladen"], Berlin, no. 4, June
1927
Cover picture
12¾" × 9½" [32 × 24 cm (page)]
sig., b. r.: "Photomontage von John Heart-
field"
Inv. no. 670
Ill. p. 126

149 *"Our Bluejackets"*
["Unsere Blauen Jungens"]
Hurray! The Armored Cruiser A is Here!
Extra issue of the German Communist Party, Berlin
1928
Design for p. 3, above
Photomontage, retouched
11" × 13¼" [27.6 × 33.4 cm]
unsig.
Inv. no. 711

150 *"A Peace Cake and Its Ingredients"*
["Eine Friedenstorte und ihre Zutaten"]
The Red Grenade [Die Rote Granate]
Berlin, August 1926
Back cover
12¾" × 9½" [32 × 24 cm]
sig., b. r.: "f. John Heartfield"
Inv. no. 3919
Ill. p. 128

151 *Jacob Dorfmann*
"In the Land of Record Figures"
["Im Lande der Rekordzahlen"]
Verlag für Literatur und Politik, Wien/Berlin 1927
2 flyleaves
7¾" × 10¼" each [19.4 × 25.9 cm each]
unsig.
Inv. nos. 1103, 1728

152 *Upton Sinclair*
"Boston"
Malik-Verlag, Berlin 1929
Dust jacket
7½" × 12¾" [19 × 31.6 cm]
unsig.
Inv. no. 235

153 *"The Trinity of the U.S.A."*
["Der Dreieinige Gott der U.S.A."]
"America, You're Better Off!"
Publications of the Piscator Theatre, Berlin, March
1928
Design for page 3
Reproduction
(Whereabouts of original unknown)

154 *"Dada ist Great and John [Heartfield] is Its*
Prophet"
["Dada ist groß und John (Heartfield) ist sein
Prophet"]
Photomontage, 1919
Reproduction

155 Upton Sinclair
"Singing Jailbirds"
["Singende Galgenvögel"]
Malik-Verlag, Berlin 1927
Book cover design
Photomontage with white and green paper
8¾" × 13¼" [21.8 × 33 cm]

Back cover sig.: "Original Heartfield Malik-
Verlag"
Inv. no. 1485

156 John Dos Passos
"Three Soldiers"
["Drei Soldaten"]
Malik-Verlag, Berlin 1929
Design for dust jacket, front
2nd version
Photomontage with painted text
7¾" × 5¼" [19.6 × 13.3 cm]
unsig.
Inv. no. 576

157 *Franz Carl Weiskopf*
"Who Has No Choice Has the Agony"
["Wer keine Wahl hat, hat die Qual"]
Malik-Verlag, Berlin 1929
Design for dust jacket, front
Photomontage with text
11" × 7¼" [27.7 × 18 cm]
unsig.
Inv. no. 598
Ill. p. 115

158 *Maxim Gorki*
"The Mother"
["Die Mutter"]
Malik-Verlag, Berlin 1927 (27th–35th thousand)
Dust jacket
7½" × 11½" [18.8 × 29 cm]
Backcover sig., b. r.: "Heartfield"
Inv. no. 3015
and
Sample for title picture from the Russian film of the
same name
Reproduction
(Whereabouts of original unknown)

159 *Marietta Shaginyan*
"Adventures of a Society Lady"
["Abenteuer einer Dame"]
Malik-Verlag, Berlin 1924
Book cover
7½" × 5¼" [19 × 13 cm]
unsig.
Reproduction

160 Ilya Grusdev
"The Life of Maxim Gorki"
["Das Leben Maxim Gorkis"]
Malik-Verlag, Berlin 1928
Dust jacket
7½" × 5" [18.8 × 12.5 cm]
unsig.
Inv. no. 3014

161 *Wilhelm Herzog*
"In Steerage to South America"
["Im Zwischendeck nach Südamerika"]
Malik-Verlag, Wien 1924
Book cover
7" × 4¾" [17.8 × 12 cm]
unsig.
Reproduction

162 *Ery H. Gulden*
"Circulatory System of Love"
["Kreislauf der Liebe"]
Rudolf-Kaemmerer-Verlag, Berlin 1927
Design for dust jacket
Photomontage with gray paper and painted text
9½" × 7" [23.5 × 17.5 cm]
sig., b. l.: "Design remains property of Heartfield"
Inv. no. 1762

163 *Fritz Slang*
"Battleship Potemkin"
["Panzerkreuzer Potemkin"]
Malik-Verlag, 3rd edition, Berlin 1927
Malik-Bücherei, Bd. 19
Book cover
7¼" × 5" [18 × 12.3 cm]
unsig.
Reproduction

164 John Reed
"Ten Days that Shook the World"
["Zehn Tage, die die Welt erschütterten"]
Verlag für Literatur und Politik, Wien/Berlin
1927
Design for dust jacket
Photomontage, retouched
8¼" × 13" [20.4 × 32.3 cm]
unsig.
Inv. no. 593

165 Upton Sinclair
"The Metropolis"
["Die Metropole"]
Malik-Verlag, Berlin 1925
Design for dust jacket
Reproduction
(Whereabouts of original unknown)
Book cover
7½" × 11" [19 × 27.5 cm]
unsig.
Inv. no. 1631
Ill. p. 120

166 Upton Sinclair
"100 %"
Malik-Verlag, Berlin 1921
Rote Roman-Serie, Bd. 2
Book cover, 1st version
7¼" × 11¼" [18 × 28 cm]
sig., b. l.: "John Heartfield"
Reproduction
Binding for 1924 edition
(21st–30th thousand)
7½" × 10½" [18.9 × 26 cm]
unsig.
Inv. no. 1613
Ill. p. 98

167 *Upton Sinclair*
"The Moneychangers"
["Die Wechsler"]
Malik-Verlag, Berlin 1925
Design for dust jacket
Photomontage with painted text
9" × 6¾" [22.8 × 16.7 cm]
unsig.
Reproduction
Dust jacket
7½" × 11½" [19 × 28.5 cm]
unsig.
Inv. no. 3116
Ill. p. 107

168 *Mynona (Salomo Friedlaender)*
"Gray Magic"
["Graue Magie"]
Rudolf-Kaemmerer-Verlag, Dresden 1922
Design for dust jacket
Photomontage with black paper
11¼" × 9½" [28 × 23.6 cm]
unsig.
Inv. no. 578

169 *Paul Rosenhayn*
"The Isle of Dreams"

["Die Insel der Träume"]
Rudolf-Kaemmerer-Verlag, Berlin 1926
Book cover
7½" × 5" [18.8 × 12.2 cm]
sig., b. r.: "Heartfield"
Reproduction

170   "Six-Day Rally. A Documentary Record by John
      Förste, Photo Illustrations by John Heartfield"
      ["6 Tage-Rennen. Eine Tatbestands-Aufnahme von
      John Förste, fotoillustriert von John Heartfield"]
      Die Arena. Das Sportmagazin, Berlin, Heft 2,
      November 1926
      Two-page spread 78/79
      9½" × 13½" [24 × 34 cm]
      Inv. no. 1546
      Two-page spread 80/81
      Reproduction

171   Raoul Hausmann, John Heartfield
      "Dadaco. Dada Handatlas"
      Publishing project of the Kurt Wolff Verlag,
      Munich, planned for January 1920, but not
      published
      Four single pages:
      top left: Giorgio de Chirico (untitled)
      top right: Francis Picabia, "Paysage" ["Land-
      scape"]
      bottom left: "Our John" ["Unser John"]
      bottom right: "Dada in School" ["Dada in den
      Schulen"]
      Reproductions
      Ill. pp. 90–93

      Displayed in the room

172   Three showcases with books from various publishing
      companies

      In front of Wall B:

      Showcase 1
      Books from Malik-Verlag, Berlin
      Authors: Upton Sinclair, Ilya Grusdev, Max Hoelz

      Showcase 2
      Books from Malik-Verlag, Berlin, Wolfgang Jess
      Verlag, Dresden, and the Vereinigung Internationa-
      ler Verlagsanstalten (Association of International
      Publishing Companies), Berlin
      Authors: Franz Weiskopf, John Dos Passos, Upton
      Sinclair, Richard Huelsenbeck, Wera Figner,
      Maxim Gorki, and Vladimir Mayakovsky

      Showcase 3
      Books from Verlag für Literatur und Politik, Vienna
      Authors: Fedor Gladkov, Aleksandr Fadeyev, Fedor
      Panferov
      Originally in front of Wall D

      Showcase 4
      Books from Malik-Verlag, Berlin, Verlag für
      Literatur und Politik, Vienna, Rudolf-Kaemmerer-
      Verlag, Berlin
      Authors: Fritz Slang, Upton Sinclair, Leo Lania,
      Franz Jung, Richard Huelsenbeck, Marietta
      Shaginyan

173   "This is What a Hero's Death Looks Like"
      ["So sieht der Heldentod aus"]
      Photographs with handscript
      5½" × 3½" [13.8 × 8.8 cm]
      unsig.
      Inv. no. 4633
      Ill. p. 15

174   Everybody His Own Football
      [Jedermann sein eigner Fussball]

Berlin and Leipzig, no. 1, February 15, 1919
4 pages
17¼" × 11¾" [43.3 × 29.3 cm]
sig. on p. 4: "Responsible for the entire contents:
Helmut Herzfeld, Berlin"
Inv. no. 3804
Ill. pp. 81–84

175   Untitled "The Last Green"
      ["Das letzte Grün"]
      approx. early 1920's
      Photo-colormontage
      9¼" × 9" [23.3 × 22.2 cm]
      unsig.
      Inv. no. 4632
      Ill. p. 292

176   "H. M."
      ["S. M."]
      The Bust [Die Pleite], Berlin, no. 7, July 1923,
      Cover
      Reprint
      sig., b. r.: "Drawing by George Grosz"
      Inv. no. 2330
      Ill. p. 124

177   "The Fascist Call"
      ["Faschistenruf"]
      The Bust, Berlin, no. 7, July 1923,
      unpag.
      18½" × 11½" [46 × 29 cm]
      sig. t. l.: "Drawing by John Heartfield"
      Inv. no. 5171
      Ill. p. 125

178   "After Ten Years: Fathers and Sons 1924"
      ["Nach zehn Jahren: Väter und Söhne 1924"]
      Photomontage, retouched
      15" × 16¼" [37.3 × 40.5 cm]
      sig. on back: "John Heartfield; Ten Years Later:
      Fathers and Sons"
      Inv. no. 515
      Ill. pp. 22–23

179   "Comrades! People! Property and Blood Have Been
      Sacrificed Incessantly for the last 5 Years"
      ["Kameraden! Leute! 5 Jahre unentwegt Gut und
      Blut geopfert"]
      Design for The Club, Berlin, no. 6, June 1926
      unpag.
      Photomontage, retouched
      12¾" × 9½" [32.5 × 24.5 cm]
      sig., t. r.: "Property Heartfield"
      Inv. no. 674
      Ill. p. 134

180   John Heartfield in front of the enlargement of his
      montage for Upton Sinclair's novel "The Millen-
      nium"
      Design for Gebrauchsgraphik, Berlin, Heft 7, 1927,
      p. 17
      Photomontage, retouched
      6½" × 9" [16.4 × 22.2 cm]
      unsig.
      Inv. no. 641
      Ill. p. 94

181   "A Peace Cake and Its Ingredients"
      ["Eine Friedenstorte und ihre Zutaten"]
      The Red Grenade, Berlin, August 1926
      Design, 1st version, revised as 2nd version for the
      "Arbeiterkalender," 1927
      Photomontage with colored paper
      16" × 15¼" [40 × 38 cm]
      unsig.
      Inv. no. 712
      Ill. p. 129

182   "Be as Determined as These Three. Vote List 5 –
      Communist Party"
      ["Seid kampfentschlossen wie diese Drei, Wählt Liste
      5 – Kommunistische Partei"]
      The Red Flag, Berlin, no. 115, May 17, 1928
      Front page
      18¾" × 12¾" [47 × 32 cm]
      sig., b. l.: "Heartfield"
      Inv. no. 4691
      Ill. p. 144

183   "Settle Accounts! Demonstrate for the Revolution!"
      ["Rechnet ab! Demonstriert für die Revolution!"]
      The Red Flag, Berlin, no. 118, Jan. 20, 1928
      Front page
      18¾" × 12¾" [47 × 32 cm]
      sig., b. r.: "John Heartfield"
      Inv. no. 3867

184   "Not a Man, not a Penny for Imperialist War
      Armaments! All Out for the Peoples' Referendum!"
      ["Keinen Mann, keinen Pfennig den imperialisti-
      schen Kriegsrüstungen! Heraus zum Volksbegeh-
      ren!"]
      The Red Flag, Berlin, October 10, 1928
      Design for front page
      Photomontage
      21¼" × 19½" [53.3 × 48.5 cm]
      sig., t. r.: "Heartfield"
      Inv. no. 414

185   "Strike at it! Subscribe!"
      ["Schlagt zu! Zeichnet Euch ein!"]
      The Red Flag, Berlin, October 14, 1928
      Design for front page
      Photomontage
      19¼" × 13¾" [48.4 × 34.5 cm]
      sig., t. r.: "Heartfield"
      Inv. no. 423
      Ill. p. 143

186   Hurray! The Armored Cruiser A is Here!
      Special issue of the German Communist Party,
      Berlin 1928
      Cover
      18¾" × 12½" [47 × 31.5 cm]
      sig., b. r.: "Heartfield"
      Inv. no. 4712
      Ill. p. 136

187   "Socialism in Sight! Always Based on Facts"
      ["Sozialismus in Sicht! Immer auf dem Boden der
      Tatsachen"]
      Same as no. 186, p. 2
      18¾" × 12½" [47 × 31.5 cm]
      sig., b. r.: "Photomontages by John Heartfield"
      Inv. no. 3864
      Ill. p. 137

188   "Our Bluejackets"
      ["Unsere Blauen Jungens"]
      Same as no. 186, p. 3
      18¾" × 12½" [47 × 31.5 cm]
      unsig.
      Inv. no. 4712
      Ill. p. 138

189   "Solution to the Ingenious Picture Puzzle"
      ["Auflösung des raffinierten Vexier-Pusselspieles"]
      Same as no. 186, p. 8
      18¾" × 12½" [47 × 31.5 cm]
      sig., b. r.: "Cut out and put together from original
      Social Democratic Party of Germany (SPD) leaflets
      by John Heartfield"
      Inv. no. 1237
      Ill. p. 139

190 *"Socialism in Sight"*
["*Sozialismus in Sicht"*]
Photo reproduction taken from news sheet (cf. no. 187), retouched (composition design for: W. Herzfelde, "John Heartfield – Leben und Werk," Dresden 1962, Pl. p. 32)
7¾" × 7¾" [19.2 × 19.2 cm]
unsig.
Inv. no. 1890

191 *Design for no. 189*
Montage from leaflets
9½" × 12½" [23.5 × 31 cm]
unsig.
Inv. no. 429
Ill. p. 135

192 "The Hand Has 5 Fingers – With 5 You Seize the Enemy! – Vote List 5! – Communist Party!"
["5 Finger hat die Hand – Mit 5 packst Du den Feind! – Wählt Liste 5 – Kommunistische Partei!"]
The Red Flag, Berlin, no. 112, May 13, 1928
Front page
18¾" × 12¾" [47 × 32 cm]
sig., b. l.: "John Heartfield"
Inv. no. 658
Ill. p. 141

193 *Same as no. 192*
Design for front page
Photo, retouched
12¾" × 8¾" [32 × 21.7 cm]
unsig.
Inv. no. 503

194 John Heartfield with Police Commissioner Zörgiebel
Photomontage, retouched
11¼" × 8½" [28 × 21.1 cm]
unsig.
Inv. no. 430
Ill. p. 122

195 *"Forced to Deliver Human Material. Courage! The State Needs the Unemployed and Soldiers!"*
["*Zwangslieferantin von Menschenmaterial. Nur Mut! Der Staat braucht Arbeitslose und Soldaten!"*]
AIZ, Berlin, no. 10, 1930, p. 183
15¼" × 10¾" [38 × 27 cm]
sig., b. r.: "John Heartfield"
Inv. no. 1244

196 *Design for no. 195*
Photomontage, retouched
20½" × 15½" [51.5 × 39 cm]
sig., b. r.: "John Heartfield"
Inv. no. 514
Ill. p. 297

197 *"Vandervelde or the Consummate Indecency"*
["*Vandervelde oder Die vollkommene Schamlosigkeit"*]
AIZ, Berlin, no. 22, 1930, p. 423
15¼" × 10¾" [38 × 27 cm]
sig., b. r.: "Mont. John Heartfield"
Inv. no. 6

198 "Macdonald-Socialism"
["Macdonald-Sozialismus"]
AIZ, Berlin, no. 28, 1930, p. 543
15¼" × 10¾" [38 × 27 cm]
sig., b. r.: "Mont. John Heartfield"
Inv. no. 288
Ill. p. 206

199 "For Bread and Freedom!"
["*Für Brot und Freiheit!"*]

Special issue of the AIZ, Berlin, autumn 1930
(appeared after no. 35)
Front page picture
15¼" × 10¾" [38 × 27 cm]
sig., b. r.: "John Heartfield"
Inv. no. 14

200 *Design for no. 199*
Photomontage, retouched
21½" × 5¾" [54 × 14.4 cm]
sig., b. r.: "Heartfield"
Inv. no. 470

201 "Six Million Nazi Voters: Fodder for a Big Mouth"
["6 Millionen Naziwähler: Futter für ein grosses Maul"]
AIZ, Berlin, no. 40, 1930, p. 783
15¼" × 10¾" [38 × 27 cm]
sig., b. r.: "John Heartfield"
Inv. no. 1249

202 "Hurray, Hurray! The Brüning Santa Claus is Here!"
["Hurra, Hurra! Der Brüning-Weihnachtsmann ist da!"]
AIZ, Berlin, no. 51, 1930, p. 1003
15¼" × 10¾" [38 × 27 cm]
sig., b. l.: "Montage: John Heartfield"
Inv. no. 15
Ill. p. 190

203 *Design for no. 202, 1st Version*
Montage setting
16" × 11¾" [40.3 × 29.2 cm]
sign., b. l.: "Montage: John Heartfield"
Inv. no. 1878
Ill. p. 191

204 *Design for no. 202, 2nd version*
Montage, arranged and mounted
16" × 12" [40 × 30.3 cm]
unsig.
Inv. no. 491

205 *The USSR in Construction*
Monthly, no. 9, Moscow 1931
Inside heading
16¾" × 12" [41.8 × 29.7 cm]
sig., b.: "Photographs [correct: Negativemontage] by John Hartfield [sic] (Moscow)"
Inv. no. 4317
Ill. p. 279

206 "One Has to Have a Particular Predisposition to Suicide . . ."
["Man muß eine besondere Veranlagung zu Selbstmord haben . . ."]
Design for AIZ, Berlin, no. 13, 1931, p. 253
Montage and press cuttings
(Variation of a 1927 montage)
18¾" × 12½" [47 × 31.5 cm]
unsig.
Inv. no. 882
Ill. p. 192

207 "On the Crisis Party Congress of SPD (German Social Democratic Party)"
["Zum Krisen-Parteitag der SPD"]
AIZ, Berlin, no. 24, 1931, p. 477
15¼" × 10¾" [38 × 27 cm]
sig., b. r.: "Photo-Montage: John Heartfield"
Inv. no. 18
Ill. p. 166

208 "Black or White – United in the Fight!"
["Ob schwarz, ob weiß – im Kampf vereint!"]
AIZ, Berlin, no. 26, 1931, p. 517
15¼" × 10¾" [38 × 27 cm]
sig., b. r.: "Photomontage: John Heartfield"
Inv. no. 19

---

209 "Resurrection"
["Auferstehung"]
Photomontage, 1932
16¾" × 23¼" [42 × 57.9 cm]
unsig.
Inv. no. 518
Ill. pp. 58–59

210 "War and Dead Bodies – The Last Hope of the Rich"
["Krieg und Leichen – Die letzte Hoffnung der Reichen"]
AIZ, Berlin, no. 18, 1932, p. 420/421
15¼" × 21½" [38 × 54 cm]
sig., t. r.: "Photomontage: John Heartfield"
Inv. no. 2259
Ill. pp. 30–31

211 *"With this Sign Shall You be Betrayed and Sold!"*
["*In diesem Zeichen will man euch verraten und verkaufen!"*]
AIZ, Berlin, no. 27, July 3, 1932, p. 627
15¼" × 10¾" [38 × 27 cm]
sig., b. r.: "Montage: John Heartfield"
Inv. no. 209

212 "Adolf the Superman: Swallows Gold and Spouts Junk"
["Adolf, der Übermensch: Schluckt Gold und redet Blech"]
AIZ, Berlin, no. 29, July 17, 1932, p. 675
15¼" × 10¾" [38 × 27 cm]
sig., t. r.: "X-ray photograph of John Heartfield"
Inv. no. 2261

213 Design for no. 212
Photomontage, retouched
28¼" × 23½" [70.5 × 59 cm]
unsig.
Inv. no. 524
Ill. p. 194

214 "H. M. Adolf. I Will Lead You to Splendid Bankruptcy!"
["S. M. Adolf. Ich führe Euch herrlichen Pleiten entgegen!"]
AIZ, Berlin, no. 34, August 21, 1932, p. 795
15¼" × 10¾" [38 × 27 cm]
sig., b. r.: "Photomontage: John Heartfield"
Inv. no. 1254

215 "The Meaning of the Hitler Salute: Little Man Requests Big Donation. Motto: Millions are Behind Me"
["Der Sinn des Hitlergrusses: Kleiner Mann bittet um grosse Gaben. Motto: Millionen stehen hinter mir!"]
AIZ, Berlin, no. 42, October 16, 1932, p. 985
15¼" × 10¾" [38 × 27 cm]
sig., b. r.: "John Heartfield"
Inv. no. 217
Ill. p. 290

216 Design for no. 215
Photomontage, retouched
18¼" × 14¼" [45.8 × 35.7 cm]
unsig.
Inv. no. 509

217 "Six Million Communist Votes"
["Sechs Millionen kommunistische Stimmen"]
AIZ, Berlin, no. 47, November 20, 1932, p. 1113
15¼" × 10¾" [38 × 27 cm]
sig., b. r.: "Montage: John Heartfield"
Inv. no. 4210

218 Design for no. 217
Photomontage, retouched
18" × 14½" [44.7 × 36 cm]

unsig.
Inv. no. 494
Ill. p. 195

219 "The Meaning of Geneva. Where the Capital
lives, There Can be No Peace!"
["Der Sinn von Genf. Wo das Kapital lebt, kann
der Friede nicht leben!"]
AIZ, Berlin, no. 48, November 27, 1932,
p. 1137
15¼" × 10¾" [38 × 27 cm]
sig., b. r.: "Montage: John Heartfield"
Inv. no. 1258
Ill. p. 182

220 Design for no. 219
Photomontage, retouched
19¾" × 14¼" [49.1 × 35.6 cm]
unsig.
Inv. no. 421
Ill. p. 183

221 "On Gregor Strasser's 'Leave of Absence' Granted by
Adolf Hitler. Little SA man, What Now?"
["Zur 'Beurlaubung' Gregor Strassers durch Adolf
Hitler. Kleiner SA-Mann, was nun?!"]
AIZ, Berlin, no. 52, December 25, 1932, p. 1227
15¼" × 10¾" [38 × 27 cm]
sig., b. r.: "Montage: John Heartfield"
Inv. no. 648
Ill. p. 164

222 "'War is the Continuation of Politics by Means of
Violence' – Lenin"
["'Der Krieg ist die Fortsetzung der Politik mit den
Mitteln der Gewalt' – Lenin"]
Illustrated Red Post, Berlin, no. 39, September
1938
(special issue "Berlin in Wartime, 19..?"), front
page
18½" × 12¾" [46 × 32 cm]
sig., b. r.: "The Destruction of Berlin – Photomontage by John Heartfield"
Inv. no. 4490 (photograph)
Ill. p. 208

223 "Advertising Construction for U.S.S.R. in Front of
the Railroad Station in Leipzig for the Trade Fair"
Design, 1927
Brushwork superimposed on pencil
18¼" × 11¼" [45,5 × 28 cm]
sig., t.: "Design John Heartfield, Berlin"
Inv. no. 1027
Ill. p. 246

224 "Not a Man, Not a Penny for Imperialist War
Armaments! All out for the People's Referendum!"
["Keinen Mann, keinen Pfennig den imperialistischen Kriegsrüstungen! Heraus zum Volksbegehren!"]
Poster, 1928
28" × 39½" [70.1 × 99 cm]
sig., t. r.: "John Heartfield"
Inv. no. 2382

225 "Fight with us! Vote Communist List 4"
["Kämpft mit uns! Wählt Kommunisten Liste 4"]
Poster for the Reichstag election on September 14,
1930
38½" × 25¾" [96 × 64.5 cm]
sig., b. r.: "John Heartfield"
Inv. no. 3939 (Reprint)
Ill. p. 146

226 "Capitalism is Robbing Them of Their Last Piece of
Bread. Fight for Yourself and Your Children! Vote
Communist! Vote Thälmann!"

["Das letzte Stück Brot raubt ihnen der Kapitalis-
mus. Kämpft für Euch und Eure Kinder! Wählt
Kommunisten! Wählt Thälmann!"]
Poster, 1932
38" × 28½" [95 × 71.5 cm]
sig., t. r.: "John Heartfield"
Inv. no. 3935 (Reprint)
Ill. p. 147

227 "Down With the Warmongers! Fight for the Soviet
Union! All Out for the Fight in May 1932"
["Nieder mit den Kriegshetzern! Kämpft für die
Sowjetunion! Heraus zum Kampfmai 1932"]
Poster
28¾" × 19¾" [71.6 × 49.2 cm]
sig., t. r.: "John Heartfield"
Inv. no. 4002 (Reprint)

228 "Prospects for the Death Business"
["Todeskonjunktur"]
AIZ, Berlin, no. 4, January 22, 1933, p. 75
15¼" × 10¾" [38 × 27 cm]
sig., b. r.: "Montage: John Heartfield"
Inv. no. 2193
Ill. p. 209

229 "Through Light to Night. Thus Spoke Dr.
Goebbels: Let Us Start New Fires so that They
Who are Blinded don't Awaken!"
["Durch Licht zur Nacht. Also sprach Dr.
Goebbels: Lasst uns aufs neue Brände
entfachen, auf dass die Verblendeten nicht
erwachen!"]
AIZ, Prague, no. 18, May 10, 1933, p. 312
15¼" × 10¾" [38 × 27 cm]
unsig.
Inv. no. 2195

230 "Morgan Announces: 'L'état c'est moi'"
["Morgan spricht: 'Der Staat bin ich'"]
AIZ, Prague, no. 22, June 8, 1933, p. 387
15¼" × 10¾" [38 × 27 cm]
sig., b. l.: "Photomontage: John Heartfield"
Inv. no. 4213

231 "On the Founding of the German State
Church. The Cross was not Heavy Enough"
["Zur Gründung der deutschen Staatskirche.
Das Kreuz war noch nicht schwer genug"]
AIZ, Prague, no. 23, June 15, 1933, p. 403
15¼" × 10¾" [38 × 27 cm]
sig., b. r.: "Photomontage: John Heartfield"
Inv. no. 766

232 "Everything's in Perfect Order!"
["Alles in schönster Ordnung!"]
AIZ, Prague, no. 25, June 29, 1933, p. 436
15¼" × 10¾" [38 × 27 cm]
sig. b. r.: "Photomontage: John Heartfield"
Inv. no. 35

233 Design for no. 232
Photomontage, retouched
17¾" × 12¼" [44.5 × 30.7 cm]
unsig.
Inv. no. 478

234 "Because He Relied on the Program of the NSDAP
(National Socialist German Workers' Party) – 'We'll
Soon Teach You Our Kind of "Socialism" in a Con-
centration Camp'"
["Weil er sich auf das Programm der NSDAP berief.
'Dir werden wir unsern "Sozialismus" im Konzen-
trationslager schon beibringen'"]
AIZ, Prague, no. 28, July 20, 1933, p. 483
14½" × 10¾" [36 × 27 cm]

sig., b. r.: "Photomontage: John Heartfield"
Inv. no. 38
Ill. p. 168

235 Design for no. 234
Photomontage, retouched
20" × 13" [49.8 × 32.5 cm]
unsig.
Inv. no. 486

236 "War"
["Der Krieg"]
AIZ, Prague, no. 29, July 27, 1933, p. 499
15¼" × 10¾" [38 × 27 cm]
sig. b.: "A painting by Franz v. Stuck.
Brought up-to-date in a montage by John
Heartfield"
Inv. no. 5168

237 Design for no. 236
Photomontage, retouched
unsig.
10¾" × 9½" [27 × 23.8 cm]
Inv. no. 493
Ill. p. 197

238 "The Cross of Murder"
["Das Mörderkreuz"]
AIZ, Prague, no. 30, August 3, 1933, p. 515
15¼" × 10¾" [38 × 27 cm]
sig., b. r.: "Photomontage: John Heartfield"
Inv. no. 39

239 "New Chair at the German Universities: Racial
Psychoanalysis"
["Neuer Lehrstuhl an den deutschen Univer-
sitäten. Völkische Tiefenschau"]
AIZ, Prague, no. 34, August 31, 1933, p. 579
15¼" × 10¾" [38 × 27 cm]
sig., b. r.: "Original photograph taken in the
Teutonic bush by John Heartfield"
Inv. no. 42
Ill. p. 186

240 Design for no. 239
Photomontage, retouched
18½" × 13¼" [46 × 33 cm]
unsig.
Inv. no. 496
Ill. p. 187

241 "Goering: The Executioner of the Third
Reich"
["Goering. Der Henker des Dritten Reichs"]
AIZ, Prague, no. 36, September 14, 1933,
p. 609
15¼" × 10¾" [38 × 27 cm]
sig., b. l.: "Photomontage: John Heartfield"
Inv. no. 1261
Ill. p. 167

242 "German Acorns 1933"
["Deutsche Eicheln 1933"]
AIZ, Prague, no. 37, September 21, 1933,
p. 627
15¼" × 10¾" [38 × 27 cm]
sig., b. r.: "Photomontage: John Heartfield"
Inv. no. 770

243 Design for no. 242
Photomontage, retouched
16" × 12¾" [40.2 × 31.7 cm]
unsig.
Inv. no. 452

244 "On the Arson Trial in Leipzig. They Twist
and Turn and Call Themselves German
Judges"

["Zum Brandstifter-Prozeß in Leipzig. Sie winden sich und drehen sich und nennen sich deutsche Richter"]
AIZ, Prague, no. 41, October 19, 1933, p. 691
15¼″ × 10¾″ [38 × 27 cm]
sig., b. r.: "Photomontage John Heartfield"
Inv. no. 1263
Ill. p. 184

245   Design for no. 244
Photomontage on black paper, retouched
20¾″ × 16½″ [51.7 × 41.2 cm]
unsig.
Inv. no. 507
Ill. p. 185

246   "The Judge/The Culprit"
["Der Richter/Der Gerichtete"]
AIZ, Prague, no. 45, November 16, 1933, p. 755
15¼″ × 10¾″ [38 × 27 cm]
sig., b. l.: "Photomontage: John Heartfield"
Inv. no. 4220

247   Design for no. 246
Photomontage, retouched
17¾″ × 14½″ [44.3 × 36 cm]
unsig.
Inv. no. 508

248   "The Executioner and Justice"
["Der Henker und die Gerechtigkeit"]
AIZ, Prague, no. 47, November 30, 1933, p. 787
15¼″ × 10¾″ [38 × 27 cm]
sig., t. r.: "Photomontage: John Heartfield"
Inv. no. 733
Ill. p. 211

249   Design for no. 250
Reversed photo of the copy for no. 250, retouched with paint
20″ × 16″ [49.9 × 40 cm]
unsig.
Inv. no. 436
Ill. p. 196

250   "The Judgment of the World: What the Court Withheld is Written in His Face."
["Das Urteil der Welt: In seinen Zügen steht geschrieben, was das Gericht verschwiegen hat."]
AIZ, Prague, no. 51, December 28, 1933, p. 851
15¼″ × 10¾″ [38 × 27 cm]
sig., b. r.: "Montage by John Heartfield"
Inv. no. 774

251   "The Reich Bishop Brings Christendom into Line. 'Hey, You Over There! The Cross More to the Right!'"
["Der Reichsbischof richtet das Christentum aus. 'He, der Mann da, das Kruzifix etwas weiter nach rechts!'"]
AIZ, Prague, no. 3, January 18, 1934, p. 35
15¼″ × 10¾″ [38 × 27 cm]
sig., b. r.: "Photomontage: John Heartfield"
Inv. no. 53

252   "The Old Slogan in the 'New' Reich: Blood and Iron"
["Der alte Wahlspruch im 'neuen' Reich: Blut und Eisen"]
AIZ, Prague, no. 10, March 8, 1934, p. 147
15¼″ × 10¾″ [38 × 27 cm]
sig., b. r.: "Photomontage: John Heartfield"
Inv. no. 2897

253   Design for no. 252
Photomontage, retouched
15″ × 13″ [37.2 × 32.5 cm]
unsig.
Inv. no. 504
Ill. p. 198

254   "Hjalmar (Schacht) or The Growing Deficit. 'I Shall Certainly not Let It Fall'"
["Hjalmar oder Das wachsende Defizit. 'Ich lasse sie auf keinen Fall fallen!'"]
AIZ, Prague, no. 14, April 5, 1934, p. 224
15¼″ × 10¾″ [38 × 27 cm]
sig., b. r.: "Photomontage: John Heartfield"
Inv. no. 1327

255   Design for no. 254
Photomontage, retouched
21½″ × 15¼″ [54 × 38.3 cm]
unsig.
Inv. no. 446
Ill. p. 203

256   "Choir of the Arms Industry: 'A Mighty Fortress is Our Geneva'"
["Chor der Rüstungsindustrie: 'Ein feste Burg ist unser Genf'"]
AIZ, Prague, no. 15, April 12, 1934, p. 240
15¼″ × 10¾″ [38 × 27 cm]
sig., t. l.: "Photomontage: John Heartfield"
Inv. no. 2900

257   Design for no. 256
Photomontage, retouched
21¼″ × 15½″ [53 × 38.8 cm]
unsig.
Inv. no. 1803
Ill. p. 199

258   "Mimicry"
["Mimikry"]
AIZ, Prague, no. 16, April 19, 1934, p. 241
15¼″ × 10¾″ [38 × 27 cm]
sig., b. l.: "Photomontage: John Heartfield"
Inv. no. 1329

259   "On the Intervention of the Third Reich. The More Pictures They Remove, the More Visible Reality Becomes!"
["Zur Intervention des Dritten Reichs. Je mehr Bilder sie weghängen, umso sichtbarer wird die Wirklichkeit!"]
AIZ, Prague, no. 18, May 3, 1934, p. 288
15¼″ × 10¾″ [38 × 27 cm]
sig., b. r.: "Photomontage: John Heartfield"
Inv. no. 779
Ill. p. 179

260   Design for no. 259
Photomontage, retouched
19″ × 13½″ [47.7 × 33.5 cm]
unsig.
Inv. no. 435

261   "As in the Middle Ages . . . So in the Third Reich"
["Wie im Mittelalter . . . so im Dritten Reich"]
AIZ, Prague, no. 22, May 31, 1934, p. 352
15¼″ × 10¾″ [38 × 27 cm]
sig., t. r.: "Photomontage: John Heartfield"
Inv. no. 780

262   Design for no. 261
Photomontage, retouched
23¾″ × 14¼″ [59.6 × 35.8 cm]
unsig.
Inv. no. 435
Ill. p. 201

263   "Dialogue at the Berlin Zoo"
["Gespräch im Berliner Zoo"]
AIZ, Prague, no. 23, June 7, 1934, p. 368
15¼″ × 10¾″ [38 × 27 cm]
sig., b. r.: "Photomontage: John Heartfield"
Inv. no. 1337

264   Design for no. 263
Photomontage, retouched
21¼″ × 17¾″ [54.5 × 44.5 cm]
unsig.
Inv. no. 441
Ill. p. 200

265   "Herr von Papen, a Diplomat but not Diplomatic"
["Herr von Papen, ein Gesandter, doch kein Geschickter"]
AIZ, Prague, no. 32, August 9, 1934, p. 520
15¼″ × 10¾″ [38 × 27 cm]
sig., b. r.: "Photomontage: John Heartfield"
Inv. no. 81

266   "German Natural History. Metamorphosis"
["Deutsche Naturgeschichte. Metamorphose"]
AIZ, Prague, no. 33, August 16, 1934, p. 536
15¼″ × 10¾″ [38 × 27 cm]
sig., b. r.: "Photomontage: John Heartfield"
Inv. no. 1345
Ill. p. 165

267   "After Twenty Years"
["Nach zwanzig Jahren"]
AIZ, Prague, no. 37, September 13, 1934, pp. 592/593
15¼″ × 21½″ [38 × 54 cm]
sig., b. l.: "Photomontage: John Heartfield"
Inv. no. 86

268   "The Thousand Year Reich"
["Das tausendjährige Reich"]
AIZ, Prague, no. 38, September 20, 1934, p. 616
15¼″ × 10¾″ [38 × 27 cm]
sig., t. r.: "Photomontage: John Heartfield"
Inv. no. 783

269   Design for no. 268
Photomontage, retouched
18½″ × 13¾″ [46 × 34.5 cm]
unsig.
Inv. no. 2182
Ill. p.205

270   "Every War Victim His Own Cross of Honor!"
["Jedem Kriegsopfer sein Ehrenkreuz!"]
AIZ, Prague, no. 39, September 27, 1934, p. 632
15¼″ × 10¾″ [38 × 27 cm]
sig., b. r.: "Photomontage: John Heartfield"
Inv. no. 88

271   Design for no. 270
Photomontage, retouched
18¼″ × 13½″ [45.8 × 34 cm]
unsig.
Inv. no. 438
Ill. p. 202

272   "A New Man – Master of a New World"
["Ein neuer Mensch – Herr einer neuen Welt"]
AIZ, Prague, no. 44, November 1, 1934, p. 697
15¼″ × 10¾″ [38 × 27 cm]
sig., b. r.: "Photomontage: John Heartfield"
Inv. no. 764
Ill. p. 169

Front page
14″ × 10½″ [34.7 × 26 cm]
unsig.
Inv. no. 4703
Ill. p. 216

300   "Five Minutes to Twelve"
      ["5 Minuten vor 12"]
      Photomontage, London 1942
      19¼″ × 16″ [48.3 × 40.3 cm]
      unsig.
      Inv. no. 473
      Ill. p. 225

301   *"Small Grosz Portfolio"*
      ["Kleine Grosz-Mappe"]
      Malik-Verlag, Berlin-Halensee, 1917
      4-page flyleaf, pp. 1/4, 2/3
      11¼″ × 17¼″ [28.4 × 43.4 cm]
      unsig.
      Inv. no. 3853
      Ill. pp. 69–72

302   *"Grosz-Heartfield mont." "The Sunny Land"*
      ["Sonniges Land"]
      Collage, 1919
      Reproduction
      Whereabouts of original unknown, dimensions unknown.
      sig., b. l.: "Grosz-Heartfield mont."
      b. r.: "Sunny land"
      Ill. p. 66

303   *Richard Huelsenbeck*
      "Dada Triumphs! A Balance Sheet on Dadaism"
      ["DADA siegt! Eine Bilanz des Dadaismus"]
      Malik-Verlag, Dada Section, Berlin 1920
      Brochure cover using no. 302 in large format
      9″ × 11½″ [22.2 × 29 cm]
      sig. on back like no. 302
      Inv. no. 4258
      Ill. p. 89

304   Alfred Polgar
      "Yesterday and Today"
      ["Gestern und Heute"]
      Rudolf-Kaemmerer Verlag, Dresden 1922
      Design for dust jacket, front
      Photo series with painted script
      11½″ × 9″ [28.7 × 22.7 cm]
      sig. b. l.: "Heartfield"
      Inv. no. 1428
      Ill. p. 103

305   *Upton Sinclair*
      "King Coal"
      ["König Kohle"]
      Malik-Verlag, Berlin 1925
      Dust jacket
      7½″ × 11½″ [19 × 29 cm]
      unsig.
      Inv. no. 724

306   Upton Sinclair
      "Oil"
      ["Petroleum"]
      Malik-Verlag, Berlin n. d. (1927)
      Dust jacket
      7½″ × 12″ [18.8 × 30.3 cm]
      unsig.
      Inv. no. 1744

307   *Richard Huelsenbeck*
      "The Leap toward the East"
      ["Der Sprung nach Osten"]
      Verlag Wolfgang Jess, Dresden 1928
      Dust jacket

8½″ × 11½″ [21 × 29 cm]
sig. on back, b. l.: "John Heartfield"
Inv. no. 1597

308   *Upton Sinclair*
      "100 %"
      Malik-Verlag, Berlin n. d.
      (1928; 36th–42nd thousand)
      Dust jacket
      7½″ × 11″ [19 × 27.7 cm]
      unsig.
      Inv. no. 233

309   Upton Sinclair
      "100 %"
      Malik-Verlag, Berlin, n. d.
      (1928; 43rd–50th thousand)
      Dust jacket
      7½″ × 11½″ [19 × 28.5 cm]
      unsig.
      Inv. no. 1616
      Ill. p. 99

310   Design for jacket front of no. 309
      Photomontage, retouched
      11¼″ × 9″ [28.4 × 22.5 cm]
      sig., b. r.: "Heartfield"
      Inv. no. 591

311   *Upton Sinclair*
      "Jimmie Higgins"
      Malik-Verlag, Berlin, n. d.
      (1928; 36th–42nd thousand)
      Dust jacket
      7½″ × 11½″ [19 × 28.8 cm]
      sig. on back and front, b. l.: "Heartfield"
      Inv. no. 1610
      Ill. p. 96

312   *Upton Sinclair*
      "The Brass Check"
      ["Der Sündenlohn"]
      Malik-Verlag, Berlin 1928
      Dust jacket
      7½″ × 11½″ [19.1 × 28.5 cm]
      unsig.
      Inv. no. 1636

313   *Heinrich Wandt*
      "Eroticism and Espionage at Ghent Base"
      ["Erotik und Spionage in der Etappe Gent"]
      Agis-Verlag, Wien/Berlin 1928
      Design for front of dust jacket, 3rd version
      Photomontage, retouched
      10″ × 8¼″ [24.8 × 20.6 cm]
      unsig.
      Inv. no. 583
      Ill. p. 301

314   John Dos Passos
      "Three Soldiers"
      ["Drei Soldaten"]
      Malik-Verlag, Berlin 1929 (11th–17th thousand)
      Dust jacket
      7½″ × 11½″ [18.7 × 28.6 cm]
      unsig.
      Inv. no. 1586
      Ill. p. 101

315   *Ilya Ehrenburg*
      "The Unusual Adventures of Julio Jurenito"
      ["Die ungewöhnlichen Abenteuer des Julio Jurenito"]
      Malik-Verlag, Berlin 1929
      Advertising leaflet
      8¼″ × 10″ [20.6 × 25 cm]

unsig.
Inv. no. 2416
Ill. p. 113

316   **Kurt Tucholsky**
–   **"A Picture Book by Kurt Tucholsky and**
326   **Many Photographers. Montage by John Heartfield"**
      ["Deutschland, Deutschland über alles. Ein Bilderbuch von Kurt Tucholsky und vielen Fotografen: Montiert von John Heartfield"]
      Neuer Deutscher Verlag, Berlin 1929

316   Dust jacket
      9½″ × 15½″ [23.5 × 39 cm]
      unsig.
      Inv. no. 1646
      Ill. pp. 148–149

317   "Sticking Together Fraternally"
      ["Brüderlich zusammenhält"]
      Design for back of dust jacket and cover
      Photomontage, retouched
      13″ × 10¼″ [32.7 × 25.7 cm]
      unsig.
      Inv. no. 600
      Ill. p. 161

318   *Pages 46–51*
      each 9½″ × 7¼″ [23.5 × 18.3 cm]
      unsig.
      Reproductions
      Ills. pp. 150–155

"This is a poor country. I am a worker, with a trade, and I have a wife and three children. Fifty days out of the year, I work not for myself. — I work a little more than two days for the army. Two other days in the year I work so that we can have a nice police station.
I have to work half a day for the church to which I don't belong anymore, and a whole week for the civil servants — for the many, unnecessary civil servants. Science and the arts are easier; they only take three hours.
This is a poor country!
In Prussia we have 28,807,988 Mark just for horse-breeding and very little to eat.
But we have 230,990 Mark to pay for religion in the army, and 2,164,000 Mark for ambassadors' and diplomats' moving expenses. What would they have to do, if they didn't move. And I am a book-keeper with a yearly salary of 3,600 Mark. My wife spends 40 Mark a week. I would have to work 433 weeks, to earn what Mr. Tirpitz, who mismanaged the German fleet, gets on pension. Mr. Loser-of-battles Ludendorff gets 17,000 Mark. We pay the old monarchists 206,931,960 Mark a year in pensions. After all, we've got the money. Well, actually, we haven't, but what are you going to do if you need a new battleship that costs 80 million Mark? And if the officers have to take morning rides, you can't expect beautiful eye clinics. We need our money for other things."

319   "German Sports"
      ["Deutscher Sport"]
      Design for p. 109
      Photomontage
      13¼″ × 8¼″ [33 × 20.4 cm]
      unsig.
      Inv. no. 602
      Ill. p. 156

320   "The Dormant Reichstag"
      ["Der schlafende Reichstag"]
      Design for p. 138
      Negative montage, retouched
      11″ × 12¾″ [27.3 × 32 cm]
      unsig.
      Inv. no. 1909
      Ill. p. 157

321 "Sweet Ink"
["Süße Tinte"]
Design for p. 107
Photomontage, retouched
13¼" × 9½" [33 × 24 cm]
unsig.
Inv. no. 573
Ill. p. 158

322 "I Only Know Legal Paragraphs"
["Ich kenne nur Paragraphen"]
Design for p. 163
Photomontage, retouched
12" × 8½" [29.8 × 21.2 cm]
unsig.
Inv. no. 601
Ill. p. 158

323 *"That? That's the Times: They Scream for Satire"*
["*Das? Das ist die Zeit, sie schreit nach Satire*"]
Design for p. 101
16¾" × 13½" [41.6 × 33.7 cm]
unsig.
Inv. no. 462
Ill. p. 158

324 "A Berlin Saying"
["Berliner Redensart"]
Design for p. 176
Photomontage, retouched
4½" × 4¾" [11 × 12 cm]
unsig.
Inv. no. 1496
Ill. p. 158

325 "Subjects"
["Untertanen"]
Design for p. 152
Photomontage
12¾" × 7" [31.8 × 17.5 cm]
unsig.
Inv. no. 502
Ill. p. 159

326 "German Talking Film"
["Deutscher Tonfilm"]
Design for p. 225
Photomontage, retouched
17" × 14" [42.8 × 34.9 cm]
unsig.
Inv. no. 489
Ill. p. 160

327 *Ilya Ehrenburg*
"Thirteen Pipes"
["*13 Pfeifen*"]
Malik-Verlag, Berlin 1930 (4th–7th thousand)
Dust jacket
7½" × 11½" [18.8 × 28.7 cm]
unsig.
Inv. no. 2241

328 *Maxim Gorki*
"In the Steppe"
["*In der Steppe*"]
Malik-Verlag, Berlin 1930
Dust jacket
7½" × 11½" [18.8 × 29 cm]
unsig.
Inv. no. 725

329 *Vsevolod Ivanov*
"The Letter G"
["*Der Buchstabe G*"]
Malik-Verlag, Berlin 1930
Dust jacket
7½" × 11½" [18.8 × 28.7 cm]

unsig.
Inv. no. 241
Ill. p. 110

330 Maria Leitner
"Hotel America"
["Hotel Amerika"]
Neuer Deutscher Verlag, Berlin 1930
Design for dust jacket
Photomontage, retouched
11" × 17¾" [27.6 × 44.5 cm]
sig., b. l.: "Heartfield"
Inv. no. 585

331 *Walter Müller*
"If we in 1918 . . ."
["*Wenn wir 1918 . . .*"]
Malik-Verlag, Berlin 1930
Dust jacket
7½" × 11¾" [19 × 29.5 cm]
unsig.
Inv. no. 1573
Ill. p. 118

332 *Fedor Panferov*
"The Cooperative of the Have-Nots"
["*Die Genossenschaft der Habenichtse*"]
Verlag für Literatur und Politik, Wien/Berlin n. d.
(1930)
Dust jacket
8" × 12½" [19.8 × 31.4 cm]
unsig.
Inv. no. 758

333 *Design for no. 332*
Photomontage
12¼" × 10" [30.5 × 25 cm]
unsig.
Inv. no. 587
Ill. p. 117

334 Larissa Reissner
"October"
["Oktober"]
Neuer Deutscher Verlag, Berlin 1930
(6th–10th thousand)
Dust jacket
7¾" × 11¾" [19.1 × 29.5 cm]
unsig.
Inv. no. 719

335 *Upton Sinclair*
"Money Writes"
["*Das Geld schreibt*"]
Malik-Verlag, Berlin 1930
Dust jacket, back, first version
7½" × 5¼" [19 × 13 cm]
unsig.
Inv. no. 230

336 *Same as no. 335*
Dust jacket, second version
(made after writer's complaint depicted on it)
7½" × 11½" [19 × 28.5 cm]
unsig.
Inv. no. 1628

337 *Ludwig Turek*
"A Worker Narrates"
["*Ein Prolet erzählt*"]
Malik-Verlag, Berlin 1930
Dust jacket
7½" × 11¾" [18.5 × 29.6 cm]
unsig.
Inv. no. 1617
Ill. p. 119

338 *Ilya Ehrenburg*
"Most Sacred Possessions"
["*Die heiligsten Güter*"]
Malik-Verlag, Berlin 1931
Dust jacket
7½" × 11½" [18.6 × 28.9 cm]
unsig.
Inv. no. 242
Ill. p. 112

339 *Ilya Ehrenburg*
"Factory of Dreams"
["*Die Traumfabrik*"]
Malik-Verlag, Berlin 1931
Dust jacket, front and spine
7½" × 6¼" [18.5 × 15.5 cm]
unsig.
Inv. no. 2515
Ill. p. 111

340 Michael Gold
"Jews Without Money"
["Juden ohne Geld"]
Neuer Deutscher Verlag, Berlin 1931
Dust jacket
7¾" × 11¾" [19.2 × 29.2 cm]
unsig.
Inv. no. 1604
Ill. p. 119

341 Upton Sinclair
"Mountain City"
["So macht man Dollars"]
Malik-Verlag, Berlin 1931
Dust jacket
7½" × 11½" [19 × 28.6 cm]
unsig.
Inv. no. 263

341a "What's Going on Here?"
["*Was geht hier vor?*"]
Design for dust jacket, front, for no. 341
Photo series, with caption
Picture above, left (middle): John Heartfield and
Wieland Herzfelde
14" × 20¼" [35.3 × 50.9 cm]
Inv. no. 488

341b Design for dust jacket, front
(cf. no. 341a photo, below right)
Photo with brushwork and airbrush
retouching
16" × 12¾" [40 × 31.6 cm]
unsig.
Inv. no. 1427

342 Upton Sinclair
"The Wet Parade"
["Alkohol"]
Malik-Verlag, Berlin 1932
Dust jacket, third version (made after second
complaint by the whisky firm named on the
label)
7½" × 11¾" [18.9 × 29.7 cm]
unsig.
Inv. no. 228
Ill. p. 121

343 *"Freedom Calling".*
"The Story of the Secret German Radio"
Frederick Muller, London 1939
Design for booklet cover, first version
Photomontage, retouched
13½" × 10¼" [34 × 25.8 cm]
unsig.
Inv. no. 4449

344 *Heartfield on the radio*
Montage detail of no. 343

5½″ × 5½″ [13.5 × 13.8 cm]
unsig.
Inv. no. 4450

345   Roger Motz
      "La Belgique Invaincue"
      Lindsay Drummond, London ca. 1942
      Design for dust jacket, spine and front
      Photomontage, retouched
      11″ × 10½″ [27.2 × 26.5 cm]
      sig., b. r.: "John Heartfield"
      Inv. no. 754
      Ill. p. 219

346   "'And Yet It Moves'!"
      ["'Und sie bewegt sich doch!'"]
      Verlag Freie Deutsche Jugend, London 1943
      Design for brochure cover
      Photomontage
      15½″ × 10¾″ [39 × 26.8 cm]
      unsig.
      Inv. no. 484
      Ill. p. 226

347   *Ivor Halstead*
      "Post Haste"
      Lindsay Drummond, London 1944
      Design for back of dust jacket
      Photomontage
      11″ × 7¾″ [27.2 × 19.5 cm]
      unsig.
      Inv. no. 1422

348   *Matthew Halton*
      "Ten Years to Alamein"
      Lindsay Drummond, London 1944
      Design for dust jacket
      Photomontage with paint
      10½″ × 15¾″ [26.1 × 39.5 cm]
      Front page sig., b. l.: "John Heartfield"
      Inv. no. 740

349   *Richard Perry*
      "I Went A'Shepherding"
      Lindsay Drummond, London 1944
      Design for dust jacket, front and spine
      Photomontage, retouched
      12¼″ × 19″ [30.5 × 47.5 cm]
      unsig.
      Inv. no. 617
      Ill. p. 222

350   *Ilya Ehrenburg*
      "The Russians Reply to Lady Gibb"
      Soviet War News, London 1945
      Design for booklet cover
      Photomontage with colored paper
      15¾″ × 11¾″ [39.5 × 29.7 cm]
      sig., b. l.: "John Heartfield"
      Inv. no. 739
      Ill. p. 220

351   *H. B. Egmont Hake*
      "The New Malaya and You"
      Lindsay Drummond, London 1945
      Design for dust jacket, front
      Photomontage, retouched
      10½″ × 7½″ [26.5 × 18.7 cm]
      unsig.
      Inv. no. 736

352   *J. J. Lynx (ed.)*
      "The Future of the Jews"
      Lindsay Drummond, London 1945
      Dust jacket, front and spine
      9″ × 6½″ [22.2 × 16 cm]
      sig.: "Book Jacket by John Heartfield"

Inv. no. 257
Ill. p. 221

353   *Design for no. 352*
      Final version, retouched
      14″ × 11½″ [34.6 × 28.7 cm]
      unsig.
      Inv. no. 1083

354   Aleksandr Pokryshkin
      "Red Air Ace"
      Soviet War News, London 1945
      Design for booklet, cover
      Photomontage with blue paper
      11¼″ × 9″ [28.3 × 22.3 cm]
      sig., b. r.: "This Original has to be returned to
      Mr. J. Heartfield"
      Inv. no. 753
      Ill. p. 218

355   Pavel Troyanovsky
      "The Last Days of Berlin"
      Soviet War News, London 1945
      Design for brochure, back cover
      Photomontage, retouched
      20¼″ × 15¼″ [50.4 × 38.2 cm]
      sig., b. l.: "John Heartfield"
      Inv. no. 4503
      Ill. p. 227

356   *Egon Larsen*
      "Inventor's Scrapbook"
      Lindsay Drummond, London 1947
      Design for dust jacket, front
      Photomontage
      11″ × 8¼″ [27.8 × 20.4 cm]
      unsig.
      Inv. no. 1958

357   Bert Stiles
      "Serenade to the Big Bird"
      Lindsay Drummond, London 1947
      Design for dust jacket, front and spine
      Brush, tempera, airbrush
      12¼″ × 9¼″ [30.8 × 23 cm]
      unsig.
      Inv. no. 1065
      Ill. p. 223

358   *David Buxton*
      "Travels in Ethiopia"
      Lindsay Drummond, London 1949
      Dust jacket, front and spine
      9″ × 6¾″ [22.5 × 17 cm]
      sig. on front flap: "Jacket design and Typography by
      John Heartfield"
      Inv. no. 925
      Ill. p. 252

359   *Bertolt Brecht*
      "Plays XII"
      ["Stücke XII"]
      Aufbau-Verlag, Berlin 1959
      Dust jacket, front and spine
      7¾″ × 6″ [19.4 × 15.1 cm]
      unsig.
      Inv. no. 927
      Ill. p. 253

360   **Gerhart Hauptmann**
  –   **"The Weavers"**
362   **["Die Weber"]**
      Grosses Schauspielhaus, Berlin 1921
      Stage set designs, probably not produced

360   *"Villa Dreißiger"*
      Reed pen superimposed on pencil, watercolor effect

11¼″ × 16¼″ [28 × 40.5 cm]
unsig.
Inv. no. 3328
Ill. p. 228

361   *"Hilly Spring Landscape with Cottages"*
      ["Bergige Frühlingslandschaft mit Hütten"]
      Reed pen, watercolor
      14″ × 20¼″ [35 × 50.6 cm]
      sig., b. l.: "John Heartfield 21"
      Inv. no. 3329
      Ill. p. 228

362   *"Winter Landscape with Cottage and Graveyard"*
      ["Winterlandschaft mit Hütte und Friedhof"]
      Reed pen, watercolor
      9½″ × 15½″ [23.9 × 39 cm]
      unsig.
      Inv. no. 3327

363   *Nikolai Pogodin*
      "My Friend"
      ["Mein Freund"]
      Theatre of the Revolution, Moscow 1931
      Set photo
      (Using a montage for stage backdrop)
      Ill. p. 231

364   **Bertolt Brecht after Maxim Gorki**
  –   **"The Mother"**
367   **["Die Mutter"]**
      Berlin Ensemble, Guest performance at the
      Deutsches Theater, Berlin 1951
      Decor and makeup: Caspar Neher; painted
      projections: Hainer Hill; film and photo pro-
      jections: John Heartfield and Wieland Herz-
      felde

364   *Set photo with projection*
      Reproduction
      Ill. p. 233

365   *Screen for background projection*
      Reconstruction
      Ill. p. 234

366   *Projection design: William II, George V,*
      Rockefeller, Clemenceau
      Photomontage, retouched, with text
      16″ × 22¾″ [39.7 × 56.7 cm]
      unsig.
      Inv. no. 5092
      Ill. p. 235

367   *Projection: Lenin, Stalin, Mao Tse-tung*
      Photomontage, retouched, with text
      20″ × 26″ [50.3 × 65 cm]
      unsig.
      Inv. no. 5094
      Ill. p. 235

368   **Arno Holz**
  –   **"Social Aristocrats"**
378   **["Sozialartistokraten"]**
      Deutsches Theater – Kammerspiele, Berlin
      1955
      Stage set, stage curtain, costumes: John
      Heartfield

368   *Stage curtain*
      Reproduction
      (Whereabouts of original unknown)

369   *Sketch of design for stage curtain*
      Watercolor on pencil
      10½″ × 16¾″ [26 × 42 cm]

unsig.
Inv. no. 4932

370 Design for stage curtain
Watercolor on pencil
19" × 25¼" [47.5 × 63 cm]
unsig.
Inv. no. 4935
Ill. p. 237

371 Stage photograph
"Fiebig's Study"
["Arbeitszimmer des Herrn Fiebig"]
Reproduction
Ill. p. 237

372 Design for no. 371
Pencil sketch
13¾" × 22¾" [34.3 × 57.1 cm]
unsig.
Inv. no. 4924
Ill. p. 238

373 Design for "Dr. Gehrke's Room"
["Zimmer des Dr. Gehrke"]
Pencil sketch
17" × 21½" [42.2 × 54 cm]
unsig.
Inv. no. 4925

374 Costume design "Fiebig"
Pencil
16½" × 10¾" [41 × 26.8 cm]
unsig.
Inv. no. 4947
Ill. p. 239

375 Costume design
"Dutch Girl with Scarf"
["Meischen mit Schultertuch"]
Pencil, colored crayon
12¾" × 10¾" [31.7 × 27 cm]
unsig.
Inv. no. 4940

376 Costume design
"Dutch Girl with Hat and Silk Blouse"
["Meischen mit Hut und Seidenbluse"]
Pencil
14" × 8¾" [35 × 22 cm]
unsig.
Inv. no. 4942

377 Costume design
"Editor"
["Redakteur"]
Pencil, touch of red crayon
16½" × 10¾" [41.5 × 26.8 cm]
unsig.
Inv. no. 4951

378 Costume design
"Writer"
["Schriftsteller"]
Pencil, touch of red crayon
16¾" × 10¾" [41.8 × 27 cm]
unsig.
Inv. no. 4948

379 David Berg
– "Mother Riba"
383 ["Mutter Riba"]
Deutsches Theater – Kammerspiele, Berlin
1955
Stage set: John Heartfield

379 Stage set
"Supermarket"
["Supermarkt"]
Stage photograph
Ill. p. 245

380 Outline of details for no. 379
"Supermarket Sign"
["Supermarkt Firmenschild"]
Tempera on pencil
10" × 20¾" [25 × 52 cm]
unsig.
Inv. no. 4987
Ill. p. 242

381 Typographical design for storefront with illustration
of supermarket show window pasted on it
Pencil
3/4½" × 33½" [8/12.2 × 83.5 cm]
unsig.
Inv. no. 5002
Ill. p. 245

382 Design in four parts for supermarket storefront
Brush, pen, tempera on pencil, partly mounted
11/11¾" × 40" [27.8/30 × 100 cm]
unsig.
Inv. no. 4989–4992
Ill. p. 242

383 Stage set design (two parts)
"Workshop 'Ajax Skirts'"
["Schneider-Werkstatt 'Ajax-Röcke'"]
Tempera on pencil
17½" × 19½" [44 × 48.5 cm] (background)
18¼" × 6¾" [45.5 × 17 cm] (workshop)
unsig.
Inv. nos. 4976, 4981
Ill. p. 241

384 David Berg
"Mother Riba"
["Mutter Riba"]
Deutsches Theater – Kammerspiele, Berlin,
Season 1954/55, Program 9
Front of playbill
8¼" × 5½" [20.5 × 13.7 cm]
sig. in imprint: "Playbill cover: John Heartfield"
Inv. no. 3368

385 "'The Mother' by Brecht Based on Themes from
Gorki's Novel"
["'Die Mutter' von Brecht nach Motiven aus Gorkis
Roman"]
Berlin Ensemble, 1951, guest performance at the
Deutsches Theater
Poster
34" × 23¾" [84.7 × 59.3 cm]
sig., b. r.: "The brothers Heartfield Herzfelde"
Inv. no. 3968
Ill. p. 232

386 Johannes R. Becher
"Winter Campaign"
["Winterschlacht"]
Berlin Ensemble, 1954
Poster
47½" × 33½" [118.5 × 84 cm]
sig., b. l.: "The brothers Heartfield Herzfelde"
Inv. no. 2000
Ill. p. 248

387 Sean O'Casey
"The Shadow of a Gunman"
["Harfe und Gewehr"]
Deutsches Theater – Kammerspiele, Berlin 1954
Poster

33½" × 23¾" [83.8 × 59.4 cm]
sig., b. r.: "The brothers Heartfield Herzfelde"
Inv. no. 4000

388 Arno Holz
"Social Aristocrats"
["Sozialaristokraten"]
Deutsches Theater – Kammerspiele, Berlin 1955
Poster
33½" × 23½" [83.5 × 58.5 cm]
sig., b. l.: "John Heartfield"
Inv. no. 3981
Ill. p. 236

389 Rolf Hochhuth
"The Deputy"
["Der Stellvertreter"]
Deutsches Theater, Berlin 1966
Poster
32½" × 23" [81 × 57.5 cm]
sig., b. l.: "John Heartfield"
Inv. no. 3978
Ill. p. 251

390 Vladimir Mayakovsky
"Lenin Poem"
["Vladimir Ilich Lenin"]
Volksbühne, Berlin 1966
Poster
33¼" × 23½" [83 × 59 cm]
sig., b. r.: "John Heartfield"
Inv. no. 3982
Ill. p. 249

391 Bertolt Brecht
"To My Countrymen"
["An meine Landsleute"]
Typographic sheet, 1950
24" × 16¾" [60 × 42 cm]
unsig.
Inv. no. 5160
Ill. p. 250

392 "If we All do not Want it, it Won't Happen"
["Wenn wir es alle nicht wollen, wird es nie sein!"]
Poster, 1957
32¾" × 24½" [82 × 61 cm]
sig., b. l.: "John Heartfield"
Inv. no. 4011
Ill. p. 254

393 "Fraternal Salute of the Social Democratic Party of
Germany (SPD)"
["Brudergrüsse der SPD"]
The Club, Berlin, no. 1, January 1927
Double-page spread
12" × 19¼" [32.8 × 49 cm]
unsig.
Inv. no. 5172

394 "Voices from the Swamp"
"Three Thousand Years of Consistent Incest Prove
the Superiority of My Race"
["Stimme aus dem Sumpf 'Dreitausend Jahre konse-
quenter Inzucht beweisen die Überlegenheit meiner
Rasse'"]
AIZ, Berlin 1936, no. 12, p. 179
15" × 10½" [38 × 27 cm]
sig. b. r.: Photomontage: John Heartfield
Inv. no. 135

395 Upton Sinclair
"Mammonart"
["Die goldne Kette"]
Malik-Verlag, Berlin 1928
Dust jacket

7½″ × 12″ [19 × 30.2 cm]
unsig.
Inv. no. 1588
Ill. p. 293

396   *Costume designs for A. Holz's "Social Aristocrats"*
      "The Bureaucrat"
      ["Der Amtsvorsteher"]
      Pencil, touched with red
      16″ × 10½″ [40.8 × 26.7 cm]
      unsig.
      Inv. no. 4949

*397   "The Good-for-nothings Convene in Brussels"
      ["Die Nachtleuchter tagen in Brüssel"]
      Photomontage, retouched, 1934
      20½″ × 13½″ [53 × 34.7 cm]
      unsig.
      Inv. no. 451*

*398   "Idyllic in the Third Reich"
      ["Idylle im Dritten Reich"]
      Photomontage, retouched, 1934
      21½″ × 15½″ [55.1 × 39.2 cm]
      Inv. no. 448*

*399   "The Nazis' Play with Fire"
      ["Das Spiel der Nazis mit dem Feuer"]
      Photomontage, retouched, 1935
      17¼″ × 13″ [44 × 33.9 cm]
      Inv. no. 435*

*400   "Hitler's X-mas Tree for His People"
      Photomontage, retouched, 1944?
      22″ × 16″ [55.9 × 41 cm]
      Inv. no. 463*

◆ 401   *"O Christmas Tree in Germany, How Crooked are Your Branches."*
      ["O Tannenbaum im deutschen Raum, wie krumm sind deine Äste!"]
      Staged montage, retouched. 1934
      21″ × 15½″ [53.3 × 40.0 cm]
      Inv. no. 475
      Ill. p. 295

◆ 402   *"Armament is a Must!"*
      ["Aufrüstung tut not!"]
      Photomontage, 1932
      14½″ × 12¾″ [38.4 × 31.5 cm]
      Inv. no. 1827

◆ 403   *"Mimicry"*
      ["Mimikry"]
      Photomontage, retouched
      18½″ × 16″ [47.8 × 40.7 cm]
      Inv. no. 455

◆ 404   *"Dr. Goebbels, the Faithhealer"*
      ["Dr. Goebbels, der Gesundbeter"]
      Photomontage, retouched, 1934
      18½″ × 12½″ [47.6 × 32.3 cm]
      Inv. no. 481a

◆ 405   *"German Natural History"*
      ["Deutsche Naturgeschichte"]
      Photomontage, retouched, 1934
      18″ × 13″ [45.7 × 33.8 cm]
      Inv. no. 516

◆ 406   *"Nazi Officers"*
      Photomontage, retouched, 1939
      19″ × 20¼″ [48.8 × 51.8 cm]
      Inv. no. 1836

◆ 407   *Barbara Nixon*
      "Rider Overhead"
      Photomontage with paint, 1943
      13″ × 10¼″ [34.5 × 26.0 cm]
      Inv. no. 735

Selected Bibliography

Dawn Ades, *Photomontage* (London, 1976)

Louis Aragon, *Les Collages* (Paris, 1965)

"Arbeiter-Illustrierte-Zeitung. Eine Dokumentation zur 'A-I-Z' und zum 'Arbeiter-Fotografen'. Bildmaterialien, Texte und Interviews, zusammengestellt von Heiner Bönke, Peter Gorsen, Eberhard Knödler-Bunte," *Ästhetik und Kommunikation* 10 (January 1973)

Lilly Becher, "Porträt einer Zeitung," *Neue Deutsche Presse* 5 (1957)

Hans J. Becker, *Mit geballter Faust: Kurt Tucholsky "Deutschland, Deutschland über alles"* (Bonn, 1978)

"Benütze Foto als Waffe!" John Heartfield – Fotomontagen, exh. cat. (Frankfurt/Main, 1989)

Hanne Bergius, *Das Lachen Dadas: die Berliner Dadaisten und ihre Aktionen* (Gießen, 1989)

Richard Davis, *John Heartfield*, Ph. Diss. (London) 1968

Ute Eskildsen with Jan Christopher Horak (eds.), *Film und Foto der zwanziger Jahre. Eine Betrachtung der Internationalen Werkbundausstellung "Film und Foto" 1929*, exh. cat. (Stuttgart, 1979)

David Evans, *AIZ. John Heartfield. Arbeiter-Illustrierte Zeitung. Volks Illustrierte* (New York, 1992)

David Evans, Sylvia Gohl, *Photomontage: a Political Weapon* (London, 1986)

Konrad Farner (ed.), *John Heartfield – Fotomontagen zur Zeitgeschichte* (Zurich, 1945)

Grosz/Heartfield: The Artist as Social Critic (Minneapolis, 1980)

John Heartfield, George Grosz, "Der Kunstlump," *Der Gegner* 10–12 (1920): 48-56

Jo Hauberg et al. (eds.), *Der Malik-Verlag 1916–1947. Chronik eines Verlages. Mit einer vollständigen Bibliographie aller im Malik-Verlag und Aurora-Verlag erschienenen Titel* (Kiel, 1986)

Frank Hermann, *Malik. Zur Geschichte eines Verlages 1916–1947* (Düsseldorf, 1989)

Wieland Herzfelde, "George Grosz, John Heartfield, Erwin Piscator, Dada und die Folgen – oder Die Macht der Freundschaft," *Sinn und Form* 23, 6 (1971): 1224-51

Wieland Herzfelde, *Immergrün. Merkwürdige Erlebnisse eines Waisenknaben* (Berlin, 1966)

Wieland Herzfelde, *John Heartfield. Leben und Werk* (Dresden, 1988)

Wieland Herzfelde, *Unterwegs. Blätter aus fünfzig Jahren* (Berlin, 1961)

Wieland Herzfelde, *Zur Sache* (Berlin/Weimar, 1976)

Stefan Heym, *Nachruf* (Munich, 1988)

Richard Hiepe, *Die Fotomontage. Geschichte und Wesen einer Kunstform* (Ingolstadt, 1969)

John Heartfield – Krieg im Frieden. Fotomontagen zur Zeit 1930–1938 (Munich, 1972)

John Heartfield und die Kunst der Fotomontage, exh. cat. Deutsche Akademie der Künste (Berlin, 1957)

John Heartfield. exh. cat. Europa Center (Berlin, 1966)

John Heartfield, exh. cat. The Arts Council of Great Britain (London, 1969)

Annegret Jürgens-Kirchhoff, *Technik und Tendenzen der Montage in der bildenden Kunst des 20. Jahrhunderts. Essay* (Gießen, 1978)

Douglas Kahn, *John Heartfield: Art and Mass Media* (New York, 1985)

Felix Kraus, "He Fought the Nazi with Photographs," *Popular Photography* 12 (1944)

Kunst im Exil in Großbritannien 1933–1945 (Berlin, 1986)

Kunst und Literatur im antifaschistischen Exil 1933–1945, Vol. 5: Exil in der Tschechoslowakei, in Großbritannien, Skandinavien und Palästina (Leipzig, 1987)

Maud Lavin, "Heartfield in Context," *Art in America* 73 (1985): 84-93

Roland März with Gertrud Heartfield (eds.), *John Heartfield. Der Schnitt entlang der Zeit. Selbstzeugnisse – Erinnerungen – Interpretationen. Eine Dokumentation* (Dresden, 1981)

Malik-Verlag 1916–1947. Berlin, Prague, New York, exh. cat. (New York, 1984)

Der Malik-Verlag 1916–1947 (Berlin, 1966)

Eckhard Neumann, *Functional Graphic Design in the 20's* (New York, 1967)

Eckhard Neumann, "John Heartfield," *Typographica* 16 (December 1967): 2-12

Revolution und Realismus. Revolutionäre Kunst in Deutschland 1917–1933 (Berlin, 1978)

Eberhard Roters, *Die visuellen Künste* (Fribourg/Berlin, 1983)

Peter Sager, "Demontage des Monteurs," *Zeitmagazin* 20 (May 1991): 60-70

Aaron Scharf, "John Heartfield, Berlin Dada and the Weapon of Photomontage," *Studio International* Vol. 176, No. 904 (October 1968)

Aaron Scharf, *Art and Photography* (London, 1968)

Aaron Scharf, *Creative Photography* (London, 1965)

Peter Selz, "John Heartfield's Photomontages," *The Massachusetts Review* 2 (1963): 309-36

Eckhard Siepmann, *Montage: John Heartfield. Vom Club Dada zur Arbeiter-Illustrierten-Zeitung* (Berlin, 1977)

Stationen der Moderne. Die bedeutenden Kunstausstellungen des 20. Jahrhunderts in Deutschland. exh. cat. (West Berlin, 1988)

Rolf Surmann, *Die Münzenberg Legende. Zur Publizistik der revolutionären deutschen Arbeiterbewegung 1921–1933* (Cologne, 1982)

Michael Töteberg, *John Heartfield in Selbstzeugnissen und Bilddokumenten* (Reinbek, 1978)

Sergei Tretyakov, "Johnny." *Die Arbeit des Schriftstellers. Aufsätze, Reportagen, Essays.* Heiner Boehnke (ed.) (Reinbek, 1972): 159-70

Sergei Tretyakov, S. Telingater, *John Heartfield. Monographie.* (Moscow, 1936)

Kurt Tucholsky, *Deutschland, Deutschland über alles,* trans. Anne Halley (Amherst, Mass., 1972)

Herta Wescher, *Collage,* trans. Robert E. Wolf (New York, 1968)

Widerstand statt Anpassung. Deutsche Kunst im Widerstand gegen den Faschismus 1933–1945 (Berlin, 1980)

Heinz Willmann, *Geschichte der Arbeiter-Illustrierten-Zeitung 1921–1938* (Berlin, 1974)

Gerhard Zwerenz, "John Heartfield," *Der plebejische Intellektuelle. Essays* (Frankfurt/Main, 1972): 50-57

Index

Photographic Credits

The Akademie der Künste zu Berlin commissioned Egon Beyer of Berlin to produce the colored photographs of John Heartfield's work and Klaus Liebig of Leipzig to produce the monochrome photographs in the table section and in the biographical chronology. The reproductions of John Heartfield's work in the essay sections are by Bernd Kuhnert of Berlin. All other photographs having to do with John Heartfield were taken from the Heartfield-Archiv of the Akademie der Künste zu Berlin.

Additional Credits